INTERPRETATION AND ITS OBJECTS

Studies in the Philosophy of
Michael Krausz

VIBS

Volume 146

Robert Ginsberg
Founding Editor

Peter A. Redpath
Executive Editor

Associate Editors

INTERPRETATION AND ITS OBJECTS

Studies in the Philosophy of
Michael Krausz

Edited with an Introduction by
Andreea Deciu Ritivoi

Amsterdam - New York, NY 2003

Cover Design: Paul Pollmann

The paper on which this book is printed meets the requirements of "ISO 9706:1994, Information and documentation - Paper for documents - Requirements for permanence".

ISBN: 90-420-1167-X
©Editions Rodopi B.V., Amsterdam - New York, NY 2003
Printed in the Netherlands

061704 - 9350 P8

Michael Krausz's influential and important work on interpretation in all its cultural manifestations is the focus of this comprehensive collection of discussion papers. In engaging with Krausz the contributors show the richness, subtlety, and depth of his thinking. There are few guides more percipient and sure-footed in this terrain than Michael Krausz.

> Peter Lamarque, Editor, *The British Journal of Aesthetics*
> Professor of Philosophy, University of York

The essays from this fittingly global array of philosophers give testimony to the richness and relevance of Michael Krausz's work on interpretation, from issues of ontology, through how to understand art and culture, to the value of life itself.

> Susan Feagin, Editor, *The Journal of Aesthetics and Art Criticism*
> Research Professor of Philosophy, Temple University

Michael Krausz, by virtue of a series of works, has become, more than anyone else I know of, a central figure in the study of interpretation theory, relativism, and multiculturalism. In Krausz's writings, they have all come together in their intricate and delicate interrelationships. This book, most appropriately in his honor, substantially advances the discussion of Krausz's ideas. The volume will become a standard work for anyone who wishes to pursue interpretation theory and its related themes.

> Jitendra Mohanty, Professor of Philosophy, Temple University, and Woodruff Professor of Philosophy and Asian Studies, Emory University

Anyone who has engaged seriously in a discussion of a particular work of art knows that the question of whether there is a single correct interpretation or even one interpretation that is better than others quickly arises. Michael Krausz's careful discussions of this issue over the past several years have advanced that debate, as have the many articles that his work has stimulated. This volume is sure to provide new insights. Both philosophers and non-philosophers are certain to benefit from the variety of approaches represented.

> Marcia Eaton, Past President, The American Society for Aesthetics
> Professor of Philosophy, University of Minnesota

Michael Krausz has developed over the years a complex, original view of the general features and uses of interpretation. Tolerant but rigorous, systematically based but historically sensitive, Krausz's account, which allows that works of art and cultural objects can often be interpreted in different ways but blocks an easy relativism, is addressed in this volume by authors from several philosophical traditions. The essays, with his detailed replies, give a lively picture of Krausz's approach. They also raise questions of substance and method that are important in their own right, address the issue of inter-cultural communication, illuminate the role of interpretation in everyday life.

> Alexander Nehamas, Edmund N. Carpenter Professor in Humanities, Philosophy, and Comparative Literature, Princeton University

CONTENTS

INTERPRETING ACROSS CULTURES

EXTENSIONS AND APPLICATIONS

PREFACE

This volume collects twenty-one original essays that discuss Michael Krausz's distinctive and provocative contribution to the theory of interpretation. At the beginning of the book Krausz offers a synoptic review of his central claims and he concludes with a substantive essay that replies to scholars from the United States, England, Germany, India, Japan, and Australia. Krausz's philosophical work centers around a distinction that divides interpreters of cultural achievements into two groups. Singularists assume that for any object of interpretation there must be only one single admissible interpretation. Multiplists assume that for some objects of interpretation more than one interpretation is admissible. A central question concerns the ontological entanglements involved in interpretive activity. Domains of application include works of art and music, as well as literary, historical, legal and religious texts. Further topics include truth commissions, ethnocentrism and interpretation across cultures.

ACKNOWLEDGEMENTS

Special thanks are extended to all contributors to this volume. Also, Giridhari Lal Pandit organized a four day international conference in relation to the work of Michael Krausz at the University of Delhi, India, in 2001. David Crocker organized a session on Krausz's work for the International Development Ethics Association at the Eastern Division meeting of the American Philosophical Association in 2001, and Julie Van Camp did so for the Western Division meeting of the American Philosophical Association in 2002. Several of the papers presented at those venues appear in this volume. Robert Ginsberg proposed the project and brought it to Rodopi Publishers. Wendy Daughenbaugh, Lisa Turner, Diana Witt, Richard Hull, and Milu Ritivoi supplied transcription, editorial, and technical assistance. At Rodopi, Peter Redpath and Eric van Broekhuizen provided steady guidance. Grateful thanks to them all.

One

INTRODUCTION

Andreea Deciu Ritivoi

"Is there a sense in which interpretation is essential to explanation in the sciences of man?" Charles Taylor asked in his 1971 essay "Interpretation and the Sciences of Man," and his answer was affirmative.[1] Taylor credited Wilhelm Dilthey—and the three twentieth century Continental philosophers, Hans-Georg Gadamer, Paul Ricoeur, and Jürgen Habermas, who had brought Dilthey's hermeneutics back on the center stage of their time in Europe and later in the United States—with the insight that meaning-making activities, efforts to render clear a reality often confusing or apparently incoherent, are at the heart of humanistic pursuits. In retrospect, from the vantage of a twenty-first century perspective, the so-called "interpretive turn" of the 1970s can be viewed as the prelude to, if not first act of many conceptual and methodological sea changes that took place in several disciplines in the humanities and the social sciences and even natural sciences, and that have been often amassed under the general rubric of "post-structuralism."

We take for granted many of the conceptual changes triggered by the interpretive turn. For instance, Hayden White's claim that our knowledge of past events is the result of an interpretive process, instead of a recapturing of what happened, and that history is packaged in narrative terms so as to pass for "realistic" presentations is virtually uncontroversial in some circles. Over the years, it has become significantly more popular than rival theses on historical accounts, which sponsor a stronger realist position. If the interpretive turn had remarkable emancipatory potential for many disciplines in the humanities and social sciences, such a large-scale shift in focus and preoccupation inevitably also had some unfortunate consequences from a conceptual and methodological standpoint. The notion of "interpretation" was diluted in an attempt to fit different agendas and assumptions. Some of the distinctions upon which the pursuit of interpretation was initially predicated in the hermeneutic tradition, either lost their relevance or were altogether modified, and sometimes the modification remained unnoted and unclear.

The question then becomes, Can we rely on a coherent and unified concept of interpretation that would transfer well across different knowledge domains? And several additional questions face us with potentially frustrating methodological choices. When we talk about the constitution of personal identity as self-interpretation (Taylor), anthropological work as interpretation of culture (Clifford Geertz), and the creation of scientific taxonomies as interpretation of the physical world (Thomas Kuhn), does the term "interpretation" retain the same referent? Can it be established what makes an interpretation correct or preferable to other interpretations? Can we even consider the notion of "correctness" or admissibility in interpretive notion of "correctness" or admissibility in interpretive endeavors? We may wish to resist any attempt to unseat a feminist interpretation of a novel, for example, over a Marxist interpretation, but is it acceptable to show similar reticence in the case of interpreting the law, moral values, historical facts, or political programs? How is our understanding of interpretive tasks influenced by epistemic and ontological commitments? Do diehard realists approach interpretive processes with the same attitude and expectations as inveterate relativists?

These are questions we tackle in the present collection of essays. They are fraught with often unspoken assumptions coming from many layers of intersecting philosophical traditions. But we take heart in our efforts to address them because they are also both intellectually challenging and relevant in a broad sense, social, moral, and political. What gives our particular inquiry focus and coherence is the common denominator we all found in addressing interpretive concerns as they emerge from the philosophical work of Michael Krausz. This book is an intellectual homage to an important thinker in the Anglo-American world, and a sharply focused conversation on the issue of interpretation, "moderated" by Krausz insofar as he both offered the topics and responded to our contributions to them.

Born during World War II in Switzerland, Michael Krausz is the son of two Jewish musicians who left Europe for the United States in the aftermath of the war and the Holocaust. His mother, Susan Krausz, is a pianist and composer, and his father, Laszlo Krausz, was a violist and conductor, who played with l'Orchestre de la Suisse Romande and the Cleveland Orchestra, and who conducted the Akron Symphony Orchestra. Krausz inherited artistic inclinations and an Old World sense of intellectual development that defies narrow specialization, yet values excellence and expertise. During his formative years, he studied both music and philosophy, and later discovered and pursued an interest in visual art, especially painting. Today, Krausz is professionally active in all three areas, philosophy, music, and art, an achievement that can appear improbable by the standards of our time and culture. While the range of his interests and abilities is reminiscent of another era, the specifics of his philosophical and artistic program speak to some of the most pressing needs and questions of the present.

Krausz's career has been shaped by his encounters and friendship with several major figures in the intellectual arena of the twentieth century. After he earned his doctorate from the University of Toronto with a thesis on R. G. Collingwood's theory of absolute presuppositions, under the supervision of William Dray, Krausz spent a year at Oxford working with Patrick Gardiner, Sir Isaiah Berlin and Rom Harré. Another stage in his philosophical formation took place in the stimulating environment of the London School of Economics at a time when the institution was the home of Sir Karl Popper, Imre Lakatos, Alan Musgrave, and J. O. Wisdom, who was Krausz's tutor. In later years, Krausz returned to Oxford to teach a joint seminar at All Souls College with his colleague and friend Bimal Matilal, with whom he began to author what became an influential book on relativism. Matilal also encouraged and facilitated Krausz's pursuit of Indian philosophies as they bear on relativism. Rom Harré replaced Matilal, as Krausz's collaborator, after Matilal's untimely death. Since 1970, Krausz has been teaching in the Philosophy department at Bryn Mawr College, where he currently holds the chair of the department and the Milton C. Nahm professorship. In his early years at Bryn Mawr it was the Spanish philosopher José Ferrater-Mora who mentored him. Currently, Krausz also teaches aesthetics at the Curtis Music Institute in Philadelphia. He is one of the co-founders of the Greater Philadelphia Philosophy Consortium, along with Joseph Margolis, whose work on interpretation came to serve as something of a foil for him.

As a musician, Krausz studied violin with Josef Gingold, concertmaster of the Cleveland Orchestra; he received his early conducting coaching from his father, Laszlo Krausz, and later from Frederick Prausnitz at the Peabody Conservatory, and Luis Biava, Resident Conductor of the Philadelphia Orchestra. Krausz has conducted many chamber orchestras, and in 1984, he founded and served as Associate Artistic Director of the Philadelphia Chamber Orchestra. In more recent years, he has been guest conductor of professional orchestras in Bulgaria, among them the Pleven, Vratsa, and Plovdiv Philharmonic Orchestras.

Although he grew up in the presence of art, his father also being a painter, Krausz discovered his interest in art as a result of an epiphanic experience at age twenty-eight, which he has described in an essay included in his edited collection *The Concept of Creativity in Science and Art*. Upon visiting a friend's painting studio and confronting a large shaped canvass, Krausz felt what he later described as an "inner necessity" to paint. To date, he has had nineteen one-person shows and ten two-person shows with his wife, artist Constance Costigan, in the United States and abroad. When I visited Krausz in his painting studio, I was introduced to a creative space that appears to combine in an intriguing intellectual symbiosis his interests in music, art, and philosophy. His paintings are philosophical reflections on the activity of artistic production and interpretation. They feature variations on an abstract image invented by Krausz to symbolize both text and sound, as the image can be perceived both as a hieroglyph and as the visual rendition of the pirouettes made by the conductor's baton. As a reviewer of one of his exhibits, Gloria Russell, noted, "asking how it is that we assign meaning to abstract marks on paper, how we learn to comprehend the nuances of meaning, [Krausz] smudges the invented hieroglyphics, so that the mock text becomes less readable. Thus he insinuates the mystery at the root of all that we know and understand." Outside the studio or the concert hall the philosopher has been attempting over the past decade to decipher this mystery, to find a rigorous conceptual framework in which to address questions about ways of understanding, conducts of inquiry, rationality, and imagination. This not only makes for an interesting intellectual dynamics, but also for a grounded approach to philosophical questions and for a refined, self-aware artistic personality. Put differently, Krausz philosophizes about things that have high stakes for him, and he makes music and art in an intensely reflective way. His readers probably owe to this cross-fertilization of artistic and intellectual concerns Krausz's writing style, which has been characterized by reviewers as austerely beautiful.

An analytic philosopher in the heterodox vein of Collingwood, in edited and authored books Krausz has systematically engaged several themes: relativism and constructivism, individual and cultural identity, sources of creativity and rationality, and interpretation. These themes, or Krausz's views of them, have co-evolved from his earlier essays in *Relativism: Cognitive and Moral* (1984), *Rationality, Relativism, and the Human Sciences* (1986), *Relativism: Interpretation and Confrontation* (1989), *Interpretation, Relativism, and the Metaphysics of Culture* (1991), and *Jewish Identity* (1993) to a full-fledged theory of interpretation that subsumes all his other interests, in *Rightness and Reasons: Interpretation in Cultural Practices* (1993) and *Limits of Rightness* (2000).

The main questions addressed in these books concern the epistemic assumptions and ontological commitments of interpretive practices. As a philosopher, Krausz is unwilling to close prematurely the investigation of issues considered settled by some scholars in other fields. For example, when I reviewed *Limits of Rightness*, from the perspective of someone familiar with theories of interpretation in communication and literary theory, I was surprised to see the author wrestling with such a question: is there one admissible interpretation of a given object, or can we tolerate several equally admissible though maybe not also equally preferable interpretations? After Richard Rorty and Stanley Fish, this question in my intellectual community has become more or less rhetorical. Relativist philosophers and their followers in literary and communication studies typically assume a multiplist stance in interpretive matters. But one of the significant lessons of Krausz's books is about what is at stake in how we deal with such a question, whether we summarily dismiss it or are willing to ponder its further implications for how we think about interpretation.

This present volume has grown out of three professional meetings and many private communications. Upon the invitation of Giridhari Lal Pandit, Krausz gave a lecture in January 1999 at the University of Delhi. As a result of the interest sparked by that lecture among the Indian audience, Pandit organized a four-day international conference on Krausz's philosophical work, with the assistance of Manasvini Yogi and other associates. Some of the papers presented on that occasion are also included here. The conference organized by Pandit in January 2001 is at the origin of this project, and the book itself is deeply indebted to his initiative. The idea of a collective volume grew further when at the 2001 Eastern division meeting of the American Philosophical Association, David Crocker chaired a session "Author Meets Critics" dedicated to the reception of Krausz's book, *Limits of Rightness*. I chaired a similar session at the 2002 Pacific division meeting of the American Philosophical Association. The papers presented on both panels are also included here. Finally, the editors have invited contributions from other scholars with a declared interest in the issue of interpretation. In the end, we have gathered an international team of scholars (philosophers of different traditions and persuasions, a rhetorician, a biologist, and a legal scholar), in a deliberate effort to keep up with the "globalization" of our subject, and to make sure that we are addressing as many diverse concerns as possible within the confines of our fields of inquiry. Our focus remains sharply on a set of detailed questions, as formulated by Krausz. I will introduce them shortly, and Krausz himself provides further elaboration in his lead synoptic essay. First, let me outline the larger, historical and intellectual context in which these questions have emerged and evolved. My goal, in providing such context, is to indicate the relevance of the questions at stake, and to alert the reader to the underlining premises and the commitments involved.

Krausz is an analytic philosopher in the Anglo-American tradition. As a topic of investigation, interpretation is inextricably connected to assumptions and questions that come to us from the Continental tradition of hermeneutics. As we will see, the questions that interest Krausz and the contributors to this volume are not that different from those found in hermeneutics. But it is important to acknowledge and understand the methodological difference between Krausz's approach and the traditional hermeneutical one. Many of us find his methodology attractive in Krausz's explorations of interpretive issues: writing in the vein of analytic investigations, he brings rigor and tight argumentation where looseness and ambiguity can be all too easily encountered.

The hermeneutical legacy, though by no means unified or uncontroversial, is predicated on a series of commonly accepted assumptions about the nature and acquisition of knowledge, the division of labor among scientific and humanistic disciplines, and the applicability of interpretive concerns to well-defined, carefully selected objects, with detailed aims and guiding principles. Dilthey's hermeneutical theory was based on the famous separation of explanation and understanding, tasks compatible with natural sciences (*Naturwissenschaften*) and, respectively, humanistic pursuits *Geisteswissenschaften*).[2] In Dilthey's intention, the separation was to be maintained; he insisted that completely different concepts and methods were adequate for each category. In his system, interpretation fell under the rubric of understanding, and in its turn understanding was the goal of those working in the humanistic realm. While the scientist explains physical phenomena by positing laws and rules, detecting causal mechanisms, and predicting future developments, the humanist understands the experience of another human being, as conveyed in art, literature, or music, through an empathic identification with that individual whose intentions are expressed in the interpreted text, painting, or music. Dilthey was much criticized for this psychologistic account of humanistic endeavors, and supporters of his theory have tried to put it in a different light in order to avoid the accusation of psychologism. However we decide to read Dilthey's theory, one of its major premises is that interpretation becomes a justified pursuit when formalizable explanations are not available. Dilthey's objective was not to engage in the kind of cultural wars that animate current attempts to separate science from the humanities. Rather, as Ricoeur reminds us, Dilthey wished to give interpretive pursuits respectability similar to that of scientific explanations. For this same reason, he could not have afforded to ignore epistemic concerns and accept arbitrariness as part of the interpretive work.

Writing under the powerful influence of Immanuel Kant, even though himself a belated Romantic interested in empathic identifications with works of art and literature, Dilthey pressed the epistemic issue: How does reliable knowledge occur as a result of interpretive activity? His major follower in the twentieth century, Gadamer, addressed this question by further narrowing the scope of hermeneutics.[3] Gadamer claimed that hermeneutics is a conceptual framework that functions well whenever we wish to understand something distant and alien, whether historically or culturally, whose meaning escapes us until we find it in interpretation. Understanding occurs, in Gadamer's account, as a result of a fusion of horizons (*Horizontverschmezung*) that involves a double transaction: of the interpreter's assumptions and expectations to those recognizable in the object of interpretation, and of the object's perceived nature and structure to the background of the interpreter. For Gadamer, interpreters are fundamentally historical creatures, immersed in traditions and linguistic communities, who bring their experience and knowledge to the encounter with the object they are interpreting, and make sense of it in light of how they have been shaped by their tradition and language. Interpretation, then, in the Gadamerian sense, is resolutely rhetorical, as Steven Mailloux would later poignantly emphasize by maintaining that "interpretive theories are not foundational but rhetorical, establishing no permanent grounding or guiding principles guaranteeing correct interpretation but certainly providing much rhetorical substance for interpretive debate."[4]

Gadamer's first edition of his major book, *Truth and Method*, was published in Germany in 1960, but it entered the intellectual arena in the United States more than a decade later. And it did not come alone, but accompanied by the echoes of Jürgen Habermas's critical review. Habermas objected to Gadamer's ontological theory of interpretation, as derived primarily from Martin Heidegger, and defended instead a notion of interpretation as critique of ideology and systematic uncovering of power structures embedded in language.[5] Habermas's concern with interpretation excludes ontology, as his social theory is founded upon a dialogical, consensual theory of truth. While Gadamer recognized the influence of cultural norms and expectations on the practice of interpretation, he did not eliminate altogether the ontological grounding of interpretation. On his account, that the fusion of horizons is ultimately realized is an ontological matter. From Habermas's perspective, on the other hand, "hermeneutical understanding ties the interpreter to the role of a partner in dialogue," and what exists beyond the dialogue, or whether anything at all is beyond the dialogue, is rendered irrelevant. The debate between Gadamer and Habermas revolves around a confrontation between epistemology and ontology.

Ricoeur attempted to resolve this confrontation by proposing in the early 1980s, as part of a more complex intervention, that we revisit the Diltheyean distinction between explanation and understanding.[6] For Ricoeur, the primary object of interpretation is a text, and the interpretation of any other possible object (an action, historical events, and others) is to be modeled on the interpretation of texts. If we consider texts, the interpretive situation in which we try to make sense of them does not match well a communicative encounter, according to Ricoeur, because the author of the text is typically absent and cannot issue clarifications, comment on our interpretive strategies, answer questions, or make any other kind of collaborative intervention from which we commonly benefit in dialogue. When we interpret a text, Ricoeur argues, as a preliminary step to understanding its meaning we do a great deal of explanatory work, ponder its articulations, taking it apart and then putting it back together in an analytical effort similar (but not identical) to the explanatory processes that operate in science. Interpretation, then, is not strictly relegated to understanding, but includes explanation. This view of interpretation is contingent upon how we define explanation, or how far we wish to take the analogy of "explaining" a text as "scientific." On Ricoeur's account, "explanation" means structural analysis, an identification of components and their inter-relations, and of the dynamics between part and whole.

The collapse of the distinction between explanation and understanding vis-à-vis the task of interpretation can be seen as easily leading to the contestation of a further demarcation, that between the humanities and the natural sciences. Post-positivist studies in the philosophy of science frequently insist on the impossibility of formulating scientific laws without interpreting phenomena. These studies claim that "facts" are created through interpretive pursuits, instead of discovered in an external world impassible to our meaning-making efforts. Such a relativist credo, even though popular in some academic circles, is by no means unanimously embraced. But the loss of faith in foundationalist separations between a scientific realm of investigation, in which facts are explained and laws formulated, and a cultural world where we deal in approximations and interpretations, has contributed significantly to the "globalization" of interpretation theory.

In his essays on relativism, Krausz, too, has consistently stood by his anti-foundationalist beliefs. Is he, then, a proponent of interpretation gone global? Despite the absence of an obvious allegiance to any trends in the hermeneutical tradition, Krausz insists, not unlike Gadamer, that for interpretation to exist there must be a reliable difference between it and its objects. Yet this concession does not automatically commit him to an ontological view of interpretation. Nor does Krausz wish to retire ontology altogether from any considerations regarding interpretation. He articulates the concept of interpretation based on three constitutive elements: *ideals, aims,* and *objects*. An ideal is a critical stance that identifies the range of admissible interpretations of a given object *prior* to the conduct of interpretive inquiry. Before I search for an interpretation, I already know, according to Krausz, whether I am willing to accept only one, or several. If I can only tolerate one, I am a singularist. If I am willing to accept several admissible, but not equally preferable interpretations, I am a multiplist. The interesting feature of this notion of interpretive ideal is its ontological neutrality. Although it would be tempting to assume that singularism fares well with realists—insofar as we construe realism as a doctrine searching for straight answers for a univocal reality—and multiplism with constructivism and with cultural objects (such as literary works, music, or art), Krausz insists that these are the orthodox positions, which do not exclude heterodox possibilities. A heterodox position, for example multiplist realism, deems objects of interpretation independent from interpretation, but tolerates incongruent interpretations. Such a distinction already indicates an intention to not use ontological constrains to define interpretive ideals. The bulk of Krausz's philosophical enterprise is devoted to what he calls the "detachability thesis": interpretive ideals, such as singularism and multiplism, do not come with implicit ontological assumptions.

To establish what are the aims of interpretation, Krausz resorts to the *Oxford English Dictionary*, as an attempt to develop his theory within the frame of commonly understood concepts, instead of on more specialized, and potentially counterintuitive, grounds. Based on the *OED* definition, he claims that the principal aim of interpretation is elucidation: to render something clear, to make sense of it. But in addition to elucidation, interpretation can also be aimed at edification when it serves some ulterior purpose. Whether aimed at elucidation or edification (and Krausz insists that edification can only be a secondary, derived aim), the process of interpretation always differs from its object—for if we entertained the possibility that they may not be different, we would also allow for ontology to play a role in our theory of interpretation. But how to "fix" an object and make sure it does not conflate with its interpretation, outside a specified ontology? And if we opt for a specified ontology, is the ontology in question not going to inform both our interpretive aims and ideals? Or, as one of the contributors, Pandit, pointed out to me, how and where do interpretive scenarios establish or define a connection with their object(s) of interpretation?

In large part, the present book addresses these questions, and participates in the larger discussion concerning the confrontation of epistemic and ontological issues in theories of interpretation. Krausz responds in his "Replies" to challenges and critiques offered by the contributors, but this book is not an attempt to close the controversy. What we seek is to offer a clear identification of the possible positions and arguments on the given topic. The book is structured as follows: we open with Krausz's synopsis, in which he summarizes his views of interpretation and explains his three-tier theoretical apparatus: interpretive ideals, interpretive aims, and objects of interpretation. The essays included in Part One further problematize the possibility of proposing a general or a specific theory of interpretation, by invoking the constraints or emancipations that come with philosophical perspectives (Sasaki, Hagberg), and the applicability to detailed objects and aims (Mukherji, Crocker, Moore). In Part Two Margolis, Pradhan, McKenna, Hanna and Harrison, and Grobstein address the problem of ontological commitments, while also exploring in depth the distinctions between singularism and multiplism, and elucidation and edification, as some argue for one element of each distinction over the other, in general or in particular, or consider the theoretical validity of the distinctions in question. Since hermeneutics has often been accused of ethnocentrism, despite Gadamer's argument that it is best understood as a framework for studying difference and cross-cultural encounters, Part Three explores theoretical assumptions (Rao, Stojanov, Chattopdhyaya), and particular analytic claims (Ritivoi) made in interpretive processes that somehow involve more than one cultural context. The essays included in Part Four focus on particular objects of interpretation and putting to test Krausz's apparatus: the law (Weston), visual art (Maxwell), music (Cox, Pandit), and religious texts (Chaturvedi).

We do not think that any of the arguments presented here represent the last word on the issues discussed. The reader may wonder, then: does this book make a genuine contribution toward eliminating the conceptual confusion, answering the many vexing questions, and solving the methodological problems associated with how we think about interpretation? We have more modest ambitions. We propose a sharply focused exchange of philosophical positions and arguments pertaining to the topic of interpretation. Our participation in this project is justified by our belief that this topic could acquire more conceptual and methodological clarity if it is sent back to the drawing board and submitted one more time to a focused and structured investigation. Such an investigation should assure us that we fully understand what is at stake before we assume critical stances and make epistemic commitments.

NOTES

1. Charles Taylor, "Interpretation and the Sciences of Man," *The Review of Metaphysics*, 25:1 (1971), pp. 3–51.

2. Wilhelm Dilthey, *Hermeneutics and the Study of History*, ed. and with intro. by Rudolf Makkreel and Fritjhof Rodi (Princeton: Princeton University Press, 1996).

3. Hans-Georg Gadamer, *Truth and Method* (New York: Seabury Press, 1975).

4. Steven Mailloux, "Interpretation," *Critical Terms for Literary Study*, ed. Frank Lentricchia and Thomas McLaughlin (Chicago: The University of Chicago Press, 1990), p. 134.

5. Jürgen Habermas, *Knowledge and Human Interests* (Boston: Beacon Press, 1972).

6. Paul Ricoeur, *The Conflict of Interpretations: Essays in Hermeneutic* (Evanston, Ill.: Northwestern University Press, 1974).

Two

INTERPRETATION AND ITS OBJECTS: A SYNOPTIC VIEW

Michael Krausz

Five general questions have motivated my recent work. First, what interpretive ideals should we adopt for pertinent objects of interpretation? Second, what sorts of ontological entanglements are involved in interpretive activity? Third, under what conditions do singularism or multiplism apply, and under what conditions does neither apply? Fourth, what bearing does the aim of interpretation have on the range of ideally admissible interpretations? And fifth, how shall we understand the directionality of life paths and projects?

This short essay reviews some of the ground that previous works have provided toward answering these questions. It does not seek to provide detailed arguments that have been published elsewhere. The "Replies and Reflections" that appear at the end of this volume address the queries and challenges of contributors who have prodded me to take yet further steps in the project. I am grateful to them for having considered my work so carefully and for affording this opportunity to ramify previous efforts.

Much of my work is meant to give pause to those who uncritically hold that singularism is required of all interpretation, and to those who hold that multiplism is required for interpretation of all cultural entities. While singularism may apply under some conditions, multiplism may apply under others. And under still further conditions neither singularism nor multiplism applies. That is the point made by the title of my book, *Limits of Rightness*.

One overarching theme of my work concerns the distinction between singularism and multiplism and its relation to the ontological theories of realism, constructivism and constructive realism. Many of the following points are meant to contribute to that concern.

1. Singularism and Multiplism

Rightness and Reasons (abbreviated as RR) and *Limits of Rightness* (abbreviated as LR) center their discussions around a distinction that divides interpreters of cultural achievements into two groups. In one group some assume that for any object of interpretation—say, a work of art, music, or literary text—there can be only one single admissible interpretation. In the other group some assume that for some objects of interpretation more than one interpretation is admissible. I call the first group singularists and the second group multiplists.

The tension between singularists and multiplists is reflected in their relative tolerances for opposing but not exclusive interpretations. Singularists think of opposition in bivalent terms, such that any second interpretation opposed to a first interpretation is contradictory to it, and so all but one should be rejected as inadmissible. The multiplist, on the other hand, holds that opposition need not be understood in such bivalent terms. He or she allows that tension may exist between some contending interpretations, a tension with opposition but without exclusivity. Multiplists deploy such multivalent values as reasonableness, appropriateness, or aptness, and they allow that more than one interpretation may be admissible. Multiplists allow that incongruent interpretations may be jointly defended, but disallow their being conjoined. Although admissible, they must remain numerically distinct.

Notice that singularism and multiplism are asymmetrical in the sense that singularism mandates a single admissible interpretation for all objects of interpretation. In contrast, multiplism affirms that multiplism need be instantiated only in pertinent cases. Multiplism allows that singularist conditions may sometimes obtain.

The interpretive tolerance afforded by the multiplist is no invitation to anarchy, for while more than one interpretation may be admissible, more are inadmissible. The multiplist is just as concerned as the singularist is to jettison inadmissible interpretations, yet he or she holds that there are interpretations which are neither inadmissible nor qualify for a single right interpretation. Further, multiplism affirms that any progress made toward converging upon a limited range of admissible interpretations does not entail singularism. And countenancing one interpretation as preferable (for good reasons) over other admissible interpretations does not result in singularism.

The multiplist condition does not arise from an epistemic lack: it does not affirm that, when all pertinent information and arguments are in, only one interpretation will indeed win out. On the contrary, the multiplist holds that in pertinent cases there are no overarching standards to adjudicate between admissible yet incongruent contending interpretations. Rather, multiplism constitutes an ideal condition.

Both singularism and multiplism deploy the concept of ideal admissibility. This latter notion might be thought to presuppose the idea of an "end of inquiry." Yet LR softens an otherwise hard reading of this idea by suggesting that the idea of an end of inquiry should be understood in pragmatic terms wherein informed practitioners may agree that all pertinent evidence or argumentation is available to make a suitably informed determination of whether a given object of interpretation answers to one or more than one interpretation. Pertinent ideals should be understood within provisional, unfolding, and changing interpretive conditions. Accordingly, I embrace Richard Rorty's pragmatist sentiment when, in speaking of the notion of a *Grenzbgriff* (or a limiting concept), he says, "To say that *we* think we're heading in the right direction is just to say, with Kuhn, that we can, by hindsight, tell the story of the past as a story of progress. To say that we still have a long way to go, that our present views should not be cast in bronze, is too platitudinous to require support by positing limit-concepts."[1]

2. Multiplism and Critical Pluralism

Multiplism does not hold that all admissible interpretations are equally preferable. On the contrary, multiplism allows for good reasons for preferring one admissible interpretation to another one without it being the case that the grounds for the preferred interpretation are so strong as to disallow other would-be admissible interpretations. This is what distinguishes multiplism from what has sometimes been called "critical pluralism" which does hold that multiple interpretations are equally preferable.[2] Accordingly, RR and LR retire the notion of "critical pluralism." In turn, that phrase should not be confused with what I have called the "pluralizing" strategy that might be deployed to install a pluralist condition (wherein a one-one relation between interpretation and its object would obtain). So understood, a pluralist condition is singularist.

3. Pluralizing and Aggregating

RR uses the notion of "pluralizing" to mark a strategy for separating out objects of interpretation or for separating out interpretations themselves. For example, a singularist might pluralize an object of interpretation that first might appear to answer to two opposing interpretations. In so doing, he or she might install a one-to-one relation between a pluralized object and one of the given interpretations, and a one-to-one relation between the other pluralized object and one of the other given interpretations.

Or, to install the singularist condition we might seek to aggregate pertinent interpretations into one. In that way, a one-to-one relation between object of interpretation and interpretation would also be installed. Conversely, when the multiplist confronts a case of an aggregated interpretation, he or she may seek to pluralize them, to separate them into distinct interpretations. In this way, a many-to-one relation between interpretations and object-of-interpretation may be installed. Such strategies may serve singularists' or multiplists' interests.

The singularist who pluralizes an object of interpretation into two or more (to install a one-to-one relation between different interpretations and their respective objects) may do so to establish that he or she is addressing different objects in turn. This procedure would undermine the multiplist's assumption that a single object is answering to more than one interpretation. In this way, the singularist would seek to dissipate the contest between otherwise competing interpretations.

4. Imputation as an Argument for Multiplism

Imputationism holds that interpretive activity may impute properties to a given object of interpretation. At different interpretive moments, the object is thought to take on different properties. Whether the same object takes on such properties, or whether in virtue of their taking on such properties the object is no longer common between interpretive moments depends upon the "hardness" (G. W. Leibniz) or the "softness" (Ludwig Wittgenstein) of our theory of commonality. According to a harder theory of commonality, when such objects take on different properties they become uncommon. According to a softer theory, when such objects take on different properties, they may still remain common. RR does not propound imputationism but does underscore the issues of identity in the face of imputationist strategies.

Some theorists find that imputationism is especially sympathetic to multiplism, but this is not so. Imputationism does not uniquely ground multiplism over singularism, since imputationism is also compatible with singularism. The claim of imputability is logically independent of the claim of multiple imputability. The former does not entail the latter. A singularist could allow that interpretive activity alters an entity's nature, but yet affirm that there is one and only one admissible way to impute properties. A singularist could also affirm that different moments of interpretive activity yield different objects of interpretation. So seen, a pluralist (i.e. a singularist) rather than a multiplist condition would obtain.

5. Intentional Objects

When speaking of objects of interpretation I refer to intentional objects, objects endowed with meaning or significance within a field of cultural codes, norms, or the like. They are objects upon which meaning has been conferred, presented as having the meaning they do. And by speaking of "objects" I do not mean to imply the thought that they are objects in a strictly synchronic atomic sense that precludes taking processes as intentional objects. Instead, objects of interpretation understood as intentional objects may be understood as nodes of networks of culturally endowed complexes. So understood, both the singularist's requirement for a one-to-one relation between interpretation and object of interpretation, and the multiplist's requirement for a one-many relation between interpretations and object of interpretation concern relations between interpretation(s) and intentional object(s).

6. Commonality

The condition of commonality of pertinent objects of interpretation underlies both singularism and multiplism. If otherwise competing interpretations do not address a common object of interpretation, then they cannot compete or disagree with one another. RR and LR thematize the issue of commonality by suggesting that, at least in cultural domains, commonality should not be "hard" or absolute or Leibnitzian. Instead, objects of interpretation may be common in the sense as suggested by Wittgenstein's notion of a family resemblance.

The sorts of examples typically adduced in RR and LR include paintings, performances, works of music, works of literature, and the like. Their individuating conditions can be specified with sufficient determinacy to speak of one or more than one interpreted objects. Yet sometimes—when the grounds are unavailable to determine whether otherwise competing interpretations actually address a common object—neither singularism nor multiplism apply. If the object is not common or if there are no grounds to determine whether interpretations address a common object, no contest between interpretations can arise.

7. Indeterminacy

Multiplism might be thought to be secured by the indeterminacy of objects of interpretation. Yet LR cautions that indeterminacy is not sufficient for multiplism. For an indeterminate object of interpretation we might install a single admissible interpretation. A singularist condition might obtain where the indeterminacy of an interpretation "matches" the indeterminacy of the object in question. The point is that multiplism is not entailed by the indeterminacy of pertinent objects.

8. Examples

RR and LR offer a range of examples that exemplify multiplism. They include incongruent interpretations of such works as Beethoven's First Symphony, Vincent Van Gogh's Potato Eaters, Wordsworth's Lucy poems, Christo's "Valley Curtain" and "Wrapped Reichstag," historical actions, and cross-cultural phenomena. LR adduces an example that concerns a dead infant baby found in the Ganges River at the Hindu holy city of Banaras in India. It addresses the question whether the baby should be interpreted as an "honored" morally unsullied individual being "returned" to the hallowed eternal life force of the Ganges (as Hindus and Buddhists might have it), or whether it should be interpreted as merely "dumped" (as a secular North American might have it), or both. Further, LR considers the paintings of Anselm Kiefer, which have been interpreted as celebrating and exorcising memories of the Third Reich. LR affirms that these are opposed but not exclusive interpretations, thus fulfilling the multiplist condition. To this tally we may add process-centered versus product-centered interpretations of creativity or of personal programs.

Sometimes the object of interpretation lacks individuating conditions so completely that judgments of commonality cannot be made at all. For example, LR outlines the case of that to which Hindus and Buddhists ultimately address themselves. On both their accounts, they each address something (Atman or Oneness for the Hindu, and Emptiness for the Buddhist) that answers to no determinate identity conditions. Both assert that language prohibits either from describing their ultimate object of interpretation, since language itself is taken to be constrained by its entrenched subject-object dualities. And on both their accounts, subject-object dualities should be overcome to achieve full realization. In such cases, a condition necessary for both singularism and multiplism would be denied, namely the condition of countability of the pertinent object of interpretation. Neither singularism nor multiplism could obtain. Such a case would have transcended the "limits of rightness." Hindu and Buddhist informants disagreeing about whether they address a common thing at all further complicate the situation. Accordingly, they disagree about whether they disagree, for without the commonality in question there could be no disagreement.

9. The Detachability Thesis

Singularism is often associated with the ontological theory of realism, and multiplism is often associated with the ontological theory of constructivism. But RR argues that these associations are not necessary. The views that for all objects of interpretation there must be one admissible interpretation, and that for a given object of interpretation there may be more than one admissible interpretation, are both consistent with realism or constructivism. The question of whether there must be one or whether there may be more than one admissible interpretation is logically detachable (as to entailment) from both realism and constructivism. LR adds that both singularism and multiplism are logically detachable from various versions of constructive realism—notably those offered by Paul Thom, Rom Harré, Bernard Harrison and Patricia Hanna, Fritz Wallner, Hilary Putnam, Chhanda Gupta, and Joseph Margolis.

I emphasize that RR and LR do not actually propound any one of these mentioned ontological theories, although I will do so in "Replies and Reflections" that appears at the end of this volume.

The thesis that the mentioned ontologies are logically detachable from singularism and multiplism should not be read as affirming that metaphysics more generally understood is irrelevant to the understanding of interpretive activity. Indeed, (1) the distinction between objects of interpretation and their interpretations, (2) the intentionality of objects of interpretation, and (3) the identity conditions of objects of interpretation all have metaphysical import. Yet, none of these points uniquely entail singularism or multiplism.

10. Distributive Claims, Objectivity and Ontology

The level of discourse at which realism, constructivism, and constructive realism are in contest is not the level at which particular distributive claims are made. Proponents of these ontological theories may agree about distributive claims while disagreeing about their ontological construals. No matter which of these ontologies they might embrace, proponents may agree that there are horses but no unicorns, that the sun rises in the East, and so on. Their disagreements arise at a second-order level of discourse concerned with the construals of the grounds for objecthood and related notions. These ontologies are not concerned with distributive claims, and none of them entails singularism or multiplism.

Insofar as objectivity is concerned with the grounds for making distributive judgments that separate particular admissible interpretations from inadmissible ones (as I use the notion of objectivity) the contest between the mentioned ontologies does not directly bear on questions of objectivity. In turn, any account of objectivity would not be located at the level of ontology but at the level of methodology.

11. Realism and Constructivism

RR rehearses the dialectic between realism and constructivism. Realists stress the logical independence of the way things are from human representations of it (e.g. John Searle). And constructivists reject the thought that there is a world that consists of a totality of version-independent objects (e.g. Nelson Goodman).

According to the constructivist view, an "object" (or for our purposes an object of interpretation) is intentionally layered in virtue of its being nested in some symbol system. For the constructivist, it is not that nothing is intentionalized. Rather, an intentional something is further intentionalized. And that is a something, not a nothing. Nowhere does the object as such "begin," independent of some symbol system or conceptual scheme. Nowhere does the uninterpreted object as such appear. And, according to the constructivist, not only is past actuality constructed "after the fact" but historical events as they unfold are constructed as well. What happens in the present and becomes past is interpretation-dependent.

12. The Constructivist's Reductio

According to the constructivist, any attempt to drive a conceptual wedge between objects as such and objects as represented will fail, for any described object as such will be a represented object, nested in a symbol system of some kind or other. This condition is inescapable. Nothing intelligible can be said about "the world" independent of world-versions. So, we should let the idea of an uninterpreted "world" or "objects as such" drop out of all accounts. Any attempt to say what a version is a version of will issue in yet another version! In short, there can be no talk of symbol system-independent objects. About such things it is best to remain silent.[3] RR and LR call this inference the constructivist's reductio (of realism). Clearly, the constructivist's reductio tends toward the conclusion that constructivism must be global and that realism cannot be injected in a piecemeal way. Yet this globalism does not preclude distinguishing nature from culture, say, in terms that are subtended under the constructivist's rubric.

13. Constructive Realism

The constructive realist, whose motto is "the real is constructed and the constructed is real," seeks a compromise between realism and constructivism. (I adopt the motto from Margolis, but offer my construal of its significance.) LR offers two versions of constructive realism, namely, internal and external. LR argues that, along with realism and constructivism, they too are logically detachable from singularism and multiplism. Internal constructive realism is detachable from singularism and multiplism because it is compatible with both. And external constructive realism is detachable from singularism and multiplism because it is compatible with neither.

You might be weary of calling constructive realism a realism at all, since at the second order it embraces a global constructivism. Yet the point of keeping its realist credential is to underscore that, at the first-order where distributive claims are made, constructive realism has all the resources necessary to distinguish between real and unreal objects.

The articulation of constructive realism helps itself to Putnam's heterodox view that existence and objecthood are internal to conceptual schemes.[4] At the same time, the claim that objecthood and existence are internal to conceptual schemes does not rule out the possibility that there is presystematic "input," as Putnam contentiously says, or pre-systematic "stuff," on the basis of which existing objects are to be constituted. To concede that objects or existents are internal to conceptual schemes is not to affirm that there is nothing external to conceptual schemes. Putnam says, ". . . why should the fact that reality cannot be described independent of our descriptions lead us to suppose that only the descriptions exist?"[5] This allows that you might embrace the views (1) that existence and objecthood are internal to conceptual schemes, and there is nothing external to conceptual schemes (internal constructive realism), or (2) that existence and objecthood are internal to conceptual schemes and there is something external to conceptual schemes (external constructive realism). This view allows the claim that there is pre-systematic "stuff" upon which our knowledge is based. (It is unclear which of these Putnam actually embraces, but that need not concern us here.) The core claim of constructive realism—again, that objecthood and existence are internal to conceptual schemes—allows but does not mandate that there is undifferentiated stuff (not yet ordained as existing or as real) beyond any conceptual scheme. In Kantian terms, if you were to posit that a noumenal realm were there—providing the undifferentiated "stuff" for the construction of real objects—you would be an external constructive realist. If you were to forswear the noumenal realm, you would be an internal constructive realist.

Yet we might ask of the external constructive realist, in what sense of "is" can it be said that there is pre-scheme stuff? In response, the external constructive realist may say that the pertinent sense of "is" is a noumenal "is" —a posit with no claim of existence. But what could that be? The external constructive realist could reply that "stuff" is an expression used to indicate the absence of any concept being applied to a subject. Its use is to show that you are not applying a significant concept to a subject. Immanuel Kant's thing-in-itself (*Ding an sich*) or the noumenal world is such a subject. Accordingly, the notion of a noumenal world is a kind of limit of thought (*Grenzbegriff*) rather than a clear concept. In response, the internal constructive realist might reply that this negative characterization of "stuff" still does not tell us in what sense we can affirm that the stuff is there, that is, exists. On the contrary, the negative characterization only tells us why we cannot say that the stuff is there or that it exists.

Here is the dilemma. It would be contradictory for the external constructive realist to say that the pre-scheme stuff exists in the internalist sense. Alternatively, if the pre-scheme stuff is still said to be there, the external constructive realist must provide a positive characterization of the different sense in which it is so. But that characterization is absent. In short, we are left with contradiction or incompleteness.

There are further problems for both internal and external constructive realists. The internal constructive realist might press the point that, even if we granted the stuff to the external constructive realist, that in itself would not explain the emergence of existent objects, for to do so would require the still further account of how undifferentiated stuff gives rise to differentiated objects, how differentiation might arise from undifferentiation. And for the internal constructive realist there is the mystery of the origin of constituted objects.

Internal and external constructive realists disagree as to whether there is "stuff" that precedes the symbol systems which construct and nest real objects. While internal constructive realists deny that there is such stuff, external constructive realists affirm that there is. The internal constructive realist holds that there can be no appeal to anything that precedes a symbol system. The external constructive realist holds that, although it cannot be countenanced as embodying real objects, some pre-systematic stuff needs to be appealed to in order to account for the construction of real objects. While the external constructive realist concedes that real objects are not outside symbol systems (or that we cannot make sense of the claim that real objects are outside symbol systems), this concession does not prohibit our positing that there is something there outside of symbol systems that constitutes the stuff from which real objects are constituted within symbol systems.

As regards the detachability thesis, notice that in external constructive realism the pre-scheme stuff remains undifferentiated. No individuation of objects operates with respect to it. Consequently, you cannot ask of its undifferentiated stuff whether it is common between its otherwise contending interpretations. External constructive realism does not admit of singularism or multiplism, for both singularism and multiplism require that otherwise contending interpretations must address a common object of interpretation. Undifferentiated stuff cannot satisfy the condition of individuation necessary for it to answer to singularism or multiplism. It remains that with respect to the once constituted objects within conceptual schemes, singularism or multiplism may obtain. Internal constructive realism is compatible with singularism or multiplism, and external constructive realism is compatible with neither singularism nor multiplism. Neither variety of constructive realism entails singularism or multiplism.

LR counts Putnam and Chhanda Gupta as external constructive realists (although there is some uncertainty about doing so), along with Paul Thom, Rom Harré, Bernard Harrison and Patricia Hannah, and Fritz Wallner. And it counts Joseph Margolis as an internal constructive realist.

14. Second-Order Constructivism

We might be tempted, in piecemeal fashion, to range some sorts of objects under a realist rubric and other sorts of objects under a constructivist rubric. But such a temptation would be frustrated by the constructivist's reductio that tends toward a globalism: realism cannot be injected in a piecemeal way.

In contrast, a second-order constructivist holds that any distinction made at the first-order between the real and the unreal, or between the real and the imaginary, or between representation-independence and representation-dependence, or between practice-independence and practice-dependence, or between non-intentional objects ("natural") and intentional objects ("cultural"), or any cognates thereof—should be subtended under a second-order constructivism. This view allows the usual first-order distinctions between the real and the unreal and it leaves distributive claims in place. The first order distinction would be subtended under a second-order constructivism. Notice that second-order constructivism is compatible with both internal and external constructive realism, but it entails neither. You might embrace second-order constructivism and deny either or both internal and external constructive realism.

Neither RR nor LR actually propounds realism, constructivism, or constructive realism. Their central concerns are with the relation of singularism and multiplism to these mentioned ontologies. They are concerned primarily with the detachability thesis.

15. Aims of Interpretation

LR observes that interpretive activity characteristically aims to make sense or to explain pertinent objects of interpretation. It calls this general aim elucidation. Yet elucidation is not the only possible use of interpretive activity. Interpretation may also be used for edification, which includes consolation or self-realization. For example, Hindu and Buddhist interpretations seek both to elucidate the nature of things in a general sense. They also aim to edify by alleviating suffering, by healing or consoling. Or, to take another example, you might favor an interpretation of one of Giovanni Bellini's many religious paintings because doing so might facilitate your "entering into" the sacred space depicted in the painting and thereby foster the viewer's religious sensibilities.[6] But such a favoring would amount to pursuing an aim extrinsic to the characteristic aim of interpretation.

Despite interpretive activity sometimes satisfying different aims, the characteristic aim of interpretation remains elucidation. If interpretive activity might edify it would do so in an ancillary way. However, the claim that interpretation is characteristically elucidatory should not be taken as essentialist. It is, instead, an empirical claim about how interpretation is characteristically pursued. Consistent with an anti-essentialist variantist view, LR allows that what it takes to be a characteristic aim of interpretive activity may change in the course of the history of interpretive practices. Interpretive activity has no intrinsic, invariant, immutable aim.

16. Paths and Projects

Finally, LR introduces a distinction parallel to that between singularism and multiplism, namely between directional singularism and directional multiplism. The latter distinction concerns life paths and projects. A directional singularist holds that, for a given individual, there must be one admissible life path. And a directional multiplism holds that for a given individual there may be more than one admissible life path. LR embraces directional multiplism. It resists the thought that such "inner necessities" as may be revealed in epiphanic experiences, for example, must be understood in singularist and essentialist terms. Instead, whatever inner necessities may be experienced are best understood in terms of the concept of a project. Accordingly, inner necessity is understood as the objective necessity of the movement toward closure of a project as set within the context of a practice, leaving open the morality of the project in question. Yet there is room for critical discussion about which projects should be taken up and which should not. So seen, the phrase "inner necessity" requires no obscure essences. There is no inherent "inner" here. Nor is there a necessity of an inherent innatist self. Accordingly, the self changes and transforms in accord with the goals and values of its adopted projects.

Such is my synopsis. Let us now turn to the essays which address one or another of these issues. In their light, I shall ramify and sometimes modify some of the salient claims I have enumerated here.

NOTES

1. Richard Rorty, "Solidarity or Objectivity?" *Relativism: Interpretation and Confrontation*, ed. Michael Krausz (Notre Dame: University of Notre Dame Press, 1989), p. 42.

2. Alexander Nehamas, "The Postulated Author: Critical Monism as a Regulative Ideal," *Critical Inquiry* 8 (Autumn 1981), pp. 133–149. Also see David Novitz, "Against Critical Pluralism," *Is There a Single Right Interpretation?* ed. Michael Krausz (University Park, Penna.: The Pennsylvania State University Press, 2002), pp. 101–121.

3. Nelson Goodman, "Notes on the Well-Made World" and "On Starmaking," *Starmaking*, ed. Peter McCormick (Cambridge, Mass.: MIT Press, 1996).

4. Hilary Putnam, *Reason, Truth, and History* (Cambridge: Cambridge University Press, 1981), p. 52. Also see Hilary Putnam, *Many Faces of Realism* (LaSalle, Ill.: Open Court, 1987), p. 19.

5. Hillary Putnam, "Irrealism and Deconstruction," in McCormick, *Starmaking*, p. 189.

6. Giovanni Bellini's "St. Francis" (New York, Frick Art Museum), "The Dead Christ and an Angel in Scarlet" (London, National Gallery), "Christ Carrying the Cross" (Collection of Duke Louis de Brissac), or "The Pieta" (Venice, Academy). All these are reproduced in Philip Hendy and Ludwig Goldscheider, *Giovanni Bellini* (Oxford: Phaidon Press Ltd., 1945).

IDEALS AND AIMS
OF INTERPRETATION

Three

RIGHTNESS RECONSIDERED: KRAUSZ, WITTGENSTEIN, AND THE QUESTION OF INTERPRETIVE UNDERSTANDING

Garry L. Hagberg

Michael Krausz's *Limits of Rightness* offers the rare combination of humane depth, cultural breadth, and analytical precision.[1] Many discussions of interpretive pluralism in philosophical aesthetics, literary theory, and cultural studies, could benefit from a fundamental point that Krausz makes clear: we must articulate interpretive pluralism in such a way that the plurality of interpretations address the same cultural entity. As Krausz shows, we can easily and mistakenly believe that pluralism's plausibility depends on there being differently constituted cultural entities.

For example, your Brothers Karamazov is different from mine in our varying subjective constitutions of the text, and so pluralism appears a natural theoretical option in that we are interpreting different objects. But with different interpretive objects, even if named similarly (like different people with the same name), interpretive singularism would be equally plausible. And, with identifiably different interpreted objects unique to our own idiosyncratic readings, multiplism would be called for only if we each had different and competing interpretations of our Brothers Karamazov. Krausz clarifies this, and then pursues the more pressing question: Can there be multiple and equally admissible interpretations of the same interpreted cultural entity?

To begin to answer such a question, we might turn to the question of the ontology of the cultural object. We might seize upon the idea that a cultural entity subject to interpretation will possess a finite set of determinate properties that determine its fixed identity before any interpretive intervention by the observer. Then, we might believe that such a fixed-property realism would imply interpretive singularism. On this view only that single interpretation formed in direct correspondence to those fixed properties is true. All others, failing the correspondence to fixity, would be false.

The polemical opposite to this singularist position quickly and naturally suggests itself as well. Seize on the idea that a cultural entity subject to interpretation will possess an indeterminate collection of properties that are in continual flux. Advance the explanation that this flux is allowed by the constructivist nature of the object and sustained by the variegated and evolving perceptual and interpretive interventions of the observer. Such a variable-property constructivism would imply multiplism. To have shown (as I will try to indicate throughout this discussion) that this analysis applies with equal force to the interpretation of works of art and to human selves is a noteworthy achievement. One that thus reveals many of their telling similarities.

But this book's signal achievement is to have demonstrated that the contest between singularism and multiplism is detachable from ontological commitments. The intuitive linkages we may too quickly grasp between realism and singularism, and between constructivism and multiplism, are the conceptual equivalent of optical illusions. To fully settle the ontological question concerning the nature of the interpreted cultural entity would not be to also settle, by implication from that ontology, the single-right-interpretation question. If the veracity of the single-right-interpretation were insured by the ontological fixity of the object, then we would also have ready to hand a stable criterion for the adjudication of any two competing interpretations. Simply stated, that interpretation that more closely approximates the ideal would be preferable. This interpretive logic would apply with equal force to the question of the interpretation of human selves, and to self-interpretation as well. But matters are not so simple.

Krausz himself looks at the issue of singularism versus multiplism from a multiplicity of perspectives. Advancing his earlier work on the subject, he shows why the interpretive ideals of singularism and multiplism do not apply only in those cases where we lack the grounds to determine if competing interpretations address one object in common beneath the two interpretations. Here, Krausz demarcates the limits of rightness. He knows that the term "interpretation" is not univocal, and that we do not follow narrow and uniform rules for its singular and correct application. The concept is used multifariously, and Krausz will not allow the unifying demands of theory to falsify the diversity of our practice.

That diversity is explored through a range of cases, including: Indian burial rites and attendant concepts of moral purification and transmigration; the paintings of Vincent Van Gogh, Paul Klee, and Anselm Keifer; Josef Gingold's Stradivarius; phlogiston and subatomic particles; contrasts between Hindu and Buddhist soteriologies; and Christo's *Wrapped Reichstag* as a problem in artistic boundary indeterminacy. In the course of his investigations into these culturally expansive cases, his analysis turns to ontological options for the theoretical construal of the interpretive artifacts that lie between the polar extremes of realism and constructivism. This project is significant for the achievement of a larger understanding of self-interpretation, precisely because the ontology of the self is too quickly articulated in fixed-property realist or (polemically opposed) variable-property constructivist terms.

Krausz takes Ludwig Wittgenstein's critique of ostensive definition (ostention alone does not individuate) as his point of departure. He revivifies our appreciation of the importance of the intentional background for the individuation of the object to which we ostensively point, be it a broom (Wittgenstein's famous example) or the Wrapped Reichstag. This opening leads into Krausz's distinctive articulation of constructive realism, which acknowledges that objects are not "given" as such. Instead, they are "taken" within the intentional frame of the observer: the symbol system, or representational system (in a manner reminiscent of Nelson Goodman), of the observer. Challenging the insistent view that we can begin any such inquiry with a basic description of an uninterpreted reality above which the interpretations float, Krausz nicely reveals some of the deep ties between problems in metaphysics and the philosophy of language. For example, the description of an uninterpreted realist world of pre-represented objects will invariably proceed within a language, within an interpretive matrix. We must relinquish the desire or overcome the temptation to speak of that pre-interpreted world. But, the process of conceptual therapy Krausz takes us through does not deliver us into an ever-new world of chaotic flux and rampant subjectivism. He is after a constructive realism, and the contingency is thus constrained.

But, on Krausz's view, is it constrained by the conditions of the preverbal world unto itself, or by what we (as ontologically empowered linguistic interventions) say about that world? Krausz wants to unearth and remove the dichotomy undergirding the formulation of this question as a formative influence on our thinking and our corresponding subsequent expectations of how an answer must proceed. The constructivist point concerns the necessity of any description of the interpreted object proceeding inside of language, never to be free of constructivist interventions no matter how scientistic our descriptive language is. The realist replies that this point concerns not what is but only what we say about what is. Krausz regards what he uncovers here, a kind of early-Wittgensteinian unsayability, as instructive. The telling impossibility of elucidating realism cleanly, in a manner free of the human hand's smudgy intervention in the proceedings, shows Krausz that the dialectic is the surface manifestation of an undergirding conceptual picture that should be excavated and eradicated.

I am casting Krausz's project in terms that are more Wittgensteinian than he uses. But, Krausz sees and says that the impulsion to ask the question originates in an underlying picture of a bifurcated separability. That separability, having first severed our many connections and relations between words and the world, then leads us to search out one fundamental and ontologically significant relation that obtains between the two metaphysical categories. In relation to the problem of selfhood and the special nature of the project of the self taking itself as its object of investigation, we would bifurcate the self as an entity that is in ontological fact hermetically sealed unto itself (analogous to the world as originally sealed from the word) and then only contingently spoken about in the ontologically separate words we use to describe it. Directly stated, the self is pictured as a fixed given unto itself, like the world on this ontologically bifurcated world-word conceptual template, and the language of the self, autobiographical writing, is pictured as ex post facto descriptions that, like the words that describe but do not in part constitute the world, are secondary to the prior facts that obtain in the pre-linguistic world. This philosophical picture engenders its polemical opposite. The linguistic constructivist will argue that words make the world, and exercise the constitutive power they are denied on the opposing realist view. The corresponding view of the self and its autobiographical writing is that autobiographical writing makes the self. The grand bifurcated categories of world and word are anything but innocent when we turn to the question of selfhood and autobiographical knowledge. On the contrary, they lay down grooves of thought of which it becomes difficult to steer clear.

I would like to know whether Krausz would accept this reformulation as one essential part of his larger project. If so, the opposition to this dichotomy would constitute a deep affinity between his view and some resurgent pragmatist views. The vital point emerging from Krausz's reflections is that we will feel impelled to espouse a radical constructivism only so long as we retain the dichotomy that the realist and constructivist share. Because the fixed referents with real properties are not accessible via language or perception, the constructivist position is in an important sense defined negatively. Constructivism is defined in terms of how we must identify and describe the interpretive object, because we could not intelligibly do it by capturing the prelinguistic in language.

Moving with Krausz beyond this dialectic of polarized opposites sharing a common foundational picture, makes possible the development of a constructive realism. In that realism the role of our interpretive practices is acknowledged without embracing a reckless interpret-what-you-will constructivism. Elements of realism, such as questions (1) of the "fit" of a description of a cultural object or entity, (2) of whether a given property is in the interpreted object, either the art work or the self, and (3) of the abiding qualities of a work or object or self that has gone unseen by its contemporary audience, all can and do arise in particular contexts of inquiry. And, elements of constructivism arise as well. We find questions about (1) the "historied" nature of the perceiving eye or ear; (2) the potentially prismatic nature of an aesthetic property we think we are seeing clearly (where the perceptual error is discerned in retrospect, thus calling into question our other perceptions of the object); and (3) the power of the particular background, interests, and sensibility of the interpreter where these powers become constitutive of that object's relational properties. All these context-specific issues that intelligibly arise only within particular contexts of inquiry, are compatible with Krausz's synthesis-ontology of constructive realism. His ontology does not entail singularism, multiplism, or, moving beyond a dichotomy and what it enforces in our expectations of an answer, either one in those cases that extend beyond the limits of rightness.

A number of such particular interpretive issues arise in the case of Christo's *Wrapped Reichstag*. Krausz uses this case to good effect to show that these issues taken together reveal an aesthetically significant boundary-indeterminacy in the work. Does it include only the German parliament building, over 60 tons of billowing silvery fabric, and over 10 miles of blue rope, all put in place around the building? Or, as Christo claims, does it include both the pre-history of the work, its conception, its long and arduous process of permissions and the files of correspondence and drawings leading to the permissions, and what we might then call the work's post-history, i.e., the revelers around the building, the art students sketching it, the storefronts displaying silver-in-blue wrapped objects, etc.? Here, as Krausz shows, where one draws the line between work and non-work is constitutive of the work. And that line could be drawn at many points. Krausz shows how such cases quickly unsettle any presumption we may have concerning the "fixed-object with a finite list of properties" model. On reflection, I think Krausz would accept this extension of his point, such cases also quickly unsettle the opposite presumption concerning the power of the interpreter of the object as envisioned by the constructivist. We can draw the lines in many plausible places. But, we cannot draw them just anywhere. For instance, we cannot possibly include the fabric and exclude the blue rope in the way we can include the fabric and the blue rope and not the documentation preceding the act of wrapping. Similar non-arbitrary constraints naturally emerge in the interpretation of selves, biographically or autobiographically.

I see Krausz's fundamental point concerning artistic boundary indeterminacy. I also see a further point concerning the context-occasioned nature of particularized questions that sometimes lean toward the realist view, sometimes toward the constructivist. The power of the judgments we make is in some respects constrained by the properties of the object. And in some different respects they exert work-determinative control over it. But a fundamental difference of epistemic priority may emerge in our thinking about such cases. Should the facts of our interpretive practices be construed as surface-level manifestations of a deeper truth to the matter yet to be analyzed, in such a way that our praxis should be organized around the principle of interpretive constraint imposed by the fixed properties of the object for the realist, or around the principle of work-constitutive interpretive power for the constructivist? Or, should those practices, for all their diversity and noncommittal stature vis-à-vis the realism/constructivism polemic, be themselves given priority as instructive sources of what knowledge we can have on this issue? The messiness and diversity of the particularities will be regarded as a more accurate, if far more unwieldy, report in some cases on the way things are, and in other cases on the way we take them? Perhaps they should not even be organized into a pattern of cases supporting the synthesis-ontology of constructive-realism of the nuanced variety Krausz favors? I endorse these less constrained views.

Krausz uses some passages of Wittgenstein's to good effect in the course of his analysis. Discussing the issue of boundary indeterminacy in relation to identity, he quotes Wittgenstein's question:

"Has the name 'Moses' got a fixed and unequivocal use for me in all possible cases?—Is it not the case that I have, so to speak, a whole series of props in readiness, and am ready to lean on one if another should be taken from under me and vice versa?" (quoted. in LR, p. 107).

Wittgenstein is directing our attention to our practices and contexts of linguistic uses, in order to glean what we can about the meaning of a word. He does so quite apart from any preconceptions we may bring to the inquiry as shaped by an underlying model of meaning as a template to organize and systematically arrange those otherwise unwieldy practices. Throughout *Limits of Rightness* Krausz sees all this clearly. Yet, we might still ask whether Krausz goes as far as the powerful collection of cases and the fundamental insight of the book concerning the limits of theoretical concision warrants. I mean something like the following.

"Interpretation" is itself a word. Given the complex and intricate interpretive practices Krausz so adroitly assembles, good reasons exist to acknowledge interpretation's diversity in practice, its wide range of possible employments, uses, and applications. Krausz acknowledges as much. Might a reasonably close look at some further passages of Wittgenstein that pertain directly to questions of interpretation prove helpful? Might those passages redirect our attention to differences and nuances that unsettle a common presumption concerning an underlying unity in the concept of interpretation, belief in which is sustainable only by insufficiently attending to the finer particularities? With regard to the question of autobiographical knowledge, this issue would prove indisputably central, since the precise way in which we understand "interpretation" will determine the way we picture or understand the concept "self-interpretation." With this in mind, we might reconsider the following case.

In investigating the case of a pupil assigned the task of writing down a sequence of numbers according to a particular rule (initially simply natural numbers in decimal notation from zero to nine), Wittgenstein observes that if the pupil copies the series 0, 1, 2, 3, 4, 5, . . . in this way, 1, 0, 3, 2, 5, 4, . . . , we will be inclined to say that he has "understood wrong[ly]," or misinterpreted our meaning. We will do so because we can easily discern a pattern to the mistake, because it is a "systematic mistake."[2] But to forestall the quickly advancing notion that in such cases we are identifying the presence of a mental state as that meaning, although the wrong one for the assigned task, Wittgenstein adds that there is "no sharp distinction between a random mistake and a systematic one," or that cases we are inclined to call "random" and cases we are inclined to call "systematic" are not sharply distinguished. (In some cases the details will tell us which is right, and in others the decision as to its random or systematic nature will be constitutive.) So far, the philosophical significance is only implicit. If we determined such cases strictly according to the presence or absence of a mental state, then categorical sharpness would exist. No such clarity exists. So we call into question the idea that a mental state exists that serves as the criterion of understanding.

The force of that question is strengthened next. If the pupil writes zero to nine in a way we find satisfactory, we will be satisfied in a larger sense only if the pupil does this correctly most of the time, "not if he does it right once in a hundred attempts" (§145). This strengthens the question because the practice of the pupil, not an inferred mental state, serves as the criterion of understanding, of the interpretation. We then want to know with some precision what serves as the criterion of correctness, of rightness for the practice. Are we not, at least initially, implicitly positing that the grasping of our own mental state, or successfully communicating it to the pupil, is the criterion of correctness? In the case of self-interpretation, on this model, correct grasp of our own prior mental state would serve as the criterion of correctness.

But we find a strong suggestion of an answer to the question concerning the criterion for correctness in the following: "Now, however, let us suppose that after some effort on the teacher's part he continues the series correctly, that is, as we do it." The words "correctly, that is, as we do it" de-psychologize the issue, resituating the emphasis on practice, eroding the presumption that it must be a mental state hidden beneath these remarks concerning practice that serves as the criterion of correctness or rightness. Reinforcing the earlier point concerning the lack of sharp distinctions between understanding, misunderstanding, and non-understanding, Wittgenstein adds that there will not exist a precise point at which we can say that the pupil has "mastered the system," that he has interpreted our intention rightly.

Wittgenstein's dialogue with his interlocutor advances rapidly. It shows Wittgenstein's position breaking off in complete independence from the presumption of interior understanding as the criterion for interpretive correctness. This example with the pupil is a "primitive language-game." It provides a microcosm within which we can see more clearly. And suppose we say with the interlocutor that, even though the pupil has shown his mastery of the system in carrying the series up to a relatively high number, still "to have got the system (or, again, to understand it) can't consist in continuing the series up to this or that number: that is only applying one's understanding." Encapsulating the insistence we may feel that the having of the understanding is one thing and the showing of it another, Wittgenstein adds in the interlocutor's voice, "The understanding itself is a state which is the source of the correct use" (§146).

Asking what one is "really thinking of here," Wittgenstein suggests that the idea behind the interlocutor's insistence is that of the derivation of a series from its algebraic formula or something analogous. This corresponds directly to the distinction between the having and the showing of understanding introduced above. But this ability to apply the formula repeatedly need not be characterized in this (fundamentally dualistic) way. Wittgenstein's argument proceeds that, even though we can think of more than one application of a formula, and even though the converse point also holds (that "every type of application can in turn be formulated algebraically,"), still, the application, not a mental state existing behind it, constitutes a "criterion of understanding."

At this stage, to agree with the interlocutor is not difficult. He is shortly given voice again. He insists, quite reasonably, that he has not "'found out' that up to now'" he has applied the formula in a certain way. He adds, again fairly reasonably if in a more metaphysically loaded way, that in his "'own case at all events I surely know that I mean such-and-such a series; it doesn't matter how far I have actually developed it'" (§147). Wittgenstein replies that the fundamental idea motivating this remark is that the knowing of the rule is "quite apart" from "remembering actual applications to particular numbers." And the reply quickly comes in turn, "Of course!" But Wittgenstein is positioned to advance the next stage of his argument, and here we can see the direct significance this may have for Krausz's analysis of rightness in interpretation.

Wittgenstein asks these questions. (1) What does the pupil's knowledge, separate from its applications, consist in? (2) When is the application is known: always, day and night, or only when the pupil is thinking of the rule? (3) Is the application known as one knows the alphabet and multiplication table? More generally, (4) Could what is here called knowledge be understood as a state of consciousness or a mental process (§148)? He goes on to point out that if we say that knowing the alphabet is a state of mind, then we must be thinking in terms of a "mental apparatus" by means of which we explain "the manifestations of that knowledge" (§149). And the objection to this way of thinking, this way of characterizing our knowing, for example, the alphabet, is that (he says confusingly) "there ought to be two different criteria for such a state."

Wittgenstein means, as the heart of this step of the argument against the larger misconception of interpretive understanding at issue, that if this is true then we should be able to gain knowledge of the "apparatus" apart from its manifestations. And upon investigation, we find, against the expectations formed by the underlying philosophical dualistic picture of understanding, that we cannot separate the manifestations from the alleged "apparatus." It is given content by a consideration of its manifestations or applications. Although Wittgenstein does not say so explicitly, this calls into question the aptness of the concept of "manifestation" in these cases. (Note that, as Wittgenstein adds, we would only further obscure matters by introducing the distinction between the conscious and the unconscious, presumably in such a way that we know the formula unconsciously and apply it consciously. He suggests that that pair of terms only covers what is of grammatical interest.)

I bring this example of the pupil with the numerical series, along with Wittgenstein's discussion of its particularities, into the discussion because such cases can give us pause of the kind Krausz's analysis gives to those who believe the singularist versus multiplist debate will be solved by realist or constructivist ontology. Krausz wants to dig beneath the oppositional dialectic of that debate. Should we not, in a broadly parallel way, ask whether the conception of interpretation, of rightly or wrongly interpreting or understanding an intended meaning at work within and beneath Krausz's analysis, needs similar re-examination? (In Wittgenstein's case the issue lies in language, but there is good reason to believe that the linguistic case holds direct significance for the interpretation and understanding of the meaning of cultural artifacts as well as the self's past actions.) Is the concept of interpretive understanding in play here excessively or exaggeratedly cognitive, or cast too strongly in intellectualist terms? Can an interpretation be non-dualistically embedded within our practices in a way that repudiates an underlying picture much like that between an understanding, construed as a mental state, and its manifestations, construed as an application? Might the practices, which Krausz masterfully puts to work, prove even more significant than his account to this point acknowledges?

Wittgenstein amplifies the preceding points by contrasting what we call mental states with what we have in his foregoing discussion of understanding. Depression, excitement, and pain are called mental states. Is "understanding a word" a natural item on such a list? True, we can say, "since yesterday I have understood this word" But this observation in itself by no means answers the four questions he put forward at the last stage of the argument. Has the word been understood continuously? We do not know quite what to say in response to that (and the point is that, if the criterion of right understanding were a state, we would immediately know how to answer). He also suggests we consider the dis-analogy between the questions "When did your pain get less?" and the marginally sensible question "When did you stop understanding that word?" The more we look into such cases, the more it becomes evident that interpretive understanding, if classified as a mental state, behaves differently from the unproblematic or natural entries under that classification. Detailed questions beyond the simple language-game of the pupil and numerical sequence further reinforce the point.

For example, consider the questions of when we know how to play chess, when we have rightly interpreted the complexly interlocking rule-governed organization of the particular pieces before us on the chessboard. Meaning, or the right interpretation, understood as a mental state, is not something we find readily intelligible once we stop to scrutinize the details. As a result of such investigations, Wittgenstein speaks of the proximity of the grammar of the word "knows" to that of "can" and "is able to. This proximity highlights matters of practice over picture-driven characterizations of knowledge generally, and, more especially for our present purposes, of a rightly grasped or understood intention.[3] He suggests that the grammar of this practice-emphasized conception of "knows" is similarly proximate to that of "understands." He adds parenthetically, for reasons we can now fathom, the phrase "'Mastery' of a technique" (PI, §150). Might it be valuable to consider the possibility of resituating interpretation of works of art, of human selves into our practices? In general, we too quickly picture it as a determinate mental act that assembles a number of particular perceptual experiences into a composite whole. In this hasty picture, the resulting cognitive structure of the interpretation mimetically mirrors the perceived artifact's structure in the world according to realism; or, the resulting cognitive structure is imposed upon the perceived elements according to constructivism. In practice, each of these competing descriptions of an interpretation can, within cases, capture the perceptual event. In suddenly seeing that a painting we mistakenly took to be abstract is in fact representational, the representational figure appears to leap out and suddenly "lock" the different elements together into an interpretation corresponding to what it in fact is.

Conversely, we can see the ambiguous line drawing, such as the perceptually reversible Necker Cube, as now having this side forward and that one in back, and then voluntarily switch the perception reversing forward and back, finding in it a case where the cognitive structure of the perceived element is constitutive of what we see. But these are only two cases: should either case be elevated to a paradigm of all perception? No more than the picture of interpretation underlying them should be elevated to a paradigm of all acts and cases of interpretation. The truth of the matter of our interpretation of interpretations, is in our interpretive practices. But we can say this and yet still retain an underlying, unifying picture or conceptual model of interpretation, where the practices are assembled as illustrations according to that model. Has Krausz done just this, or does he want to move to the stronger claim for the practices, which I would endorse, that would entail the exacting scrutiny of the kind Wittgenstein gives his case: the model found more or less applicable in some cases (like the painting or Necker-Cube example) and utterly beside the point in others.

Wittgenstein shows in his case that the model or picture, not the practice, is dispensable. He weaves the different strands of his position together, identifying: (1) the motivations for the initial search for the mental process or state that allegedly constitutes an interpreted under-standing; (2) the instructive problems endemic to the characterization of that state as hidden somewhere other than in the practices where they lie open to view; (3) the problem of an essentialistic or unitary definition of correct interpretive understanding and the resultant subordination of all cases and their nuances to that overriding definition; and (4) the illusory nature of the driven attempt to locate the mental process or state. And then (5), Wittgenstein sets a distinct tone of self-diagnostic analytical distance:

> We are trying to get hold of the mental process of understanding, which appears to be hidden behind the coarser and more readily visible accompaniments. But we do not succeed; it does not get as far as a real attempt. For even supposing I had found something that happened in all those cases of understanding—why should it be the understanding? And

how can the process of understanding have been hidden, when I said "Now I understand" because I understand?! And if I say it is hidden— then how do I know what I have to look for? I am in a muddle. (PI, §153)

The specially problematic nature of the idea of the hidden process or state is most devastating for the interlocutor's intuitions here. If we say "Now I understand" because we understand, how could it even make sense to say that at the moment of that utterance—an utterance made because of the internal recognition of the understanding—the state of understanding was hidden? This does not and could not describe the moment of under-standing, of interpretive rightness. The concept of hiddenness, as construed in this particular way, is thus bound to severely mislead any attempt to shed light on the moment at which a work of art or a human being is understood, the interpreter's moment of felt rightness.

Yet there remains the sense that the interlocutor's insistence has not been exhaustively diagnosed and treated. Is there not something else "behind," or if that is thought too metaphysically freighted a formulation, something else in addition to, the practices? Are we not in pursuit of something—a determinate and unitary process, act, or event—apart from them, like the understanding apart from its manifestations? The next step of Wittgenstein's discussion acknowledges and to a degree assuages this sense, and it clarifies what Wittgenstein was referring to as the "muddle."

If, Wittgenstein writes, the phrase "Now I understand the principle" is not equivalent to, or is not exhaustively captured by, "The formula . . . occurred to me" or "I say the formula," and so on, we should then ask, Does it follow that we thus use the sentences "Now I understand" or "Now I can go on" as a description of, or as a report on, the inward existence of a process or state that occurs either "behind or side by side with that of saying the formula?" (PI, §154). He addresses the sense that there must be something in addition to the practices. The implied answer is clearly negative. And at this final step of the argument Wittgenstein can say that, if anything exists behind, beside, or in addition to the formula, then it is "particular circumstances, which justify me in saying I can go on—when the formula occurs to me." Here is what legitimately gives rise to a good part of the interlocutor's insistence that more than (brute) practice must exist to the accounting of the phenomena of understanding. This final step in de-psychologizing our conception of the understanding that is interpretive rightness leads us to ask not about the presence, absence, or nature of a hidden inner state or process, but to inquire instead into the circumstances of our acting on, and speaking about, understanding. "Try," Wittgenstein adds, "not to think of understanding as a 'mental process' at all. For that is the expression which confuses you." He suggests that we ask ourselves in what sort of circumstances we could say that famous phrase "Now I know how to go on."

Krausz's lucid, precise, and powerful new book gives pause to those who would think too quickly about singularist or multiplist interpretation in relation to realist and constructivist construals of cultural artifacts of any kind. It casts much light and clears much ground, and in its final chapter turns explicitly to a discussion of life paths and projects, and whether such paths and projects need be understood in relation to a self that possesses a singularist essence, a realist artifact displaying definitionally invariant properties. Or, as we have seen the question approached in a number of ways in the foregoing, Is the self, by contrast, a construction whose organizing cognitive structure is imposed by the interpreter? That insistent dichotomy is misleading in self-interpretation as well, and what I have described as Krausz's conceptually therapeutic project frees us of it with the following progression of thought. In understanding, in rightly interpreting a life, the orthodox essentialist would insist that essences—of character, of life-paths, of potential in a continual process of realization—are there in the person to be found.

But, as Krausz says, "rather than actualizing antecedent innate potentialities, antecedent potentialities are posited in light of who the person has become. It is a posit in light of the foreknowledge of actuality. One retroactively infers the past potential in light of the present actual" (LR, p. 143). We will then want to know: Did the past potential preexist its realization as a kind of determining essence of the self, conceived in a fashion resonantly similar to understanding or right interpretation existing metaphysically and temporally apart from its alleged mental content? No, Krausz answers, "such retrospective positing does not establish a preexistent essence of who one was to become" (LR, p. 143). Instead, "when telling the story of one's own actualization, one posits a prior narrative self, but that does not entail a substantive essentialized self. That self as the subject of the story is a posit from the vantage point of the present actualized self" (LR, p. 143–144). Much like the reversing Necker Cube, the cognitive structure within which we organize all we know of a life—either our own or that of another—is imposed from without: the self as construction. Sounding like a late-in-the-game endorsement of a radical constructivism of selfhood, Krausz continues: "so understood, the subject of the story is no inherent being but is a construction of the presently told story" (LR, p. 144).

So, with regard to selfhood, we come to the bedrock-level question: Does saying so make it so? One might believe the answer is affirmative from what Krausz says next: "One postdictively postulates the self, the grammatical subject, that makes the narrative intelligible" (LR, p. 144). But, pulling back from one theoretical polar extreme, Krausz adds in a style reminiscent of pragmatism's relational conception of selfhood, "at the same time, this does not mean that just any story will do. The natures of selves are postdictive constructs of plausibly entertained present narratives." He goes on to describe constraints that, within particular contexts of self-inquiry, are loose enough to allow a self emergent from its practices and its discourse and yet tight enough to make distinctions between what is and is not true of a self.

So we must finally ask: is Krausz, at the culmination of his account, having his cake and eating it too? The self is in one sense an individual corresponding to a realist model and in another constituted and reconstituted through and within its practices, discursive and otherwise. The answer is, No. This would appear cake-eating-and-having only to one indissolubly wedded to the polarized conceptual bifurcation from which Krausz's work is designed to free us. Given the particularities of my intentional background, that, in a manner at once reasonably free and yet (I hope) rationally constrained, is my interpretation of Krausz's position and its relation to Wittgenstein's contribution to our understanding of the "logic" of interpretation and understanding. And both, taken together, significantly advance the cause of reconsidering— in a manner that has gained freedom from misleading conceptual models— the nature of interpretive rightness.

NOTES

1. Michael Krausz, *Limits of Rightnesss* (LR) (Lanham, Md.: Rowman and Littlefield, 2000).
2. Ludwig Wittgenstein, *Philosophical Investigations* (PI), trans. G. E. M. Anscombe (Oxford: Blackwell, 1968), §142.
3. For a fuller discussion, see Garry Hagberg, *Meaning and Interpretation: Wittgenstein, Henry James and Literary Knowledge*, Chapter 5 (Ithaca: Cornell University Press, 1994).

Four

IS THERE A GENERAL NOTION OF INTERPRETATION?

Nirmalangshu Mukherji

Much of what we grasp, understand, and act upon is a result of some interpretive activity directed on some object of interpretation. As Immanuel Kant taught us, little of the world comes to us via sensory channels only, so to speak. We interpret vagaries of nature, traffic signals, musical scores and performances, visual arts, speeches and writings, smiles and tears, gestures and attitudes, practices and symbols, aches and twinges, and so forth; each of these categories come in a bewildering variety of individual forms. Interpretive activities differ not only with respect to the objects, but with the features of interpreters as well—their age, gender, interests and preparations, cultural location, and the like. Discerning a general pattern in these activities is hard.

This is not to deny that there could be a general pattern, or a network of patterns, involved in all these. There must be; human interpretive practices cannot fail to have a common cause entrenched in the design of a human. But a discovery of that common cause could well be the agenda for a final science, if at all; "if at all" because such a science may well fall beyond the scope of human design.

In the meantime, settling for some version of what may be called pluralism, the idea that human interpretive practices differ as interpreters and objects of those practices differ, is natural. In some favorable cases, such as several basic levels of human linguistic interpretations or visual interpretations, we may hope to reach a more general thesis that detects commonalities between, say, sundry linguistic interpretations. Even there, as hinted, the claim of generality may well be restricted to some "basic" levels such as grammatical interpretation, and may fail to cover pragmatic aspects of interpretations. For the rest of our interpretive practices, some forms of literary criticism, and some reflective enumeration of "forms of life" are all that we are likely to get. In sum, reasons exist to be suspicious about any claim of generality for this area of human conduct.

In what follows, I examine one aspect of Michael Krausz's work from the stated direction.[1] Krausz offers a general thesis on human interpretive activities that pays careful attention to some aspects of the diversity of those practices. Krausz's thesis is perhaps the most disarming general thesis currently in circulation. Yet, I will argue, even this disarming generality fails.

Krausz opens *Limits of Rightness* with the question, "Must there be a single right interpretation for such cultural entities as works of art, literature, music, or other cultural phenomena?" (LR, p. 1). The form of the question suggests that Krausz expects a general answer: yes or no or something in between. Krausz settles for the third option as follows. Singularism is the thesis that a given "cultural entity" admits of exactly one interpretation; multiplism is the thesis that cultural entities admit of more than one interpretation. Armed with these theses, Krausz concludes that while singularism applies in some cases, multiplism applies in some others. Some entities appear to escape this dichotomy when, in considering whether they admit of several interpretations, we are unsure if the same entity is involved in each of the allegedly competing interpretations.

Several points need to be noted to get some bearing on what these ideas mean. First, for reasons that follow, I presented Krausz's general thesis, following his opening remark, in terms of cultural entities alone. Krausz wishes to extend the thesis to any object of interpretation whatsoever, cultural or non-cultural. I review this extension briefly below only to set it aside.

Second, Krausz's formulation of singularism and multiplism involves admissibility of interpretations, not just the availability of them. As I understand this interesting move, singularism and multiplism are to be viewed as the end-results of a long and reflective interpretive process, not in terms of the beginning of this process. Consider the non-cultural example of the snake-rope problem widely discussed in classical Indian philosophy. You have the visual experience of some longish, greenish object lying in front you. "Is this a snake or a rope?" you wonder. A given experience here gives rise to two possible interpretations. But this will not be an example of multiplism since the interpretations have not been (simultaneously) admitted. In this case both the interpretations cannot be admitted: just one of the interpretations can be right. We proceed to inspect and admit one, if at all. Despite the availability of two possible interpretations, this at best is a case of singularism.

The proposed picture is as follows. We begin with, say, two available interpretations, and commence a process of investigation. First, we attempt to reject one or both interpretations. Suppose we are left with one: singularism. Suppose we are unable to reject any. Then we try to put the two together to form a single coherent interpretation—called the strategy of aggregating. If the attempt succeeds, we get singularism again. If the attempt fails, we go back and try to pluralize the original object so as to attach different interpretations to different objects. If the attempt succeeds, we get singularism again. Otherwise, we get multiplism, where we are compelled to admit two opposing interpretations at the same time. Krausz is cautious to add that, here as well, we might prefer one of the interpretations over the other, although we can no longer explain our preference in terms of rightness. These processes, Krausz believes, apply to any object of interpretation.

I deliberately presented Krausz's proposals in an "algorithmic" form to bring out the point that, on the face of it, the generality of his thesis concerns strategies of interpretations, instead of interpretations themselves. Since the evidence of objects of interpretations typically underdetermine the range of possible interpretations, we are likely to come up with more than one interpretation in most cases and proceed along the lines just suggested. This is just a methodological suggestion, which says nothing about the character of interpretations reached by this methodological route. For example, it does not prevent all interpretations to be exclusively singularist, or exclusively multiplist, or neither. Nothing in the description of possible choices tells us how these choices are likely to be distributed. In that, Krausz's thesis by itself does not answer his leading question, "Must there be a single right interpretation?"

Not surprisingly, Krausz's thesis applies across the board, since we employ such strategies of rational inquiry in almost every sphere of possible dispute, as any ombudsman can tell. Nor are we surprised that these strategies are immune from classical philosophical disputes around realism, since these disputes have to do with (the content of) interpretations themselves. In sum, making a list of logically possible options does not generate any substantive result. How do we add substance to Krausz's proposal?

Suppose Krausz suggested that, for any choice of object of interpretation, that object will always give rise to all of singularism, multiplism, and neither. But Krausz does not say that, as we saw. He cannot say that since, being oppositions, singularism and multiplism cannot apply to the same object when we fix the interpreter; multiplism obtains when all attempts at singularism fail.

Krausz's proposals could have meant that, given the totality of all objects of interpretation, some give rise to singularism, some to multiplism, and so on. This suggestion, though non-trivial, is far from being an interesting one. We saw already that the snake-rope case generates singularism at best. Classical figure-ground cases (duck-rabbit, face-vase, and so on) generate multiplism. As we will see, Krausz himself holds, correctly in my view, that all music is multiplist. These facts immediately satisfy the alternative suggestion under discussion. But to say as much is to list some well-known facts; it does not say how these facts cohere. We may discern a more substantive contribution in Krausz's work when we take a closer look at the organization of his discussion. What follows is a possible reconstruction of Krausz's work. First, although Krausz had a general thesis concerning all objects in mind, he opens the discussion in terms of cultural entities such as literature, works of art, and music. Second, the greater part of Krausz's discussion on these issues over the years concerns cultural objects; he has only a marginal interest in non-cultural objects such as objects of scientific interpretation, middle-sized objects of common life, and the like. Third, even when Krausz ventures into non-cultural domains, he shows more interest in those cases, such as figure-ground cases, that have an intuitive pull toward cultural entities. These selective interests can be discerned much beyond Krausz to a variety of "anti-essentialist" positions in recent decades. Such interests show where Krausz's sympathy lies. How do we interpret this body of textual evidence?

For obvious reasons, cultural objects—literature, marriage ceremonies, and religious practices—are generally viewed as grounds for the idea that interpretations vary as cultural locations vary. Cultural objects naturally breed multiplicity. This alleged fact of multiplicity of cultural objects has led many authors in recent decades to several claims of multiplism, relativism, incommensurability, indeterminacy, and the like, for all human interpretive acts, including acts of scientific interpretation. A discussion of this turbulent literature is beyond the scope and interest of this essay.

Krausz's contribution lies in distinguishing between multiplicity and multiplism even for cultural entities; just the availability of multiple interpretations is no ground for the suspension of rightness. That limit is reached when other options fail. To identify cultural entities with multiplism is a confusion. The category of cultural entities—its ontology—has no direct links with the character of interpretive activities directed on them. Most philosophical theories, such as constructivism, constructive realism, and the like, that depend on a close tie between the category and its allegedly characteristic interpretation, are mistaken. This is not to suggest that these theories themselves are mistaken. They could well be right on independent metaphysical considerations; but those considerations are detached from the interpretability of cultural entities.

Earlier, I characterized Krausz's work as disarming; we can see why. Interpretive activities directed on cultural entities are spread over several choices. Some of these choices decisively admit rightness, some do not. As we saw, several reflective options are available within these choices. In some sense, the rich variety of human interpretive activities is given its due.

Krausz disarms not only constructivists in their several guises, but the realist as well. The argument proceeds in two steps. First, which is the central concern of this paper, Krausz maintains that "multiplism is perhaps characteristic rather than definitive of the cultural" (LR, p. 12), although "multiplism is no criterion of the cultural" (LR, p. 11). The tension in these claims is difficult to miss. The only way I can interpret this set of puzzling claims is to think of a picture in which cases of multiplism and cultural entities cluster so that most cultural entities are cases of multiplism, and vice-versa. To take an analogy, consider two oppositions: male-female and masculine-feminine. We could say that the female and the feminine cluster, although feminine males and masculine females are to be found. Multiplism characterizes the cultural without being definitive of it.

In this picture, cultural multiplism is viewed as the central core of human interpretive activities. The rest of the activities trickle out of this core formation. Krausz is in agreement with the choice of the domain of the cultural relativist: this is where human interpretive activities are at their salient best. But Krausz is able to avoid the position of the relativist by allowing the core picture to diffuse at both ends: not only that singularism applies to some cultural entities, multiplism applies to some non-cultural entities. Krausz is able to disarm the realist and the relativist, and any combination of the two (such as constructivist-realist), while staying in the domain of cultural multiplism. The disarming subliminal message is that all interpretive activities are more or less cultural, but that concession does not by itself lead to any definite metaphysical position.

This is the substantive consequence of Krausz's proposals regarding interpretive strategies. Given a conception of cultural entities (a category), the application of interpretive strategies to them generates singularism and multiplism, though predominantly multiplism. For expository purposes, I am ignoring Krausz's third option of neither singularism nor multiplism. The availability of this category enables a conception of non-cultural entities. When the strategies are applied there in turn, we get singularism and multiplism again. Even if multiplism clusters with cultural entities, multiplism is not identified with cultural entities. A quite general picture of human interpretive activities stretches across all domains of those activities, though with unequal weight.

These applications of interpretive strategies generate four areas: singularist non-cultural, multiplist non-cultural, singularist cultural, and multiplist cultural. The entire taxonomy flows from the initial conception of cultural multiplism, the fourth area. Is that conception tenable? If the answer is negative, we need not look at the other areas to examine the validity of Krausz's picture.

The crucial issue is that the conception of the category of cultural entities has to do with human interpretive activities in this area. Assume that something called cultural interpretation exists that applies to each of the entities that fall under this category. This means that some notion of interpretation remains invariant across the entities in this category. Krausz's program requires, as with many other programs in this area of philosophy, some coherent notion of culture that can be tied to the form of interpretive activity that takes place there. Traditionally, that tie had been sought in multiplism itself, namely, that cultural interpretations are distinguished by their abundance. But this is one of the "orthodox" views that Krausz categorically rejects— correctly in my view. So, the only way Krausz can uphold a coherent notion of cultural interpretation is in terms of the nature of the interpretations themselves.

I will argue that the notion of interpretation varies so much across literature, painting, and especially music that unitary notions of singularism and multiplism would apply everywhere is implausible. To take an analogy, consider Albert Einstein's claim that quantum theory is incomplete, and Kurt

Gödel's claim that some formal systems are incomplete. It does not follow that a general notion of incompleteness applies to both the domains. If our concept of multiplism is understood in terms of the way it applies to literature, then that the twin concepts of singularism and multiplism apply to music at all is hard to see. I will develop the argument from three different directions, and show that they converge.

1. Some Examples

To get a preliminary idea of the sort of problems I have in mind, consider some of Krausz's crucial examples that purportedly illustrate multiplism for different kinds of entities. Recall that Krausz's list of cultural entities includes other cultural phenomena besides literature, works of art, and music.

For general cultural multiplism, Krausz cites the interesting case of a dead baby floating in the Ganges river (LR, p. 35–36). While Krausz himself, a North American, was plainly shocked with the sight of a "dumped" baby, the locals explained to him that, being "morally pure beings," dead babies are accorded the honor of being returned to the life source of the Ganges. The implication is that, while the North American Krausz was shocked, the locals would perhaps interpret the sight as a holy gesture. Krausz asks: "If we saw the same thing but interpreted it differently, who is right? Or is more than one interpretation admissible?" Plainly, large and irreconcilable belief systems of different cultures as embodied in their texts, convictions, and practices are involved here: you cannot be shocked and filled with religious admiration at the same time.

Suppose in this case that everyone sees a dead baby afloat. That is the sight. Then the question of whether the sight is repulsive or respectable depends on the cultural lens we use. Beginning with the visual experience then, we find two layers of interpretation: (a) the interpretation as a floating dead baby, and (b) the interpretation regarding how we evaluate (a). Multiplism in the sense concerned occurs, if at all, at (b). If the sequence of interpretations terminated with (a), multiplism will not apply. Moreover, even if multiplism exists at (a)—say, between a dead baby and a rotting idol shaped as a baby, the notions of interpretation involved here will be quite different from the one applying at (b).

Next, consider Krausz's example of a "pluralizing maneuver" regarding Vincent Van Gogh's *Potato Eaters*. He suggests that the work of art may be subject to any one of formalist, psychoanalytic, Marxist, feminist, or other interpretations. To think of each of these interpretations as cultural interpretations in the sense encountered in the previous example raises several problems. For one, the formalist interpretation hardly involves any other belief system except the one solely geared for such artistic objects; for example, the formalist interpretation is likely to be concerned with tonality, strength of drawing, spatial arrangement, distribution of light, and the like. It will not apply to political systems, or family relations. In that, the formalist interpretation is quite different in character from the other interpretations. The other interpretations may be viewed as highlighting different aspects of the work such that, as Krausz suggests (LR, p. 13), reaching an aggregating interpretation, say, Marxist-feminist, is a possibility. Multiplism in this case can disappear in two different ways. This, as noted, cannot be the case at stage (b) of the previous example.

Consider some examples from music. In the musical case, Krausz has admitted to multiplism.[2] But he also says that the notion of interpretation involved in musical multiplism attaches exclusively to performances of music, not to the scores themselves. In enforcing the restriction, Krausz is suggesting subliminally that the notion of interpretation in music might be significantly different from the interpretation of a work of literature. In the case of dramatic works, for example, we find a relevant notion of performance; we find a relevant notion of interpretation in the sense of performance: actors interpret a play by acting it out in a particular way. But a play also admits of varied cultural interpretations of the text itself: Marxist, feminist, Buddhist, and the like. The point is too obvious to require illustration. Pieces of music typically admit of only one of these forms of interpretation—as performance—even when we label pieces of music "romantic," "baroque," and so forth. This is not to deny that works of music admit of critical interpretations as well. Such critical interpretations, though distinct from performance interpretations, are closely tied to them. The present point is that even critical interpretations are quite different from "cultural" interpretations such as Marxist or feminist. Music is a wholly different kind of cultural entity than a work of art or fiction.

The point can be illustrated by considering the factors that Krausz lists as contributing to multiplism in music. Starting with the idea that multiplism in music arises because "musical scores are characteristically incomplete," Krausz suggests several "different resources" in which "different interpreters" interpret their music.[3] These include choice of tempi, choice of timbre or volume of a given instrument, physical position of a musician in an orchestra, choice of bow movements for string instruments (up or down), duration and speed of a vibrato, pressures of bows and fingers, room temperature, well-accepted violations of the score, historical practices of a tradition, idiosyncrasies of a teacher, pressures on rehearsal time (LR, p. 19–21), and the like. Cumulatively, Krausz calls these things "extra-score practices." His general conclusion is, since "extra-score practices vary historically," it will be incorrect to "insist that the range of ideally admissible interpretations must always be singular" (RR, Ch. 1).

For the purposes of this essay, I will not question whether such extra-score practices lead genuinely to different interpretations. Let us assume so. Even then this notion of interpretation—and the related notion of multiplism—could not be the one that applies to *Potato Eaters* or floating babies. I will attempt to give some theoretical shape to this concern.

2. Forms of Inquiry

An irony of human inquiry is that different groups of people reflect on the same object without having anything to say to one another. A classic example is the complete lack of conversation between astrophysicists and astrologers, though both deal with motions of stars. Astrologers think that stars have something to do with human fate; astrophysicists think that they are nothing but great balls of fire, totally incapable of influencing the course of psychic events.

In the star case, which inquiry is the valid one is reasonably evident. In some cases, both inquiries could be equally valid, up to a point. Consider the distinction between theory of language and theory of literature. Both fields are concerned, in some sense, with the workings of language. Yet, they are looking at quite different aspects of language and its use. A language theorist is basically concerned with a cognitive system; a literary theorist is concerned with a cultural-historical product with a cultural-historical content. Roughly the same holds for the more advanced forms of visual arts such as painting, sculpture and architecture. Literature and the visual arts may make comments, albeit in quite different ways, on the futility of war, wickedness of power, grandeur of nature, personal grief, and so forth. There could be an inquiry focused exclusively on these comments and the explicit, articulated forms of making them. This inquiry would not need to concern itself with the properties of the cognitive systems of language and vision that underlie the ability to make these comments. We can also discern a difference between literature and the visual arts with regard to the distinction between cognitive structure and cultural comment.

For literature, the distinction is overriding. How considerations from cognitive linguistics will bear upon the examination of the thoughts expressed in literature is hard to see. To bring out Coleridge's form of what he calls "romantic imagination," Maurice Bowra examines Coleridge's use of language, including his poetic style, at great depth. "*The Ancient Mariner*," Bowra suggests, "draws attention to neglected or undiscovered truths."[4] The way a poet "reveals" such "secrets of the universe" is to "work through myths" such as that of the ancient mariner. This myth is to be thought of as "an extension of the use of symbols," where a symbol, according to Coleridge, is "characterized by a translucence of the special in the individual." In *The Ancient Mariner*, Coleridge "shapes these symbols into a consistent whole" resulting in "a myth about a dark and troubling crisis in the human soul." Plainly, Bowra is concerned with "world-views" as they get uniquely expressed in Coleridge's use of language. Although such concerns often re-

quire study of metaphor, irony, analogy, and imagery, at no point do they require going into the structure of semantic interpretation, grammatical rules,
and pragmatic competence in ways in which linguists understand these things.
This distinction is less marked in our understanding and appreciation of the
visual arts. Cinema raises problems of classification that I will set aside in this
discussion.

Outstanding examples of art, such as Pablo Picasso's *Guernica*, Michel-
angelo Buonarroti's *Pieta*, Van Gogh's *Cypress Tree*, cave-paintings of
Ajanta, and the like, are often understood in terms of their "messages" on
matters of human interest, as we saw for Van Gogh's *Potato Eaters*. Even in
these exemplary cases the predominant interest is in the form of the artistic
piece instead of in its content. In the large majority of artistic examples, especially for the more abstract and non-representational pieces, the interest is
entirely in the form. That artistic pieces may be non-representational brings
out the point under discussion. This point has little to do with the issue of
realism in arts; a representational piece need not be realistic, as some of Van
Gogh's and most of Salvador Dali's paintings show.

The form of an artistic piece is intimately connected to how it appears to
its viewers, to its perceptual properties. In this sense, much of the visual arts
may be thought of as skilled manipulation of perception. Considerations such
as the above led E. H. Gombrich to cite John Constable with approval: "Painting is a science and should be pursued as an inquiry into the laws of nature.
Why, then, may not landscape painting be considered as a branch of natural
philosophy, of which pictures are but the experiments?"[5] The interest is that
Constable's work, as Gombrich puts it, "is surely more like a photograph than
the works of a Cubist or a medieval artist."[6] Even then, as Gombrich's subsequent analysis of Constable's *Wivenhoe Park* brings out, "the painter's experiments adjoin those of the physicists." In this sense, the artist's achievement lies "in the 'discovery of appearances' that is really the discovery of the
ambiguities of vision."[7]

I am not suggesting that an artistic work ought to be viewed on a par
with the science of the relevant domain, such as the human visual system. The
artist's scientific explorations at best underlie his artistic expression; unlike
the scientist, he is not describing the visual system. Although the artist's "discovery of appearances" often requires some understanding of the concerned
cognitive system, this understanding is exploited instead of expressed, much
as advertising campaigns exploit the laws of human gullibility.

It does follow, as Gombrich's extensive analysis shows, that one significant way of explaining a work of art is to explain the psychological understanding that goes into its making. In that sense, the distance between a psychological study of visual arts and their aesthetic study is not as far removed
as for literature. Aesthetic explanation is likely to converge onto psychological explanation at prominent joints. As we saw, the more a work of art is seen

as a formal object—in contrast to a cultural product—the more amenable to psychological explanation. This raises the possibility that the distance between these forms of explanations becomes indistinguishable when a work of art is not viewed in terms of its message at all.

In the case of music, to make a distinction between a cognitive system and a cultural product is more difficult. Though no human enterprise can fail to be a cultural-historical product (music is no exception), it is difficult to maintain that music has a cultural-historical content in that it makes comments on the futility of war, as an example, although the cultural-historical context of a war might lead someone, such as Igor Stravinsky, to compose a particular brand of music. This point about music can be brought out in several ways.

The widely tested ability of quite young children to intuitively grasp and perform fairly advanced forms of music even when they have little "world-knowledge" to grasp advanced forms of literature and the visual arts, is one quick piece of evidence. This "non-representational" character of music is a puzzle of great theoretical interest that raises doubts about the distinction between a cognitive system and a cultural product. For this reason, it has been a persistent problem to incorporate music in aesthetic and critical approaches that begin with architecture and Greek tragedy.

The non-representational character of music is also the underlying reason for an ancient interest in the "language-likeness" of music that Leonard Bernstein finally explicitly raised.[8] Interestingly, the grammatical complexity of language (long-distance reflexives, triple embedding, double negation, and so on) poses no problem for young children even when they have troubles with metaphors, analogies, deliberate ambiguities, ironies, and the like.

Current work in linguistics and musical cognition can be fruitfully linked to some of Wittgenstein's insights to develop the idea of "language-likeness" in the grammatical sense just outlined. The perspective that ensues helps explain why musical interpretation is fundamentally different from literary interpretation. Musical interpretation, I will argue, stops at a level analogous to the grammatical level of interpretation.

3. The Psychological Version

The suggested parallel between just the grammatical part of language and the whole of music can be approached from Ray Jackendoff's discussion of these issues.[9] He distinguishes between two versions of "the fundamental question for a theory of mind." The philosophical version poses the question, "What is the relationship of the mind to the world . . . such that our sentences can be true or false?" The psychological version poses the question: "How does the brain function as a physical device, such that the world seems to us the way it does?" With this distinction in hand, Jackendoff argues, "it hardly makes sense to say that the representations we construct in response to hearing a performance of the *Eroica* are true or false."[10] Mention of Ludwig van Beethoven's (later) work is especially relevant here since Beethoven wrote the symphony "in the absence of any overt musical signal." To ask if the piece suddenly acquired a truth-value when the score was written or the first performance took place is absurd. The philosophical version of the fundamental question does not apply to music at all; only the psychological version does.

The inapplicability of the philosophical version to music is nearly obvious. In his influential work, Roger Scruton has forcefully argued that musical symbolism does not imply that its symbols stand for anything in the world.[11] Working through well-known examples of music where aspects of nature are allegedly depicted (blowing of wind, sound of waterfalls, bird calls, cries of animals), Scruton argued that no intelligible sense can be made of the idea that these sections of music resemble or represent aspects of nature. Further, even if we grant that such music imitates nature in some way, we cannot say that the music says something about those aspects of nature. In sum, musical symbolism lacks predication in the desired sense. Since predication does not occur, there cannot be any satisfaction in Alfred Tarski's sense; the notions of truth and falsity do not apply to music.

Jackendoff makes a similar claim for language. Suppose language consists of three parts: grammar, phonology, and semantics. Jackendoff claims that the psychological version, as against the philosophical version, holds for each of these parts. The claim is most controversial for the third of these parts; Jackendoff's arguments for the psychological version of semantics are the weakest. We strongly intuit that "dog" is true of dogs and "dogs are feline" is false. Except for the general suggestion that terms such as "true" or "false" need to be "embedded" "in a general theory of concepts," Jackendoff has done nothing to dispel this intuition. I do not, thereby, mean to endorse the "philosophical version" for semantics. My complaint is that Jackendoff's arguments for the psychological version are insufficient. In my opinion, Noam Chomsky presents a more powerful perspective in favor of the psychological version.

Not surprisingly, Jackendoff's claim for phonological representations is more plausible since what it means for the *noise* "dog" to be true or false is totally unclear: it is "difficult to see how the predicates 'true' and 'false' apply to one's phonological representations in response to an incoming stimuli."[12] Jackendoff concludes that "the notion of computation need not have anything to do with "respecting semantic relations" at least in the domains of phonology and syntax."[13] Consider the aspirated sound "p" as in "Patrick." Jackendoff's central point is that these phonological objects themselves do not stand for something else. A sound-meaning correlation exists between "p" and an aspirated sound; no further correlation between the sound and something else in the world is to be found. "Patrick" is just an arrangement of sounds. The point is obviously even more compelling for objects in syntactic structures:

"There is no such thing as an NP, a VP, or an Adjective in the environment."
In sum, "speakers do not believe (or believe in) NPs or phonological distinctive features or rules of aspiration."[14]

With these considerations in hand, asking if the significance of a piece
of music—and its possible interpretations—ought to be phrased in any external terms that refer to elements apart from the musical symbolism itself is
worthwhile. For example, Jackendoff shows that explanation of some aspects
of musical affect—why some pieces of music do not lose their pleasing effects even after repeated hearing—can be explained solely in terms of the
combinatorial properties of notes, and the modular character of musical processing.[15] We can explain why we *want* to hear the same music from the properties of musical processing alone, not *because* the piece invokes—although it
may—pictures of reality, desires, and the like.

"And the like" is beginning to include moods and emotions that are
thought to be the hallmarks of musical significance in most common and philosophical conceptions of music. Granting that the external significance of
music cannot be captured in terms of representations of aspects of reality,
music represent*s* emotions in a way that can be recognized by listeners. As
Diana Raffman proceeds to cite Roger Scruton, it is "one of the given facts of
musical culture" that the hearing of music is "the occasion for sympathy."[16]
The literature on the emotional significance of music include: being merry,
joyous, sad, pathetic, spiritual, lofty, dignified, dreamy, tender, or dramatic;
feelings of utter hopelessness, foreboding, anxiety, terrified gesture, and the
like. For Scruton, if someone finds the last movement of *The Jupiter Symphony* "morose and life-negating," he would be wrong.

In recent years, cognitive theorists of music have generally rejected this
tradition. The basic objection to the idea can be stated in Raffman's terms as
follows: "Musicians argue about phrasings and dynamics and resolutions.
They do *not* argue about the emotions they feel or otherwise ascribe to music."[17] As Raffman elaborates, musicians may argue that a given phrase ends
at a particular E-natural because the note prepares a modulation to the dominant; the argument never takes the form that the note expresses ultimate joy,
or whatever. None of this is meant to deny that listeners often have emotional
responses to music. The fact need not be traced to music itself.

4. Wittgenstein on Language and Music

Ludwig Wittgenstein reached this point several decades before the onset of
cognitive psychology of music. In his *Blue and Brown Books*, he remarked:
"It has sometimes been said that what music conveys to us are feelings of joy-
fulness, melancholy, triumph etc., etc. and what repels us in this account is
that it seems to say that music is an instrument for producing in us sequences
of feelings. . . . To such an account we are tempted to reply 'Music conveys to

us *itself*."[18] According to him, a "strange illusion" possesses us when "we say 'This tune says *something*,' and it is as though I had to find *what* it says." Since what a tune says cannot be said in words, "this would mean no more than saying 'It expresses itself.'" To bring out the sense of a melody then is to "whistle it in a particular way" (BBB, p. 166).

To see what Wittgenstein might have meant by his claim that music "expresses itself," note that he extends the claim to language as well—to the understanding of a sentence, for example. He suggests that what we call "understanding a sentence" has, in many cases, a much greater similarity to understanding a musical theme "than we might be inclined to think." The point is that we already know that understanding a musical theme cannot involve the making of "pictures." The suggested similarity between music and language is meant to promote a similar view of language as well, namely, no "pictures" are made even in understanding a sentence. "Understanding a sentence," he says, "means getting hold of its content; and the content of the sentence is *in* the sentence" (BBB, p. 167).

Several ways of interpreting these difficult claims can be discerned. Wittgenstein's way is to draw attention to "gestalt" features of object-perception that, in a way, leap into our minds. Wittgenstein devotes a major part of his analysis to properties of visual perception in an attempt to draw lessons to apply in turn to music and language. Even if we grant that lessons from vision might work for music, how can it work for language? For example, despite Wittgenstein's valiant attempts, how the notion of expression, as in "what a face or a flower expresses," applies to what a sentence expresses is hard to see.

The suggested parallel between understanding a sentence and a piece of music such that they convey themselves can be explained from an altogether different theoretical perspective. In this perspective, significance of a sentence can be brought out in several layers, beginning with a layer that has no external significance at all. We can then view the other layers in terms of progressive addition of external significance. Each layer admits of multiplism that attaches exclusively to that level. Multiplism in music is quite like the multiplism of language at the initial level.

Consider the sentence "who knows John gave what to whom." The sentence admits multiple interpretations depending on the relative scopes of the embedded *wh*–phrases. Since these are questions, I have also included a possible answer in each case to display the differences of interpretation more perspicuously.

(1) Representation: who$_i$ e$_i$ knows to whom$_j$ [John gave what e$_j$]
     Interpretation: For which persons x and y, x knows John gave what to y
     Answer: Bill knows John gave what to Mary

(2)   Representation: who$_i$ e$_i$ knows what$_j$ [John gave e$_j$ to whom]
      Interpretation: For which person x and what thing y, x knows
      John gave y to whom
      Answer: Tom knows John gave the book to whom

Someone's knowledge of John's gifts is under query here. In (1), the query is about the recipient of those gifts; in (2), the query concerns the gift-item. The sentence (= text) under discussion omits of multiplism. Representations (1) and (2) are linguistic expressions *par excellence*—called LF-representations in linguistics. Many aspects of the interpretations that can be attached to them are linguistic in character as well. In particular, we do not expect the shape of these expressions to be available in any other symbolic domain.

I wish to draw attention to some general features of this example that, in my opinion, are available beyond language. First, (1) and (2) are structurally distinct in that the relative positions of the symbolic objects in them differ. Second, these structural differences are directly related to the way a representation is to be interpreted. One of the global economy principles stipulates that a representation may not contain any element that cannot be interpreted. Third, the interpretations do not make any reference to how the world is like, the beliefs of people interpreting them, the vagaries of the associated culture, and the like. In order to differ, the interpretations do not require that there be an external world at all. Multiple interpretations are attached to the same symbolic object solely in terms of the ambiguity of its representational structure.

Consider the possible dispute between musicians that Raffman suggested to show the irrelevance of emotivism for musical interpretations. The dispute concerned the identification of a musical phrase, whether it ends with a particular (occurrence of) E-natural. In principle then, the dispute can be traced back exclusively to the structural features of how a group of notes are to be represented. Three possibilities arise: the phrase ends before the E-natural, the phrase ends at the E-natural, and the phrase extends beyond the E-natural. As anyone familiar with music knows, these structural differences make big differences in the interpretations of music. Depending on the group of notes at issue, and the location of the group in a passage, some of the structural decisions may even lead to bad music. This is because these decisions often make a difference as to how a given sequence of notes is to be resolved. Any moderately experienced listener of music can tell the differences phenomenologically, though its explicit explanation requires technical knowledge of music (such as modulation to the dominant).

This explains why composers and performers spend a lot of time marking a score to show how exactly they wish a sequence of notes to be grouped. Lerdahl and Jackendoff's work shows how different groupings impose different hierarchies on musical surfaces such that each hierarchical organization gets linked to an interpretation of the surface. The phenomenon is explicit in musical traditions that use scores. But it can be observed in any tradition by attending its training sessions. Training means attention to the pitch of individual notes and how notes are to be organized. When the music becomes complex, and it begins to tax memory and attention, several devices are used to highlight the salient properties of symbolic organization. These include emphasis typically by suitable ornamentation, organization of music in delineable cycles such as rondo, display of unity of larger sections by cadences, exploiting the cyclic features of the accompanying beat, and so on. The list is obviously quite incomplete, but music is nothing else. Interpretations in music are sensitive solely to the syntactic properties of representations.

Plainly, linguistic interpretations involve a lot more. Consider Chomsky's example "drinks will be served at five."[19] As Chomsky observed, the sentence can be used as "a promise, a prediction, a warning, a threat, a statement, or an invitation," among others. A decision about which of these varied interpretations of the given sentence is most salient will depend on the features of the extra-linguistic environment. These features include the states of mind of the speaker and her audience, a knowledge of the locale in which the sentence is uttered, some knowledge of the culture in which the given community of people generally participate, facial expressions, past utterances, and so forth. In sum, the linguistic object "drinks will be served at five" needs to interact with other systems of knowledge and belief for these interpretations to be available.

The array of these systems can get progressively thicker to include social relations, cultural choices, religious pronouncements, proto-scientific beliefs, conceptions of the future, and the like. At some point in such a dense field of interactions, we get works of literature. These works themselves can then seep into the general culture to generate even wider belief systems—most cultures are textual cultures, in that sense. Since we do not have the faintest idea of how these systems are organized with respect to each other, let us say that interpretations of literary and cultural texts form a continuum with items of common life such as "drinks will be served at five." The entire continuum may be viewed as distinct from syntax-governed interpretations outlined above. No general notion of interpretation spans literature and music, even if we want to place them under the common head "cultural entities."

NOTES

1. Michael Krausz, *Limits of Rightness* (LR) (Lanham, Md.: Rowman and Littlefield, 2000).

2. Michael Krausz, "Making Music: Beyond Intentions," *The Linacre Journal,* ed. Rom Harré and John Shosky (Oxford: Linacre College, 2002), pp. 17–27.

3. Michael Krausz, "Rightness and Reasons in Musical Interpretation," *The Interpretation of Music*, ed. Michael Krausz (Oxford: Claredon Press, 1993), p. 22.

4. Maurice Bowra, *The Romantic Imagination* (London: Oxford University Press, 1950), p. 68.

5. E. H. Gombrich, *Art and Illusion: A Study in the Psychology of Pictorial Representation* (Princeton: Princeton University Press, 1960), p. 33.

6. *Ibid.*, p. 34.

7. *Ibid.*, p. 314.

8. Leonard Bernstein, *The Unanswered Question* (Cambridge: Harvard University Press, 1976).

9. Ray Jackendoff, *Languages of the Mind* (Cambridge: MIT Press, 1983), pp. 157–165.

10. *Ibid.*, p. 165.

11. Roger Scruton, *The Aesthetic Understanding* (Manchester: Carcanet Press, 1983), Chapter 7.

12. Jackendoff, *Languages of the Mind*, p. 164.

13. *Ibid*, p. 29.

14. *Ibid.*, p. 165.

15. Fred Lehrdal and Ray Jackendoff, *A Generative Theory of Tonal Music* (Cambridge: MIT Press, 1983).

16. Diana Raffman, *Language, Music, and Mind* (Cambridge: MIT Press, 1993), p. 42.

17. *Ibid.*, p. 59.

18. Ludwig Wittgenstein, *The Blue and Brown Books* (BBB) (Oxford: Basil Blackwell, 1958), p. 178.

19. Noam Chomsky, *Reflections on Language* (New York: Pantheon Press, 1975), p. 65.

Five

INTERPRETIVE IDEALS AND TRUTH COMMISSIONS

David A. Crocker

Michael Krausz's *Limits of Rightness* is an incisive and challenging book about interpretation—its varieties, foundations, and uses.[1] In the present essay I identify and explore some issues that emerge when the perspectives of *Limits of Rightness* are applied to official truth commissions. My particular interest is the challenges such investigative bodies in post-conflict societies face in revealing the truth about human rights violations committed by a government or its opponents during times of armed conflict. Krausz's theory of interpretive ideals illuminates several issues that truth commissions must address better than they have done in the past. Through the lens of Krausz's theory, we see (or are reminded of) the importance of getting clear about objectives: truth commissions must understand properly their interpretive ideal and goals and the means they are willing to use to achieve their aims. In addition, a consideration of the work of truth commissions may contribute usefully to Krausz's work, inviting clarification, extension, and perhaps modification of his framework in future work.

1. What Are Truth Commissions?

In *Rightness and Reason*, Krausz remarks that "the judgment whether singularism or multiplism is an appropriate ideal for a given practice requires that one has sufficient information about the pertinent practice."[2] Let us consider official truth commissions—of which there have been more than twenty in the past twenty-five years—as a practice.[3] How should we understand these investigative bodies? Like historical writing, including biography, some (historical) novels, and some trials, truth commissions interpret past actions and events. These bodies are one tool that societies, in transition from one government to another or from war to peace, have used to reckon with past wrongs.[4] Such wrongs typically include state-sponsored massacres, "disappearances," and such crimes against humanity as rape, torture, and genocide. Priscilla Hayner, the leading scholar of truth commissions, describes truth commissions as those "official bodies set up to investigate and report on a pattern of past human rights abuses."[5]

She also argues that these bodies have four common traits. First, truth commissions focus on the past (but in ways that differ from that of historical investigation or court proceedings) and not on current events, as does most journalism. Second, unlike some historical accounts, which investigate one or a few events, truth commissions look for a "a pattern of abuses over a period of time."[6] The question is not whether the accused is guilty as charged, but whether you can narrate and explain patterns of actions that occurred during a designated time frame. Third, unlike courts and many historical research centers, truth commissions are temporary bodies that typically last for no more than two years. Such time constraints limit what a commission can do. Fourth, neither individual investigators nor merely private citizens, truth commissions are collective bodies that a government or a peace accord authorizes and legally empowers.

The tasks and responsibilities with which truth commissions have been charged vary greatly. Some allow victims a voice and compensate them for their losses. Some advise on the rule of law and establish standards of judicial justice. Many commissions recommend reforms and seek to promote reconciliation and strengthen democratisation.[7] But arguably the most crucial function of truth commissions, and the one from which they receive their generic name, is that of "discover[ing], clarify[ing] and formally acknowledg[ing]" the truth about a pattern of past abuses.[8]

Truth commissions try to realize this aim by following different procedures, which yield revelations about the past, and by making a final report, which offers findings and recommendations to the public. Truth commissions may take testimony from victims, (alleged) perpetrators of rights violations, and bystanders; seek confirmation of testimony; examine documentary and forensic evidence; and permit civil society to subject the commission's procedures and tentative findings to scrutiny and assessment. Typically a commission ends its work by issuing an official report that offers an interpretation or narrative in the sense of "a coherent account in which earlier events are cited to account for later ones."[9] The final report usually ascribes responsibility for past wrongs to different institutions and groups and sometimes, as in El Salvador, "names names." Insofar as it documents and expresses the (past) government's guilt in committing or not preventing past crimes, a truth commission offers not merely knowledge but also acknowledgement of past wrongs.[10]

Although official mandates often permit these commissions to define some of their ends and means, these official terms of reference more or less guide and constrain these bodies in the conduct of their work and scope of their final reports. The parliamentary, executive, or negotiated terms of reference make the relevant commission responsible—usually within a period of less than two years—to find and report truth about past abuses during a determinant period. These mandates exhibit considerable differences in relation, inter alia, to the types of abuses to be investigated. Such crimes may include killings for political purposes, genocide, kidnappings (and possibly resulting in death, although a body might never be recovered), torture (with or without resulting death), and, more recently, rape and sexual servitude. Typically, forced displacements are beyond the scope of a commission's work. Sometimes, the mandate directs a commission to investigate the systemic repressive structure that issued in particular violations.

Implicit in most mandates and explicit in the terms proposed for a Bosnian truth commission is the idea that the final report should be "one agreed-upon and well-documented account" with respect to the sorts of crimes to be investigated.[11] Where and when did the violation occur? How was the violation accomplished? The Truth and Reconciliation Commission in South Africa called the findings that answered these questions "factual or forensic truths."[12] What groups (and sometimes what individual agents) were responsible? What were the likely causes—national and international, proximate and more ultimate—of the crimes? What have been the effects on individuals and institutions of the human rights violations? Sometimes the answers to these questions are called "interpretations," because some believe that "interpretations" are more difficult to support than "facts." Sometimes responses are termed "personal or narrative truth," because they include individuals "telling their own stories;" or "social or 'dialogical'" truth, insofar as the truth emerges from a consultative and democratic process.[13]

2. Ideals of Interpretation: Singularism and Multiplism

This brief account of truth commissions allows us to ask the question: What ideal(s) of interpretation are or should be part of the work of a truth commission? Krausz offers a general account of interpretation that distinguishes between two fundamentally different interpretive ideals: singularism and multiplism. What does Krausz mean by "singularism" and "multiplism" and what relevance might this distinction have for the work of truth commissions?

According to the definition given in Krausz's synoptic essay in this volume, singularism allows only one single admissible interpretation. Applied to the work of truth commissions, the singularist insists that ideally one and only one right interpretation of a past abuse or a pattern of past abuses exists, and a truth commission should aspire to achieve that one correct interpretation. It may fail, but a commission should come as close as it can to "getting it right." Multiplism, on the other hand, allows that "for some objects of interpretation more than one interpretation is admissible" (LR, pp. 1–2). Applied to the work of truth commissions, the multiplist accepts that some of the historical events that the commission interprets may have more than one adequate account. From the multiplist perspective, a commission's report permits and even embraces contending and opposing interpretations of some objects.

Notably, although singularism completely excludes multiplism, multiplism permits singularism. The multiplist may admit that for some (but not all) objects of interpretation, there exists only one admissible interpretation. But multiplism is defined in such a way that the multiplist must say that for some (not all) objects of interpretation more than one interpretation is admissible.

The casual reader might fail to notice that each of Krausz's two interpretive ideals captures some of the virtue of the other. For all objects of interpretation, singularism posits one and only one admissible interpretation. But
even as it aspires to realize this ideal, singularism may accept the usefulness
of a multiplicity of interpretations. Let a thousand flowers bloom, not because
(after weeding) each bloom is justified, but because the evaluation of the diversity will contribute to achievement of the one prize bloom. Operating under the singularist ideal, interpreters can fall back on more than one temporar-
ily approved interpretation as a way station before trying again to achieve the
one admissible rendering.

Likewise, that multiplism makes no room for the notion of "correct interpretation" is incorrect. We have already seen that, for Krausz, multiplism
permits in some cases only one admissible interpretation. For example,
Krausz himself might be a multiplist about many objects of interpretation but
believe that only one right interpretation of his book exists. Multiplism is not
to be confused with what Krausz calls the anarchist view that anything goes
or that any interpretation is as good or as bad as any other. A multiplist may
make judgments about worse and better interpretations even about those objects that permit more than one admissible interpretation, for multiplism permits that the ideal interpretation can and should narrow the field of contending and conflicting interpretations such that some (perhaps many) may be
judged inadmissible and only some judged admissible.

Where multiplism parts company from singularism is that with respect
to some objects of interpretation, following scrutiny of all contestants for
admissible interpretation, more than one contestant can and should remain.
Multiplism can accommodate singularism in an even stronger way. In his
synopsis, Krausz insists that operating under the multiplist ideal is compatible
with "countenancing one interpretation as preferable (for good reasons) over
other admissible interpretations" (IO, p.12). We might ask whether this multiplist accommodation to singularism does not go too far, since it appears to
accept one and only one interpretation as preferable and that there need exist
any theoretical or practical differences between multiplist preferability among
admissible alternatives and singularist exclusive admissibility is not evident.
Perhaps the singularist's one admissible interpretation comes to no more than
the multiplists's most preferable interpretation. In short, Krausz's sharp distinction might collapse into two points on a continuum (determined by degree
of preferability supplied by reasons).

3. Ideals of Interpretation and Truth Commissions

Krausz's theory of interpretation has direct application to the practice of truth
commissions, and I hope his future work will take them into account.

Truth commissions should be of interest to Krausz because they are, as
noted above, governmentally-authorized practices with official mandates.

How should we understand interpretive practices that are the work of governmentally-authorized commissions, not of private individuals or unofficial bodies? To what extent, if any, does the validity of a commission's findings and narrative account depend on the commission's status as an official body? Does the legitimacy or democratic character of a regime contribute to the acceptability of a truth commission's process or final report?

Regardless of their terms of reference, truth commissions explicitly express neither the singularist nor multiplist ideals of interpretation. On first blush, it appears that truth commissions presuppose singularism. Some have argued, for instance, that the proposed Bosnian truth commission should arrive at one account of the nature and causes of the 1992–95 Bosnian war. To do otherwise would induce grandchildren of Bosnian Serbs, Croats, and Muslims to fight on the graves of their antecedents for a partisan account of the past.[14] More generally, one commentator remarks that "truth commissions are tools that traumatized countries use to set the historical record straight ... overturning the lies told by previous regimes to cover up their abuses."[15]

Similarly, a singularist spin can be given to the Guatemalan commission's mandate: "[The commission should] clarify with all objectivity, equity and impartiality the human rights violations and acts of violence that have caused the Guatemalan population to suffer, connected with the armed conflict."[16] Investigative bodies frequently frame their interpretation of facts in a unified and comprehensive narrative, replete with moral judgments and ascriptions of responsibility. Disagreements internal to a commission's work would be acceptable only as a means to achieve an agreed-upon report. On this singularist interpretation of truth commissions, a commission would have failed if its final report expressed disagreements let alone endorsed contending interpretations.

That truth commissions uniformly or consistently presuppose singularism is not so evident when we consider other features of truth commissions (or features of other truth commissions). First, two scholars who headed the research department of the South African Truth and Reconciliation Commission (TRC) argue the TRC's Final Report sought, among other things, to capture the diversity of interpretations that contending parties have offered with respect to apartheid and individual abuses. The TRC Final Report is "not the imposition of a single official 'truth' but "supports the case for the recognition of the depth of past differences."[17] The Final Report is a "map" that readers can use to examine contending and incompatible perspectives on the past and the conflicting motives of the protagonists. The Final Report can express and contribute to "the shared acknowledgement" that South Africa's story is one of "a multitude of nuances and many layers of truth that capture the motives and perspectives of those who shaped the agony and triumphs of the past."[18]

A second reason for ascribing multiplism to some truth commissions is the claim that truth commissions do not pursue—let alone achieve—a single truth about the past but instead rule out lies. Frequently quoted (almost always with approval) is Michael Ignatieff's remark: "All that a truth commission can achieve is to reduce the number of lies that can be circulated unchallenged in public discourse. In Argentina, its work has made it impossible to claim, for example, that the military did not throw half-dead victims in the sea from helicopters. In Chile, it is no longer permissible to assert in public that the Pinochet regime did not dispatch thousands of entirely innocent people."[19]

If we extend Ignatieff's claim from "factual truth" to interpretations of patterns and explanations of facts, we could craft a sophisticated multiplist point that truth commissions—through reasonable arguments—critically narrow the range of permissible interpretations, but allow and even encourage more than one admissible or plausible interpretation to survive the winnowing.

A third reason to contend that truth commissions do or should presuppose a multiplist ideal concerns the ways that truth commissions address disagreements among their commissioners. A singularist might insist that disagreements be resolved with one and only one right answer with respect to each object of interpretation. Perhaps none of the disputants currently have the right interpretation; but, Krausz would contend, a singularist commission would encourage the search for the right interpretation, perhaps employing a "pluralizing strategy" (LR, pp. 12–13) to show that the apparently competing interpretations concern diverse objects, such as different events or periods.

A multiplist, in contrast, tolerates all and only those diverse and competing interpretations that cross the threshold of admissibility. Toleration can be expressed in three ways.[20] A truth commission (that of Chile is an example) may paper over the disagreement by adopting vague or ambiguous language that the contending sides can accept. Second, admitting it has failed to reach consensus, a truth commission may agree to disagree, describe the two (or more) conflicting interpretations, and, perhaps, encourage public debate of the disagreement after the release of the final report. Finally, a commission may include a minority interpretation in the final report and (as does the U.S. Supreme Court) designate a dissenting view as a minority opinion. The singularist views these resolutions as steps toward eventual "correct" resolution, but the multiplist might include these diverse views as plausible resolutions themselves.

Perhaps the best approach to understanding truth commissions in the light of Krausz's two ideals is to conclude that, at times, the singularist approach is best, and at others, the multiplist. Employing Krausz's pluralizing strategy, a commission might decide that some past actualities (ideally) yield one and only one interpretation while other objects (ideally) permit more than one right interpretation. The TRC appears to have incorporated both approaches. Its Final Report distinguishes between factual truths and narrative truths. Questions concerning "who did what to whom, when, and how" arguably embody the singularist's demand for one and only one right answer. The TRC Final Report draws on a sophisticated database and reports its "findings." New evidence might overturn the judgments of factual truth, but such revisability remains compatible with the singularist ideal. In other circumstances and in relation to other objects of interpretation, the multiplist ideal might make more sense. Several incompatible but plausible and even reasonable interpretations explain why Argentina descended into barbarism in 1976. Why not say, with Aristotle, that different objects demand different ideals of interpretation? Why not pluralize the objects and keep both interpretive ideals? We may then conclude that truth commissions presuppose and exemplify both multiplism and singularism because these ideals are appropriate for different sorts of objects of interpretation.

Krausz objects to this way of using his distinction. As noted above, he defines multiplism in such a way that it permits the existence of a single correct interpretation for some objects (LR, p. 5). For Krausz, I believe, a truth commission would exemplify or embrace only singularism or only multiplism. And, if the second, such a truth commission may accept that some objects are susceptible to only one interpretation and others can be acceptably interpreted in more than one way. An asymmetry, then, exists in Krausz's account between singularism and multiplism; the first ultimately excludes the second, but multiplism may include singularist aspects in the sense that the multiplist can concede to the singularist that some (but only some) objects of interpretation should occasion one and only one right construal.

Instead of relying on this asymmetry, Krausz would do better to conceive singularism and multiplism as end points on a continuum. Instead of defining A and B in such a way that B may include A, it might be more perspicuous to identify pure A and pure B as ends of a continuum with the possibility of different ways of combining the two. In between black and white are different shades of grey. On this softening of the distinction, pure singularism would permit one and only one admissible interpretation of all objects of interpretation, and pure multiplism insists on more than one admissible interpretation of all objects of interpretation. In between the ends of the continuum would be different combinations of two end points depending on kinds or domains of objects. In the natural sciences most of the objects treated might call for singularism as an ideal of inquiry, but a view—such as the origin of the universe—might call for more than one interpretation. In cultural studies the multiplist ideal might be most suitable for the vast majority of objects investigated. But even in this "softer" inquiry, singularism sometimes is the relevant ideal, for example, in determining the nationality of Hamlet's prince.

In personal communication, Krausz has mentioned two objections to my suggested way to conceive of the relation of the two types of inquiry. First, he contends that on my construal the two "polar" extremes would be contradictories and the middle points could not shade into each other (like black and white) or be mixed with each other in different proportions (salt and pepper). On my alternative, pure singularism and pure multiplism would be contraries instead of contradictories. Two statements are contradictories when they both cannot be true and they both cannot be false. In contrast, two statements are contraries when they both cannot be true but can both be false. My rendition of the singularist-pluralist distinction is a case of contraries: singularism ("All objects admit of one and only one interpretation") and pure multiplism ("No objects admit of one and only one interpretation") cannot both be true, but they can both be false, for arguably some objects yield one right construal while others permit and even encourage more than one. Krausz correctly sees the world of objects as one composed of both sorts of objects, those that conduce to only one admissible construal and those that conduce to more than one. He could make this point more perspicuously by conceiving singularism and multiplism as contraries and that both should be taken as false.

A second reason that Krausz gives in rejecting my recasting of his distinction is that while what I call "pure" singularism and he calls "singularism" is a "live option" in a particular domain of inquiry, what I call "pure" multiplism is not a "live option." By "live option" Krausz means the same as did William James, namely, an intellectual position that many people take seriously and that some endorse. I have no more than impressionistic evidence on this point, but a discouragingly large number of people—and not just Richard Rorty's "occasional cooperative freshman"—believe that two sides to every issue exist (except the issue of whether relativism is true) and both sides are equally good.[21]

Whether Krausz accepts this modification of his fundamental dichotomy, yet another issue emerges in interpreting truth commissions through the lens of his theory. Consider the multiplist ideal in relation to those objects of interpretation that permit more than one admissible interpretation. Krausz, as we have seen, does not saddle multiplism with accepting any interpretation whatever or with ascribing equal worth to all admissible interpretations. For any object of interpretation, the multiplist may reject some interpretations as just plain crazy or beyond the pale. Among those that rise to the level of admissibility, one alternative may be preferable to all others. But, what makes one interpretation preferable to another? All Krausz tells us is that preferability is related to "good reasons" offered by expert practitioners (LR p. 7). Although a good one, this answer is only a start. I would urge Krausz to go further and decide what should count as good reasons or to invite relevant practitioners (truth commissioners, commission researchers, the democratic public) to deliberate and decide these matters (or both). With respect to truth commissions, among the questions concerning standards and procedures that Krausz or a commission itself might take up are the following questions.

How much evidence is sufficient to decide whether to accept the testimony or interpretation of a fact ("forensic truth") as admissible or preferable? Hayner describes two rules for (quantity of evidence) that different truth commissions have employed: "[T]he El Salvador commission established a two-source rule, requiring two credible and independent sources as confirmation of a fact. In contrast, the South African commission required only one source, both for corroborating victims' accounts and for deciding the culpability of perpetrators, providing the source was sufficiently compelling."[22]

What constitutes an appropriate "standard of proof"? Among the options are "beyond reasonable doubt" and "balance of probabilities" ("preponderance of evidence").[23] The El Salvador commission went further than this bivalent approach and, as Hayner describes: "established three levels of certainty—where there was overwhelming, substantial, or sufficient evidence to back up finding—and stated its degree of certainty for each of its findings throughout the report."[24] For example, the Salvadoran Commission has been one of the few truth commissions that identified perpetrators, and it did so only when evidence rose to the highest level of certainty.

By contrast, as Hayner points out, a truth commission might list, with the relevant evidence, two sets of names: the names of those people repeatedly identified in testimony as guilty of abuses; the names of people, a smaller group, about whom the commission has investigated further and drawn its conclusions with respect to culpability. Regarding both amount and rules of evidence, Hayner sagaciously recommends that: "Future commissions should state in their reports the amount or quality of evidence that backs up their findings (such as one or two primary or secondary sources), and what level of certainty their findings represent."[25]

What procedures should a truth commission follow to decide these questions about the quantity and quality of evidence and whether to name names? Is absolute consensus required among members of the commission and its researchers? If so, by what procedures can and should it be obtained? What role might democratic deliberation play? Lacking such unanimity, how should the commission proceed? If by voting, should the majority rule? Should the majority take into account the views of the minority and adopt a compromise position that all can accept? Should expression of preferences or the give-and-take of deliberative reason giving be emph-asized?[26] When should a commission agree to disagree? What role, if any, should non-commission citizens (civil society) play in the commission's deliberations and decisions?

In bringing Krausz's theory and the practices of truth commissions' into reciprocal focus, I have a final and most basic worry about Krausz's distinction between singularism and multiplism (whether the dichotomy is replaced by a continuum). When applied to truth commissions, does Krausz's view of the difference between singularism and multiplism constitute a meaningful or useful distinction? Recall that the singularist can accept multiple interpretations as a means to determine the one and only correct interpretation. Interpreters who are singularists might also modestly admit that they are not sure whether they have the right answer or whether they have made a proper approximation and these singularists might be open to the truth of rival views. And since multiplism accepts only one admissible interpretation regarding some objects of interpretation, rejects "interpretative anarchism" (RR, pp. 49–53), requires a distinction between inadmissible and admissible interpretations, and under some circumstances permits that expert practitioners give reasons for the preferability of one interpretation, the divide between singularism and multiplism erodes entirely. What is the theoretical or practical distinction between the ideals if both may guide interpreters to aspire to one interpretation and both accommodate conflicting interpretations?

I see two ways that Krausz might respond to these worries and maintain the sharpness of the distinction between singularism and multiplism or between—what I have dubbed—pure singularism and pure multiplism. First, he might distinguish his two interpretive ideals on the basis that only multiplism is fallible and revisable while the successful realization of the ideal of singularism somehow transports the interpreter beyond human finitude, error, and history. This strategy goes against Krausz's expressed affirmation that fallibilism is involved in choosing and trying to realize either ideal. For Krausz, in his synopsis, conceives both ideals not in relation to the ahistorical pursuit of a Platonic form or to the convergence on one option at the "end of inquiry," but to a pragmatist idea that both ideals "should be understood within provisional, unfolding, and changing interpretive conditions" (IO, p.12). Recall Krausz's statement, again in the synopsis, that, in the choice of an ideal, "informed practitioners may agree that all pertinent evidence or argumentation is available as to whether a given object of interpretation answers to one or more than one interpretation" (IO, p.12).

Truth commissions cannot catapult themselves outside of a particular historical moment to an infallible God's-eye view to determine whether its judgments match a Platonic Idea or whether its inquiry converges on one admissible interpretation (singularism) or on a limited range of admissible interpretations (multiplism). Singularism and multiplism are best understood as differing in degree and not kind, for the conditions in which they are chosen are changing, those who choose interpretive ideals and interpretations are fallible, the choices of ideals and interpretations are provisional, and the content of each ideal may reflect this fallibility.

A second way, which might truly distinguish singularism from multiplism, occurs in RR (p. 44–53) but not (explicitly) in LR. In RR, Krausz contends that only the singularist ideal allows for the "conclusive overthrow" (RR, p. 43) of all competing interpretation. What is "conclusiveness"? For Krausz, conclusiveness is not a psychological notion having to do with states of mind such as "decisiveness," "certainty," or "convincingness" but a "logical notion" (RR, p. 50). Although Krausz could explain and defend this "logical notion" more fully, he makes a start in RR and goes further in his comments on my draft paper.

On one account, "conclusive overthrow" would occur if and only if deductively valid arguments from irrefutable or self-evident premises proved one interpretation to be superior to contending interpretations. Let us dub this as the "knockdown proof" construal of "conclusivity." Which of two interpretations of Beethoven's First Symphony should a director accept and why? Should she interpret the work on the basis of Beethoven's printed score or on the basis of aesthetic considerations and, if the latter, which aesthetic criteria? A singularist director would adopt that interpretation that was (successfully) based on knockdown proof.

Attributing this sort of "conclusivity" to singularism would distinguish it from multiplism, for in multiplism rational preferability would never rise to the level of irrefutable proof. Yet such a demarcation between singularism and multiplism would come with an unacceptably high price. Singularism would apply only to those circumstances in which one interpretation would win by knockdown argument, and such circumstances may be exceedingly rare if they exist at all. Multiplism would reign in the arenas of past wrongs—and, more generally, of historical events—to be investigated by a truth commission. Arguably, on this "knockdown argument" interpretation of the difference between multiplism and singularism, only multiplism would be relevant not just to truth commissions but to all or most arenas of human affairs and to all or most human inquiries (including the natural sciences). For in most if not all human inquiries apodictic methods take a back seat to humanly good but fallible and revisable judgment.

In RR, Krausz himself puts forth a considerably weaker criterion of "conclusive overthrow" of contending interpretations. On this account of singularism, what the singularist believes is that standards exist by which the (singularist) interpreter can adjudicate between conflicting interpretations. In contrast, a multiplist ascribes to "inconclusivity" in the sense that "no overarching standards exist in virtue of which we might adjudicate between contending interpretations" or, presumably, if such standards do exist, they yield no conclusive adjudication. The singularist ideal aims for only one admissible interpretation—although inadmissible interpretations may help achieve that goal. Although the multiplist ideal is compatible with one interpretation being advanced—with good reason—as the best, the multiplist tolerates and even celebrates more than one admissible interpretation. An admissible interpretation is one that has some good reasons, but not necessarily the best reasons, to support it. If one admissible interpretation is judged best, that superiority is not conclusive in the sense that all alternative interpretations are judged inadmissible.

Does this weaker notion of conclusivity provide Krausz with a reasonable way to distinguish—both theoretically and practically—singularism from multiplism without elevating singularism to infallibilism or deductivity or reducing multiplism to "anarchism"? I still have some worries. On the one hand, "(conclusive) adjudication in relation to standards" is not quite different from "knockdown argument." Although such adjudication may be practiced by human beings, even in the hard sciences, to have one and only interpretation completely vanquish its rivals is difficult and rare. Defeated interpretations still have something to offer, albeit in a pedagogical, distorted, one-sided, or incomplete way. Successful theories are seen to be so only in relation to strengths and weaknesses of their bested rivals. Singularism, in assuming conclusive overthrow and casting its rivals into inadmissibility, is in danger of ceasing to be a live option in both scientific and cultural interpretation. On the other hand, if singularism were to be more tolerant about the truth and value of vanquished rivals, it would avoid remoteness from human experience but be threatened by being only different in degree from that kind of multiplism that elevates one interpretation as (far) better than its rivals.

If singularism and multiplism merely occupy "ideal" extremes of a continuum (in which every point between the extremes represents some mixture of multiple admissible interpretations with respect to some objects and single admissibility with respect to others), then there appears to be no difference in kind between singularist fallibilist adjudication by standards and multiplist tolerance of many interpretations but reason-based preference for one of them. The first might affirm the partial insights of its rivals and be open to arguments that the rivals are superior, while multiplism, on the other hand, might wholeheartedly promote one interpretation as best, even though no assurance exists that its standards or reasons are the only game in town.

Is there a practical difference between the ways in which singularists and multiplists would proceed in relation to rival interpretations? Krausz might answer that the multiplist interpreter who says, "I prefer this interpretation over all others, and I have good reasons for doing so—yet I allow that certain others are also admissible" expresses a quite different attitude from the singularist interpreter who says, "Only one admissible interpretation exists."

Krausz rightly concedes that a multiplist bent on the best interpretation could fail to tolerate admissible rivals and could arrogantly ignore the worth of their positions. And a singularist who was genuinely fallibilist could be so humbly open to the virtues of his foes that he failed to be sufficiently whole-hearted in advancing what he believed to be true. Yet, a singularist, committed to fallibilism and respect for rivals, and a multiplist, intent on getting the best interpretation, would likely express the same practical attitudes of openness to a rival's possibly better ideas, wholehearted argument for the best that has been discovered, and a willingness to reduce and even reconcile whatever differences remain.

If this point is accepted, the differences that interpreters have toward rival interpretations have less to do with interpretive ideals than with the cognitive virtue of fallibilism and the moral virtue of respect for others. A truth commission of multiplists does not guarantee interpretive toleration or reconciliation of differences. A truth commission of singularists necessitates neither close-mindedness nor intolerance. A truth commission of fallible and sagacious citizens would democratically choose when to aim for interpretive consensus, when and how to accommodate disagreement, and how to understand and value the reconciliation of former foes.

Perhaps I have interpreted Krausz's distinction between singularism and multiplism incorrectly or misapplied it to truth commissions. Or perhaps this object of interpretation (Krausz's text) permits more than one admissible interpretation and mine (*ojalá que sí*) is one of them. A third possibility, that I favor, is that I have given good but not conclusive reasons for one (the best?) interpretation of a theme in Krausz's book and a well-reasoned but fallible assessment of his theory and its relevance for an interpretation of truth commissions. If I am right, some recommendations for Krausz and for truth commissions follow. Krausz should revise his key distinction, view singularism and multiplism as limiting points on a continuum, and consider in some detail the advantages and disadvantages of different ways of moving from inadmissible to admissible interpretations and thence to the most reasonable interpretation (should there exist just one) or interpretations (should there be more than one). Truth commissions should clarify, more than they typically do, their interpretive, cognitive, and moral ideals, their strategies to realize them, and their ways of coping with differing interpretations both within the commission and the larger society.

NOTES

References to Krausz's synoptic article (Chapter 2) at the beginning of this volume are preceded in the body of this article by "IO."

1. Michael Krausz, *Limits of Rightness* (LR) (Lanham, Md.: Rowman and Littlefield, 2000).

2. Michael Krausz, *Rightness and Reasons: Interpretation in Cultural Practices* (RR) (Ithaca: Cornell University Press, 1993).

3. Priscilla Hayner, *Unspeakable Truths: Confronting State Terror and Atrocity* (New York: Routledge, 2001).

4. David A. Crocker, "Reckoning with Past Wrongs, "*Ethics & International Affairs*, 13 (1999), pp. 43–64. See also Timothy Garton Ash, "The Truth About Dictatorship," *New York Review of Books*, 45: (19 February 1998), p. 35.

5. Hayner, *Unspeakable Truths*, pp. 5, 23.

6. *Ibid.,* p. 14.

7. *Ibid.*, pp. 15–16, 24–31. See also David A. Crocker, "Truth Commissions, Transitional Justice, and Civil Society," Robert I. Rotberg and Dennis Thompson, eds., *Truth vs. Justice: The Morality of Truth Commissions* (Princeton: Princeton University Press, 2000), pp. 100–109; and Crocker, "Reckoning with Past Wrongs," pp. 49–62.

8. Hayner, *Unspeakable Truths*, p. 24.

9. Charles S. Maier, "Doing History, Doing Justice: The Narrative of the Historian and the Truth Commission," *Truth v. Justice*, p. 271.

10. Hayner, *Unspeakable Truths*, p. 26–29.

11. *Ibid.*, p. 27.

12. Alex Boraine, *A Country Unmasked: Inside South Africa's Truth and Reconciliation Commission* (Oxford: Oxford University Press, 2000), p. 288.

13. *Ibid.*, p. 289–290.

14. Neil J. Kritz and William A. Steubner, "A Truth Commission for Bosnia and Herzegovina: Why, How, and When?" paper presented at the Victimology Symposium, Sarajevo, Bosnia, 9–10 May 1998.

15. Tepperman, "Truth and Consequences," p. 130.

16. Cited in Hayner, *Unspeakable Truths*, p. 305. See Guatemala Memoria del Silencio, *Informe de la Comisión para el Esclarecimiento Histórico* (Guatemala City, 1999), CEH/UNOPS, 1, p. 42.

17. Charles Villa-Vicencio and Wilhelm Verwoerd, "Constructing a Report: Writing Up the 'Truth,'" *Truth v. Justice*, p. 279–294.

18. *Ibid.*, pp. 289, 279.

19. Michael Ignatieff, "Articles of Faith," *Index on Censorship* 5 (1996), p. 113.

20. Crocker, "Truth Commissions," p. 102.

21. Richard Rorty, *Consequences of Pragmatism: Essays 1972–1980* (Minneapolis: University of Minnesota Press, 1982), p. 166.

22. Hayner, *Unspeakable Truths*, p. 130.

23. *Ibid.*, p. 131.

24. *Ibid.*

25. *Ibid.*

26. Amy Gutmann and Dennis Thompson, "The Moral Foundations of Truth Commissions," *Truth v. Justice*, pp. 22–45. See also James Bohman, *Public Deliberation: Pluralism, Complexity, and Democracy* (Cambridge: MIT Press, 1996).

Six

LIMITS OF INTERPRETATION

Ken-ichi Sasaki

1. Hermeneutics as Philosophy

Michael Krausz's *Limits of Rightness*, a book full of insights based on logical clarity and formed against a vast knowledge of arguments on interpretation, has incited me to rethink several basic concepts, not only that of interpretation, but also constructivism and realism, multiplism and singularism.[1] I will concentrate on the conception shown on the title "Limits of Rightness," which sounds almost poetic. I take the philosophical stance expressed in this title as an index of the author's critical attitude vis-à-vis philosophical hermeneutics. Krausz tries to go beyond the limits of rightness through a critical examination of the discourses on interpretation. Although I might not be able to do anything more than raise some questions, I will critique his arguments in favor of this spirit. I must add that I stay outside the American philosophical world, and I am not as well acquainted with the literature on this topic as other contributors to this volume are. I fear I might not be heterodox enough against Krausz.

I have the impression that on the international arena, the United States provides the most fervent discussions of interpretation. In this context, the following remark by Joseph Margolis appears to me even enigmatic: "It is not, I should say, usual for American or Anglo-American philosophers, writing on mainstream topics, to write on either interpretation or history."[2] In 1991, three philosophers insisted upon the importance of interpretation in the modern history of Western philosophy, so much so that they spoke of the "interpretive turn."[3] Besides, the rich repertory of works Krausz takes up and examines in his book disproves Margolis.

The wave of hermeneutics landed in Japan, where I pursue my academic life, toward the end of the 1970s. Unlike in the United States, in Japan this vogue was passed leaving behind just a slight change in intellectual life. Familiarity, though, does not necessarily afford understanding. I have felt foggy about the topic of interpretation. It was not difficult to follow the historical description of hermeneutics from Friedrich Schleiermacher, via Wilhelm Dilthey and Martin Heidegger, to Hans-Georg Gadamer. Several theories of interpretation in poetics, rhetoric, philosophy of language, and history of art were interesting to me. I did not know how to relate the ideas of these thinkers to particular examples. I could not relate, for example, Heidegger's hermeneutics of "Dasein," or the hermeneutic circle, to more concrete discussions on a painting by an Erwin Panofsky, or on poetics and rhetoric by a Jean Cohen, on metaphor by an I. A. Richards and a Max Black, or finally on literary criticism by a Monroe Beardsley. In short, I learned separately about many issues connected with interpretation, without procuring the map of cases on which to situate them. Such a map can explain why hermeneutics is crucial, and its absence gave me a foggy feeling about hermeneutics.

Other philosophers might have acquired such a map. I dare to confess my ignorance because I wish to discuss the work of Krausz in relation to this map. We can form an image of this global background from another remark by Margolis, which continues the above-mentioned points: ". . . interpretation appears marginal only because the analytic tradition is strongly disposed to believe that we confront the world directly and have no deep need (except for accommodating the transient contingencies of ignorance and lack of evidence) to construe our cognitive interventions as interpretively freighted."[4] Margolis suggests that all "our cognitive interventions" are more or less interpretations. This basic and universal character of interpretation makes interpretation of such philosophical importance. We should distinguish new hermeneutics, as a philosophy, from traditional hermeneutics as methodology in several particular fields of study, such as religious exegesis, law, literature, and art. Interpretation is being discussed in these particular fields today because hermeneutics as a philosophy has entered into the main stream of thought.

We are interested in interpretation in different forms, as we are strongly incited in the contemporary world we live, to construe our cognitions epistemologically in terms of interpretation, as claimed by Margolis. Interpretation implies the existence of different interpretations: conflict is an essential feature of interpretation.[5] In ordinary language, we do not call any evident (one that brings forth no conflict) perception or cognition an interpretation. When Newton got the intuition of universal gravitation observing an apple falling from the tree, he interpreted the phenomenon, because his intuition was different from simple ordinary perception taking the phenomenon just as the fall of an apple. Pan-interpretationists wish to take even perception for an interpretation. I do not agree with this view, since it neglects the basic fact that an interpretation appears with the recognition of difference.

Does Margolis ally with pan-interpretationism? His phrase quoted above, "our cognitive interventions as interpretively freighted," is ambiguous: he appears not to admit that all cognitions are interpretations. Then, if we talk about "constructivism" instead of pan-interpretationism, we do not have to hesitate to count him among its representative advocates. Krausz qualifies him as an "internal constructive realist." Interpretation is the mode of procedure of the construction or constitution, or its essential ingredient.

From this point of perspective, we can understand and situate the advent of philosophical hermeneutics in the modern tradition of the West: it marks a final finish of the modern philosophy inaugurated by Immanuel Kant. Kant, strictly speaking, established the conception of construction or constitution. Margolis appears to understand this historical development properly, when he acknowledges that "Kant is already committed to a constructed world."[6] His reservation comes from his excessive attention to Kant's notion of noumenal reality. But the Kantian critique of perception insists upon the concepts of category and schema. In Kant, the epistemological critique is one thing, and the ontological posit of the noumenon is another. Kant was not committed to a constructed world, but he created the constructed world. He conceived for the first time in the history of Western philosophy the explication of perception in terms of active "constructive" intervention the subject gives to sensible materia (*Anschauung*), instead of passive reception of "phantasma," or images given as such.

A crucial difference exists between Kant and contemporary constructivism. While Kant was concerned with the a priori structure of perceptive cognition that should assure its possibility ("transcendental aesthetics"), contemporary constructivists in the broadest sense are mainly occupied with the empirical dimension of schematism, which consists in the cultural or historical determinateness of our perception. One of the concepts showing the most striking affinity with the Kantian "schema" is the "mental set" (*Einstellung*) by E. H. Gombrich.[7] According to this art historian, our perception is conditioned by the "mental set," or structuring tendency formed through experiences. This "mental set" made people see the fin of a whale as an ear: the knowledge of the whale as mammal had "set" the mind (or "mens") tending to interpret a projection behind the eye of a whale as its ear. It concerns evidently a phenomenon of empirical schematism. We see that all the above-mentioned theoretical topics relating to interpretation, such as semiotics, symbol theory, theory of metaphor, rhetoric, and so on, are to be most properly interpreted as fields of schematism.

Philosophical hermeneutics represents the modern or post-Kantian climate of the Western way of thinking. I will examine *Limits of Rightness* with regard to this philosophical background, which he shares and wishes to go beyond. Western modernity was or is a civilization, or a culture of pure humanity; it emphasizes human creativity for the sake of the good life of human beings.[8] The leading slogan of "mastery of nature" proclaimed by René Descartes, when viewed retrospectively from the present point, sounds arrogant. The setting of Kantian epistemology might express the acknowledgment of limited human faculties (we cannot grasp directly the thing as such), but it also might appear to be expressing excessive pride (we are the universal measure). I find arrogant some contemporary theories of interpretation that do not appear to respect the work worthy of this name, whether artistic or philosophical. The work in a strong sense of the word means the human product that transcends the intention of the author and has become creative itself. Through the notion of "limits of rightness," Krausz expresses his critical or skeptical attitude toward such an arrogant modernity. But is he not arrested by his standpoint of the theory of interpretation?

2. Where Are the Limits of Rightness?

Limits of Rightness develops by centering on twin pairs of concepts: singularism versus multiplism, and realism versus constructivism. The first concerns the "ideals of interpretation," and the second concerns basic views of epistemology and ontology. A great portion of Krausz's effort addresses the argument aimed to distinguish (or "detach") these two concepts, so that he can hold that "orthodox positions," as singularist-realist and multiplist-constructivist, and all other "heterodox combinations" are possible (LR, p. 3). His differentiation allows him to go so far as to admit the combination between two ontological positions: "constructive realism." The same spirit of discrimination leads him to an acknowledgment of the "limits of rightness."

Krausz does not explain his interest in this subject. He does not tell us his motives. But to surmise the motive behind his efforts to establish the "detachability" thesis is not difficult. Speaking of the "two ideals of interpretation" found "all along the course of history," which correspond to Krausz's singularism and multiplism, Umberto Eco remarks that "the first option is instantiated by different kinds of fundamentalism and of different forms of metaphysical realism."[9] The "orthodox combination" of singularism and realism is a commonplace, to which Krausz's claim of "detachability" raises as a provocation and a logical challenge.

But still another point in Krausz's intention is obscure: the relation between this "detachability" thesis and the idea of "limits of rightness." He addressed his main efforts to prove the "detachability" of the ideals of interpretation from the metaphysical theories. But throughout this work, he wishes to talk about the "limits of rightness." I notice a shift, which he neither explains nor notices. The opposition between singularism and multiplism concerns the rightness of interpretation. But, to detach it from the metaphysics of realism and constructivism is neither to attest to, nor to go beyond "the limits of rightness." I think this point is quite crucial, because the idea of "the limits of rightness" reveals all the more true philosophical fulcrum of Krausz's arguments. We will return to this fundamental point, after a critical examination of Krausz's argument.

Krausz mentions the limits of rightness in three passages, and in two different contexts. First, he refers to it in a paragraph featuring it as the headword: "The title of this book, *Limits of Rightness*, signals that sometimes neither the ideals of singularism nor multiplism apply. They do not apply where the grounds are unavailable to determine whether otherwise competing interpretations address a common object. If the object is not common or if there are no grounds to determine whether interpretations address a common object, no contest can arise" (LR, p. 16).

Krausz defines singularism and multiplism as follows: "Singularism is the view that that which is interpreted should always answer to one and only one ideally admissible interpretation. . . . In contrast, multiplism is the view that that which is interpreted need not always answer to one and only one fully congruent ideally admissible interpretation" (LR, pp. 1–2).

He adds this comment: "Multiplism requires that competing interpretations address the same thing" (LR, p. 2). Even concerning the same painting as Vincent Van Gogh's *Potato Eaters*, which prompted several interpretations such as "formalist, psychoanalytic, Marxist, feminist, or others," "the singularist might attempt to install the singularist condition by pluralizing the object of interpretation" (LR, pp. 12–13). Hence, the "limit."

Krausz mentions limits in this context about the sameness of the object of interpretation. This time the term concerns a more radical case, the possibility of individuation of that which is interpreted. He talks about the two opposing ultimate principles of being in Hinduism and Buddhism: "Atma" or "the cosmic self" for the first, "Anatma" or "Emptiness" for the second. These principles concern "the nature of things," and "'the nature of things' is not individuable as one thing instead of another" (LR, p. 123). "Such cases would be beyond the scope of singularism or multiplism. They would be beyond the limits of rightness" (LR, p. 124). "Since the Hindu and the Buddhist disagree about whether they are talking about the same thing, they disagree about whether they disagree" (*Ibid.*).

Krausz adds a further complication concerning the Hindu-Buddhist controversy. Given the radical disagreement between them, "the question of ideal admissibility could not arise. So the question of interpretive admissibility can arise only relative to the soteriological place of the inquirer, and at that it can arise only at a 'relative' or 'conventional' level. Here is another limit of rightness" (*Ibid.*). I paraphrase this argument as follows: while a Hindu considers "Atma" true, a Buddhist sees "Anatma" as true. These concern their respective visions of the world, and it would be meaningless for an outside judge to pronounce either admissible, because these visions represent personal choices based on existential decisions. The Hindu or the Buddhist might fail in attaining the final object of their salvation. But such failure is not the result of the lack of rightness or the inadmissibility of their choice.

Unless I overlooked other mentions the author might have made elsewhere, these three are all the passages where Krausz touches upon the "limits of rightness." They fall into two different categories of limits of rightness, not three: individuation or determinability of the object of interpretation (or more exactly, "that which is interpreted") on the one side, and the soteriological world vision on the other. I suggest that Krausz's idea of the "limits of rightness" does not fit with his frame of argument consisting in the problem of the ideal of interpretation: the first order of problem is based upon a wrong problem setting, and the second is beyond the reach of interpretation.

3. Individuation As Pseudo-Problem

I begin with questioning the reason we cannot individuate the object of interpretation, in the above-mentioned two cases: Vincent Van Gogh's painting,
Potato Eaters, and the confrontation between the Hindu and the Buddhist
soteriology. In the case of Hinduism and Buddhism, the impossibility of individuation is said to come from their addressing "the nature of things." The
nature of things is uncountable and cannot be individuated. I wonder if
exactly the same thing is at stake in Van Gogh's painting. "Limits of rightness" appear when we claim that we cannot tell whether a Marxist and a psy-
choanalyst, for example, see the same thing in *The Potato Eaters*. Why can
we not tell that? Is it not because their interpretations concern a kind of "nature of things?" While the Hindu and Buddhist dare to decipher the enigma of
the universe and answer with "Atma" or "Anatma," art critics try to interpret
Van Gogh's painting and give their answer with Marxist or psychoanalytic
interpretations. If "Atma" and "Anatma" address the "natures of things,"
these interpretations of art do so as well.

Here I see something strange: a reverse operation between the object
and the interpretation. Does the impossibility of individuation of the object of
interpretation, which is said to bring us beyond the "limits of rightness," not
concern the interpretive content instead of its object? I wonder whether
Krausz (or more exactly, the singularist supposed by him as wishing to hold
fast to his or her view by pluralizing the object), discussing this impossibility
of fixing the object, does not refer to the result of interpretation. But the object comes first. The enigma or charm of an object sets off the interpretation.
At the level of the prepositional form of the interpretive utterance, the object
gives rise to the subject, the interpretation, the predicate. The object (or the
subject of the proposition) is one, while the interpretation is diverse. Taking
the results of interpretation for its objects, we necessarily arrive at the impossibility of individuating the object of interpretation. To explain the reason
such inversion happens is easy: it comes from the dialectical relation between
the object and its cognition (or interpretation): with a deeper experience, we
do not see its object any more as we did before. The object of cognition is
always being reformed by cognition. This is a complementary side of the
hermeneutical circle.

Sometimes interpretations of one and the same object are so heteroge-
neous that they appear to be talking about different objects. This is an ordinary way of speaking, but it is only a way of speaking or a kind of metaphor
that does not express the ontological structure. If we allow such diversity in
the object, we will be led to a radical solipsism. There would be no single
identical object: even this object I point to before my eyes is not one, but
many different objects—one for each perceiver. Such view logically implies
that we cannot communicate with anyone about the world: everyone would
always talk about a unique thing unknown to anyone else. All theories or

opinions would be soliloquies, and there could be no disputes or controversies.

This extreme particularism is not only epistemologically unsound, but also contradicts the facts. For instance, Marxist and formalist interpretations of *The Potato Eaters* oppose one another. A Marxist will deny and criticize the formalist view of the painting because of the bourgeois spirit that ignores the content representing the reality of society. For a formalist, by contrast, the Marxist view is erroneous because it does not take into account the painting as such or the art history constituting its real context. They believe they can (or even should) dispute one another. Such belief also means they assume that they talk about the same object: Van Gogh's *Potato Eaters*.

We are led to the interesting issue of the self-contradiction or self-refutation of singularism, which comes in two forms. Recall the argument of Krausz's singularist. He or she dared to suppose that a Marxist and a formalist, for example, interpret different objects, in order to rescue his or her singularism from the competition of different interpretations. This trial of rescuing singularism destroys, in the first place, the basis of the dispute, which I think constitutes singularism. A singularist is singularist by claiming that there exists only one "right" interpretation about one and the same object and by being ready to refute different interpretations as not "right." Second, such a procedure of rescuing singularism destroys the basis for the opposition between singularism and multiplism. This Krausz rightly perceives when he talks about "limits of rightness." This self-refutation of singularism suggests something is wrong with the distinction between singularism and multiplism.

4. Singularism and Multiplism as Apparent Oppositions

I assume that the opposition between singularism and multiplism is hypothetical and asymmetrical. By "hypothetical" I mean that the distinction is drawn and supposed only by Krausz, and not necessarily shared by other authors. He examines seven authors whom he considers "constructive realists" in detail from Chapters 6 to 9. The object of his examination is to verify the "detachability" of the ideals of interpretation (singularism or multiplism) from theories of epistemology and ontology (realism, constructivism, and constructive realism). These authors do not talk about "ideals of interpretation," but Krausz reviews their theories in terms of singularism and multiplism. Among the authors quoted in this book, we find just one who presents his singularist ideal of interpretation (while calling it "critical monism"): Alexander Nehamas (LR, pp. 5–10); and just one who upholds multiplism in the case of "cultural" objects of interpretation: David Norton (LR, p. 11). Comparing their views so far as quoted and examined by Krausz, I see a crucial asymmetry between singularism and multiplism. "While singularism claims that all objects of interpretation are singularly interpretable, multiplism holds that some objects of interpretation may answer to more than one admissible interpretation" (LR, p. 5). The asymmetry noticed by Krausz concerns the extension of these ideals. My asymmetry is different, and concerns the difference of context or standpoint. A singularist and a multiplist do not talk about the choice on the same problem. On this issue, the position of Nehamas is especially instructive, because his singularism is "regulative": "he distinguishes between pursuing the single right interpretation from asserting that there is a single right interpretation. He notes that the pursuit of a posited single right interpretation does not commit him to the claim that there is one such interpretation" (LR, p. 5). Singularism is an (or the) ideal of interpretation. But multiplism is not: its claim is, let us say, "existential." Norton regards multiplism as "the epistemic condition" of all interpretation on cultural objects (LR, p. 11). We can consider it and a simple acknowledgment that plural interpretations exist. That many different interpretations of the same cultural object exist serves as a condition for further different interpretations.

In brief, while singularism is an, or perhaps even the ideal of interpretation, multiplism is not. Their opposition is only apparent, and they are not contradictory. We can talk about "multiplist singularism." I fear that this hypothetical and asymmetrical character of the concepts of singularism and multiplism might make *Limits of Rightness* less persuasive than the admirable fine sense of logical discrimination of the author led us to believe.

5. Soteriology Beyond Hermeneutics

Krausz surprised me by referring to his experience in Banares at the Ganges River, in the context of his discussion of the distinction between realism and constructivism (LR, p. 35 ff). It was the last thing I expected from an American philosopher at work on interpretation. Banares is the holy city of the Hindu, where "it is thought that dying and being cremated [there] will guarantee pure beings as holy people and babies are given "the honor of being returned directly to the life source of the Ganges," by means of their wrapped corpses "weighted with heavy stones" being thrown into the holy river" (LR, p. 36). Krausz asks himself: "Did I see something different from what the Indian saw? Or did we see the same thing but interpret it differently? If we saw the same thing but interpreted it differently, who is right? Or is more than one interpretation admissible?" (LR, p. 36).

This impressive example not only fits the context, but also reveals the deep reach of the problem of interpretation and rightness in Krausz himself. Without doubt, it arises from the same philosophical interest that prompts him to introduce the soteriological problem, instantiated by the controversy between the Hindu and the Buddhist. But I think that the problem is different in nature. Krausz claims two "aims of interpretation" exist: "elucidation and edification" (LR, p. 113). His "soteriology" evidently belongs to the second aim. First, I immediately felt an irrelevancy of this assertion, because in my view, interpretation has the unique aim of "elucidation" and this is implied in its concept. To interpret a text or a phenomenon is not as such an act of "edi-fication." Even if the edificatory concern may intervene, it can be as a use of the elucidatory result. (Our author himself quotes the definition of interpreta-tion given in the *Oxford English Dictionary*, "explanation, exposition, con-struction put upon, representation.") I do not think that raising this problem is futile, but that it transcends the domain of interpretation. As I have said, Krausz considers that the Hindu "Atma" and Buddhist "Anatma" are, respec-tively, interpretations of "the nature of things." My problem is not so much whether these metaphysical concepts are soteriological, but whether they are interpretations. In order to construe them as interpretations, Krausz posits that "Atma" and "Anatma" concern the "nature of things." As I remarked above, every interpretation concerns the nature of something: this "something" calls for an interpretation, and becomes its object. Interpretation of something re-sults in a propositional formulation, of which the predicate is given by the interpreted "nature." I doubt whether "Atma" or "Anatma" is given as an answer to the question concerning "the nature of things." Are they not instead the answer to a question too general, too fundamental, too comprehensive, and too universal for its subject to be determined in its interpretive proposi-tion? Are they not pure intuition without any object (of cognition) or subject (of proposition)?

Some cognitive cultures are inclined to substantiate states or the natures of things, and to subjectify predicates. Perhaps such is a universal tendency in human understanding. The most typical case is given by the metaphysical concept of "being" in Western philosophy. Although representing the purest "state" of things, "being" is immediately transformed into the most funda-mental substance. A typical case is that found in the famous passage, Exodus 3:14: "And God said unto Moses, I AM THAT I AM: and he said, Thus shalt thou say unto the children of Israel, I AM hath sent me unto thou." Such for-mulation in subject-predicate form must be a logical (or propositional) recon-struction of the original intuition of "being." If we concentrate on the original intuition, we should conceive it as something like "Eureka!" As far as I know, the intuition is an immediate grasp or a sudden illumination of a state—a revelation of a pure predicate. Although I have experienced neither "Atma" nor "Anatma," I am convinced that if such cognition exists, that cognition is obtained as an intuition, not through interpretation. Besides, is not this dis-tinction the reason that this particular cognition can have a soteriological meaning?

6. Limits of Interpretation

While Krausz speaks of limits of rightness with regard to the reach of inter-pretation, I am inclined to think of the limits of interpretation itself. I have already referred to Eco's notion of "the limits of interpretation." Mine is dif-ferent from his. By "limits of rightness," Eco, author of a book called *The*

Open Work, means that the act of interpreting a work presupposes the constraint of the text, so that "the Peircean idea of unlimited semiosis" or the Derridean "drift" represents only a half of the dialectic.[10] While Eco thinks of the series, considered as *ad infinitum* (an interpretation is an interpretation of an interpretation of . . .), I, being inspired by the reading of Krausz's book, think of the limited reach of (the concept of) interpretation,.

In my opinion, interpretation implies multiplism, and the opposition between singularism and multiplism is only apparent. We find the simplest evidence for this claim because we do not call interpretation any opinion of which we do not have or can imagine any different view. When Newton discovered the law of universal gravitation, he was interpreting a phenomenon for which there were different explanations. But when all people accepted his view, it became a law and stopped being an interpretation. Accordingly, singularism is a self-defeating concept. The only possible way to be a singularist is in the "regulative" sense. Its "existential" version does not obtain. The only way for it to function existentially is by pluralizing its object, and this is contradictory for a different reason: the pluralizing process concerns an offer of different interpretations for different objects. In short, singularism is only "regulative," and "existential" can only be multiplism. The only limits of rightness, rightly claimed by Krausz, concern soteriology. The limits of rightness are real, because the problem is found beyond the reach of interpretation.

NOTES

1. Michael Krausz, *Limits of Rightness* (LR) (Lanham, Md.: Rowman and Littlefield, 2000).

2. Joseph Margolis, *Interpretation Radical But Not Unruly. The New Puzzle of the Arts and History* (Berkeley: University of California Press, 1995), p. ix.

3. D. R. Hiley, J. F. Bohman, and R. Schusterman, eds., *The Interpretive Turn, Philosophy, Science Culture* (Ithaca: Cornell University Press, 1991).

4. Margolis, *Interpretation*, p. ix.

5. Paul Ricoeur, *Le conflict des interpretations: Essais d'hermeneutiques* (Paris: Seuil, 1969).

6. Margolis, *Interpretation,* p. 9.

7. E. M. Gombrich, *Art and Illusion* (London: Phaidon, 1962).

8. Ken-Ichi Sasaki, "Relativism as the Fate of Modernity," JTLA, 23/24 (1998/1999), Department of Aesthetics and Philosophy of Art, the University of Tokyo.

9. Umberto Eco, *The Limits of Interpretation* (Bloomington: Indiana University Press, 1990), p. 24.

10. *Ibid.*, p. 6.

Seven

INTERPRETIVE IDEALS AND LIFE PROJECTS

Ronald Moore

Protracted philosophical battles, like their political counterparts, are likely to seem chaotic, confusing, and ultimately wearisome, especially to the sideline observer. The longer the battles proceed, the more the larger goals of combat become obscured behind a welter of logistic details. Where first reports advertise grand advances toward (or retreat from) easily appreciated objectives, later reports dwell on finer and finer discriminations of strategic position, combatant identity, and relative firepower. Eventually the endless proliferation of strikes and counterstrikes, alignments and realignments, and endless remapping of the field of combat prove daunting, even to the most attentive observer. In time, initial passion dissipates into dispassion and ultimately indifference. The war goes on. Casualties pile up. But, the combatants have lost their fervor and noncombatants are going on to other things.

This is the current state of affairs in a quite protracted philosophical battle over the conceptualization of cultural phenomena in which Michael Krausz has been a leading reporter and one of the most decorated of generals. As it started out, this conflict was over whether each object of phenomenal awareness is one, though available to multiple descriptions and appraisals (multiplism), or is instead a multiplicity of things, each reflective of someone's interpretive take (singularism, via the pluralizing strategy). This simple division between the camps has, proliferated a formidable array of subdivisions and complex alliances. Good soldier that he is, Krausz has spent a great deal of time documenting and responding to them all. He has left no old trench unexplored and no new outpost unchallenged. The enterprise is remarkable, worthwhile, and it has contributed to the shape and character of the battle. But, like most good combatants, Krausz has been so absorbed with the details of combat that he has left himself little time to explain how the battle plays out in relation to its general objectives.

In *Limits of Rightness*, Krausz begins to redress this deficiency.[1] And, although the bulk of the text is taken up with combat minutiae, we find here the beginning of a return to the basic questions the combat is meant to answer. Why should we care about the battle between singularism and multiplism, let alone all of their excruciatingly different subsidiary spawn? Unless we are what Rom Harré so felicitously calls "ontological bookkeepers," it must be because thinking one way instead of the other provides a better line on leading a good and worthwhile life. One way—or some articulated version of that

way—must offer a prospect for making sense of practical and interpretive activity the other lacks. I think this is one crucial thing (among many) that
Krausz is driving after in this book and something that he has been leading up
in the works that precede it. In the end, reflections on the multiplicity of interpretation, to be worth the effort, should connect with the perennial project of
organizing life in ways conducive to enjoying its bounty and avoiding its mis-
adventures. In LR, Krausz turns back to the issue connecting interpretive and
normative theory, albeit tentatively and prospectively. He also points out, albeit tentatively and prospectively, why this connection is a good reason for
accepting his general interpretive theory.

In this essay, I explore the merits of Krausz's most recent battlefront reports by considering ways in which something might be differently perceived
or interpreted and ways in which these different perceptions and interpretations might be practically organized. The distinctions between these ways
seem to me to mark crucial differences between normative options for living,
and not just lines drawn in the epistemological or ontological sand. This range
of options incorporate and draw upon aesthetic and ethical norms. Recently a
good deal of philosophical discussion has been directed at ways in which
fields of value intersect. I intend to show here that the vector of argument in
LR extends in a direction that converges with crucial contemporary philosophical discussion on the connection between ways of thinking of things and
ways of acting.

1. Aims of Interpretation

Krausz identifies five questions that motivated the production of LR. Put as
succinctly as possible, these questions have to do with (1) the business of interpretation and its ingredient ideals, (2) the ways in which interpretation involves ontology, (3) the potential split in interpretation between singularism
and multiplism, (4) the relation between interpretation and its aim, and (5) the
way in which all of this should help us to "understand the directionality of our
life paths and projects." The last of these is the most crucial, and is what motivates the rest. But this conclusion is not supported by the general organization of LR. The great bulk of the book is taken up with the detailed articulation
of different combinations of ontological and interpretive theory and by arguments aimed at the liberation of interpretive theory from different ontological
constraints. The issue of the application of liberated interpretive theory to the
business of directing life choices, is taken up only quite late in the book and in
what appears to be a sketchy, preliminary way. Still, here the payoff for all the
earlier labor is to be found. And the payoff is not just an apt conclusion for the
present study; but is or should be the culmination of a long expedition into the
myriad *isms* of epistemology, ontology, and interpretive theory pursued
through several books and many articles and the provision of sound philoso-

phical advice about living a good life.

Let us begin with an example. Suppose a bright red maple tree exists at the corner of Third and Main. To A, a botanist, the tree is a fine specimen of *Acer rubrum* . To B, the tree is just a nice, old-fashioned tree, reminiscent of the good old days when such trees abounded in urban neighborhoods. To C the tree is the terrible object into which Larry fatally drove his Corvette. Well, then, what is it? Are we bound to say the tree is all these things? Or is it instead one thing to which different interpretations can be affixed? Is there no one thing at all, but only an endless variety of experiences with different contents, unified because they are focused in a given spatio-temporal direction? And equally crucially, why should it matter how we answer these questions? It would take the utmost phenomenological perversity to deny the existence of such things as people, that these people have experiences, that the experiences they have will, due to differences in the points of view from which they arise, have different contents, and that these people are able to communicate with each other in ways that reflect, and depend upon, a substantial sharing of experience through discourse and art. The real objective behind all the epistemological and ontological skirmishing is to find the best way to make sense of this set of individually obvious but jointly puzzling facts.

Things as they occur in our lives are charged with an unending array of meanings, associations, ways of comprehending. The world does not sort itself out for us in any simple way. We persistently and habitually mix what we recognize with what we value, and what we value with what we hope. Things are how we take them. And yet, things are something other than, or more than, how we take them. The bright red maple tree at the corner of Third and Main is what it is. That it not be made out to be something other than what it is, is crucial. Yet it is what it is to everyone who sees it. And each viewer is different from every other viewer. Each comes from a different background, has led a different life, and perceives things from a different spatio-temporal vantage. So, in some sense, the tree is in some sense a different thing to each interpreter. And it can be as many other things as perspectives that pertain to it. But, on the other hand, the tree is not just anything we please. The tree is not a prayer shawl, my thumb, a logarithm, London, or Sidney Morgenbesser. The endless quarrel between singularists and multiplists is ultimately a conflict over the best way to make sense of this condition in which to insist that the objects of interpretive experience are one and many is crucial.

Singularists (led by Monroe Beardsley and Alexander Nehamas) claim that the aim of philosophical theory is to find some one right interpretation of each thing, whatever things are taken to be. On such an account, an object of interpretation might rightly be described as, say, "the bright red maple tree on the corner," and all the other descriptions are relegated to the secondary status of associated notions, renditions, seeings-as, and the like. This way of looking at the world has no shortage of champions. Something like this view is advanced in the philosophy of science by Rudolf Carnap and Karl R. Popper, in the philosophy of history by Simon Nowell-Smith, in the philosophy of literature by E. D. Hirsch, in the philosophy of law by all the originalists, and so on. Multiplists (led by Joseph Margolis) claim that some_objects of interpretation may answer to more than one admissible interpretation. Much of LR is consumed with demonstrating the detachability (with respect to entailment) of several inventoried ontologies from singularism and multiplism. Krausz argues at length that singularism and multiplism are compatible with realism and constructivism, as well as with a host of other ontological theories he goes on to survey. He argues that singularism and multiplism require the commonality of objects addressed by competing interpretations, whichever view of commonality ultimately prevails. And he argues that neither the "pluralizing maneuver" (by which singulists spurn evidence favoring multiplism by the multiplication of objects of interpretation) nor the "aggregating maneuver" (by which multiplists respond to pluralization by urging that the putative intentionalized objects be aggregated) can settle their differences.

The net result of these arguments is to disencumber and clarify the basic conflict between singularism and multiplism. The ultimate point of Krausz's detachability argument is not that no connections between these ideals and a range of ontological and epistemological positions are plausible. However compatible these two ideals turn out to be with these different positions, the first and not the second must do the work in making interpretation useful in charting life's paths and projects. Krausz tells us that interpretations can sometimes serve edificatory purposes (even though doing so is not their core aim). But the fundamental issue toward which the whole analysis must be taken as driving, is the question of how interpretation can be edifying. How is it that conceiving things first this way then that, or even in a variety of ways simultaneously, can—at least sometimes—be conducive to the general betterment of life? Although not a major part of its declared project, LR provides several crucial and insightful suggestions regarding this issue. Krausz makes it abundantly evident that the sketch he provides of connections between interpretive ideals and ideals central to life paths and projects falls well outside the book's center of gravity, it opens a door on some especially intriguing prospects-one which we may hope Krausz will continue to pursue in later works. The rest of my comments are, for these reasons, directed toward this theme, which I take to be inherently crucial and because of the connections it suggests with some of the most exciting and worthwhile work being done today in axiological theory.

2. Acts of Aspection

The first step in understanding any of his philosophical projects is to realize that Krausz is an artist who takes art seriously. Because he has repeatedly confronted the challenges of execution inherent in the practice of painting as well as the perplexities of anticipating audience response to his work, he has a perspective on this particular interpretation-saturated enterprise only an insider can have. He can say with authority that art objects are altered by their interpretations. He can say that the value of the art object lies in the transaction it invites between artists and viewers with a broad range of perspectives.

Art traditionally and persistently involves what Krausz calls "intentional layering," the embedding of representation within representation in the artwork. Our appreciation of the importance of responding to artworks in ways that pick up on their several layers of meaning—both those intended by the artist and those that accrue to the work for other, cultural and idiosyncratic, reasons-prepares us for appreciating intentional layering generally. What Krausz says about our response to Vincent Van Gogh's *Potato Eaters* has a deep connection with our response to corpses of babies floating in the waters of a river. The connection is that responding appropriately to both phenomena demands aesthetic dexterity of a particular kind. It demands that we are willing to perform what Virgil Aldrich used to call "acts of aspection," seeing a thing first as this representation then as that, where the ability of the object to serve as a vessel for multiple meanings and our ability for grasping the several meanings cooperate in making these experiences edifying and memorable.[2] The intentional layering we perceive in the world of art reveals as much about us as it does about its objects. The artist, the audience, and the artwork are all engaged in an aspective transaction through which several meanings are crowded into a lesser number of objects.

This combinatory feature of the artistic enterprise is edifying precisely because to deploy the same mode of regard in relation to non-art objects is often appropriate and instructive. Dead babies in the water can be seen as just a bunch of tissue, molecules, and chemicals, and so forth, or as the sad ends of parents' aspirations, or as blessed and honored beings, or as dumped waste, or even as evocations of Ophelia or Moses, or any number of other things. The capaciousness of representational imagination in dealing with intentional layering is what raises the "rightness" question Krausz addresses throughout the book and mentions in its title. Reflecting on his experience of seeing a swaddled infant corpse in the Ganges, Krausz asks himself, "What did I actually see? Did I ... see something different from what the Indian saw? Or did we see the same thing but interpret it differently? If we saw the same thing but interpreted it differently, who is right?" (LR, p. 36). Is any way of regarding the phenomenon observed as good as any other? Evidently not. But, then again, we can readily refer to nothing that adjudicates between competing interpretations.

But what is it that orders or organizes the intentional layering into coherent and comprehensive wholes? To answer this question, Krausz turns repeatedly to the synthesizing notions of story and story telling. In explaining how

our awareness of multiple interpretations of the dead-baby-in-the-water phenomenon can be edifying, he points up the role of the "supplementing intentional story" in providing "individuation," or the conceptual unity that renders
the descriptive account comprehensible (LR, p. 42). And, in explaining how
the contrast between two dead-baby-in-the-water stories can be especially edifying, he tells another story, a meta-story, about the way two geographically
and temporally disparate experiences play off against each other dialectically
their respective objects of interpretation are distinguished (LR, p. 37-38). The
arts generally, and not only narrative literature, owe the impact they have in
our lives to the stories they present, stories that require us to indulge different
points of view, different unaccustomed experiences, and different new appraisals of the familiar. And not only art draws upon the enterprise of storytelling to reveal and explain the multiplicity of meaning in our lives.

In a duly famous essay about the cultural peculiarities of cockfights in
Bali, Clifford Geertz points out that the horrific spectacle of trained fighting
birds tearing each other apart is, in this one cultural setting, something that
renders everyday experience comprehensible by becoming "a Balinese reading
of Balinese experience, a story they tell themselves about themselves."[3] For
the Balinese, so graceful and pacific in their outward lives, the cockfight is a
story steeped in interpretations that may be almost unattainable in other arenas
of behavior. Geertz maintains that "what it does is what, for other peoples with
other temperaments and other conventions, Lear and Crime and Punishment
do; it catches up these themes-death, masculinity, rage, pride, loss, benefi-
cence, chance-and, ordering them into an encompassing structure, presents
them in such a way as to throw into relief a particular view of their essential
nature."[4]

Like Geertz, Krausz views the elements of art—and aesthetic experience
generally—as woven together in the stories we tell about ourselves and about
the events in our lives. He cites with favor an observation Bronwyn Davies
and Rom Harré make about the role stories perform in the grounding of the
individual personality: "An individual emerges through the processes of social
interaction …as one who is constituted and reconstituted through the various
discursive practices in which they [sic] participate. Accordingly, who one is is
always an open question with a shifting answer depending upon the positions
made available within one's own and other's discursive practices, the stories
through which we make sense of our and other's lives" (quoted in LR, p. 143).

So, in a sense, we make ourselves (and others) up as we go along, interpreting all the welter of experience in ways that produce this or that (tentative
and shifting) narrative. Krausz points out that the selves in these life-stories-
the present narrating self and the various prior narrative selves-are inevitably
"postdictive constructs of plausibly entertained present narratives" (LR, p.
144). I take it he means we are like authors of endless stories, whose current
shape is indebted to prior story elements, but whose emerging shape depends

on how all the elements seem at present to connect best with newly interpreted experience.

As Krausz is quick to point out, not just any story will do. A life story may be coherent, interesting, touching, exciting, and many other things while remaining out of touch with individual experience and social enterprise. Psychotics, for example, are often quite good storytellers; but their stories are unedifying because they are disconnected from any experience the rest of us can share. This takes us to the final theme in Krausz's analysis, that of a *practice*. In *Rightness and Reasons*, Krausz tells us that "the very ideas of singularism and multiplism rest upon the idea of a practice" and he identifies these theories as "praxial ideals," ideals within practices.[5]

Practices, he points out, provide the aims and orientations of their ingredient programs; they set the range of admissible solutions to the problem-situations they engage and orient practitioners to those features of a given domain of inquiry that are significant and salient. Admittedly, "practice" is a suspiciously elastic concept, and one about which philosophers differ heatedly; but the use to which Krausz puts it here can be understood in a way that avoids much of the controversy. Think of it this way: Individuals do things; when they order their doings by making plans, developing routines, and interacting with others in interpretive communities so that their doings are subject to recognition and appraisal as projects, these doings become practices. Practices are inherently social, communicative, and purposive. Musical interpretation is paradigmatically a practice, and so are carpentry, baseball, and joke telling. These socially rooted interactions provide the appropriate contextual matrix for the stories we tell about our selves and others; and through them the issue of "which stories will do" gets resolved. The admissibility of possibilities is a function of human practices. Our stories are tied to our projects, and these projects are developed within, and make sense in, communicative social settings. Just as there can be no private language, there can be no intelligible private stories, and no private art.

3. Contributions

Krausz's effort to explain the connection between the singularism-multiplism controversy and the directing of life's paths and projects is soundly and plausibly argued, as far as it goes. The threat of conceptual anarchy posed by multiple interpretations is allayed by seeing the interpretive process through the lens of art, which welcomes the intentional layering of its objects and finds ways to present them informatively to a public. Recognizing the roles of stories and storytelling as organizing devices averts the prospect of limitless and irrelevant layering of meaning. And the concern that only some stories count, only some connect with lived experience is allayed by recalling the controlling influence of practice, the inter-communicative, purposive, social enterprise within which our stories are told and played out, and within which our art makes us as much as we make it.

This acknowledgment is only a start, like a good map that shows how to get to the big green square that is the promised land but leaves that square itself a monochromatic blank. As I read it, this book's promised land is the idea that all of the fussing about isms is worth the trouble it takes because it can lead us to crucial insights about leading worthwhile, meaningful, lives. And what is missing is the linkage between the multiplicity of interpretation (as a key aspect of the way we artistically tell stories that connect to our practices) and the conclusion that we are better off for that multiplicity. LR lays the foundation for this linkage and, in its last chapters, hints at what might be built on such a foundation, but leaves the job itself largely undone. In this section, I offer two modest contributions toward the completion of this crucial work. The first is a brief analysis of the underlying problem of explaining why the recognition of multiple interpretations of a given object should be taken to be edifying. The second is a summary of some work by other philosophers that connects with and extend Krausz's line of argument.

The edification problem I have in mind is this: Even if we agree with Krausz that the living of an intelligent and responsive life involves an artful rendering of multiple interpretations wedding narrative and practice, s why thinking of one thing in multiple ways conduces to a good and meaningful life is not obvious. Why would it not be just as likely to conduce to a life crippled by ambiguity, confusion, and mystery? Among different ways interpretive multiplicity might affect our lives, three come to mind that are distinctively salubrious.

First, the confrontation with multiple interpretations of a given thing may expose us to cognitive dexterity in ourselves and others. When, for example, we are induced to see an ambiguous drawing asfirst a duck then a rabbit, then a duck again, and so forth, we learn something about ourselves. We learn that we are aesthetically and cognitively capable of re-identifying elements of experience. This is no small feat in itself. In the *Critique of Judgment*, Immanuel Kant argues that, in moments of confrontation with sublimity, our experience of having our intellectual capacities overwhelmed, then coming to realize that we are capable of appreciating the cognitive conditions that make this possible reveals something deep about ourselves. He goes so far as to allege that in this switching back and forth of apprehension we discover the fact of shared human dignity. I do not want to suggest that in seeing the face of the moon first as a rabbit body profile then as a smiling human face we discover something profound about ourselves. But, I do think we discover something about the versatility of human perceptions, and that versatility is itself the first step toward crucial elements of normative self-awareness and social interaction.

Second, the confrontation with multiple interpretations can inspire reflection that results in the reduction of conflict or dissidence. In William James's famous story, two hunters violently disagreed over the question of whether a hunter who had circumambulated a tree trying to get a squirrel in his sights when the squirrel managed to keep the tree between himself and the hunter (circumambulating it on a smaller radius) had, or had not, gone around the squirrel. A third hunter then pointed out a distinction between two ways of thinking of the notion of "going around." On one, the hunter did, and on the other, he did not go around the squirrel. If you take "going around" to mean moving in a way that describes a geometric figure within which the movements of the thing gone around are enclosed, the hunter has gone around the squirrel. If you take "going around" to mean facing the squirrel first head on, then to one side, to the back, to the other side, and then to the front again, he has gone around it. Drawing the distinction makes peace between the contending parties by pointing out that each is right on a separate interpretation. The ability to discriminate among different interpretations of a thing that may not have been raised to the level of explicit awareness can produce undeniable value in social contexts by laying our grounds for reconciliation, compromise, conciliation, and tolerance. Adversaries may be more willing to make peace if they can bring themselves to see that more than one way of looking at disputed objects exists.

Third, and most crucial, the awareness that one thing may be understood in many ways presents the foundation of moral and aesthetic maturity, an awareness of the potency of layered meaning in informed and culturally responsive life generally. When we realize that a portrait can be understood as a compliment and as an insult to its sitter, we comprehend a basic requirement of art, or at least great art—that it invites us to take a point of view and destabilizes that point of view. The business of art is to take us out of our comfortable and routine modes of perceptions, forcing us to recognize the legitimacy of seeing things as valued and valuable in radically different ways. It is the first move in cultural sophistication; the modern world systematically excludes the naïve assumption that this is this and that is that. That assumption is psychologically essential in managing the sea changes in experience that aesthetic formalists, deconstructionists, and free-market economists have all taken to be central to the formation of perceptiveness and good character. But, most crucial, that assumption is an essential piece of moral and aesthetic education. Youth is a domain of natural monocularity; children generally look at things one way and assume that that one way is the right way. Art's greatest contribution to society is its undermining of this innocence.

Finally, I want to point out some of the vectors in which others are exploring the implications I have found in Krausz's work. For the sake of brevity I will mention only three. The first is in the work of Martha Nussbaum. Krausz deals summarily with her ideas on the relation between art, interpretation, and life paths. He introduces her only to make a narrow point about antirealist ontology, observing that "Nussbaum presses her 'internal essentialism' with the thought of defining humans in terms of necessary or essential conditions"(LR, p. 139). But, Nussbaum's recent work has been less dedicated to essentialism than to its defense of the creative-and by that she means disruptive and subversive--aspects of the artistic (interpretive) enterprise. She, perhaps more than any other contemporary philosopher, has caught on to the necessity of contextualizing normative problems.

Good literature, Nussbaum says, "disconcerts and puzzles. It inspires distrust of conventional pieties and exacts a frequently painful confrontation with one's own thoughts and intentions. One may be told many things about people in one's own society and yet keep that knowledge at a distance. Literary works . . . cut through those self-protective stratagems, requiring us to respond to many things that may be difficult to confront."[6]

Nussbaum argues that literary art brings general ideas about human flourishing to bear on concrete situations in such a way that the reader is forced to deploy imagination in regarding and re-regarding those situations. She insists that this form of intellectual activity is "a valuable form of public reasoning, both within a single culture and across cultures."[7] So here, the multiplicity of interpretation is seen as making a crucial moral point. Rejecting the naive principle that things are what they are, we are plunged into a painful confrontation with diversity. Nussbaum points out that the first responsibility of literature is to make us face choice. Just as every option for interpretation and further development in the course of a novel is open, so our lives are open.

Marcia Eaton has also addressed the relations of interpretation and narration to aesthetic and moral value. No one has recently done more to bring the issues of aesthetic interpretation and moral interpretation together. In *Merit, Aesthetic and Ethical*, she argues at length for the view that art stimulates a versatility of mind that conduces to, or links up with, qualities of mind that we routinely commend ethically (and possibly politically, religiously, and so on).[8] Her idea is that artworks, by forcing us to see things as this and that—and possibly as both this and that—extend our intellectual and emotional repertoire. Because we have been required to put on different glasses, try out foreign perspectives, be someone else, we enrich our lives. Eaton dwells at some length on the importance of storytelling in the construction of moral and aesthetic identity. The "urge to narrative," she says, "is not a mere social grace, but a vital component of moral and political engagement."[9] All ethical deliberation arguably involves what amounts to storytelling. "Even when one attempts to come to a decision about what particular action to perform in a specific set of circumstances, one imagines scenarios about various possible consequences. . . . Acts must be joined together for us to make sense of personhood at all. No story, no meaning. In a very real sense, whether a life is meaningful depends first and foremost on there being a story to be told."[10]

Because ethical deliberation is a way of telling and extending the stories we tell about ourselves and others, the density of interpretation can have a decided impact on the development of life paths. Eaton observes that people typically express a longing to have lives that lend themselves to a "crisp as well as rich narrative."[11] A good narrative, she says, is one that pauses repeatedly to pose for itself the multiplicity of ways of going on. The aesthetic imagination is not disconnected from the moral imagination at these points. And because the sense of what we are is tightly connected to the stories we tell ourselves about our selves and others, that sense is necessarily affected by the openness and imaginativeness of these narratives. Eaton argues that the combination of past and future conceptions of self cannot be achieved without binding together moral and aesthetic values.

Mark Johnson has a different take on this intersection of issues. As he sees it, human activity is rich with imaginative opportunities; we have to select paths to follow, and in doing so we forge our ways among ideas and ideals that surround us at every turn. We develop skills for living that incorporate the ability to managing multiple interpretations. If what we face is a disorganized welter of ingredients, we need to find the right story to bring them together in a way that will make sense. "We each want very badly for our particular life stories to be exciting, meaningful, and exemplary of the values we prize. Morality is a matter of how well or how poorly we construct (i.e. live out) a narrative that solves our problem of living a meaningful and significant life."[12]

Johnson's view is that aesthetic complexity may complement moral focus by providing a suitably rich and provocative line of life stories to which morality responds. This view aims to resolve normative complexity in a way that mirrors the ways the more sophisticated versions of Krausz's interpretive ideals aim to resolve complexity. In particular, Johnson's position seems most similar to what Krausz calls "directional singularism." By incorporating the recognition that we face a rich range of options in thinking about, or acting on, every one of life's turns and the recognition that we want our resolution of all of this deliberation to be coherent and defensible, we see the payoff at the end of the protracted battle over interpretive ideals Krausz has fought and documented.

The observations I have offered about three ways of deriving normative value from interpretive multiplicity (whether it be multiplistic or directionally singularistic) and my summary acknowledgements of work by Nussbaum, Eaton, and Johnson to this end are meant to mark the trailhead of a worthwhile philosophical exploration. Krausz has shown that his previous work leads us to this trail; but he has yet to take more than a few, tentative steps down it. LR makes a case for getting from the stage of conceptual analysis regarding all of the isms surrounding interpretive experience to the point where our convictions about all of that frame our experience more generally. While some of its readers will relish the account of furious combat that runs from the outset of the book to its last chapter, other readers will see the warfare as a (perhaps necessary) prelude to crucial moral and aesthetic claims about life's paths and projects. That this book does not explore these claims in any detail is no indictment of its overall achievement.

NOTES

1. Michael Krausz, *Limits of Rightness* (LR) (Lanham, Md.: Rowman and Littlefield, 2000).

2. Virgil Aldrich, *Philosophy of Art* (Englewood Cliffs, NJ: Prentice Hall, 1963).

3. Clifford Geertz, "Deep Play: Notes on the Balinese Cockfight," *The Interpretation of Cultures* (New York: Basic Books, 1973), p. 448.

4. *Ibid.*, p. 443.

5. Michael Krausz, *Reason and Rightness: Interpretation in Cultural Practices* (RR) (Ithaca, N. Y.: Cornell University Press, 1993), p. 143.

6. Martha C. Nussbaum, *Poetic Justice: The Literary Imagination and Public Life* (Boston: Beacon Press, 1995), p. 5-6.

7. *Ibid.*, p. 8.

8. Marcia Muelder Eaton, *Merit, Aesthetic, and Ethical* (Oxford: Oxford University Press, 2001).

9. *Ibid.*, p. 157.

10. *Ibid.*, p. 160.

11. *Ibid.*, p. 162.

12. Mark Johnson, *Moral Imagination* (Chicago: University of Chicago Press, 1993), p. 192.

INTERPRETATION WITHOUT ONTOLOGY?

Eight

INTERPRETATION AND ONTOLOGY: TWO QUERIES FOR KRAUSZ

Bernard Harrison and Patricia Hanna

1. Motivating Multiplism and Singularism

Michael Krausz's latest book, by its author's account, is meant to erect obstacles to those who hold that there can only be a single correct response to any question of interpretation, and to those who hold that multiplism, the admission of two or more equally correct, but not necessarily equally preferable, interpretations, is required in the interpretation of cultural entities.[1] Both doctrines have their roots in a particular picture of how language is related to "reality" or "the world." One thought that motivates the first doctrine is that, since conceptual contents, if they are to have any bearing on reality, must single out real entities or features, two divergent interpretations cannot both be faithful to the nature of those entities or features. One thought that motivates the second is that many or most of the entities invoked by the discourses of "culture"—literature, music and the other arts, politics, religion, morals—are constructs upon practices, fabrications of human conceptual spontaneity, concerning which, since they are founded in the nature of no really—that is objectively—existing thing, divergent interpretations are not only possible but to be expected.

Krausz suggests a "characteristic or orthodox" association of singularism with realism and multiplism with constructivism (LR, p. 33). We might add that an equally characteristic association of multiplism with subjectivity exists. Where what we say about the world is not constrained to singularism by the nature of its subject-matter—so that stage of the argument would go— that subject-matter must have to do, not with the way the world is, but with the way cultures or individuals perceive it as being.

Krausz argues (1) that realism and constructivism are not exclusive alternatives, but admit combination in several versions of "constructive realism"; and (2) that neither realism nor constructivism, nor any version of the two, entail singularism or multiplism. We are in broad agreement with these claims. Our criticism is that they do not go far enough. Krausz retains two assumptions central to the "characteristic or orthodox" view that have little to recommend them.

The first assumption is that multiplism and singularism are exclusive alternatives with respect to the object of interpretation; that with respect to a given object of interpretation we must opt for one or the other. As Krausz puts it in introducing the notions, "the singularist ideal holds that for any object of interpretation, there must be one and only one ideally admissible interpretation of it . . . . In contrast the multiplist ideal holds that some objects of interpretation may answer to more than one (opposed but not exclusive) ideally admissible interpretation of them." (LR, p. 5).

The position here is that, for any given object of interpretation, the ideal of singularism or the ideal of multiplism must hold, but both cannot. We will argue for a reinterpretation in terms of the inclusive "or." One and the same object of interpretation may answer to singularism or to multiplism, because (roughly speaking) the choice depends not on the type of object whose nature we are concerned to interpret, but on the structure of the linguistic practice through which our interrogation of the object under interpretation is conducted.

The second assumption is that the distinction between "internal" and "external" versions of constructive realism turns on whether a given version postulates a structureless or undifferentiated "world," or "kind of stuff" external to conceptual schemes; in Kantian terms a noumenal object, as distinct from the phenomenal objects constituted in accordance with those schemes. The two issues are connected. We argue both that a version of constructive realism shorn of the notion of the noumenal is conceivable, and that in consequence multiplism and singularism may in some circumstances be dependent upon one another in more, and more complex ways, than Krausz has so far envisaged.

2. Measurement and Moduli

Both the points we hope to make can be explained and defended in terms of a single, simple example: that of linear measurement. Linear measurement offers, among other things, a counterexample to what we might call the specular conception of the relationship between language and reality. According to the specular conception, the logical form of the sentences by means of which we describe reality must mirror the form of the realities those sentences describe.

For instance, the subject-predicate form, as exemplified in "That cube is red," might be taken to mirror the relationship between real items, such as the cube of which we speak, and real properties, such as redness. If so, it would follow that, as many philosophers have supposed, it ought to be possible to provide a learner with everything needed to allow him to grasp the meaning, the propositional content, of such a statement, just by presenting him with instances of the sort of situation it describes. For there, "out in the world" are "states of affairs" or "facts" that possess exactly the same structure as the sentence. According to the specular conception, the mirroring by sentence-structure of fact-structure allows the sentence to say what it says, confers upon it its assertoric content. The specular conception allows us to make sense of the idea that some descriptions—those that employ sentences whose form and content exactly mirror the form and content of "reality itself" or "the world"—describe things as they really are; whereas other descriptions, whose form and content mirror nothing in reality, but derive from the way in which the sentences concerned are enmeshed in conventional practices of our devising, describe not real things, but only the dream-things, the intentional entities, of culture. From that idea it is a short step to two of the orthodox views that Krausz is out to subvert; that singularism marches in step with realism, and that multiplism, in turn, is always and only in order in the interpretation of intentional, or cultural objects.

How does linear measurement supply a counter instance to the specular conception? Could we explain to someone with no conception of linear measurement what it means to say "X is 5 cm. long," just by exhibiting 5-centimeter long objects? Why should the learner pay attention to the length of these objects at all? After all, he or she has, *ex hypothesi*, no prior conception of length. Will he or she take the sentence, at best, as asserting whatever material similarity or similarities the members of this otherwise arbitrary collection of objects happen to exhibit?

How might we set about getting the learner past this block? By acquainting him with the practice of linear measurement. But what will that involve? Teaching him to carry out measuring operations with rulers and measuring-tapes? Not only that. Someone who knew only how to go through the motions of measuring, even if trained to say aloud or otherwise note the numbers corresponding to gradations on the yardstick, would not understand what measurement *is*. That person would have been converted into a kind of measuring-device himself: a tool, an element in the practice of linear measurement, not its master. To be a master of the practice, a fully-fledged member of the human community whose practice it is, that person needs to understand the point of the practice: on the one hand, the purposes it serves in our lives, and on the other, what it is about that practice that enables it to serve those purposes. Only then will the learner be able to deploy the practice in the service of typical human purposes.

What has to be grasped by the learner to satisfy these conditions is that linear measurement, whatever techniques it may employ, always involves the comparison of two objects by relating them to a third, usually more easily manipulable one. In its simplest form, linear measurement is the repeated placing, end over end, of an object *M*, generally chosen for its ease of manipulation, against one side or edge of another, less easily manipulable one, *O*, to see how many iterations of M are required to span *O*. Even in the simplest contingencies of human life, such a practice has its uses. For one thing it can be used to establish whether a heavy object will or will not pass through a given space. Once the practice is in use, other uses, and with them new refinements, will follow. One of the first will involve laying the arbitrarily chosen M repeatedly against a straight length of wood or metal, *Y*, and marking off along *Y* the points reached by the end of M at each iteration. *Y* becomes a yardstick, constituted in terms of a particular modulus of measurement, the one supplied by the arbitrarily chosen object M. The length of any object, now, is the number of iterations of M required to span it. The practice of linear measurement is, put in the most general terms, the practice of comparing the lengths of different objects by relating them via the repeated laying-on of some modulus.

3. Measurement, Multiplism, and Singularism

A statement of the form "O is nM long," giving the length of an object O in terms of a number, n, of iterations of a particular modulus M, presumably states, if true, a truth about the world, or reality. In Krausz's terms, it offers an interpretation of a given object of interpretation, O, with respect to one of its features or properties, namely its length. It would be difficult to find an example of a more objective truth: the notion of measurement is built at a fundamental level into both our everyday and our scientific notions of objectivity.

Are we to say, then, that given an object O, there must be a unique, in Krausz's terms a singular, truth about the length of O? What is fatal to this supposition is the possibility of devising new techniques of measurement, often involving the adoption of new moduli, in response to practical demands for greater precision in measurement. Consider an example. Let us say a given table is claimed to be three feet long, and that the truth of that statement can be established by anyone capable of using the sort of measuring tape you buy from a hardware store. Other procedures, based on other, more precise measuring devices, maybe involving optical instruments, might produce results expressed in microns. The result of accurately measuring O with a measuring tape might fail of identity with that obtained by measuring it in microns using an optical method of far greater precision and converting microns to inches. This discrepancy occurs not because the system of moduli, which includes the micron, is not fully mathematically intraconvertible with that which includes the inch. We can imagine pairs of moduli for which that might not be so, but that is not the point. What ensures the possibility of a disparity between the results (in inches) obtained by measuring (with optimal accuracy) with a hardware-store tape and those (in microns) obtained by measuring (with optimal accuracy) with the optical device, is simply the greater precision of the second technique of measurement.

We are left with a curious interplay between singularism and multiplism. As long as we stick with a range of techniques operating within similar limits of precision and employing interconvertible moduli, singularism rules for linear measurement. Once we admit different techniques of measurement operating within widely differing limits of precision, then, with or without intra- or interconvertibility of moduli, multiplism rules. Both singularism and multiplism here seem compatible with objectivity, since, we take it, both the statement that the table is *n* inches long and the statement that the table is *m* microns long have to be accepted, subject only to revision in the light of more careful (accurate) deployment of the respective measuring techniques, as objectively true.

Ultimately, these reflections suggest that multiplism and singularism are not, as Krausz and others tend to suppose, exclusive alternatives, but may be so mutually involved and involving as to be, in effect, implicit in one another. In this way both multiplism and singularism lie coiled as potentialities within the practice of linear measurement, within the possibility of differing degrees of precision latent in that practice. Once we have fixed on a set of techniques, with an appropriate modulus, for determining length, singularism rules so far as questions about length raised within those terms are concerned. At the same time the evolution of special demands for more precise forms of measurement, with associated new moduli, opens the way to a plurality of equally "correct" answers to the question "How long is x?"—answers, that is, that remain distinct even allowing for the systematic intraconvertibility of the moduli in terms of which they are expressed. At the same time what the example supports is multiplism, and not what Krausz, following Alexander Nehamas, terms "critical pluralism."[2] Measurements employing different moduli associated with different limits of precision may not be equally preferable or admissible (critical pluralism); good grounds may exist in a particular case for preferring a measurement in inches over one in microns; but in no such case will such grounds be conclusive, identifying one or the other as the only correct one.

The choice between singularism and multiplism is not a function of the type of object of interpretation under interrogation, but of the possibilities inherent in the structure of the linguistic practice by means of which the interrogation is being conducted.

4. Measurement and Realism

We can easily imagine an objector in whose throat this conclusion sticks. And the objection will be likely to focus on what is seen as its abandonment of scientific realism: an abandonment the more scandalous because it pretends to involve a notion, that of accuracy in measurement, central to the claim of science to provide objective knowledge. We have made it the basis of our argument that science advances by introducing techniques of measurement serving our demand for greater precision. But does the idea of such an advance imply the existence of a reality altogether external to any measuring practice, whose dimensions such practices aim to record more accurately? Does that in turn presuppose a point at which perfect accuracy will be reached? At that point will our alleged multiplism drop out, leaving singularism in possession of the field?

That demand rests on an ancient and pervasive philosophical picture:

the one that we earlier termed the specular conception of the relationship between language and reality. It affirms the possibility of a final truth: final because articulated in a language conforming in its terms and logical grammar to the structure of reality.

The notion of a final truth, motivated in that way, has long served as the central, motivating myth of Western metaphysics. And if that were its sole sphere of influence it would not, perhaps, matter much. But the boundary between metaphysics and other spheres of intellectual and moral life is far more fluid and porous than we are apt to imagine. Our scientific, our moral, our religious, our literary thinking all suffer repeatedly from our readiness to desert a notion of truth founded in concrete practical activity in order to embark on the perennially unprofitable pursuit of the eerie gleam of absolute finality that equally perennially beckons to us from the pages of Plato or Bertrand Russell, and whose ultimate lair is in the picture of a logically perfect, that is, a perfectly specular, language. And such a picture seems the more persuasive because we imagine the only alternative to it consists in acquiescence in subjectivism or relativism in some form that restricts the reach of knowledge to the interior of human culture.

We can hardly hope to argue away the influence of that picture on our minds. But we can show how a reply should go in the case of the particular example that has been occupying us. What would it be to demand a real, a final truth about linear dimension? The problem here is not inaccessibility of such a truth, whether for practical or metaphysical reasons, but the lack of any clear sense to the demand for it. What makes it look as if there might be some sense to be attached to it, is the temptation we feel to treat the measurement of the table in inches and its measurement in microns as if the accessibility of the second somehow impugned the truth of the first: making it merely a truth, an interim determination only: one falling short, in some quasi-Bradleian sense, of absolute truth, truth-preceded-by-the-definite-article: *the* truth. Looking at the matter in that way leads fairly directly to an absurdity: supposing that because more and more precise techniques of linear measurement can be devised, there must be some point at which the ladder of increasing degrees of precision of measurement comes to an end, in a technique that yields not just a determination of length within assigned limits of precision, but an absolutely accurate determination of length: one that tells us the real length of whatever object is at stake.

This is obvious nonsense. There can be no such thing as the real length of anything, because there can be no such thing as length determined without reference to some modulus or other. We cannot speak, because it makes no sense, of length *tout court*, but only of length-in-inches, or in-microns. But if that is the case, must we not have risked falling into error when we were tempted to construe the statement of an object's length in inches and the statement of its length in microns as advancing competing claims to truth? Why should we not regard both, not as relative truths, or stabs at the truth, or as way stations on the road to some quasi-Bradleian Absolute, but as simply true? On the specular conception we would answer: because they are not (or may not be, given the differing degrees of precision of the methods of measurement that yielded them as results) numerically equivalent, and there can only be one correct answer to the question "How long is x?" But the last, crucial step of this argument stands in need of justification. The question needs clarification, and this clarification can only take the form of providing a modulus of measurement. Absent a modulus in terms of which O is to be measured, the question cannot be answered. Once we are provided with a modulus, we see that the original question does not, indeed cannot, require a unique answer. Why should not different answers, serving practical needs differing in ways making the extreme degree of precision essential in one case superfluous in another, be equally true? The only obvious reply available is that there must be a final, unique truth about every property of anything that can be regarded as an existing constituent of reality, a final truth about the dimensional properties of things. The intelligibility of this claim is precisely what is at issue. Degrees of precision do not correspond to degrees of accuracy, whether accuracy is seen simply as care in the application of the techniques of measurement, or as the specular conception would have it, as a limiting concept.

Suppose we simply dismiss the idea of a final truth expressible in a language whose conceptual contents and logical syntax mirror appropriately fundamental features of the natural world. What follows? What is the problem supposed to be with taking two nonequivalent determinations of an object's length to be, both equally, true? Both record outcomes of measuring procedures. The person who conducts such a procedure does not have the power to decree what its outcome will be. If it were, since the results of measuring might in principle differ arbitrarily from observer to observer, such procedures would lose their practical point, and the concept of linear measurement would lapse into vacuity.

Can we not say that the nature of the world, and not our wishes, determines the outcome of a measuring procedure? Putting it that way makes it look as if there might be something further to be said about the "nature" in question: something that would explain why and in what way "the nature of things" determines that outcome and not another. But this also is an illusion. No digging further into "the nature of things" is to be done at this point. We have reached one of those points in our thinking at which, as Ludwig Wittgenstein says, "the spade turns." What makes an object deliver, relative to a given procedure of measurement, the result that it is n inches long, or m microns long, is simply because it *is* n inches, or m microns, long. No further fact about the world needs to be uncovered, nor would another language, a logically perfect or perspicuous one, be better adapted to plumb those putatively hidden depths than the ordinary languages of linear measurement.

We do not need another language in which to talk about the real world, because we are already talking about the real world. Our language, to deploy another Wittgensteinian tag, is already "perfectly in order as it stands." Despite the fact that we could not indicate the length of anything in the absence of methods of measurement, and the general practice of linear measurement within which such methods find a place and practical purposes, and despite the fact that those methods are productions of human conceptual spontaneity, no gap exists between what we truly say concerning the lengths of things and the way they are "in themselves." No such gap exists because, although we do determine what is to count as truth-warranting for such sayings, which sayings of that kind are warranted is determined by the outcome of procedures over whose outcomes our wishes have no influence, and no influence on "the way things are in themselves" in the only use of that phrase capable of being assigned a clear sense.

5. Constructive Realism and the Noumenal

That brings us to the second of the qualified disagreements with Krausz that we mentioned earlier. Krausz talks as if there were a distinction to be drawn between internal and external constructive realism, on the grounds that, whereas the internal constructive realist holds reality to be, root-and-branch, constituted by human practices, or conceptual schemes, the external constructive realist wishes to admit, or half admit, because she does not quite want to make it a world of objects, the existence of a world external to, and operated on, by those schemes. External constructive realism so characterized is strongly redolent of the Kantian distinction between phenomenon and noumenon. Krausz says, "The internal constructive realist would say that there can be no appeal to anything—real or otherwise—that precedes the symbol system. The external constructive realist would say that, although it cannot be countenanced as real objects, some presystematic "materia" needs to be appealed to in order to account for the construction of real objects" (LR, p. 57, 87).

This characterization may well catch some philosophers. Krausz tends to offer Hilary Putnam as an instance of an external constructive realist in the required sense, and there may be some truth in this label. But we have already shown that this is not the only way of setting up external constructive realism. Lengths are constructed entities, to which we have access only via a socially constituted and maintained practice, the practice of linear measurement, which operates, among other things, to give sense to items in a "symbol system," including such expressions as "O is 5 cm. long," "'Meter' is the name of a modulus." Physical objects, on the other hand, exist prior to the institution of any symbol system. And yet physical objects are among the things that possess lengths: are (on occasion) truly described by such remarks as "My boat is a 15-foot dinghy." Physical objects have to be "countenanced as objects" by anyone who holds the sort of position we have been sketching here, since otherwise, to put it crudely (we will see in a moment precisely what this caveat comes to), the practices that introduce lengths would have nothing to operate on. No "presystematic materia" "needs to be appealed to in order to account for the constitution of lengths," but cannot "be countenanced as embodying *real objects*" because presystematic materia is *ex hypothesi* external to the "system of representation." A type of external constructive realism (the one we hold) escapes the terms of Krausz's way of distinguishing between the internal and the external constructive realist.

This line of reasoning may seem at first sight like a prevarication. If the characterizations we give of the world in terms of sortal and attributive concepts have meaning only within, and relative to, systems of practices through which we impose these categories upon the world, then the world that exists prior to that imposition must be in some deep sense unstructured or undifferentiated. The word lurking in the background of the discussion at this point is, one wants to say, "ineffable." But if constructive realism makes the nature of reality, as distinct from the way we describe it, ineffable, does it offer a form of realism, as distinct from a version of transcendental idealism, at all?

The difficulty lies with the terms "unstructured" and "undifferentiated," which are systematically ambiguous, though not in an obvious way. Krausz, in correspondence with one of the authors, put the issue this way: "What is the relationship between the undifferentiated reality and the differentiated claims about it?" The answer is that (according to us) no direct relationship holds between claims (statements, propositions, whatever) and the reality that they concern. We see a pair of relationships, the first between words and some practice, the second between that practice and the realities on which it operates.

In the present example, such terms as "length," "modulus" take on meaning not from their relationship to any feature of the world that predates the institution of the practice of linear measurement, but from the roles assigned to them within the structure of that practice. The practice of linear measurement in turn relates to reality or the world through the practical operation of measuring techniques of all kinds. With respect to the schema of concepts, including those of length and modulus introduced by the practice of linear measurement, the world as it exists prior to the introduction of that practice, is indeed, in one sense, undifferentiated: conceptually undifferentiated. But that is not to say that the schema of concepts is undifferentiated with respect to the practical techniques and manipulations that connect the practice to that schema. On the contrary, the world as it exists prior to the institution of the practice is replete with the sort of structure that reveals itself to optical, manual, auditory, manipulation. The world is not praxially undifferentiated. We may think of the world relative to practical techniques, including techniques of measurement, as a realm of outcomes.

Such a realm will deliver the same outcome in response to a given manipulation in wholly reliable ways, ways reliable, that is, from observer to observer, given equal accuracy in the conduct of the manipulation in question. If the world were not, in this sense, a realm of outcomes, it would be impossible to invent the complex practices that bestow sense and conceptual content on the terms that acquire a use in connection with them. One thing offered by the example of linear measurement is a way of grasping how talk of concepts and conceptual schemes might prove systematically reconstruable as disguised talk concerning the diverse ways in which verbal expressions come to be involved in practices.

On such a view, the institution of conceptual schemes contributes to human life the concepts of assertoric force and truth. By providing us with a sense for a range of potentially assertoric expressions of the form "O is n M's long," and with a range of techniques for attaching truth-values to such expressions in particular contexts, the practice of linear measurement functions, in effect, to transform the world from a realm of outcomes into a realm of truth-conditions, and, as such, into a world to which conceptual distinctions apply. In a sense, the world prior to the institution of linguistic practices *is* "ineffable," but only in the sense that, as yet, nothing can be said of it. That world is not "ineffable" in the sense of "unknowable," for it is already richly knowable as a realm of outcomes, and its characteristics *qua* realm of outcomes are precisely what will determine what propositions we will find to be true or false of it when we are sufficiently equipped with linguistic practices to have a use for such notions as proposition, truth, and falsity.

So much for the alleged association of constructive realism with transcendental idealism. The example of linear measurement shows, in effect, that the Kantian schema of phenomenon and noumenon is irrelevant to the task of elucidating the relationship between language and reality because that relationship is not—or need not be construed as—one of representation.

This point can be put another way. Kantianism can be seen as, overall, an attempt to answer the question how far thought can be taken to provide an adequate representation of reality. John McDowell's much praised book *Mind and World* offers a good instance of the tendency, common in recent philosophy, to transfer that problematic wholesale to the philosophy of language.[3] As McDowell puts it, the problem is to see how events in the world can be construed as truth-conditions, unless some formal isomorphy obtains between reality and propositions considered as that of which truth and falsity are predicated. If there were no such isomorphy, so the argument runs, the conceptually ordered real world that we imagine ourselves to inhabit would fall apart into, on the one hand, a conceptually unstructurable, since wholly extra-conceptual World, and a neatly conceptually-ordered Mind whose conceptual categories would have no bearing on anything beyond it.

Thinking about how linear measurement relates to what is measured enables us, in effect, to think beyond the terms of McDowell's version of Immanuel Kant's problem. Establishing the length of something, O, is not a matter of there being something about O that, as it were, fits it by nature to

bear upon the truth or falsity of statements about length. A practical operation—of measuring—yields a certain result. What makes that result truth-
determining for a given statement of length—"*O* is 5cm. long,"—is nothing
"in nature" at all, but the way in which the operation that yielded it fits into
the practice of linear measurement. What the example shows is that we can
admit the world to be conceptually unstructured prior to the elaboration of
language, while continuing to hold with perfect justice that, on occasion,
what we say about the world correctly characterizes it—correctly characterizes, that is, something external to the symbol-system—because of the
(preconceptual) praxial structure of the world, the conceptually structured
claims that the introduction of appropriate linguistic practices will in due
course put us in a position to assert of it will ultimately turn out to be true or
false.

Our practices mediate between a conceptually unstructured world and
the conceptually structured truths we assert of it. The notion of truth has no
bearing on the world prior to the invention of such practices as linear measurement. The whole point of such practices is to equip us with machinery of
truth-determination, including yardsticks and other measuring devices, that
takes out of our hands the question of which propositions will turn out to be
true of what. The notion of objective truth-determination is part and parcel of
the notion of truth itself. Both are conjured into existence through the institution of such practices as that of linear measurement. Without such practices to
mediate between the propositional and the natural, we would be faced by
something like McDowell's version of Kant's problem. But since we have
them, we are not.

The suggestion implicit in what we have had to say about linear measurement is that the relationship between language and the world is not specular, but practical. But if that is true, then so is most of what Michael Krausz
has to say about the issue between singularism and multiplism. What is correct, on the present view, is what the truth-determining machinery associated
with our linguistic devices reveals to be correct. In some cases, as in the case
of linear measurement, there will be an irreducible multiplicity of correct
results, depending, in that particular case on choice of measuring technique
plus modulus. In other cases, as in the application of the number system to
sets of discrete objects via the technique of counting, singularism will obtain.
Whether multiplism or singularism obtains, in short, is a matter having to do,
not with ontology, with the nature of objects of interpretation, but with the
nature of our linguistic practices and of the techniques of truth-determination
with which they equip us.

But from that it follows, just as Krausz argues, that neither realism nor
the objectivity of science demand singularism (and, *per contra*, that multiplism is compatible with both). And, as we have argued, that, since whether a
given object of interpretation answers to multiplism, or to singularism, or to
both, may be a function not of its nature, but of that of the practice through

which we interrogate it, multiplism and singularism may on occasion be so closely intertwined, as potentialities implicit in the nature of a linguistic practice, as to be part and parcel of one another.

6. Multiplism, Singularism, and Cultural Entities

We have argued in support of Krausz, and against the characteristic or orthodox association of singularism with realism, that, in the description of the natural world, multiplism may at times not only be compatible with objectivity, but compatible equally with both realism and constructivism, and that that pair may, on some interpretations be equally compatible with one another. What about the equally orthodox association of multiplism with culture? An obvious argument for orthodoxy is that culture is, by its nature, humanly constituted. A literary, or religious, or aesthetic tradition develops by reinterpretation, and as reinterpretations multiply and cohere into new structures of response or belief, so the entities that populate the discourses of culture change their nature or divide amoebically into daughter-entities. As long as we stay within the limits of a particular hermeneutic strategy singularism may seem to obtain; but the possibility of multiple, equally correct interpretations always lurks in what Jacques Derrida has taught us to call the margins of such discourse. The possibility of multiplism is inseparable from cultural discourse because multiplism is the lifeblood of such discourses: their principle of growth, development and self-transformation.

Nothing is wrong with this argument as far as it goes. Put in those terms, the argument is simply correct. Some of its supposed consequences, however, are more suspect. As often put, the argument is assumed to differentiate cultural from scientific or factually descriptive discourse, in which singularism is presumed to exercise unrestricted sway. This, as we have seen, it does not. Multiplism is as much at home in the discourse of measurement as in the interpretation of the literary and biblical texts discussed by the Cambridge critic Frank Kermode.[4] A second presumption of the argument as usually put is that the permanent possibility of multiplism in cultural discourses necessarily undercuts and erodes any foothold that singularism may find within their bounds. That this is also a mistake can also be shown by counterexample. Take, for instance, the notion of irony, frequently central as that is to serious discourse of any degree of sophistication, whether the discourse in question counts as literary, as in the case of Jane Austen or Thomas Love Peacock or philosophical, as in the case of David Hume, or something between the two as in the case of Friedrich Nietzsche. And take, as an instance of irony, something as familiar, as unquestionably ironic as the first sentence of *Pride and Prejudice*: "It is a truth universally acknowledged that a single man in possession of a good fortune, must be in want of a wife."

What makes us read this as irony? Why should not Austen, in writing this down on the page, be simply stating her belief, a belief both in the wide acceptance of this dictum and in its truth? The difficulty is that the text itself defeats the attempt to read it straight.

Let us look into this more closely. Multiplism, as Krausz conceives it, is the thesis that there can be two or more ideally admissible, but not necessarily equally preferable interpretations of a given object of interpretation. The admission that one interpretation may, for all sorts of reasons, be preferable to others, as we have already noted, distinguishes multiplism from critical pluralism. The trouble with an ironic utterance is not its ambiguous or equivocal character.

An instance of ambiguity, celebrated for a time thirty years ago because of its use by the linguist Noam Chomsky is "They are flying planes." Here we have a straightforward case of critical pluralism. Two interpretations offer themselves, corresponding to the two possible ways of construing the syntax of the sentence, neither in any way preferable, *qua* interpretation, to the other. But by that fact there is nothing in the least ironic about "They are flying planes." What irony requires is not only that what is said or written should be capable of being read in more than one way—that there should be more than one ideally admissible interpretation, as Krausz puts it, and that these interpretations should not be equally preferable—but that the alternative readings should obstruct, run counter to one another, in such a way that, though the process of interpretation may come to rest in one, the others remain active in the mind; are not simply discarded in favor of the maximally preferable one. For this to happen the grounds for preferring one interpretation to another must operate to partially undercut one another, so that the mind is left hanging in an unstable and endlessly shifting movement between the admissible alternatives.

Your first thought, on reading the opening sentence of *Pride and Prejudice*, is that you are confronting a maxim in the manner of La Rochefoucauld: one of those cynical but sadly undeniable distillations of worldly experience of which the example everyone knows is: "In the adversity of our best friends we find something that does not displease us." Call this Interpretation 1. But, in order to ape La Rochefoucauld, one's productions must share the same solid basis in fact. As Jonathan Swift put it, "As Rochefoucauld his maxims drew From Nature, I believe 'em true . . . ."[5]

But Austen's purported Rochefoucauldianism does not, in that sort of way, have the ring of truth about it. On the contrary, to imagine that any single man in possession of a good fortune must be in want of a wife is just silly. So perhaps what is confronting us is a hopeless stab at imitating La Rochefoucauld. Call this Interpretation 2. Interpretation 2, however, immediately runs up against the misleading innocence of the five pompous little words "It is a truth universally acknowledged." These have the effect of shifting the burden of belief in the truth of a patently silly maxim from the author to the social world she means to survey. But in that case we are dealing with a Rochefoucauldian maxim after all: a sound if cynical abstract of social experience pithily expressed, whose true thrust is toward exposing what non-sense people, if they are to be judged by their actions, and the assumptions those actions imply, will elevate to the status of a universal truth, provided their self-interest, in this case their interest in marrying off their daughters well, is sufficiently engaged. Call this Interpretation 3.

"It is a truth . . ." is ironic because it cannot be taken straight, that is univocally; and it is not simply ambiguous between two equally preferable interpretations. It admits no single interpretation, but generates a set of distinct interpretations whose inconsistencies drive the mind of the reader across the set from one to another in a particular order and direction. We have, in short, multiplism: multiple, but not equally preferable interpretations. Interpretation 3 is the one the reading mind comes to rest in (the ultimately most preferable one), but the mind's coming to rest in that interpretation would lose entirely the irony and the comic effect of the sentence if that point of rest, with its realization that the author is not, after all, speaking *in propria persona*, were not reached by way of a flight, or tumble, across the other two possible interpretations.

We must begin by taking the dictum seriously as a straight attempt at imitating La Rouchefoucauld if we are to advance first to the realization that since the dictum is too silly to sustain the solemnity of the style in which it is introduced, and from that to the realization that Austen is not speaking in her voice, but in that of a social world whose willingness to accept manifest non-sense as universal truth is all of a piece with its willingness to dignify that propensity with a degree of solemnity well caricatured by couching its ab-surdities in the style of La Rochefoucauld; with the additional grace-note that La Rochefoucauld was the opposite of one capable of being tricked by self-interested hope into granting credence to nonsense. All of this happens quite quickly as we read. We pass quickly from taking the sentence seriously to taking it as bathetic and ironic in ways that allow it to tumble us immediately into the central concerns of the plot. But, as we hope we have shown, an irre-ducible multiplism in interpretation is essential to the possibility of that pas-sage.

So far, so good. Ironic doubleness "answers to multiplism," so the first sentence of *Pride and Prejudice,* considered as an object of interpretation answers to multiplism. But when we ask whether that sentence is to be read as irony, it "answers to singularism," for there can be only one answer to that question. In the case of a "cultural" object, that object may answer equally to singularism or to multiplism, depending on the nature, not of the object, but of that of the questions we put to it and of the practices that give point to those questions by supplying us with the means of resolving them. As Krausz suggests, the idea that singularism is peculiarly foreign to cultural matters can be seen to be an illusion.

Many writers on literary and critical theory have recently talked as if the choice between reading something straight and treating it as irony must be a completely imponderable one, settleable only *ad hoc*, by arbitrary selection of a hermeneutic strategy, because the only way of settling it objectively would involve access to Jane Austen's interiority—her mind, her intentions—a recourse manifestly denied us in her case by death and the passage of time, and denied us anyway, in any such case, by the simple absence of the author from her text once that has passed from her hand. That absence is commonly emphasized by replacing with talk of texts and textuality an older discourse, currently regarded in some literary critical circles as antediluvian in its naivety, of books and their authors. But what we have seen is that the conclusion that Jane Austen's intentions in writing down the first sentence of *Pride and Prejudice* were ironic in no way depends upon access to her mental states, since it can be arrived at with perfect certainty on purely textual grounds. Textuality indeed rules, and with it, on some of the levels upon which we question a text, mutiplism in interpretation. But neither rules out singularism at other levels, or the perfect confidence we may sometimes enjoy in assessing, on purely textual grounds, the intentions of a long-dead author.

NOTES

1. Michael Krausz, *Limits of Rightness* (LR) (Lanham, Md.: Rowman and Littlefield, 2000).

2. Alexander Nehamas, "The Postulated Author: Critical Monism as Regulative Principle," *Critical Inquiry*, 8 (Autumn 1981), pp. 133–149.

3. John McDowell, *Mind and World* (Cambridge, Mass.: Harvard University Press, 1994).

4. Frank Kermode, *The Genesis of Secrecy: On the Interpretation of Narrative* (Cambridge: Harvard University Press, 1979).

5. Jonathan Swift, "Verses on the Death of Dr. Swift," *Poetical Works of Jonathan Swift*, ed. Herbert Davis (London, New York: Oxford University Press, 1967).

Nine

CONSTITUENTS OF INTERPRETATION

Paul Thom

What is the structure of interpretation? What must exist for an interpretation to exist? I offer an answer to these questions within an ontology of actions. I will pursue the question as it relates to interpretation. I am interested in what are the conditions for an interpretation, not in what must exist *tout court*. The latter is a metaphysical question facing all theorists, not just theorists of interpretation. The metaphysical question may be entailed in questions about interpretation, but only because entailed in all questions. Entailment in this broad sense (what logicians call strict implication) is not the same as relevance. (Suppose that necessarily God exists. Then the existence of God is entailed by any consideration at all, even a consideration about washing. But the existence of God is not relevant to washing, in the way that soap is relevant.)

In *Limits of Rightness*, Michael Krausz describes a case in which an Indian and a North American come across a baby's body wrapped in cloth and floating among debris in the Ganges.[1] The North American sees the situation as one in which the body has been dumped in the river. The Indian reminds him of the religious context, where dead babies and other morally pure beings are honored by having their uncremated bodies placed in the waters of the sacred river.

This case conforms to the three-tier structure that I have proposed for operations of interpretation in my book *Making Sense: A Theory of Interpretation.*[2] That which is interpreted (the "object of interpretation") is represented in a particular way such that, as so represented, it can be subsumed (relative to a particular significance-system) under a governing concept that makes sense of it, and thence indirectly makes sense of the object of interpretation. What I am here calling the object I elsewhere called the "further object." That expression has led some, Krausz among them, to attribute to me a belief in transcendent objects of interpretation. But I see no reason for theorists of interpretation as such to engage in metaphysical issues, of which the existence of transcendent objects is one. The object of interpretation, on my account, is a "further" object only in the sense that the object of interpretation is further removed from the governing concept than is the object-as-represented.

One reason for distinguishing between objects of interpretation as such, and objects-as-represented, is to deal with the puzzle posed by the existence of "hermeneutic circles." Interpreters often appear to adapt the object of interpretation to suit the interpretation being proposed for it. This appears to be a fact about even the best interpretive practices. But, on the face of it, such an adaptation appears illegitimate, like begging the question, or changing the question to suit a pre-determined answer. If the best instances of a particular practice are suspect, then the whole practice is suspect. Could it be that interpretation as such is a tainted practice?

If we distinguish the object as such from the object-as-represented, we appear to be able to address this problem. We can then recognize the existence of this type of circularity in interpretive activity, and explain it as an adaptation of the object-as-represented, but not of the object as such, to the interpretive task in hand. An object that cannot be fitted under a given concept may be able to be so subsumed once it has been represented in a particular way.

Another reason for distinguishing objects of interpretation from objects-as-represented is that, if our aim is not merely to give a descriptive account of interpretive processes but to construct a normative theory, then we have to acknowledge that (logically speaking) interpretation stands in need of mediation. This mediation is provided by the interpreter's representation of the object. An example of this need for mediation is provided by Galileo's comment in *Il Saggiatore* that the universe is a wide-open book that is written in mathematical language.[3] The interpretation of nature, he realized, needed to proceed by first representing natural phenomena in quantitative terms.

By "that which is interpreted" I do not mean the output, but the input, of an operation of interpretation. To avoid that ambiguity, we might speak of that which is to be interpreted, instead of that which is interpreted. In doing so, we would have dispelled one ambiguity, only to spawn another: "that which is to be interpreted" suggests something whose nature demands interpretation. The present discussion will not be confined to things whose nature requires that an interpretation be given of them. The discussion is more global than that, and is supposed to cover anything of which an interpretation is given, even if its nature does not demand it.

In calling that which is interpreted "the object of interpretation" I am using the word "object" in what is fundamentally a grammatical sense, namely the sense in which we speak of the object of a verb. If I want coffee then the object of my desire is coffee. In this sense, whether any material object corresponds to such a grammatical object is an open question. Maybe when I want coffee, there is no coffee. Also open is the question whether the grammatical object takes the form of a count noun or a mass noun. "Coffee," in one of its uses, is a mass noun.

Commenting on my notion of an object of interpretation, Krausz writes: "the point is not so much whether there is or could be an *object* . . . . Instead, it is whether there is anything at all that in interpretive contexts could be constructed into an object" (LR, p. 31). We are at cross-purposes here. Krausz is building more than I do into the notion of an object. Objects, in the grammatical sense, need not be existent countable entities.

1. What Interpreters Do

Two different ways of approaching this question exist. On one approach we are interested in descriptions of what interpreters do in capturing the different types of fluctuating process, the formation of an interpretation, the varying extent to which interpretations are decided upon or discovered through their enactment. On the second approach, our interest is normative instead of descriptive. We aim to articulate the constituents that are required in order that an interpretation should succeed. I will take up this second approach next.

A. Identification

An interpreter identifies that which is interpreted via a set of features, which (so the interpreter believes) are uniquely satisfied in the context. Call this set of features the profile. The interpreter can use a definite description to specify what the interpretation is supposed to be an interpretation of. If the complex of identifying features is P the interpreter can specify the object of interpretation as "the P," for example, "the writing on the wall," "the seven starving cattle," "the phenomenon of calcination." Such a specification may be metaphorical, as when one uses the description "the red leather encyclopedia" to identify a know-all who wears a red leather jacket. On an alternative treatment of this example, the set of features relied on by the interpreter are literally those of being red, leather, and an encyclopedia. One of these (the last) is not literally possessed by the individual being identified. Yet identification is successful. The two treatments are equivalent to one another. According to one, a property of the individual (being a know-all) is metaphorically picked out by the expression "encyclopedia." According to the other account, this expression literally picks out a property that belongs metaphorically to the individual. It may be negative, as when theologians specify the object of their interpretations by the *via negativa*. It may be impressionistic, or it may only be a vague indication, as in Plato's specifications of transcendent ideas.

Maybe nothing possesses the features mentioned in the previous example—or maybe more than one such thing exists. But maybe there is just one
such thing in the context. If so, then that thing is the external object of interpretation.

Accordingly, we can distinguish three possible senses of "that which is
interpreted": (1) the set of features that the interpreter uses to identify the object of interpretation (the *profile*); (2) the definite description, or its sense,
that the interpreter takes to uniquely identify an individual satisfying the profile in the context (this is the *intentional object* of interpretation); (3) any existing individual that fits the profile (the *external object*). Both the intentional
and the external objects are defined in terms of the profile. This reflects the
primacy of the interpreter's perspective relative to that of an observer. The
external object may be defined in terms of the profile used by the interpreter,
but the reverse definition is not possible. An observer's characterization of the
object of interpretation is compatible with several different profiles that might
have been used by the interpreter.

   If I were to rely on a profile, without believing that anything fits it,
there may be an external object, namely if something fits the profile. What
there would not be is an intentional object, since I do not believe there is an
external object.

   The two interpreters in Krausz's example share an external object of interpretation: the baby's body floating in the river. Whether their interpretations also share a profile, we do not know. We are not told what set of features the two interpreters use in identifying the object of their interpretations.
Maybe one of the interpreters identifies the baby via a feature that escapes the
other interpreter's attention. In that case, their profiles differ from each other;
and, to the extent that this happens, their intentional objects also differ in a
way, even if the external objects are the same.

   The identity of intentional objects can be judged materially or formally.
Materially, they are identical provided that their external objects are the same;
formally, their identity requires that they share their profiles. Formal identity
is evidently a matter of degree, since the profile used by one interpreter may
be pretty much the same as that used by another, without their being identical
in every detail.

                                B. Representation

The two interpreters in Krausz's example may be supposed, without theoretical difficulty, to have intentional objects that are pretty much the same as each
other. Where they differ is in the ways they represent this common object.

Representation, like identification, proceeds by way of sets of features. In representing an intentional object, an interpreter may make use of features that were not relied on in the object's identification, so long as the interpreter believes those features to be possessed by the object of interpretation. The interpreter can specify the object-as-represented by a definite description followed by a *qua*-phrase, "the P *qua* R."

Krausz's two interpreters represent the common object of interpretation differently by foregrounding different features of the case: what is salient for one interpreter is the material surroundings of the body (the floating debris and garbage), what is salient for the other is the baby's moral purity. I express this by saying that the two interpreters have different objects-as-represented.

Commenting on this expression, Krausz writes: "one might hold that, rather than saying that there is a distinction between the further object and the object as represented, what is really going on is that one simply 'sees' the properties of the further object. That is, there is no constructed object-as-represented. There is only the object seen one way or another" (LR, p. 26). I accept this point. Throughout, I am not using the word "object" in the sense of an entity except when I talk of external objects.

C. Subsumption and Application

The two interpreters make sense of that which is interpreted, and do so in different ways. One interpreter, having represented the floating baby as occupying a space used for garbage, sees its presence there as due to an act of dumping (since that is the significance of putting things in such a space). The other interpreter, having represented the baby as a morally pure being, interprets its presence in the Ganges as an act of honoring (since that is the significance of placing such beings in the Ganges). In both cases the object-as-represented is fitted into a significance-system and thereby subsumed under a governing concept. The governing concept is on that basis applied to the object of interpretation.

In outline, this is the "three-tier" analysis that I have proposed—the three tiers being the (further) object, the object-as-represented, and the governing concept.

According to this account, an act of interpretation can be analyzed into four constituent acts: (1) an act of identifying an (intentional) object as that which (putatively) fits a given profile, and does so in a contextually unique way; (2) an act of representing this object in some way (for example, by foregrounding some of its putative features); (3) an act of subsuming the object-as-represented, via a significance-scheme, under a governing concept ("the P *qua* R is C"); (4) an act of applying the governing concept to the intentional object ("the P is C").

I do not claim that interpreters consciously perform these acts in just this sequence—only that operations of interpretation can be seen as being made up of these constituents. Note that, for an act of interpretation to occur, there must be an intentional object but there may or may not be an external object.

2. Conflicting Interpretations

Let us ask what must exist in order to have two conflicting interpretations. Krausz insists that the object of two rival interpretations must be assumed to exist and to be singular. He charges me with overlooking this requirement: "The further object must be singular if it is to perform the job of "grounding" the objects-as-represented. If the further object is not singular, then Thom's pluralism (again, my multiplism) could not be generated. But Thom provides no grounds for individuating further objects. He assumes that one and only one further object affords and is represented by objects-as-represented. If one successfully argued that more than one further object were in place, or that there were no way of counting the further object, then the job that Thom assigns to the further object could not be performed. Put otherwise, Thom's principle of pluralism (or my multiplism) cannot be sustained if one were to disallow the countability and singularity of the further object" (LR, p. 30).

Contrary to what Krausz says on this point, there need not be an existent object, and the object need not be countable. Two competing interpretations may concern a nonexistent object. A paranoid husband may believe that his wife is unfaithful, and may successively explore alternative explanations for this nonexistent state of affairs ("she is bored with me," or alternatively "she is trying to attract my attention"). The grammatical object of an interpretation-verb may be a mass noun (like "death") instead of a count noun. Aboutness does not imply existence, and sameness does not imply countability.

What is necessary is that the two interpretations point to or are about the same object. The three-tier analysis does not deprive us of the everyday means of identifying objects of interpretation. The object of interpretation is in the first instance an intentional object, and this remains so for pairs of rival interpretations. In order for two interpretations to point to the same object, their profiles must be equivalent, that is, it must be the case that whatever fits one fits both.

Identity of object is, not sufficient to ensure that two interpretations are competitors. They also must have identical aims. We can see this in the case of the baby in the river.

Krausz asks which of the two interpretations in his example is right. It might appear that the two interpretations are incommensurable, one being religious, and the other secular. But this would be to overlook a crucial feature of the case. It is not as if the Indian views the sight with complaisance while the North American alone is shocked by it. The Indian is described as being "dismayed" when he notices the body (LR, p. 35). Why would the Indian be dismayed at the sight? Because what he sees in not just an instance of a religious practice, but one that has gone wrong. The body was supposed to sink to the bottom of the river and stay there, but the ballast has come loose and the body has floated to the surface. What we have from both interpreters, then, is an intentional explanation: in both cases the proposed interpretation is of the form "explained as being the outcome of such-and-such intentions." Both interpret the object of interpretation as being explained by an intentional action, in one case an act of dumping, in the other an act of implementing a religious practice designed to honor the dead child. The second interpretation is complicated because the interpreter sees the implementation of that practice as having gone wrong and as having produced an unintended result.

The two proposed intentional explanations are mutually incompatible: if the mother's act was a botched implementation of a religious practice then it was not an act of dumping a body. So the example of the baby in the river shows *inter alia* interpretive disputes about a single intentional object do occur.

A. Conflicting Intentional Explanations

Which interpretation, then, is right? There may well be an answer to this question, but we can only speculate. If we are to go beyond speculation, we will need to know something about the act of placing the body in the river. Maybe, as the Indian supposes, the mother was following a religious practice. Maybe, as the North American supposes, she was dumping the dead body. Maybe she was dumping the body in a way that would be seen by others as following a religious practice. Maybe she was confused. In any case, to the extent that the mother acted with an intention, something is a truth of the matter concerning her intention and concerning her execution of that intention. This is the truth both interpreters are trying to get at.

3. Non-conflicting Interpretations: Consolation and Understanding

That is the case if what is being interpreted is the corpse in the river, and what is sought is an intentional explanation. But maybe Krausz does not mean the example to be taken this way. Maybe he wishes us to focus on the belief-systems of the Indian (described as "Hindu/Buddhist") and the North American (described as "secular"). Those belief-systems can be seen as different interpretations of another object of interpretation—the phenomenon of death.

Looking at matters this way, we can ask again which interpretation is right. But this time we find no straightforward answer. What does an interpretation of the fact of death aim at? Does it aim at understanding, or consolation? Those who have knowledge about the causes of death, about the phases in the process, about the phenomenology of death, and so forth might achieve an understanding of death. We may not find such knowledge consoling as we approach our death. Consolation requires not knowledge but hope. A consoling message is not so much one that we know is true, as one that we hope will be fulfilled. We must believe fulfillment of the message to be possible. But belief in a possibility is a far cry from knowledge. The consolations offered by the great religions often concern matters about which no knowledge is possible, one way or the other. Precisely because we cannot know that their claims are false, we can cling to the hope that they may be realized.

Krausz distinguishes two aims of interpretation—elucidation and edification (LR, p. 113). He notes that Hinduism and Buddhism share both of these aims (LR, p. 115). Further, both these religions share views on the nature of death: "Both agree that the individual is no inherent existent and thus it does not die as one might think an inherent autonomous individual might die" (LR, p. 132).

I take it that what Krausz calls edification includes what I am calling consolation.

If the secular interpretation aims only at understanding, and the Hindu-Buddhist interpretation aims at both understanding and consolation, then in a way they are not rival interpretations—namely, to the extent that the Hindu-Buddhist interpretation has an aim not shared by the secular interpretation. You can try to make sense of death by telling a believable (but not knowable) story about its meaning, a story that gives us hope. Or you can try to make sense of death by recounting all that is known about it, in a way that gives us understanding. But there need be no conflict between the two aims.

An attempt to provide consolation might come into conflict with an attempt to provide understanding, if for example it offered consolation on the basis of some proposition that can be known to be false. The consolation will be ineffective as soon as its recipient discovers that it is based on a falsehood. Such would-be consolers should ensure that they offer their wares only to the ignorant.

But, so long as the recipient does not know that the basis of the consolation is false—even better, if that basis cannot be known to be false, because it is unfalsifiable—then no conflict occurs between consolation and understanding. I can know all to be known about death, and still take consolation from an interpretation that offers me hope, so long as that consolation is not based on falsifiable propositions. If knowledge offers me no hope, I derive hope from elsewhere.

NOTES

1. Michael Krausz, *Limits of Rightness* (LR) (Lanham, Md.: Rowman and Littlefield, 2000).

2. Paul Thom, *Making Sense: A Theory of Interpretation* (Lanham, Md.: Rowman and Littlefield, 2000).

3. Galileo Galilei, *Il Saggiatore* (Ricciardi editore, 1953). E-text at URL = http://www.liberliber.it/biblioteca/g/galilei/il_saggiatore/html/index.htm, p. 6.

Ten

NOTES ON KRAUSZ'S DETACHABILITY THESIS

Joseph Margolis

Whoever has shared the grand puzzle of explaining the nature of interpretation in the company of another soul equally ardent to hit on a reasonable theory, someone not entirely in agreement with your views but close enough to make the difference provocative and productive for both, will understand how impossible (and risky) to hold the evolving debate to positions once held in an uncertain past by either party—positions plainly superseded at present, these lengthening years, almost in tribute to what the intervening discoveries have made possible. I have enjoyed such an exchange with Michael Krausz; and I am pleased to see that the dispute continues in the spirit in which it began; also, that the most strategic aspects of the matter are clearer now than they probably were before. As far as possible I will confine my remarks to Krausz's synopsis in the present volume, "Interpretation and Its Objects: A Synoptic View," with an eye to what may be congruent with it, in *Limits of Rightness*, with what I still believe to be essential to an adequate answer, and with why the matter is important.[1] The conceptual questions Krausz collects are good ones, enough to focus the differences between us, which he and I would wish to put in the clearest light. They are questions we have never been able to count fully answered. Here, I am especially interested in the question of "detachability."

Krausz sets the stage for his claim in the following terms: in the interpretation of cultural "things," he says, broadly speaking, two opposed views exist: "In one group some assume that for any object of interpretation—say, a work of art, music, or literary text—there can be only one single admissible interpretation. In the other group some assume that for some objects of interpretation more than one interpretation is admissible. I call the first group singularists and the second multiplists." (IO, p. 11). Let me worry these remarks a little, though I am perfectly willing to confine myself to the issues they introduce.

You will notice that Krausz speaks of "objects of interpretation," which he takes to be denumerable—a particular piece of music or a literary text or a painting or the like. He fleshes out what he means in two ways. He notes that singularists support their claim on the strength of the necessity of adhering to a bivalent logic: given some "admissible" interpretation (say, a valid one), any would-be interpretation incompatible with that will be "inadmissible" (say, invalid). I do not mean to press the obvious sense of "invalid" for the moment;

I introduce it initially to fix the direction of Krausz's thought—thus far. But the argument will oblige us to recover a more robust sense of "valid" and "invalid." The rest is familiar to those who know my proposal. I spare them the details.

Second, Krausz says quite plainly, in *Limits of Rightness*, that (even) "multiplism requires that competing interpretations address the same thing. Where different interpretations address different things, no multiplism obtains" (LR, p. 2). Of course. In "Interpretation and Its Objects," Krausz confirms the same point: familiar arguments between Hindus and Buddhists, he notes, presumably interpreting what both "ultimately address themselves" to, fail to meet "a condition necessary for both singularism and multiplism . . . namely the condition of countability of the pertinent object[s] of interpretation" (IO, p. 16). This remark must be read in the sense of imposing an "ontological" constraint on "admissible" interpretations—not merely "countability" but what, about interpretable things, makes them determinately countable and permits us to distinguish between admissible and inadmissible interpretations of such things. For the moment, I merely acknowledge that we need an explanation of these terms of art: "admissibility," "countability," "ideality" regarding particular things.

Krausz's characterization of singularism appears to be modeled on Aristotle's argument in *Metaphysics* Gamma as far as the modal reading of bivalence is concerned: whatever it means to say that interpretation "addresses" an object, and whatever it means to say that, in doing that, an interpretation is "admissible" or "inadmissible," it must be Krausz's intention to hold that the admissibility of a would-be interpretation depends on the discernible attributes or nature of a particular countable thing.

I cannot see any other way of making sense of the thesis. But if so, then the theory of "admissible" interpretation is (on my reading) metaphysically or ontologically constrained; and both the singularist and multiplist options make sense, in opposing each other, only on the assumption of some particular account of the "nature" of an artwork deemed convincing as a pertinent ontology. For the moment, I do not care what ontology either partisan favors; I say only that they cannot be speaking about anything remotely arguable if they "detach" (the key term of Krausz's central claim) the sense of singularism and multiplism from any and all accounts of the countable things we interpret!

In laying out any such metaphysics, if we are speaking about the real nature of interpretable things, we are talking about what version of realism the singularist and the multiplist are committed to or contesting between themselves, in virtue of which we may assess their claims. Krausz explicitly but mistakenly holds that "The question of whether there must be one or whether there may be more than one admissible interpretation [of the countable objects of interpretation] is logically detachable (as to entailment) from both realism and constructivism" (IO, p. 16).

This is checkmate in one move, unless Krausz means to say that the "general" entailment does go through, although it does not follow (so Krausz might say) that singularism (as defined) entails what he calls "realism" and that multiplism (as defined) entails "constructivism." I can only answer: singularism and multiplism must entail some limited set of metaphysical options; whether they entail precisely what Krausz means by "realism" and "constructivism" depends on just how he defines those terms!

Admittedly, "realism" and "constructivism" (as Krausz reads these notions) cannot be directly derived from what he says about singularism and multiplism. But the reason is this: nothing "ontological" follows from the definitions given of singularism and multiplism. The difficulty is that they are vacuous in the relevant sense. The quarrel cannot be joined if singularism and multiplism convey no ontological constraints at all, convey no reason for thinking either claim relevantly bears on the interpretation of artworks or histories or the like. They cannot for instance tell us anything about "admissible interpretations" either. The reductio is there: wherever the definitions of singularism and multiplism are robust enough to bear on the choice between singularist and multiplist theories of interpretation, they will do so in virtue of one or another metaphysics of the kind Krausz claims they can be "detached" from! Krausz is just wrong about that. I find no explicit argument to support his claim.

Neither singularism nor multiplism makes any sense until we say what we take to be the nature of the countable things we are examining, in virtue of which we rightly decide whether singularism or multiplism is the better position. Singularism and multiplism must impose some metaphysical constraints on the "object" of interpretation, in virtue of which their respective claims could make consistent sense.

Here, a complication arises. For Krausz reminds us that "indeterminacy is not sufficient for multiplism [to obtain]": "multiplism is not entailed by the indeterminacy of pertinent objects" (IO, p. 15). Apparently, indeterminacy does not even preclude singularism. The complication is not primarily due to saying this, but to the need to spell out what is meant by the "indeterminacy of interpreted objects." (LR, p. 1–2). I may have misled Krausz here in some unintended way by something I have said or written earlier. Perhaps he means by "indeterminacy" what I mean by "determinability" (as distinct from "determinacy")—especially in speaking of Intentional properties as opposed to physical properties (on the usual account of the latter).

I am not clear as to what Krausz means by "indeterminacy." He says: "A singularist condition might well obtain where the indeterminacy of an interpretation 'matches' the indeterminacy of the object in question" (IO, p. 15). I do not know what this can mean, apart from a purely abstract (really an uninterpreted) formula that says that if an artwork had (whatever that may mean) an "indeterminate" nature, then if there was only one "indeterminate" interpreta-

tion (!) that could fit such a nature (never mind what that means), then singularism might accommodate even that. Notice two things here: first, the thesis
still intends some match between the choice of singularism and multiplism and
the "metaphysics" of the interpretable object; and, second, in order to answer
the question, we would have to know much more about what an "indeterminate" object was—which would amount to an ontology again.

The burden is on Krausz: I take an "indeterminate interpretation" to be
no interpretation at all (or one we cannot make out); and an "indeterminate
object," one that does not exist at all (or one we are inclined to believe is real
but whose nature and existence we cannot quite make out). When I speak of
"indeterminacy," I never mean to be speaking of an ontic attribute: I always
mean something that cannot (on a given account) be determined (made determinate) in the way thought possible on the strength of the theory being challenged. For example, on the adoption of a relativistic logic, the disjunctive
choice between incompatible interpretations becomes logically indeterminate
on purely formal grounds (can no longer be determined: assigned a truth-value
that would be permitted under bivalence, or under excluded middle).

Indeterminacy is primarily a question of would-be knowledge or understanding or methodology and logic or conception or the like. To take a famous
case: if the speckles of a speckled hen can be counted, then although in seeing
a speckled hen the number seen may be indeterminate, the speckles are not
indeterminate in number; "speckled" may be a vague enough term that no determinate number can or need be made out, but then "being speckled" would
not be indeterminate, only (determinately) vague. Nothing that exists (a particular object) can be indeterminate in number or lack the properties it has in
virtue of which it is the particular thing it is. To favor constructivism or the
doctrine of the flux, or to admit intentionality or historicity, does not adversely
affect any of these distinctions.

I do not wish to intrude my account here, because doing that may appear
to depart from the scruple set at the start of this discussion. Though I cannot
claim to have reread all the things I have written about interpretable objects, I
cannot imagine ever speaking of real but indeterminate objects. I can imagine
saying that if (as I believe) Intentional properties (or objects that possess Intentional properties)—culturally significant, interpretable properties—are not
determinate in the same sense in which physical properties are said to be determinate, are at best only determinable (justifiably "imputed" alternative determinations by interpretive means), then a kind of logical "indeterminacy"
results from replacing the strictures of bivalence by the laxness of a relativistic
logic. But I do not think anything that exists is indeterminate (or incomplete)
in any sense that its existing would require.

I cannot make sense of an artwork or interpretation that is indeterminate
tout court. To exist is to be "determinate" enough to do so! For instance, that
an artwork or interpretation is determinate in "number," in the sense that it can

be identified and reidentified, is a purely logical matter. In *Limits of Rightness*, Krausz challenges the idea: he thinks that the mere interpretive "determinability" of an artwork's. Intentional "nature" (which he regularly equates with "indeterminacy" read in an ontic sense, despite going on to cite my explicit denial of any such equivalence) may well threaten the "determinability" (or "indeterminacy") of "number" as well! "Margolis's thesis of pan-fluxism," he remarks, "tends toward the conclusion that determinability as to nature entails determinability as to number" (LR, p. 98). He means that the "determinability" of Intentional properties threatens the "determinacy" of Intentional things (in regard to "number"), just as admitting a "fluxive" world does (as he supposes). But that confuses reference and predication and ignores the import of admitting that Intentional properties (as I argue) are indissolubly "incarnate" in physical properties ("determinate" if any properties are).

Krausz's worry is misplaced. Nothing is identified numerically on merely predicative grounds. The question of what an artwork's nature is presupposes its being the particular thing it is: there could not be any coherent question about the determinable peculiarities of an artwork's Intentional properties (its "nature") if it were not determinate in "number." Intentional objects are determinate in their novel way precisely in being interpretively "determinable." Just the difference between the logical roles of reference (or denotation) and predication permits us to entertain the idea that cultural denotata, Intentionally qualified objects, artworks for instance, can have determinable (as opposed to determinate) natures (which affects the logic of interpretation) at the same time that they remain determinate in number—as determinate as physical objects are.

I do not deny any of the well-known complications that beset our stating the conditions under which any object is individuated and identified and said to have correctly predicated of it any properties that we take it to have; but that is not a special problem for Intentional objects or for a "fluxive" view of the real world. To see all this is to begin to see why the choice between singularism and multiplism is (must be) ontologically constrained. If Krausz would reconsider this point alone, I think he might find my argument more compelling. But if he allows it, he cannot then support the "detachability thesis," as he means to do.

In *Limits of Rightness*, Krausz pointedly says: "The thesis that ontology is detachable from ideality does not mean that metaphysics more generally understood is irrelevant to the understanding of interpretive activity. For example, the intentionality of cultural entities—their settings in regard to rules, norms, and the like—is a broadly metaphysical consideration without which one could not countenance pertinent entities as cultural to begin with" (LR, p. 150).

I concede the point, but I do not see how it meets the deeper complaint. For the choice between singularism and multiplism, or the partisan advocacy of either, requires that we take into consideration a theory of the "nature" of Intentional (cultural) objects relative to their countability—which begins to fill out, relevantly, what Krausz means by "ontology"; otherwise, we have nothing to talk about! Anything that would spell out what Krausz means by "ideality," detached from "ontology" in this sense, would be irrelevant to Krausz's issue.

Almost nothing in *Limits of Rightness* explains the sense of "ideality" as distinct from ontology (which Krausz effectively confines to choices between "realism" and "constructivism" and the like). What is offered is confined exclusively to the question of whether "one ideal interpretation" of an interpretable object exists, or whether "there may be more than one ideal interpretation of it"—which is to ask whether singularism or multiplism is the better thesis. But "better" or "tenable" in what respect? Krausz offers no operative or operable sense in which the would-be defense of either doctrine over the other can be pursued at all: say, in terms of "ideality" as opposed to "ontology." What have I missed?

We are in the middle of a large thicket here. We may easily fail to see all at stake. Let me draw your attention to two further complications that may help to round out a reasonable account of interpretation. One concerns what Krausz calls "ideality":

> The multiplist condition does not arise from an epistemic lack: it does not affirm that, when all pertinent information and arguments are in, only one interpretation will indeed win out. On the contrary, the multiplist holds that in pertinent cases there are no overarching standards to adjudicate between admissible yet incongruent contending interpretations. Rather, multiplism constitutes an ideal condition ["the concept of ideal admissibility"] (IO, p. 12).

This is not as straightforward as it sounds. A difficulty arises because, on the one hand, in explaining what he means by multiplism, Krausz raises the question of the "objectivity" (IO, p.17) of an interpretation (whether singularist or multiplist) but does not spell out what might be the conditions on which an objective interpretation may be rendered; and, on the other hand, in explaining the sense in which "multiplism constitutes an ideal condition" (regarding admissible interpretations) in which "both singularism and multiplism [are said to] deploy the concept of ideal admissibility"—he says: "I embrace Richard Rorty's pragmatist sentiment [regarding] the notion of a *Grenzbegriff* (or a limiting concept)" (IO, p. 12). (He is apparently explaining "ideality.") On my reading, these are completely incompatible views, because Krausz wishes to be as flexible as possible about the objective grounds for would-be singularist and multiplist claims; whereas Rorty means to reject the entire question of objective claims, to reject any and every pretense that we can provide cognitive grounds for choosing between (say) singularism and multiplism— anywhere!

The idea of a *Grenzbegriff* was Hilary Putnam's unfortunate suggestion regarding how, borrowing from William James (who uses the term, which, in turn, is cobbled from Immanuel Kant) as a "regulative" but not a "constitutive" constraint on the application of "true"—it was a suggestion meant to accommodate an objective pluralism.[2] Whenever Richard Rorty says "there is only the dialogue" (which Krausz cites favorably), he means to reject outright the legitimative relevance of any analysis of objective grounds (say, objectivist or pluralist or relativist) for any judgments at all).[3]

Rorty is speaking as his kind of "postmodernist" (sometimes said to be a kind of "pragmatist"); whereas, on the evidence we have, Krausz is not a postmodernist in Rorty's sense at all. For that reason Krausz says, a bit later: "any account of objectivity would not be located at the level of ontology but at the level of methodology" (IO, p. 17). I think Krausz is mistaken about the separability of metaphysics and methodology; but, apart from that, Rorty will have nothing to do with methodology any more than with ontology!

The trouble is that "ideality" hangs in the air. There is no way to bring "ideality" (as altogether different from ontology) to bear on the appraisal of singularism's and multiplism's claims. I cannot see how Krausz means to proceed. Putnam had made an unguarded, wholly indefensible proposal of a purely regulative *Grenzbegriff* regarding truth. He did so because he wished to avoid any form of objectivism ("the God's eye point of view") and wished to endorse a form of objective pluralism (a metaphysics). Rorty saw the conceptual weakness at once and pounced on Putnam. Putnam saw that Rorty had gained a dialectical advantage in favor of "ethnocentric solidarity"—which abandons any pretence of the relevance of epistemology—but he had already lost the round.

In cognitive matters, it makes no sense to introduce a "regulative" *Grenzbegriff* if it cannot also claim a "constitutive" function. (So Rorty was right in thinking that Putnam was even more arbitrary than he!) Krausz cannot afford to draw on Rorty's maneuver, because it would wipe out completely any grounds—ontological, epistemological, logical, methodological—on which (alone) some reasonable argument in favor of singularism or multiplism would make sense. The dispute between singularists and multiplists is an epistemological and methodological dispute (to give Krausz his due); but if so, on the argument I am advancing, it cannot fail to depend on metaphysical grounds as well—which Krausz denies. Krausz must believe that logical and methodological issues—and perhaps semantic and epistemological ones—can be resolved in the context of "ideality" detached from "ontology"; but I believe that to be a serious mistake (if we suppose we are speaking about the real world at all).

In order for Krausz's argument to have any legs at all, it must be possible to separate ("detach") metaphysics and epistemology. Not only is that impossible, Krausz himself opposes the idea. I think he muddies the account in several unnecessary ways: as by invoking Nelson Goodman's idea of "world-making," which idea is incoherent; and by attributing to me the doctrine that "the real is constructed and the constructed is real" (IO, p. 18), an idealist formula obviously false about the physical world. I waive these complications here.

Krausz subscribes to Putnam's observation (which is directed—correctly—against Rorty): namely, "why should the fact that reality cannot be described independently of our descriptions lead us to suppose that only the descriptions exist?" (IO, p. 18). Krausz grasps the Kantian import of Putnam's remark that we cannot describe noumena at all (*Ibid.*). Krausz's view and mine would instantly converge if, for instance, he subscribed to Georg Wilhelm Friedrich Hegel's rejection of any principled disjunction between appearance and reality (*Erscheinungen and Objekte*). (He could have reached the same conclusion by invoking the Buddhist sources he admires.) Post-Hegel, the recovery of realism must take a constructivist turn. Krausz admits the constructivist turn but not quite the Hegelian lesson (IO, p. 18). But to subscribe to a constructivism, a constructive realism, is not to say that the real world is itself constructed! It is also not to deny that the cultural world is humanly constructed.

If these corrections are made, then "ideality" cannot be disjoined from "ontology"; the appraisal of singularism and multiplism with respect to objective interpretation cannot be coherently pursued without providing a metaphysics of interpretable things.

If I read him correctly, Krausz views "realism" as committed to the claim that we can know noumena—know how real things "are" independently of our descriptions and perceptions and experiences of the world (IO, p. 17). Both Kant and Hegel showed knowing noumena to be impossible, a finding Krausz himself shares. But if he does, then "realism" cannot provide a proper ground for singularism or multiplism. "Realism" (in this pre-Kantian sense) could not possibly be "entailed" by a defensible singularism (say) because it could not be defended at any cost! But that means that showing that neither singularism nor multiplism entails "realism" (in the sense supplied) is a trivial matter.

When he moves over to define "constructivism," the picture becomes unnecessarily muddied because he links the notion too closely to Goodman's options or to idealism's options (IO, p. 17). But what Krausz means (if he will allow me to restate his view) is that what we take to be the real or independent world is a construction under Kantian (or, better, Hegelian) constraints—which is not to say that the real world is itself a construction! Well then, "ideality"—regarding truth and rightness and "admissibility"—cannot be anything but a piece of our ontological/epistemological/methodological/logical/semantic construction adjusted (on Krausz's view) to resolving the question of the objectivity of interpretations. QED.

NOTES

References to Krausz's synoptic article (Chapter 2) at the beginning of this volume are preceded in the body of this article by "IO."

1. Michael Krausz, *Limits of Rightness* (LR) (Lanham, Md.: Rowman and Littlefield, 2000); Michael Krausz, "Interpretation and Its Objects: A Synoptic View," (IO), *Interpretation and Its Objects: Studies in the Philosophy of Michael Krausz* (Atlanta, Amsterdam: Rodopi Press, (2003).
2. Hilary Putnam, *Reason, Truth, and History* (Cambridge: Cambridge University Press, 1980).
3. Richard Rorty, "Hilary Putnam and the Relativist Menace," *Philosophical Papers*, vol. 3 (Cambridge: Cambridge University Press, 1998).
4. Richard Rorty, "Solidarity or Objectivity?" in *Philosophical Papers*, vol. 1 (Cambridge: Cambridge University Press, 1991)

Eleven

A METAPHYSICS FOR KRAUSZ

Michael McKenna

In *Limits of Rightness*, Michael Krausz explores the array of positions possible at the intersection between two lines of philosophical inquiry.[1] One concerns issues within the theory of interpretation. The basic contestants are singularists and multiplists as regards the status of competing, but mutually conflicting, interpretations of items within some domain (life's plans, electrons, works of art, or ordinary middle-sized objects like toasters or aardvarks). The central question Krausz considers in this philosophical arena might be put as follows: Does rightness entail exclusivity? The other line of inquiry concerns ontology. The basic contestants in this arena are realists and constructivists as regards the status of the objects encountered in our world, both in the context of the mundane, and at the fringes of human experience. The central question Krausz considers here might be cast as such: Is the world, and are the objects in it, found or made? Krausz's contention, in his earlier *Rightness and Reason*, is that the fundamental positions in each arena are, as he puts it, "logically detachable."[2] That is, our commitment to a stance on the singularism versus multiplism controversy has no bearing on our stance on the realism versus constructivism position. The same applies vice versa. According to Krausz, in his latest treatment, *Limits of Rightness*, the detachability thesis applies to the more nuanced hybrid forms of constructive realism (with exception for a thesis Krausz calls "external constructive realism").

I do not dispute Krausz's detachability thesis; sufficient coherently describable combinations of theses are found at this philosophical intersection to confirm that constraints of logical consistency alone will not disallow the full range of permutations Krausz considers. Naturally, the orthodox combinations are less challenging for the philosophical imagination. If you are a realist, and if you believe that there is *a* way the world is, that there must be a single right interpretation of every thing, aspect, happening within it will be quite natural. Similarly, if the items encountered in the world are constructed from conceptual schemes or linguistic frameworks, we should not be surprised that we can, so to speak, cook our interpretations of the world (and what we find in it) in a variety of manners that will, though jointly conflicting, have reasonable claims to rightness. Krausz displays the characteristic finesse of a seasoned philosophical master in artfully showing how the unorthodox positions might be conjoined. I applaud him. But a coherent description does not a true one make. Which one is true?

I confess to a craving for a stronger metaphysical commitment from Krausz. By this point in his career as a seasoned philosopher, he should have bitten several bullets! As with the Richard Rortys, Hilary Putnams and the like, he should be at the stage of squirming, finessing, and backpedaling. These weaselings are what allows young pups like myself to make a career feeding off the gaffes of our precursors. But Krausz will not stick his neck out for us. Krausz's strategy is characteristically thoughtful and conciliatory. He is like a peacemaker that has shown up at the OK Corral. All the hotheads are itchin' for a fight, but he is not giving anyone a reason to shoot. In this dialectical space, I have been invited to act as critic in assessing *Limits of Rightness*. Faced with such a cautious, carefully crafted piece of work, what's a guy (or gal) to do? If Krausz will not commit to a metaphysics at which I can take aim, I might as well give him one. What follows is a metaphysics for Krausz. I present it unabashedly as the truth, lean on argument and fat with bold assertion. Let Krausz have at it, take what he may, and leave the rest.

1. Rocks and Socks and Seagull Flocks

Individuals exist. In a description of the ultimate nature of reality, we must make room for the notion of a countable, datable item, a particular, a thing, an entity—one of a possible many. Even this notion has been challenged in the history of philosophy. But it is a thesis that, for current purposes, we can count as axiomatic. Included in what exists are rocks, socks, and seagull flocks. These items fall into different categories. The crucial categories are between those items falling within the domain of natural kinds and those falling within the domain of the artificial. Rocks fall within the camp of natural kinds; socks in the camp of artifacts. Seagull flocks are, likely, a logically complex case involving the natural kind "seagull" and the artificial kind "flock". (I am prepared to have a zoologist set me straight on the matter of flocks.) An intuitive, pretheoretical characterization (some would say "caricature") of this division would have it that natural kinds and their members are discovered and not created, and that artifacts are created and not discovered. The division is not clean, and wonderful cases exist that might challenge the boundaries. Perhaps good philosophical reason could provide a basis for unseating this bit of conceptual organization, but it would have to be quite powerful, and stand beside independent reasons for indicting this straightforward bit of ontological parsimony. As a starting point, it should be embraced.

One form of realism that Krausz does acknowledge (not quite in the form presented here), but does not endorse, is a restricted form in which the realists' domain of the way the world is is restricted to the spectrum of natural kinds (LR, pp. 43, 51–56). This restricted form of realism can be cautiously extended to the properties or universals that serve some kind of explanatory role in the casual powers or interanimations of the natural items, events, states, and processes that constitute reality. Let the constructivist loose on the artifacts; allow them to loosen identity conditions on works of art, making hay with all kinds of imputed properties and multiply admissible interpretations of *Hamlet* plays, Beatles tunes, or ships owned by characters named Nuerath. But the laws of thermodynamics, and the genetic constitution of bunny rabbits and weasels are not up for grabs, are not subject to revision and construction from the conventions constituting our "conceptual schemes." Bunny rabbits would have such and such DNA and would go hippity-hop with or without English or Urdu, or with or without the speakers of any or all languages. These facts of nature, of the universe, of "the way the world is," or whatever idiom one prefers, are to be discovered, not made. This is a form of constructive realism according to Krausz's taxonomy.

In our first pass at a metaphysics, we restrict the range of realist commitments to the domain of the naturally occurring. Let constructivism rule in the realm of human fabrication and convention. In the realm of convention we find the items that are truly at the heart of Krausz's project, intentional objects, that is, objects as presented, and, most crucially, works of art. Let us call this metaphysical mapping, Plain Jane Metaphysics. While Krausz does acknowledge a Plain Jane ontological mapping, and does place it in the category of constructive realism (LR, pp. 45–49, 51–55), he develops and articulates different forms of constructive realism that diverge from Plain Jane Metaphysics. Plain Jane is left behind.

2. The Constructive Realisms Krausz Likes

The forms of constructive realism that Krausz considers promising share two questionable features: First, they allow for mere intentional layering "all the way down." Using Krausz's example of an honored soul, a baby, left in the Ganges River, in Benares, India, in contrast with an infant "dumped" in Cobb's Creek, near Philadelphia, Pennsylvania, Krausz suggests that a layered form of discourse can articulate the realists' sense of sameness alongside the constructivists' sense of difference (LR, pp. 45–46). Where categories and particular cases differ, is in a layer of intentionality in which objects like infants are assigned meanings or saliences of a higher level. So some *homo sapien* infants are, at a higher, culturally intentionalized level of discourse, members of a special kind whose identity conditions are given within that higher level. The dumped baby in Cobb's Creek does not have the property of being an honored soul; nor does the honored soul in the Ganges have the property of having been dumped. We arrive at the relevant level of difference. What about the realists' sense of sameness? At a lower level of discourse, of intentional layering, there exists the more primitive notion of an infant: Both the honored soul, and the dumped baby are infants, and "infant" is a phasal concept capturing a period of time within the normally progressing life span of the natural kind "human being" (or "*homo sapien*") (LR, p. 56). How to gloss this lower level of discourse is a further contested matter between realists and constructivists. But, according to Krausz, for the constructivist to hold that the level of discourse in which "infant" is nested is itself constructed and not real, or is made and not found is entirely consistent.

The second feature of the constructive realisms Krausz finds promising is that they are unwilling to acknowledge, in a most basic account of "the way the world is," kinds like bunny rabbit or aardvark or quark or walnut tree or hunk of gold (LR, pp. 56–58). Both the internal and the external constructive realisms Krausz considers find no ontological categories in the ultimate nature of reality. Any such categories, in particular any apparently natural kinds, are the upshots of conceptual schemes, symbol systems, or linguistic conventions. Internal and external constructive realists will posit some kind of undifferentiable "stuff." Krausz calls it "materia"; Rom Harré makes use of the elegant term "glub." Let us call it "da stuff," so as to differentiate it from the uncontroversially identifiable stuff I have in my briefcase. The internal constructive realists will hold that da stuff is, itself, only intelligible from within some symbol system; external constructive realists will hold that da stuff is intelligible independently of any symbol system. (From what I can tell, internal constructive realists favor the basic project of constructivism; external constructive realists favor the basic project of realism.)

Each of these features of the conceptual realisms Krausz considers, left unqualified, do violence to Plain Jane Metaphysics. The tool of layering of intentionalized levels of discourse is not a threat to Plain Jane Metaphysics and is useful in its cultivation. The treatment of the dumped baby in Cobb's Creek and the honored soul returned to the Ganges are sufficient to make the point. But no reason is to be found to assume that this layering, qua mere intentionalized construct, goes "all the way down." In particular, applied to the case under consideration, no reason exists to think that the level of discourse in which "infant" occurs is also mere layering. According to Plain Jane Metaphysics, some reason exists to think not. (I will return to a defense of this point.)

What about the appeal to da stuff? According to Plain Jane Metaphysics, there were trees, rocks dinosaurs, geological periods, bugs, and stars before there were any symbol systems about at all. (Naturally, if we were Platonists about symbol systems, then there always were such symbol systems; but that is a story no one wants to talk about. In all honesty, going that route makes Plain Jane blush a bit.) There were not just bunches of, or one sprawling mass of, da stuff around out of which would have been constituted these kinds of things had there then been such symbol systems. There were these kinds of things—that is, there were token particulars of these kinds. Really. So is the world according to Plain Jane Metaphysics.

The layering all the way down compliments the thought that what a realist must do is hold on to the idea of da stuff. If we assume mere intentionalized layering all the way down, and if we want the realist idea of an independent world to be confronted by a symbol system or a conceptual scheme, then we have to turn to da stuff. Otherwise we will have nothing. But Plain Jane should avoid da stuff and the all the way down outlook. Once she embraces it, she will find that she is addicted to da stuff and that she might never recover a world worth wanting. No. Plain Jane needs to do some hard philosophical work; she needs to resist the assumptions that drive her to da stuff.

The idea that what realists would have left to embrace is da stuff is puzzling in that it resonates with a building-block picture of reality that has its origins in atomistic conceptions of nature: Namely, all of reality is constituted out of primitive bits of matter. Da stuff is a philosophical analog of atoms, or little bits of material that, like flour in a piece of pastry, get plugged together with more bits of stuff in more complicated ways. Why is this puzzling? Because the thought that a realist would find a safer home for the way the world is by holding out for the primitive notion of da stuff is driven by a deep and powerful picture of the universe. This concession—this bowing before that picture—belies an allegiance to constructivism! Why? Because da stuff invites the intellectual crutch of scientism in the worst way: It is just nature in its "brute form" that is "real." The rest is convention and fabrication. Here is a worldview caught in a constructed paradigm if there ever was one. No doubt, according to Plain Jane Metaphysics, da stuff exists in the ultimate nature of reality, but right up with da stuff are rich, robust items like pterodactyls, crocodiles, stars, and masses of gold. Also, properties like the color red, or being lighter than gold, exist; truths, like the second law of thermodynamics, exist; and so forth.

3. A Bad Argument That Krausz Allows to Do Too Much Work

Nelson Goodman advances one argument to which Krausz gives too much credence. Krausz calls it Goodman's *reductio* on realism. Krausz himself does not endorse it; he acknowledges its weakness (LR, p. 48). Still, in his reflection on the dialectic between realist and constructivist, he takes the power of Goodman's argument to be a reasonable basis to move the realist to recast the realist thesis so as to retreat from a robust ontological commitment as to the content of the world as it is (LR, p. 56). Though Krausz does not state this explicitly, as he presents the dialectic, the fundamental intuition found in Goodman's argument is at play in all the different forms of constructive realism Krausz does consider, such as Putnam's and Joseph Margolis's. Goodman's argument turns upon the observation that no "way things are" can be expressed without being expressed in a language. From this a great deal of weight is placed upon the inescapable link between a symbol system and even the most rudimentary bits of reality. Goodman makes use of it for a full-blown form of constructivism. Goodman's argument should go like this:

> That the world is a particular way is an admissible assertion.
> Any admissible assertion can be asserted only within the framework of a symbol system.
> Therefore, that the world is a particular way can be asserted only within the framework of a symbol system.

This is a valid argument, likely sound as well. It also poses no threat to realism. It calls attention to nothing but the transparent. But what Goodman wants is the following argument:

> That the world is a particular way is an admissible assertion.
> Any admissible assertion can be asserted only within the framework of a symbol system.
> Therefore, that the world is a particular way is inevitably linked to a symbol system.

The conclusion to this second argument would have it that realism is a hopeless enterprise. But notice that this second argument, unlike the first, is not valid. Here is what is needed to make it so:

> That the world is a particular way is an admissible assertion.
> Any admissible assertion can be asserted only within the framework of a symbol system.
> Therefore, that the world is a particular way can be asserted only within the framework of a symbol system.
> If a proposition (or statement) p can only be asserted within the framework of a symbol system, then p's referents are inevitably linked to a symbol system.
> Therefore, that the world is a particular way is inevitably linked to a symbol system.

The fourth premise in the above argument is question begging. A realist would insist that this third argument is valid but not sound as the fourth premise is false. The basic problem with Goodman's argument is that it starts with the following mundane point: To say something about anything (including the world), it has to be said. Naturally, said things are said in languages. From these two morsels we are to move to the quite dubious point that no aspect of the world is free of the conventions of a symbol system or a conceptual scheme. But this conclusion comes only after an indictment of something like Plain Jane Metaphysics.

What kind of attack on Plain Jane Metaphysics would be sufficient for a defense of the fourth premise above? Consider just this one: no theory of reference is able to make intelligible the distinction between a non-linguistic referent, and the linguistic referential resources that do the referring. (Enter the puzzles inherited from Gottlob Frege, Bertrand Russell, and Ludwig Wittgenstein.) Why think that a failure to explain the simple, intuitive picture of reference would lead to an acceptance of a collapse (or an inescapable melding) of the distinction between a referring device and referent? If the two were to collapse, then there would be no possibility of making any assertions about the way that things are that did not pack into those things the linguistic resources made use of in the act of asserting. But the obvious point of resistance is in the assumption that, in the absence of a positive, philosophical analysis or explication of reference, we ought to assume no such thing as reference exists (as pretheoretically construed). Maybe more philosophical work needs to be done.

Perhaps the notion of reference is a primitive concept, incapable of much philosophical illumination. Similar things have been said about truth. Once we come across a concept that does truly resist philosophical illumination, we have two ways to explain its resistance. We might hold that it is a corrupt concept that can be eliminated, or seriously revised so as to bring a variation of it within the scope of theoretical machinery in which the revised concept is analyzable. Alternatively, we can judge that we have hit conceptual rock bottom. We have come upon a concept that is so fundamental to inquiry that it cannot be analyzed or explicated (to any great extent): a condition or an essential constituent of philosophical analysis and explication. Nothing stands in a more basic relation to such a concept that it can be analyzed in other terms. Few other concepts exist on a conceptual par. Few resources are left for illuminating philosophical explication. Which way we ought to go—elimination or primitive status—will depend on the centrality of the concept to the entire conceptual framework in which we operate. Truth is a candidate for preserving and treating as primitive. So is meaning. Is reference? The question comes to this: Can we preserve our conceptual framework while giving up the idea that language allows us to speak of an extra-linguistic reality? Notice that a negative answer to this question would belie an already established allegiance to constructivism; a negative answer cannot be used in an argument advanced on behalf of constructivism.

Another possibility is that reference is analyzable, or explicable, but only by beings smarter than we are; we philosophers have reached a limitation of human intelligence, not an insight about the constructed metaphysical nature of it all.

Finally, even if it were true that it is not possible to make assertions about the way things are without imbedding into those things the symbol systems we use, that would not be reason to think that things don't exist in an independent way, only that reality's being that way is inexpressible, or inexpressible for us. But what does it matter to the ultimate nature of reality whether we can express its nature? Metaphysical truth need not bend to our frailties and limitations.

I think that Goodman's argument is a poor one, and that many theorists in this dialectic are too impressed with the fundamental thought contained in it. Without the power of Goodman's argument, why realists have to retreat to da stuff is not evident. According to Plain Jane Metaphysics, realists can, without shame, assert that the world is a particular way, fully acknowledging that they might be wrong in detail, but not in the simple thought that that world can itself be carved in ways that conform to a true nature. That's right: Nature can be carved at the joints. Where the carving does hit the joints, we have no reason to believe that the level of discourse in which the carving is expressed is mere intentional layering. We have intentional layering, but driven by a world found, not one made. I turn next to an elaboration of this point.

4. Plain Jane Metaphysics Advanced

Much of Plain Jane Metaphysics has already been unpacked by way of contrast with the above remarks. Plain Jane Metaphysics is a codification and theoretical development of the pretheoretical worldview of ordinary persons: an expression of what P. F. Strawson might call "descriptive metaphysics." What more can be said about the division between the natural and the artificial, and the restriction of realism to the domain of the natural, and of constructivism to the domain of the artificial?

Here is one starting point: How does Plain Jane Metaphysics explain why it is not mere intentional layering all the way down? Consider the layerings that, on appearance, fall within the domain of the artificial. Take the properties of being dumped and being honored as applied to the Benares-Cobb's Creek example considered above. Contrast these properties with the property of being an infant. Plain Jane Metaphysics will tell us that the causal origin of an item's being dumped or honored, and the causal origin of the properties of being dumped or honored, essentially includes the role of social convention and construction. But the causal origin of an item's being an infant, and the causal origin of the property of being an infant, does not include the role of social convention. Being an infant is explained by the laws of nature and by state descriptions of the world at particular times (state descriptions for instance, in terms of spatial and temporal relations). The best explanations in each case dovetail with the intuitions of realism for the naturally occurring, and with intuitions of constructivism for the artificially created.

The distinction between the real and the constructed (as regards realism and constructivism) is the distinction between the intentional layerings whose descriptions are the results of an independent causal order on to which our linguistic resources are designed to map (even if the mapping is imperfect), as opposed to the intentional layerings whose descriptions are the upshots of social conventions that need not pay heed to the structures of an independently constrained world. We (a society, or a community of interpreters, or what have you) can do as we wish with, and playful dicker over, the conceptual constraints on games, or Anselm Keifer's works, or Charles Dickens' novels, or chairs, or even what we mean when we say, "Stand roughly there." But we cannot do that with chickens and the Ebola virus. If convention could allow it that a chicken could be a monkey wrench, then, according to Plain Jane Metaphysics, all hell breaks loose.

5. Plain Jane Metaphysics and Identity Conditions

Plain Jane Metaphysics is also fairly rigid about identity conditions for the natural, and quite flexible about identity conditions for the artificial. Any chicken is only contingently feathered and two eyed. A chicken could lack either property by being shaved or by losing an eye, and still remain a chicken. But a chicken could not lack the property of being a bird, or an animal, or a creature with a heart, and still be a chicken. Some properties that a chicken has are essential to its being a chicken in such a way that they establish the boundary conditions for any item's being a member of the natural kind "chicken." This identity is an upshot of the pretheoretical thought that a natural thing can only undergo particular kinds of changes; other changes result in the perishing of such things. Again, on this score, nature will not sway to the vagaries of social convention. But Plain Jane Metaphysics is quite open to the prospect that what a poem is, or a loving gesture, or an epoch or era, or a watch with several replaced parts, is revisable and that no tight identity conditions for such items are discoverable. We as a society of interpreters could change the rules.

Note that when Krausz turns his attention in chapter ten to questions of indeterminacy and identity, he first considers an essentialist treatment of identity conditions (LR, p. 106), but then moves to a family resemblance view espoused by Wittgenstein and advanced by Harré and others (LR, pp. 106–110). The question of identity has interesting implications for Krausz's treatment of the singularism versus multiplism controversy in light of the possibility of indeterminate objects, but what is illuminating here is Krausz's preparedness to treat the views of identity on a par. Krausz favors the family resemblance view. Plain Jane Metaphysics will favor essentialist conditions for the domain of natural kinds, and be open to a Wittgensteinian treatment of identity for the artificial.

With all the attention Wittgenstein received for those famed passages about games, it is unusual that he and his followers made off so well with an indictment on essentialist accounts of identity. Has no one noticed that games are artifacts? Why there might be no essential features required of all games is easy to understand. In the passages Krausz quotes (LR, p. 107), the examples Wittgenstein offers after his discussion of games are: Moses, Egypt, the Israelites, red, dark, and sweet.[3] But Wittgenstein defends only the case of games in any detail. According to Plain Jane Metaphysics, Egypt and the Israelites are candidates for the family resemblance treatment since the identity conditions of these things contain a large conventional factor. Moses is a troublesome case turning on tricky matters regarding the meaning of proper names. Red, dark, and sweet are a mixed bag. They are also properties and not things. Nowhere did Wittgenstein speak of a family resemblance account of identity for gold, or titmouse, or elephant. For these types of items, the essentialist account of identity squares much better with Plain Jane Metaphysics, and rightly so. If nature presents itself to us with joints that we might carve, and if what it presents will not sway to our conventions, then nature sets the limits; we do not. Essentialism is an expression of nature's limitations on what is ontologically possible for natural items.

Essentialism helps to show why nature is not mere intentional layering all the way down. Some of the layers that we "construct" within our "symbol systems" will be built around an effort to capture the essential identity conditions for members of natural kinds. Following Saul Kripke, we can fully acknowledge that this is an empirical matter. We can get it wrong. We must, then, in the spirit of W. V. O. Quine, stand prepared to acquiesce, on the basis of good evidence, to a revision of our best scientific theories, acknowledging that the essential features of the items we countenance in nature might be different than what we believed. But that is merely the interface between epistemology and metaphysics, between knowledge and the world. This is not a surprise.

6. Plain Jane Metaphysics and the Appearance of Competing Ontological Mappings

Plain Jane Metaphysics also has a clean explanation for why different symbol systems or conceptual schemes or theoretical frameworks will yield different ways of parsing the world, even for the natural. In *Sameness and Substance*, David Wiggins offers the following analogy: Think of our conceptual applications to the world as a set of differently sized nets that we cast into the sea, some with finer, others with coarser weavings. What we draw from the sea will be a function of how fine our conceptual net is. Different sized nets will draw from the sea different creatures within it. But that does not mean that our nets shape what is in the sea; our nets shape what we can get from it. So it goes with our symbol systems, theoretical apparatuses, conceptual schemes, and so on, in relation to extra-linguistic reality. That different conceptual resources will parse up the world differently is not evidence against the world being the way it is. Cellular biologists fix upon different aspects of biological life than do botanists, but neither denies *tout court* the reality of the other's distinctions and discoveries.

Some might press Plain Jane's Metaphysics here, inviting her to give up her conventional worldview. For, how are all of these differing conceptual systems to fit together? If, for instance, what counts as illness in Chinese medicine does not dovetail with Western practice, how can we acknowledge the legitimacy of both when each is applied to the same patient's symptoms or maladies? How, for that matter, do we even reconcile the ontological parsing of the cellular biologist with that of the botanist? If a plant is composed of nothing but cells, then, if the cellular biologist gets her theory correct, what ontological meat is left for the botanist?

Plain Jane has to go to graduate school and study philosophy to go much further here. She will depart from the ordinary intuitions that might be found in pretheoretical conviction. But Sophisticated, albeit Formerly Plain, Jane Metaphysics will make every effort to advance views only to the extent that they bolster central elements of the picture as already sketched, while at the same time doing as little violence to ordinary thought as possible. Sophisticated Jane Metaphysics does have an explanation for the relations between the different ontological mappings that nature presents to us. Sometimes she will use the term "supervenience." But that term has taken on such a technical meaning, and debates over it have become so highly derived, that the basic intuition behind it has become lost. A more plausible term is "constitution." A plant is constituted out of a set of cells. A plant cannot be identified with or reduced to a set of cells since such a plant could lose a few cells and still remain the same plant, or it could have been damaged just slightly and, in healing, grown a different set of cells, and yet remain the same plant. So, what a plant is, and its identity conditions, are not the same conditions as applied to a collection of cells that constitute the plant.

In general, the relation of constitution allows Plain Jane Metaphysics to sustain a rich ontological inventory allowing for levels of nature. Lower levels of nature serve as a constitutive basis for higher levels of nature. Chemical properties are constituted out of physical ones; biological out of chemical; biological properties of animal and plant life are constituted out of cellular biological properties. The ontological status of the higher levels of nature cannot be reduced by an exhaustive characterization of those levels from the perspective of the framework of lower levels. Why? Because, as indicated in the previous paragraph, no attempt at reduction will be supported by true counterfactuals. No plant is identical with some set of cells, since any plant— while remaining the same plant—could have had a different set of cells than the particular set that it had. Here Sophisticated Jane Metaphysics has offered a way to save, in realist fashion, the legitimacy of a good deal of the inten-

tional layering that her critics have called attention to as mere intentional layering, and as a reason to leave Plain Jane Metaphysics behind.

7. Sophisticated Jane's Defense of the Relation of Constitution and the Importance of Levels of Nature

It is by way of the constitution relation that Donald Davidson, Daniel Dennett
and others have saved the legitimacy of folk psychological concepts from a
skeptical form of reductivism to the purely neurobiological. A similar move is
adrift, inspired by John McDowell, Wiggins, Richard Boyd, Nicholas Stur-
geon and others, as to the relationship between moral and natural properties.
Jagewon Kim has attempted to discredit standard accounts of the relation of
supervenience. We might object that the supervenience relation is just a more
logically precise relation than the messy constitution relation, and that Kim's
attack on supervenience can apply just as readily to constitution. So, the objection will go, Kim has cast doubt on the legitimacy of the supervening properties in light of what looks to be their casual impotence in relation to the su-
pervened properties. Does Kim's criticism apply to the constitution relation?
Perhaps. Note that one assumption driving Kim's work is that explanatory
relevance is exhausted by causal explanation. Need the metaphysical enterprise of ontology demand the same standard?

If, in terms of causal efficacy, according to Kim, no beliefs (or other folk
psychological notions) explain human behavior, because brain chemistry is all
that is needed to do so, should the ontologist grant that no beliefs exist, or that
beliefs are not constituted out of some kind of physical states? This would be
rash. Here is one quick argument for why it would be so. Consider the entire
set of psychological states of some possible world. Make the possible world
our actual one. Imagine that the states can be exhaustively explained purely in
terms of neurobiological state descriptions and laws. Absorb Kim's charge
that, in terms of causality, beliefs appear to be purely epiphenomenal. Is it
possible that some other set of physical states different from those at work in
the actual world could also provide the same kind of causal basis for a like
range of "human" behavior? If so, then, at an ontological level, mental properties, states and events cannot be eliminated, even if, in any particular possible world, they are fully explicable in terms of some more basic level of nature.

By defending the legitimacy of the constitution relation, and making
plausible the ontological reality of levels of nature, Sophisticated Jane Metaphysics is able to sustain much of what Plain Jane wanted to protect. By doing
so, Plain Jane Metaphysics can even sustain an open-minded attitude toward
such apparent discrepancies as those arising in cases where both Western and
Chinese medicine are applied to the same patient's malady. Given the constitution relation, possibly different kinds of properties, revealed by different

biomedical parsings (revealed by different theoretical frameworks) are each constituted by the same physical creature. We have no reason to assume that different theories are giving rise to different medical "realities." We have just one medical reality—the one applied to the single patient. Different properties, revealed by different conceptual tools, might apply to that person.

The constitution relation does enormous work in explaining the layering between levels of nature. But it can also be applied to explain the relation between the natural and the artificial. Here is where Plain Jane Metaphysics can truly engage Krausz's provocative enterprise in *Limits of Rightness*. All artifacts have to have some natural constitutive basis. People perform plays on stages. Music requires acoustic excitations. Novels are realized on some paper. Poems, in conception, came from some thought, some brain. Chairs are made of wood, or other materials. Canvasses are made of something. Turn to the layering that Krausz considered in discussing the relation between the natural and the artificial. Consider the category infant and either of the categories, "dumped baby" or "honored soul" in the Benares-Cobb's Creek case. In each case the honored soul and the dumped baby were constituted out of the biological item, infant. An account of the possibility of multiplism is close at hand.

Consider this quite striking application of Sophisticated Jane's Metaphysical commitment to levels of nature. Many would identify a person with a *homo sapien*. But simple science fiction stories are sufficient to unseat anyone from this common view. Just as a cell is constituted out of particular matter, but is not identical with that matter, and just as an animal is constituted out of a particular set of cells, but is not identical with those cells, so too is a person constituted out of the human animal *homo sapien*, but is not identical with that animal. This fairly derived philosophical thesis helps to explain how people can have the thought that a person suffering from severe Alzheimer's disease is "not really there" anymore. It also is able to explain why some find abortion morally unproblematic: A fetus is a distinct human being all right, but not a person. Some will retort that here intuition is deeply divided. For each reflective person willing to hold that a fetus is not a person, we can find another who strenuously disagrees. No single interpretation of the moral domain is mandated, and arguments that force exclusivity of interpretive significance appear contrived at best, and downright mean-spirited at times.

Here is an explanation for the above dispute, an explanation that fits with these reflections regarding levels of nature and the relation of constitution, and that invites the interpretive thesis of multiplism: The category of person, unlike the category human being or *homo sapien*, is not a natural kind. The category is an artifact. In the case of person in the typical as opposed to the science fiction cases, a natural kind serves as a constitutive basis for a constructed item. And, as with all matters of social convention, especially those in which we are so deeply invested as we are in the intimate concept of a person, the boundaries of how the conventions get applied are a matter of social and political artistry and conflict. Here, in the contact between our animal nature and our morality, is a touchstone betwixt realism and constructivism.

This discussion of the concept of a person, as emerging out of Sophisticated Jane Metaphysics, is not meant as a digression. I believe that it can be used as a model speaking to the heart of the issues in *Limits of Rightness.*

8. Sophisticated Jane Metaphysics and the Possibility of Multiplism, Imputed Properties, and Oh, So Much More!

In both *Rightness and Reason* and *Limits of Rightness,* Krausz's adversaries are those resistant to the unorthodox mixes in the debate about interpretation and the debate about ontology. In particular, in his earlier work, Krausz was arguing for the possibility of constructivism coupled with singularism, or realism coupled with multiplism. In his recent work, he has taken on constructive realists who embrace more subtly shaded variations on those two camps. If I might issue one serious criticism of Krausz's enterprise, he has set the standards of his inquiry too low. Krausz's detachability thesis is a thesis regarding what is logically possible. But this is an inadequate litmus test for worthy theories at the crossroads of ontology and interpretation. A worthy theory should not just show that, for instance, multiplism coupled with realism is possible. It should show that coupling to be plausible. Throughout Krausz's work, in his writing, he wavers between these two standards.

This essay is a metaphysics for Krausz. Here is one way to be a realist and a multiplist, meant to make the coupling plausible, offered as the truth. This is a form of constructive realism in that it restricts the scope of realism to the natural, and permits constructivism to reign in the domain of the artificial. The crescendo comes by making use of the levels of nature and the relation of constitution to suggest how objects of interpretation can be constituted out of, but not reducible to, the natural items on which they are built. Constructivism allows us to make sense, quite easily, of multiplism. Multiple interpretations of objects of interpretation are not tied to the determinacies of natural objects because they are not natural objects, even though they are tied to them in a quite basic way, as in the way that a statue that is made out of bronze is tied to the bronze. But the aesthetic properties in virtue of which the statue is an object of interpretation cannot be reduced to the properties of the bronze, for they are different.

This is how Krausz and Paul Thom should meet Robert Stecker's challenge regarding the possibility of imputed properties. Imputed properties are properties an intentional object acquires by virtue of interpretations of it. Stecker claims, for simple reasons associated with Leibniz's Law, that an object cannot both be predicated of, and at the same time, have a property imputed to it in the act of predication. The object has the property, and the predication is true in virtue of that; or it does not, in which case, no amount of saying it has it will give it something it does not have. Krausz and Thom have it almost right. They postulate an "object as such" and an "intentional object" (though this is not Thom's terminology). This postulation fits with the metaphysical machinery of the relation of constitution as advanced by Sophisticated Jane Metaphysics. It also suggests that the relation of constitution here is one in which a shift is made between the natural and the artificial. (Think of the relation between *homo sapien* and person as sketched above.) But when Stecker attacks Krausz's and Thom's openness to the disputed phenomena of imputed properties, Krausz and Thom hold that the predication applies to the intentional object, and the imputed properties are confirmed by virtue of the fact that the imputation relates only indirectly to the object as such. Using the example of a bronze statue of a horse, the predication is of the piece of art, the statue; but the imputation is confirmed only indirectly as it relates to the hunk of matter, the bronze, that can constitute different works of art, and be the object of predication for different imputed properties.

Here is a better view: The predication and the imputation (and an exemplar candidate for the confirmation of multiplism) all occur at the same level—at the level of the work of art, that is, at the level of the intentional object. The reply to Stecker should be that he is imposing the constraints of identity for a realist account of natural kinds onto objects of invention. Our interpretive practices and the rough and tumble struggles among those producing art and those interpreting it do not need to hold fast to the metaphysical constraints of a world fixed by a nature unconcerned with our interpretive practices. In the world of art, and thingamagigies, chairs, and nation states, we set the rules. So we can fudge them. This is a stronger form of multiplism than the one that Krausz and Thom endorse. In a way, they give up the game to Stecker. By holding that multiplism can be confirmed only indirectly in terms of different ways that an object as such could come to constitute an intentional object, they admit that the intentional object itself could not admit of imputed properties, and multiply admissible, but jointly conflicting interpretations. I advise them to shamelessly embrace this transgression against dear Leibniz. No worries. He was not all that concerned with the nutty stuff we twentieth-century free spirits can cook up. He was worried about the facts that fix an entire reality viewed by the divine. Fudging in that case would be blasphemous. But in the world of art, fudging is merely play.

9. Why a Realist's Reliance on Da Stuff is Dangerous and How Constructivist Can a Realist Get?

Earlier I warned the realist of relying exclusively upon da stuff, undifferentiated materia, glub, or whatever the preferred term happens to be. One reason is exhibited in the previous discussion. If a rich ontology can be preserved in an account of the nature of extra-linguistic reality, we have available a robust metaphysical theory that offers a great deal of explanatory power. The power jibes with the pretheoretical thought and talk expressive of ordinary persons' worldviews. We can object that this "ordinary person" is nothing more than twentieth-century Western man. (The gendered description is intended.) Reliance merely on da stuff in the "ultimate nature of it all" guarantees that we avoid bias. The issues here are too vast, but grant that avoiding social and moral bias is a worthy project, even for the cold, heartless work of the metaphysician. A realist of the Plain Jane persuasion will reply that the bias can be avoided while preserving a rich metaphysics, and that the willingness to cast out such a metaphysics to avoid this bias indicates a willingness to shape reality to the moral order we desire. That is backwards. It might even be dangerous.

One argument against reliance on the austere thesis that only da stuff exists at bottom requires a premise that some will not grant. That premise is the one I made use of to instigate Plain Jane Metaphysics: individuals exist. For those who will insist that, in the ultimate nature of reality, we do not need to make room for the basic or primitive thought that particulars exist. I invite them to think through what this would involve. I am suspicious. I doubt that we could even design a purely constructed ontology. Where would we start? Could there be a where in such open logical space? What would we pick out first? Whence our thought of a particular or countable item? This was Strawson's concern in *Individuals*.[4]

If we want a metaphysics to map onto anything remotely like what is featured in our lives, we need the concept of an individual. Once this is granted, then merely working with da stuff will not do, because no items can be differentiated at all without being differentiated by virtue of some feature. A feature is a property. Properties apply to countable items. Now we have individuals and kinds. If, at the most primitive level, a metaphysics acknowledging particulars requires a commitment to properties or features, then da stuff comes differentiated. However da stuff is, the world comes framed in kinds, not just in raw gunk out of which kinds get formed. Why not assume that the kinds are determined by a reality that tells us where the joints are? I think we should. If this all-too-fast scream through a powerful metaphysical strategy is on the right track, you cannot be a realist and have only da stuff. You will never recover a world and will play into the constructivists' camp.

If you do embrace a parceled way that the world is, right at its primitive core, then those parcelings in terms of kinds represent genuine conceptual structures of a reality that is given to us as cognizers and symbol system makers. In this way, even within the domain of the naturally occurring, a realist can embrace much of the spirit of constructivism. A realist cannot hold that things can get constructed in any old way. At the most primitive metaphysical level, our concepts are given by the nature of it all; we do not structure the nature of it all. Given how we have all managed to treat each other over the history of human kind, how scary it would be if it were otherwise.

10. Concluding Methodological Reflections

Why go the route of Plain Jane at all? Why adopt a philosophical strategy that attempts, as best as possible, to track ordinary intuition? The contrast between Plain Jane Metaphysics, and the radical, revisionary pictures of philosophers such as Nelson Goodman is like the contrast between David Hume the naturalist, as opposed to Hume the skeptic, or between Strawson the descriptive metaphysician, in contrast with Quine, the unabashed revisionist. A simple principle of intellectual economy and conservation underlies Plain Jane Metaphysics: Preserve the most by altering the least. We are thereby able to offer the richest worldview with the least philosophical effort. But, in truth, that does not speak to the heart of Plain Jane methodological proclivities. I suspect that the Plain Jane Metaphysician is humbled by the collective wisdom of her history, and by its lived expression in ordinary life. Plain Jane is blue collar and working class. At bottom, the Plain Jane strategy may reflect a philosopher's affections more than it does her reasoned convictions.

In my case, the first philosopher from whom I learned anything was my grandfather, Poppy. He was a bricklayer with an eighth grade education. But he had views. In all honesty, he has always been my audience. If I could not imagine making it plausible to him, then I could not imagine how it might be so. For me, some form of realism must be defended. I cannot imagine how I could tell Poppy, after all of those years of struggling and toil, back aching and fingers bleeding, after he had worked so hard to see me and the rest of his family through it all, that there is no "way the world is." After all those years of hard labor, what I, his grandson, went off to school to learn—what those fancy ivory tower stiffs taught me—was that, really, there were no rocks and trees and stars, not "really." I can imagine convincing him that the bricks in his hands, that the mortar he threw down, that they were just things that we cooked up. He would be disturbed to hear that the chimney place he just built could actually be a carburetor. But, were he alive today, if I sincerely tried to convince him that doggies and fern plants, the moon and sky were just things we constructed, what with all his toil to get me here, I am guessing that he would look at me with a stare of apoplexy that could only be followed by coronary arrest.

Don't worry, Poppy. Something like the worldview that helped you through all those years, something like that is the right one. Maybe the wood box we stuck you in is really a giant bobsled, or could be. But the dirt we threw over it, the earth around you and grass above, and the sky beyond that, well we mortals might be able to soil them horribly, even sinfully, but we cannot change what they are. There, we must bend to the world, and, like you, so will I.

NOTES

1. Michael Krausz, *Limits of Rightness* (LR) (Lanham, Md.: Rowman and Littlefield, 2000).

2. Michael Krausz, *Rightness and Reason: Interpretation in Cultural Practices* (Ithaca: Cornell University Press, 1993).

3. Ludwig Wittgenstein, *Philosophical Investigations*, trans. G. E. M. Anscombe (Oxford: Blackwell, 1968), § 66.79, 87.

4. P. F. Strawson, *Individuals: An Essay in Descriptive Metaphysics* (London: Methuen, 1959).

Twelve

HOW NOT TO BE
A METAPHYSICAL REALIST:
KRAUSZ ON CONSTRUCTIVE REALISM

R. C. Pradhan

In his *Limits of Rightness*, Michael Krausz contrasts constructive realism with classical metaphysical realism ("realism" in his terminology).[1] In this paper I would like to spell out the contours of constructive realism in light of Krausz's explorations and to reiterate the thesis that singularism and multiplism are detachable from realism and constructive realism.

The constructive realist, according to Krausz, argues that in no way can we can understand objects as such, because objects are constituted in some symbol system or a conceptual scheme. This observation imposes a constraint on our interpretations of objects. We do not have an unconstrained way of understanding objects. Objects remain structured within a symbol system or conceptual scheme and cannot remain unaffected by the concepts we use in describing them. To describe is to represent and to represent is to construct. Objects can never be separated from the way they are described. In turn, the external constructive realist allows "stuff" independent of symbol systems—not yet amounting to objects. And the internal constructive realist disallows such "stuff."

According to Krausz, the constructive realist of either variety rejects the idea that objects as such are presented to us in a purely unconceptualized form. Objects and concepts are networked together and are inextricably involved in the process of interpretation. An object X is interpreted I in a symbol system S provided X is nested in S according to the rules of I. The I-rules are codified into S because the interpretation is a rule-embedded process.[2] The constructive realist allows that objects are given only within symbol systems. The interpretive system and its interpreted objects constitute one integrated phenomenon. The object is already impregnated with the concepts with which the object is interpreted. Concepts are the mechanisms through which objects gain their significance.

The constructive realist correctly holds that an object has no defined nature except in the context of the method of interpretation. As an example, Krausz cites the case of the baby in the Ganges. No baby as such exists, only the Hindu understanding of a baby consigned to the holy Ganges for salvation, or the non-Hindu North American understanding of a baby perfunctorily thrown into the Ganges. The difference in the ways of seeing the baby is due to your perspective. For the Hindu, consignation to the Ganges is a mark of respect, but for the North American, that baby is tossed into the Ganges after its death. No doubt, a baby is floating in water, but your perspective adds meaning and constitutes the object.

For the realist, the object is found because it is already there before interpretation takes place, but for the constructive realist the object is made in terms of your interpretation. The idea of making an object arises because objects are "nested in a symbol system" which means that objects have no existence independent of the system to which they belong. This explains why the constructive realist holds that objects have no intrinsic nature except the one conferred on them by a symbol system.

Paul Thom's idea of a "further object" merits attention.[3] He advocates the thesis that interpretation will not be possible if an object does not already exist before interpretation takes place. Interpretation can take place only if an object that is to be interpreted already exists. Interpretations are applied on to the object available for the interpreter. In the case of the baby in the Ganges, the object is the dead baby and the interpretations regard that object (the baby). Interpretations vary because the ways of seeing the object vary. Thom argues that the object is in the background of interpretations; it does not vary along with the interpretations. So the object has to be treated as a "further object" as distinguished from the object as represented. Thom's argument is cogent to the extent that it makes a distinction between the object as such and the object as represented. The uninterpreted object is different from the interpreted one because the second is situated in the symbol system and the first is not. The idea of "further object" suggests that objects like stones or trees are not constructed *per se*. They are already there before we begin to think; they are pre-interpretational or pre-conceptual. In that sense, they are not matters of construction. What are constructed are the objects as interpreted by us, that is, the objects that are made available in our symbol system.

The constructive realist does not accept the idea of a "further object," thinking that it will lead to the old Kantian puzzle regarding the thing-in-itself as distinguished from the thing-as-known. The thing-in-itself has given rise to many speculations as to whether it is something altogether different from the objects known. The constructive realist disowns Immanuel Kant's distinction because he thinks the objects are not out there beyond our conceptual system. For the constructive realist, no distinction exists between objects as they appear and objects as they are. Thom favors the Kantian idea of thing-in-itself (*Ding an sich*), as he cannot explain how the thing can be interpreted in the absence of a thing-in-itself because the thing-in-itself is the "further object" which is beyond the system of interpretation. Thom admits: "The important point is that interpretation displays a three-tier structure. For present purposes I am calling three levels "interpretation," "object-as-represented," and "further object." The labels are not vital; the number of levels is."[4] Thom's three-tier distinction is a response to the constructive realist's plea that there is no object apart from the object-as-represented. For the constructive realist any pre-systemic "stuff" is no object with an identity.

Now the question arises whether there are imputed properties of the object? The constructive realist admits to imputed properties, which are derived from the system in which the objects are represented. For example, in the case of the baby in the Ganges, the Hindu imputes the property of being consigned to the sacred river, whereas the North American imputes the property of being "dumped" in the Ganges. These two properties are such that they do not attach intrinsically to any object as such. The constructive realist questions the distinction between the imputed and non-imputed properties. According to the constructive realist, we can in no way make the distinction in the absence of our being outside the symbol system. If we remain all the while within the system, we can never venture out of it in search for intrinsic properties of the objects apart from the properties that the objects have as occurring within the system. All properties of the object are constructed instead of discovered.

The realist resists the idea that objects have no intrinsic properties as such. Appealing to John Locke's distinction between primary and secondary qualities, the realist argues that primary qualities exist that are independent of our knowledge and interpretation. Interpretations presuppose prior properties that precede attribution of new properties. According to the realist, the property-relativism assumed by the constructive realist must be surrendered for the sake of the proper understanding of the objects concerned.

Constructive realists answer the realist account of the pre-systemic existence of objects and properties by claiming that objects have a system-dependent existence and are constructed by the systems of reference. This logic leads to conceptual relativism. Conceptual relativists claim that objects have, as W. V. O. Quine would put it, a relative existence only in the conceptual scheme.[5] The objects have no existence unless they are embedded in the system of concepts. The concepts determine the objects insofar as objects have only a dependent existence. From conceptual relativism ontological relativism follows. Yet, I suggest, while the nature of objects is a matter concerning the system in which they are posited, it hardly follows that they are manufactured in the system itself; the system contains the objects without making them. Quine does not specify in what way the objects are manufactured.

The realist blocks these moves of relativists and constructive realists by claiming that objects are not system-dependent for their existence and that the system presupposes the existence of objects. Realists admit the need of interpretation but not at the cost of the system-dependence of objects. The second condition is independent of any system of interpretation we adopt. Interpretations do not affect the existence of objects. No reason is to be found why the existence of objects should be relative to any system of interpretation.

In contrast, Hilary Putnam maintains that while objects have no existence outside the system, they exist because they are manufactured. Objects have existence within the system. Putnam writes: "What objects does the world consist of? is a question that it makes sense to ask within a theory or description. Many 'internalist' philosophers, though not all, hold further that there is more than one 'true' theory or description of the world." [6] The availability of many alternative theories or descriptions of the world suggests that the world and its objects cannot be ready-made in the realist sense. Putnam questions the assumption of the realist that objects have a ready-made existence in the world. The world must be described in some theory or other and so we have to presuppose a theory for any set of objects to be described.

Putnam's so-called "internal realism" explains that the world is a matter of description. Already a conceptual element is to be found in all descriptions that makes the world a matter of internal organization. Objects are relativized to systems of description. Krausz interprets Putnam's internal realism as a case of constructive realism because Putnam invokes an internal making of the objects within the symbol system. For an internal realist the objects are to be located within the system and have to be interpreted in terms of the internal rules of the system. This internal realism ensures that no ready-made objects are found in the world. So-called ready-made objects are made within the system. However, Putnam admits "inputs" which exist prior to the system without which the objects cannot be made. He writes: "Internalism does not deny that there are experiential *inputs* to knowledge; knowledge is not a story with no constraints except internal coherence; but it does deny that there are inputs which are not themselves to some extent shaped by our concepts, by the vocabulary we use to report and describe them, or any inputs which admit of only one description, independent of all conceptual choices. . . . The very inputs upon which our knowledge is based are conceptually contaminated inputs; but contaminated inputs are better than none."[7]

The internalist position opposes the possible realist claim that objects are to be described in one and only one way. Putnam denies any intrinsic and essential structure of the world—understood as a collection of objects—that is independent of our conceptual network. Such a world is constructed in terms of our conceptual vocabulary. The internal realist must disown the realist's picture of the world. The realist characteristically claims that the objects of the world have a fixed nature and that they can be represented in a unique way. The unique representation of the world supposedly adheres to a correspondence theory of truth. Putnam opposes this theory to make room for the possibility that the world could be described in many ways. The constructive realist endorses the view that objects must be situated in the conceptual framework in which they are described, and agrees with Putnam that the relativity of objects to concepts must be secured.

In what way can we measure the rightness of the many descriptions of the world or world-versions? Some world-versions must be better than others. Extreme relativism, which claims that anything goes, is absurd because we do evaluate pertinent claims according to available criteria. Putnam's proposal for making truth an ideal limit of all evaluations sets a limit to admissible world-versions. At the same time, Krausz is right to claim that singularism is not incompatible with internal realism or constructivism, and that singularism does not negate the constructivist ideal. A singular description of the world does not commit us to realism per se. Descriptions may converge. All descriptions may not be equally admissible.

The constructive realist accepts that objects do not exist prior to conceptual activity. They arise from such activity. And the world comprised of such objects arises from such activity. Its frameworks carry norms and rules through which we interpret. Limited only by rationality, interpretive schemas exhibit primacy. Krausz's *Limits of Rightness* is a testimony to the demand of reason for fixing the limits of what is right.

NOTES

1. Michael Krausz, *Limits of Rightness* (LR) (Lanham, Md.: Rowman and Littlefield, 2000).

2. Krausz, *Limits of Rightness*, pp. 51–58.

3. Paul Thom, *Making Sense: A Theory of Interpretation* (Lanham, Md.: Rowman and Littlefield, 2000).

4. Paul Thom, "Review of Michael Krausz, *Rightness and Reason*, Joseph Margolis, *Interpretation Radical But Not Unruly*, and Robert Stecker, *The Constructivist Dilemma*," *Literature and Aesthetics: The Journal of the Sydney Society of Literature and Aesthetics* (October 1997), p. 183.

5. W. V. O. Quine, *Ontological Relativity and Other Essays* (New York: University of Columbia Press, 1969).

6. Hilary Putnam, *Reason, Truth, and History.* (Cambridge: Cambridge University Press, 1981), p. 49.

7. *Ibid.*, p. 54.

Thirteen

GETTING IT LESS WRONG,
THE BRAIN'S WAY:
SCIENCE, PRAGMATISM, AND MULTIPLISM

Paul Grobstein

> One's conduct of inquiry is largely shaped by one's answer to the question of whether there must always be a single admissible interpretation. . . . Must there be a single right interpretation for such cultural entities as works of art, literature, music, or other cultural phenomena?[1]

> In both fields [neurobiology and developmental biology], there has been some tendency for investigators to presume that a complex process is "designed" to have a particular, single, and well-defined outcome, and hence to search for some equivalent of a cog and wheel machine which yields that outcome for particular inputs and starting conditions . . . this can cause problems if . . . the nature of [the systems being investigated] is such as to put a premium not on uniformity but on diversity . . . .[2]

> Physical concepts are free creations of the human mind, and are not, however it may seem, uniquely determined by the external world.[3]

Albert Einstein's assertion that "physical concepts" are not "uniquely determined by the external world" may be surprising to people whose experience with science is largely "from the outside." That view is an operational reality of science, one that has wider implications extending well into cultural and philosophical realms. Being professionally a scientist instead of a humanist or philosopher, I will confine myself in this essay largely to science and how it works, and to considerations of brain function that relate to how science works. The context for doing so is Michael Krausz's above-quoted assertion (with which I agree) and question (for which I believe the discussion of science and brain function is relevant). Toward the end of this essay, I sketch some directions that warrant further exploration in connection with issues of the interpretation of cultural entities as opposed to material ones, and of the conduct of inquiry more generally.

1. Science and "Pragmatic" Multiplism

Einstein ought properly to have said "Physical concepts are, as best I can make sense of things from my experiences, free creations of the human mind .

. .". In the present context it is crucial that, to a scientist, understandings are always "summaries of experiences" and have no greater (or lesser) significance than that. One major corollary that follows from science as "making sense of experience" is that all scientific understandings, whether they are called concepts or laws or theories or hypotheses, have in common the same validity within their respective realms of observations made. They effectively summarize existing observations (and make testable predictions about future observations). All scientific understandings have as well the same fundamental vulnerability to being wrong, when tested by further observations.

An additional less obvious corollary of science as evolving summaries of experience is the operational reality Einstein characterized: a given set of observations can always be summarized, in principle, in a multiply admissible way. Not all scientists would agree that this corollary—multiple acceptable stories—follows necessarily from how science works, but virtually all embrace it in practice. Scientists aspire, to one degree or another to findings that do not fit the current understanding (concept, theory, hypothesis, story) in their area of expertise, and require replacement of that understanding with a new and different one, which adequately summarizes both the old observations and the new ones. For this ambition to be entertainable, scientists must believe (consciously or unconsciously) that there exist at any given time summaries different from, but as appropriate as (and, in the long run, better than), those that are currently generally accepted.

Scientists always presume, for operational purposes, that there exist two admissible hypotheses: the one that effectively summarizes observations made to date and the (perhaps not yet described) different one that will also effectively summarize those observations, and some new observations yet to be made. To put it differently, science, which one might have taken to represent the quintessentially singularist mode of inquiry, has at its core a quite profound pragmatic multiplism in its conduct of inquiry, over the short run. Whether science has or does not have, needs or does not need, a presumption of singularism over extended time is a question I return to. For this reason, and for present purposes, I use the term "pragmatic multiplism" to distinguish what is involved in science from Krausz's unmodified multiplism, which (like singularism) is an expectation about the relation between interpretation and the thing being interpreted. The significance of pragmatic multiplism, as it emerges from consideration of some relevant aspects of brain function, is such as to make it quite unlikely, perhaps impossible, to provide a sufficiently certain description of the thing being interpreted so as to say what is its relation to an interpretation of it.

2. The Brain as Inquirer

Pragmatic multiplism is not a characteristic of science alone, but is an inevitable and inescapable characteristic of all human inquiry into material things, because it is a fundamental aspect of the organization of the brain, which is itself the inquirer. I will not defend the assertion that the material brain (instead of the mind or the spirit or the soul or some other material or nonmaterial entity) is the exclusive and sole inquirer.[4] For reasons of space, I will take that as a given and concede, as a necessary stipulation, that my argument for the inevitability of pragmatic multiplism holds only if the given is so. This choice will clear the way to a more focused consideration of some especially relevant aspects of brain organization to which I want to call attention.

One other preliminary is needed before we get to the main argument. As a professional neurobiologist, it would be irresponsible of me not to note that the description of brain organization I am about to give is not the summary of experience that many other neurobiologists would provide (as the summaries of many scientists would not include Einstein's corollary of the nature of science itself). It is crucial to understand, both for professional reasons and as an illustration of the larger argument, that any disagreements here (among neurobiologists) have to do not with the existence or validity of relevant observations, or even with the immediate interpretation of particular observations, but with the degree of priority one gives to particular observations or interpretations in creating the overall summary of experience. This paper is not the place for an extended discussion of theories of brain function, but I will try to make evident the idiosyncrasies of my prioritization as they become relevant. I will also return, with further illustrations, to the central role that the action of giving priority plays in brain function, and in pragmatic multiplism.

3. The Painter and the Audience

Preliminaries completed, let us start with what I call the picture in the head, by which I mean what many people experience when they are looking at some aspect of the world (and at other times, such as when dreaming). A large body of observations of a variety of different kinds are well summarized, to almost any neurobiologist, by saying that the picture in the head corresponds, no more and no less, to some pattern of activity in some quite large number of neurons widely distributed in the brain, in the sense that different pictures correspond one to one with different patterns of activity and that, in the absence of one or another of some large (probably infinite, but bounded) set of patterns of activity, no picture exists in the head.[5]

Two questions arise from this. Who is the painter, or the entity that creates the picture in the head? And who is the audience, or the entity that looks at it? Phrasing the questions this way raises a new set of issues that, like the question of whether anything other than the material brain exists, I do not have the space to pursue here. Are there two, or more "people" in the brain? Do they each, or all have all of the properties we normally mean by personhood? Do one or more have all the properties we normally mean by "painter," by "audience"? These are, I believe, all entertainable and, in principle, an-swerable questions. But the answers to most of them are not central to the arguments I am developing here. Particular characteristics of being a painter and being an audience are crucial to my argument, and I will make evident in the following what these are, and why I want to use these terms. I also do not intend by the phrasing of the questions some sleight of hand that leads to a dramatic but trivial conclusion: both the painter and the audience are the brain. I follow this path to reach a point that is both reasonably robust and distinctly non-trivial: while both the painter and the audience are in the brain, they are neither coextensive with each other, nor with the brain as a whole. The painter of the picture in the head and the audience that peruses it are largely distinct aspects of the brain.

The assertion that the painter and the audience for the picture in the head correspond to distinguishable brain processes summarizes several quite different sets of observations. Perhaps the simplest and most dramatic has to do with phenomena related to the optic nerve head or "blind spot" of the eye.[6] No photoreceptors capable of transducing light into neural signals exist at this anatomical location in the back of the eye. The fact of this piece of anatomy, taken together with the optics of the eye, of what one is looking at, shows the brain receives no direct information whatsoever about a significant portion of the retina. The picture in the head has no hole or unfilled space. Instead, processes within the brain use the incomplete information provided to them to render a continuous and complete picture in the head. Even if you are fully aware that the hole is being rendered invisible, you have no sign whatsoever of that activity in the picture in the head. I call attention to this dissociation by using the terms "painter" and "audience." The tools and creator of aspects of the picture in the head constituting one set of brain processes are invisible to the audience observing the picture, which represents a second, distinct set of brain processes.

I have deliberately used a vague term, brain processes, instead of a more concrete one, such as brain regions or locations. The reason is largely technical. Given existing observations, we find uncertainties about how well localized the picture in the head, such as a discussion of the effects of brain lesions, and about whether the processes involved in elaborating the complete picture in the head are fully distinct or have same significant degree of overlap with those involved in observing it. Neurobiologists familiar with the relevant observations would generally concur with a summary to the effect that brain processes involved in creating from visual input abstracted signals that are adequate to interact successfully with the world are different from those involved in having a picture in the head. And all would be comfortable with the summary that the first, located largely in subcortical parts of the brain, are crucial inputs to the second, largely dependent on the neocortex. The information cannot reach the neocortex except via subcortical processes, and we have abundant evidence that subcortical processing does influence the picture in the head.[7]

4. Tacit Processing and the I-Function

For ease of reference in the following, it will be helpful to have some descriptors for the two distinguishable sets of brain processes. Here are difficult issues that I wish to detour around as not essential to the argument. Let us refer to those processes that contribute to the picture but which one is unaware of and largely cannot control as "unconscious" brain processes and a reminder as "conscious" brain processes. The difficulty is that both terms are freighted with innumerable alternate and corollary meanings that make them both controversial and potentially misleading in the present, rather simple case. A parallel distinction between "implicit" and "explicit" processing is employed in the literature of psychology and cognitive science, but it also is freighted with more meaning and associated controversy than I want or need to deal with.[8] With the hope of keeping things simple, while preserving the useful parallelisms, I will follow the philosopher Michael Polanyi and use "tacit" for the brain processes and sometimes the resultants of which one is unaware. I will use "I-function" for the brain processes that constitute observable internal experiences, such as the picture in the head.[9] While the particular words and usages are idiosyncratic, most neurobiologists would agree that available observations require some kind of dichotomy along these lines. In these terms, I am equating the painter with tacit brain processes and the audience with the I-function.

A second set of observations provides further support for the dichotomy between tacit I-function, and will also serve to lay out the core of the argument for the fundamental character of pragmatic multiplism. Most people are familiar with ambiguous figures, images that are sometimes seen as one thing and sometimes as another (the duck/rabbit, the old/young woman, and so forth.[10] In the present context, familiar observations reveal that, despite a constancy in the inputs from the eye to the implicit processing part of the brain, the picture in the head is bi-stable. Different pictures can and do result from the same input. Here again the observations are both compelling and interesting in their right. For purposes of the present argument, though, what is significant is that the picture in the head contains no sign of the ambiguity itself or of the act of repainting the picture as it goes from one stable state to the other. As in the case of the blind spot, the painter and tools are missing from the picture in the head. The observation of a picture is the business of the I-function, but the tools and a large portion of the painter, the origin of the picture, is elsewhere, in the brain's tacit processing.

5. The Existence of Multiple Admissible Interpretations in Perception

The case of ambiguous figures adds to the understanding of brain function, over and above the painter-audience distinction, the recognition of a step of ambiguity prior to the presentation of the picture to the audience: its appearance in the I-function. For ambiguous figures, the painter can make two admissible pictures of the input. The I-function is not in general aware of the existence of multiple admissible interpretations until it is pointed out, or until one is startled by a change in appearance when seen a second time. The painter (tacit brain processing) "interprets" the input without letting the audience (the I-function) know that there was any ambiguity at all. This characteristic is the second of the two that make the metaphor of the "painter" and the "audience" an appealing one: tacit brain processes not only create the picture without themselves being visible to the audience (the I-function); in doing so, they also commit to one of several admissible possibilities, without that fact being visible to the audience. This feature implies that the existence of more than one admissible interpretation is, whether one is aware of it, a significant factor in perception itself, at a stage in the inquiry process long before it might have been thought that issues of singularism and multiplism arise.

We have reached a key element in the argument that pragmatic multiplism is the way brains work and is fundamental to human inquiry. The point is not only that what the I-function sees is not reality, but also what it does see is the outcome of a prior process of which it is not generally aware and in which multiple admissible possibilities of which the I-function again is not generally aware are reduced to a single observed picture. Tacit brain processes, as revealed by ambiguous figures, are fundamentally multiplist in character, able to generate more than one admissible interpretation of what they are painting.

What is involved in the transition within the brain from multiple admissible paintings inherent in the tacit processing to a single outcome in the I-function? Ambiguous figures tolerate two or more admissible interpretations and, in typical cases, each interpretation involves a different identification of what in the picture constitutes the foreground and what the background. In an approving discussion of "imputational interpretation," Krausz describes this phenomenon as one that "assigns salience to certain aspects of the figures."[11] I referred to the same phenomenon earlier, though in a broader intellectual context, as the degree of priority one gives to particular observations or interpretations in creating the overall summary of experience. So, the transition from multiple admissible paintings to a single outcome (always?) involves some assignment of special significance to some feature of the picture/observations in comparison to others; by changing the priority the picture or summary of observations changes. To avoid misunderstanding, I should emphasize that while the prioritization process may have a "conscious" (I-function) involvement, it need not (as it does not in the example of ambiguous figures). We have increasing reason to believe that the prioritization process, while influenced by a variety of definable factors (cultural, psychological, and so on), also has a degree of indeterminacy or randomness associated with it.[12] Prioritization, in the sense used here, can result in genuinely unexpected and novel pictures or summaries. The significance of prioritization in broader contexts will further emerge toward the end of this essay.

From this point of the argument, the path to my conclusion, that pragmatic multiplism is a central aspect of brain function and so an "inevitable and inescapable characteristic of all human inquiry into material things" should be fairly evident. So, too, should be some of the remaining obstacles along that path. The first, and easiest to deal with, is the issue of whether the blind spot and ambiguous figures are special cases, unique in the property of having a painter (tacit brain processes) tacitly resolving ambiguities before presenting a painting to an audience (the I-function). The answer to this question is a resounding no; the blind spot and ambiguous figures created by humans are usefully unusual. They stand for situations where the underlying brain processes can readily be made apparent, but are in no other way special cases.

It is not, for example, the case that only the creations of artists interested in ambiguity are ambiguous in the sense of having multiple admissible interpretations. All visual input, including that from non-manmade sources, has this property. An instructive, if extreme example, is that of a neurobiologist. Such a person, myself, for example, can and does accept as an admissible interpretation of any scene both a representation of it as a set of well-defined and recognizable objects, and an interpretation of it as a quite large array of independent point sources of light each emitting different sets of photons of distinctive number and wavelength. The second interpretation is the problem to be solved by the brain. In general, lots of pictures in the head can solve it, and one of them is that description itself. It is noteworthy that not even a neurobiologist is likely to be offered by implicit processing the photon interpretation as a picture in the head, despite its being the most real.

Nor is it the case that such ambiguity is limited to visual input. Identical phenomena occur in all sensory realms. The sound of a clarinet playing the note A, for example, consists of a fundamental tone together with a series of overtones sounding at the same time. Under appropriate circumstances it can be heard as a clarinet playing an A or as a series of simultaneously perceived pure tones. Imagine a symphony orchestra, in which a large number of instruments are simultaneously each generating a fundamental tone and a series of overtones. Unbeknownst to the I-function, implicit brain processes have made an enormously complex set of decisions about which overtones to associate with which tones in order to eliminate ambiguity. An enormous number of different, but equally good, symphonies exist in the head, depending on which overtones have been associated with which fundamentals.[13]

6. Ambiguity and Reality

A second and greater obstacle in the path to my conclusion about the fundamental character of pragmatic multiplism has both a professional and a more general aspect to it. Many neurobiologists would argue that the ambiguities to which I am calling attention are in principle not meaningful ones, that the brain is designed by evolution with a series of mechanisms that in practice eliminate most or all of the alternate interpretations, yielding the real picture (or symphony). Correspondingly, many non-neurobiologists (those who are not philosophers interested in multiplism) would contend that the picture (or symphony) in the head is of a real thing; so, that the brain can generate alternative construals is, while interesting and perhaps unsettling, an oddity of the limited capabilities of the material brain, one without broader significance.

My response to these concerns, in both professional and non-professional contexts, is the same. It has to do not with disagreements about observations or about interpretations of observations, but with how one prioritizes in painting the painting that is the summary of those observations. If one starts with the presumption of a reality out there, then the organizational characteristics of the brain to which I have called attention can be regarded as oddities of the material "inquirer" (the brain). Many neurobiologists can continue to study and describe aspects of brain organization that have evolved to make the picture of that reality more real. In doing so both groups are ignoring (or choosing in their painting to deprioritize) the general implication of the phenomena I am describing: the brain does not know that a reality exists out there, and so it cannot, without reservations, assume that it itself has been designed (by evolution) to paint pictures of it.

The point here is important and odd enough to add some extra brushstrokes so that a key portion of the picture I am painting in this essay can be seen in more detail. For a neurobiologist, the only needed input link between the brain and things outside the brain is a set of sensory neurons, signals in these sensory neurons, perhaps together with architectural features of the brain themselves dependent on genetic information constitute the only information the brain has about anything outside of itself. Particular patterns of signals in these sensory neurons are (under most circumstances) the prelude to the picture in the head. And these signals contain nothing special. They can in principle be brought into existence by light from objects in the outside world impinging on sensory neurons in the retina or by, for example, a neurobiologist using electrical stimuli to activate sensory neurons, or for that matter, by processes within the neurons themselves that cause them to generate signals autonomously. In short, the brain does not get any unambiguous information about exactly what is out there; it gets only signals in sensory neurons that it needs to make sense of. It gets no unambiguous information indicating that an "out there" exists.

Perhaps the most significant thing implied by observations on the brain is that the concept of an unambiguous reality, a reality of any kind, is itself an hypothesis made and continually being retested by the inquirer, a painting, one of many possible paintings created by the brain. External reality, ambiguous or otherwise, is a good hypothesis supported by an overwhelming number of observations over a quite long period of time, but external reality is not the starting point for how the brain, and the inquirer, at the deepest level, works. What is real to the brain is the signals it receives and generates, signals that are always ambiguous in the sense of having multiple interpretations. The brain has evolved not to lessen its imperfections in painting pictures of reality, but to make of the ambiguous information it has candidate unambiguous paintings, not one but many, which it can then test by additional observations. The brain is not designed to have a single picture of reality as an outcome, but to explore an infinite variety of candidate pictures. Ambiguity and uncertainty are not the ripples of the imperfect glass through which the brain tries to perceive reality. They are the fundamental reality, both the grist and the tool by which the brain creates all of its paintings. In this light, pragmatic multiplism is not one possible interpretational posture among which inquirers into material things can choose, but instead is the fundamental posture from which all others emerge as alternate possibilities.

7. Science and Pragmatic Multiplism More Completely

I hope the reader understands that, in accord with the overall message of this essay, my aspiration is not to reach conclusions in the sense in which the term is frequently understood. I have painted a picture from a clearly described set of observations. This picture can legitimately be painted from the observations. I do not assert, as I have tried to make evident from the beginning and as follows from my argument, that mine is the only such picture. To put it differently, I assert neither that the argument has any exclusive claim to being true, nor the picture any exclusive claim to being real. Instead, I assert that the picture is an admissible summary of the observations and that a large number of otherwise entertainable pictures are not. I also assert that the picture is viewable by anyone inclined to try and see it for what it is (subject to the limitations of my skill as a painter), and that the picture is of potential use, to myself and others, in helping to define available options for further paintings.

No claim of truth or real? To some, the above may appear such a disclaimer as to make the whole exercise appear worthless. My response to them is that the argument I have developed allows, at the moment, no greater claims than those given, not only in the case of this particular inquiry by me but also, as Einstein suggested, in the case of any other inquiry into material entities by anyone else. Other people, in contrast, may find the directions pointed by my painting so sweeping and unsettling that they reject it out of hand for that opposite reason. Can one do science at all in the absence of some conception of truth or reality against which particular claims can be evaluated? Does this line of thinking not tumble us all into abject and valueless relativism? My answer to these challenges is not only that one can do science in the absence of the concepts of truth and reality, but also, whatever one may think, that is, operationally, the way science is done. Progress in science is not measured by increasing closeness to truth or to the real. It cannot be, because neither truth nor the real is a known location against which proximity can be measured. Progress in science has instead always been measured in terms of distance from ignorance. Science proceeds not by proving truth or reality but by disproving falsity, not by painting the right picture but by painting a picture less wrong than prior pictures. This process, instead of objectivity or some other privileged access to reality, is the basis of the demonstrable power of science.

This assertion is another way of describing pragmatic multiplism, the notion that inquiry proceeds by assuming that, at any given time, there exist two admissible interpretations of available observations: the one currently used and the different one that will, by accounting for available observations and some new ones, replace it. And that returns me to a question posed and deferred earlier in this essay. I have argued that pragmatic multiplism is the operational strategy of science operating in the short run. It demonstrably works, not because of abject relativism but because of a quite rigorous method of continually conceiving and evaluating summaries of increasingly large numbers of observations. Does science have or need a singularist presumption in some absolute sense, in the long run? Many scientists presume, as Einstein may have, that the answer to both questions is yes, that what is going on is the use of pragmatic multiplism to achieve successively closer approximations of reality, and that what drives science is the aspiration to achieve the single perfect painting of it, after which the task is effectively over. Among the observations prioritized in painting such a picture is the history of unification in physics, the achievement of progressively smaller pictures summarizing increasing larger number of observations, creating a sense that a final and complete picture might be achieved.

My answer to the question of whether science has or needs a long-range singularist posture is no and no. The difference between my painting and that of many other scientists is again one of prioritization, instead of the validity of observations or interpretations involved in creating the different paintings. My painting does not highlight the history of unification in physics, or other comparable historical patterns, but modern understandings of the evolutionary process, and some extensions of the kinds of brain operations discussed in this essay. Evolution treats change over time not as the deterministic playing out of a fixed and eternal set of rules but as an exploration that may go in many different directions dependent on chance events, and one that is both modified by and modifier of what it explores.[14] And some neurobiology and cognitive science treats the brain not as a passive observer but as an inquirer, an explorer who learns by acting on what is being observed and, in so doing, necessarily changes to one degree or another the topic of inquiry.[15] This point is most obvious in thinking about explorations of the brain, by the brain, but has much more general applicability in, among other places, quantum physics. In my painting, the historical convergence in physics is not an exemplar of science in general but the possible playing out of the usefulness of a particular painting style.

I regard this set of issues not as settled, but as permitting at the moment two currently admissible interpretations. Whether there will be, at some time in the future, a singularist outcome to science, at which point it will cease to be a significant human activity, is an open question, one that only time will answer, or fail to answer. As for the issue of whether science needs the presumption of singularism in the long run, I argued elsewhere "that this agnostic approach works ought not to be surprising, since it is the way humans first make sense of the world, and the way most humans continue to do so in their day-to-day lives. Children make no presumption about an inevitably fixed number of alternative explanations for a given phenomenon or that there exist basic building blocks of reality. They instead imagine and play, constructing and destroying hypotheses at all levels of organization based on their day-to-day interactions with the world."[16]

Did the brain perhaps evolve as a pragmatic multiplist because that is the most productive posture in a reality that is itself characterized by continual change and exploration? Is inquiry not only an exploration of what is out there, but itself part of the continual change, a creative and a revelatory process?

The issue of whether pragmatic multiplism suffices for the long run has quite broad significance for science, given its implications for thinking about the nature of scientific revolutions and the existence or lack thereof of ways to translate one set of scientific understandings into another. And these issues, in turn, have implications for science education, and for how the place of science is understood in the broader context of culture. My guess is that science would proceed more rapidly (along its infinitely extended trajectory or toward reaching the final picture if such exists) if scientists were generally more aware of what they are about in practice. I also think that the understanding of science by non-scientists, and their engagement with it, would both be desirably enhanced if science's core activity of pragmatic multiplism were better understood. All that, though, is a new painting, and I mention it here as evidence that the current painting is of potential use in conceiving future ones.

8. Pragmatic Multiplism, Multiplism, and Culture

The remaining issue to address is the significance of pragmatic multiplism as evolved in science to Krausz's question whether there must be a single right interpretation for such cultural entities as works of art, literature, music, or other cultural phenomenon. By this point, I assume it can be guessed that, from my perspective, the simplest answer goes roughly as follows: Pragmatic multiplism is inherent in the organization of the material inquirer (the brain) and suffuses all of the primary acts (seeing, hearing, construing) that are involved in inquiring into material objects. Since cultural artifacts are themselves material objects, pragmatic multiplism is an inevitable and inescapable characteristic of the interpretation of cultural objects, and of other material objects. Since we require the interpretation of cultural artifacts to paint not only a picture of the material object itself but also of its creator and context, we tend to expect that the number of admissible interpretations for cultural artifacts is greater than that for other material objects.

Notice, though, that I have, as I mentioned at the outset of this essay, been discussing an interpretational posture, pragmatic multiplism, which has significant overlap with Krausz's multiplism but also a key difference. Krausz poses the question of interpretational postures in terms of whether there exist multiple admissible interpretations inherent in the things being interpreted that. The argument I have developed precludes the possibility for material things of knowing with any reasonable degree of certainty what is or is not inherent in the things being interpreted. All we have are interpretations, and no way, other than via the interpretations and the trajectory of interpretations, to answer the question of whether the things being interpreted inherently require a multiplist interpretational posture. To put it differently, pragmatic multiplism makes it impossible to assert the validity of, or even the desirability of, a multiplist interpretational posture as Krausz defines it. On the other hand, it yields an alternate approach that, for all practical purposes, comes out in the same place: we are, in the interpretation of cultural artifacts, as in the interpretation of material ones, always best off proceeding from the interpretational posture that there exist multiple admissible interpretations.

In this realm, though, I substantially mistrust the range of my observations, and so am inclined to offer the arguments above not as a painting but as a sketch, to be modified, filled in, or rejected entirely by others whose experience with the interpretation of cultural artifacts is greater than mine. For their use, I can think of several places where the sketches may be faulty or need to be filled in. Conceivably (though I do not quite see how), the characteristic of cultural artifacts having been constructed by a human in a particular sociocultural context somehow lessens, instead of adds to, the number of admissible interpretations. The approach here would appeal to intentionality as a distinct and distinguishing property of cultural artifacts and their creation. I do not think such to be true, but that is a whole different painting and, even if we were persuaded of the category distinction, an account would need to be given of why such a property reduces the number of admissible interpretations, since more than one is already present given the existence of the cultural artifact as a material entity.

The sketch might also be discarded on the grounds that it presumes that the problems of cultural interpretation occur on top of the previously existing problems of interpretation of a material object. How to create a painting that does not have this characteristic is not evident to me. My sense is that it would, at a minimum, have to provide a way to portray inquiry into cultural artifacts as involving distinctive brain activities that occur independently of, instead of in sequential relationship to, those involved in inquiry into material objects. Perhaps an admissible painting of this sort can be generated, but I do not think I can do it.

The sketch might be discarded on the grounds mentioned at the outset of this essay, the assumption that the brain (no more and no less) is the inquirer. Related to this is the still deeper assumption that the brain is a material entity, inquiring into things that are themselves, at the core, material entities. Could an admissible painting be done that does not similarly prioritize existing observations on the material nature of human existence, but also does not leave them out? If you accept with me that pragmatic multiplism is inevitable and inescapable, then the answer must be yes. But I am, given the evolution of my painting style over many years, even less likely to be able to do it. Telling and retelling my story, with second thoughts and modifications based on new observations, is far easier (while also listening to the stories of others with an open mind or brain), and I can be awed and fundamentally changed by the experience. As with the inquiry into material artifacts, this is a good path for finding truth if it exists, and a better one than singularism if it turns out that in the interpretation of cultural artifacts, as in material ones, part of the point of the inquiry is the creation of new things into which to inquire.

NOTES

1. Michael Krausz, *Limits of Rightness* (Lanham, Md: Rowman and Littlefield, 2000), p. 1.

2. Paul Grobstein, "From the Head to the Heart: Some Thoughts on Similarities between Brain Function and Morphogenesis, and on Their Significance for Research Methodology and Biological Theory," *Experientia* 44 (1998), p. 962. The full paper is available on line at the URL http://serendip.brynmawr.edu/complexity/hth.html.

3. Albert Einstein and Leopold Infeld, *The Evolution of Physics* (New York: Simon and Schuster, 1938), p. 33.

4. William James, *Pragmatism: A New Name for Some Old Ways of Thinking* (New York: Longman Green, 1907).

5. Karl Popper and John C. Eccles, *The Self and Its Brain* (New York: Springer, 1978); David J. Chalmers, *The Conscious Mind: In Search of a Fundamental Theory* (New York: Oxford University Press, 1996); Francis Crick, *The Astonishing Hypothesis* (New York: Scribner, 1994); Daniel Dennett, *Consciousness Explained* (New York: Little, Brown, 1991); Tor Nørretranders, *The User Illusion: Cutting Consciousness Down to Size* (New York: Viking, 1998); Antonio Damasio, *Descartes' Error: Emotion, Reason, and the Human Brain* (New York: G.P. Putnam, 1994); Antonio Damasio, *The Feeling of What Happens: Body and Emotion in the Making of Consciousness* (New York: Harcourt Brace, 1999); V. S. Ramachandran and Sandra Blakeslee, *Phantoms in the Brain, Probing the Mysteries of the Human Mind* (New York: Wil-

liam Morrow, 1998); Oliver Sacks, *An Anthropologist on Mars* (New York: Knopf, 1995).

6. V. S. Ramachandran, "Blind Spots," *Scientific American* (May 1992), pp. 86–91.

7. Floyd Ratliff, "Contour and Contrast," *Scientific American* (June 1972), pp. 102–109.

8. Zoltan Dienes and Josef Pernar (1999). "A Theory of Implicit and Explicit Knowledge," *Behavioral and Brain Sciences* 22 (1999), pp. 735–755.

9. Michael Polanyi, *The Tacit Dimension* (New York: Doubleday, 1966).

10. Richard Gregory, *Eye and Brain: The Psychology of Seeing* (New York: McGraw-Hill, 1966); Dawn Ades, *Dali's Optical Illusions* (New Haven: Yale University Press, 2000); Bruno Ernst, *The Eye Beguiled* (Köln: Benedikt Taschen, 1992); E. H. Gombrich, *Art and Illusion: A Study in the Psychology of Pictorial Representation* (Princeton: Princeton University Press, 1969).

11. Michael Krausz, *Rightness and Reason* (Ithaca., N. Y.: Cornell University Press, 1993), p. 68.

12. Paul Grobstein, "Variability in Brain Function and Behavior," *The Encyclopedia of Human Behavior*, Vol. 4, ed. V. S. Ramachandran (New York: Academic Press, 1994), pp. 447–458; R. H. S. Carpenter, "A Neural Mechanism That Randomizes Behavior," *Journal of Consciousness Studies* 6 (1999) 13–22.

13. Diana Deutsch, "The Tritone Paradox: A Link Between Music and Speech," *Current Directions in Psychological Science* (1998), pp. 174–180; Diana Deutsch, *Musical Illusions and Paradoxes*, CD (Philomel Records, 1995); see her work at URL = http://psy.ucsd.edu/~ddeutsch/psychology/deutsch_research1.html.

14. Richard Lewontin, *The Triple Helix: Gene, Organism, and Environment* (Cambridge: Harvard University Press, 2001).

15. Margaret A. Boden, *The Creative Mind: Myths and Mechanisms* (New York: Basic Books, 1992); C. R. Gallistell, *The Organization of Learning* (Cambridge: MIT Press, 1990); Gerald Edelman and Giulio Tononi, *A Universe of Consciousness: How Matter Becomes Imagination* (New York: Basic Books, 2000).

16. Grobstein, "From the Head to the Heart," p. 968.

INTERPRETING ACROSS CULTURES

Fourteen

ETHNOCENTRISM AND THE INTERPRETATION OF CULTURAL PRACTICES

V. A. Rao

In this paper I will focus mainly on the differences between Michael Krausz and E. D. Hirsch, Jr., insofar as these differences concern the problem of ethnocentrism and a related problem, namely whether any over-arching standards exist in the interpretation of cultural practices. I will confine myself to Krausz's *Rightness and Reasons* where his philosophical position finds a most trenchant expression.[1] If we were to locate a single common source for the differences between Krausz and Hirsch, we might perhaps find it in their respective attitudes to Immanuel Kant. Krausz steadfastly refuses to privilege, as a requirement of philosophical explanation, what have been traditionally regarded as the seminal Kantian ideas: universality and necessity. In contrast, Hirsch's interpretive theory is largely shaped by these ideas.

As for Krausz's contention that there can be no overarching standards in the interpretation of cultural practices we may concede that measurement is a prerequisite in physical sciences and that it has since graduated to the social sciences making the task of philosophy even more difficult than ever. Equally, there cannot be in principle any overarching standards in aesthetic judgments. Kant himself has ruled out any universally applicable formula in aesthetic matters for these are governed by the principle of taste which in itself is not easy to define.[2] This distinction does not mean that a search for norms or standards must wait till such time as we can discover laws governing aesthetics. We may assume provisionally that just as social norms exist that emerge over a period of time, aesthetic norms also exist. Norms imply control, and if we defer the issue of institutional control for the moment, we may see what a "norm" stands for in Krausz and Hirsch. Krausz favors "consensus," by which he means an agreement over what is an ideally admissible interpretation by informed practitioners (RR, p. 39). This "consensus" invites comparison with Hirsch's "principle of sharability," by which is meant a principle underlying the norms of language.[3]

In spite of the family resemblances, a wide divergence of meaning exists between "consensus" and "sharability" in the way the terms are used. Both terms comprehend some notion of public language, if by public language we mean a language shared by a group or community with common interests or coincidence of interests. In Krausz's "consensus" this notion of public language is implied but the same would exclude any notion of a "pri-

vate language" on grounds of inaccessible mental content. Further, his statement that he finds epistemic difficulties in recovering the original intentions
of creators suggests the inevitability of having to fall back on a linguistic
community for conceptual clarity (RR, p. 47). Intelligibility for Krausz is in
proportion to our accessibility of "social intentionality" and "cultural context"
(RR, p. 63). This view has significant implications. A work of art as a product
of a sociocultural environment carries with it a distinctive mark or signature
and for this reason is untranslatable or irreproducible. Since there can be no
commensurateness in the absence of "correct" translations, not only is pre-
suming to judge artifacts of alien cultures or cultural practices of another
clime absurd; arriving at any objective critical standards is also impossible,
because such standards would require an independent or neutral system.
When no ultimate standards exist, relativism is inescapable.

According to Krausz, ethnocentrism is also ineliminable (RR, p. 107).
The absence of overarching standards and ethnocentrism are closely interre-
lated in Krausz (RR, p. 115). The emphasis in Hirsch's "principle of sharability" on the other hand is on the "function of speech" instead of on linguistic
or syntactical peculiarities, by which Hirsch means that the multiplicity of
syntactical patterns that may be found in several linguistic media the world
over in no way limits cross-cultural understanding.[4] As for norms or standards, Hirsch argues that the meaning of a text is best obtained by following
the author's intended meaning and this intention provides the "discriminating
norm."[5]

Intention, intentionality, and norms are contentious issues in literary and
aesthetic criticism, and it would be well to clarify some basic points in this
regard. When we say, for instance, that the author provides his or her norm or
standard, it would mean that the meaning has its internal reference, which
defies any formulable public language. One implication of such a statement is
that the meaning is somehow accessible through the experience of the work
itself.[6] Experience necessarily varies with each reader and so does the interpretation. The meaning intended by the author is what is to be aimed at as
against, or in preference over, the multiplicity of meanings.

But here is a problem. Supposing we say that intention cannot be known
until realized in a concrete form in the work itself, then what we are in effect
proposing is that a text is known only by the functions determined for them in
the whole. This is exactly the nature of the hermeneutic circle formulated by
Hans-Georg Gadamer on the basis of Heidegger's philosophy. Since Hirsch is
resolutely opposed to Gadamer's theoretical position, the author's intention
advanced by Hirsch must have other implications.[7] By intention, Hirsch suggests that the meaning intended by the author is in the object, determined by
his will, a "determining will."[8] Its verbal import or meaning is sharable on
account of the universality of its characteristics—"type"—even when its
uniqueness, its distinguishing qualities, belong to the conventions of its embodied discourse.[9] Hirsch speaks of "the huge and unencompassable areas of

meaning," and of "this immensity" that language represents.[10] Such phenomena make for the universality of participation at the verbal level, the sheer human ability to adopt alien cultural categories to understand culturally alien meanings provides the necessary calculus for judgment.[11] Hirsch gets around the problem of ethnocentrism with these moves. The problems raised by Krausz in relation to ethnocentrism and overarching standards are in a way intractable if only because the ontology that he draws upon stands in direct opposition to Hirsch's. We will try to gain a perspective on these rival ontologies.

First let us take a look at the "indeterminacy of meaning." For Hirsch, indeterminate meaning is not sharable because it is not self-identical.[12] Meaning is variable when at the mercy of "contexts"; we are left with no normative principle of judgment.[13] Such linguistic skills as the author can command or such linguistic possibilities as his language can reveal are precisely those that enable him to provide a "determinate object" which makes for a valid interpretation.[14] Refusal to entertain a "stable normative principle" results in the so-called indeterminacy of meaning, which legitimizes multiplicity of meanings.[15] To this, Krausz replies that the distinction between determinacy and indeterminacy is a matter of degree and that indeterminate meanings may be "sufficiently determinate and self-identical for requisite interpretive purposes" (RR, p. 129). "Self-identity" and "indeterminacy of meaning" are evidently terms each with specific connotations, and in need of a closer analysis. In this task, a possible help may be found in Krausz's concept of "object-of-interpretation" which forms part of his general theory of multiplism (RR, p. 39). It would appear that this concept is meant to meet the challenge of Hirsch's "determinate object" which roughly stands for the claims of singularist ideal.[16]

The distinctive aspect of object-of-interpretation is its "ontological neutrality" (RR, p. 39 fn). For Krausz, the sheer inaccessibility of intentions gives the lie to any a priori knowledge and this argument in turn enables him not only to posit object-of-interpretation in an ontologically neutral space, but also to transfer the interpretive responsibility on to "informed practitioners" (RR, p. 39). Knowledge becomes socially constituted. Another aspect to Krausz's concept of object-of-interpretation has far-reaching implications. This aspect concerns the idea of "order." Krausz holds that the presuppositions of ontological realism—that affirms a prior order, and of ontological constructionism—that denies such an order—are irrelevant to the consideration of object-of-interpretation as an intentional object (RR, pp. 119–120).

Hirsch's notion of "determinate object" is Kantian and is identified with individual meaning.[17] In its original Kantian formulation, a "determinate object" is what would secure image and thought in one representation, in which "image" roughly corresponds to intuition, while "thought" is reflective capability or understanding that struggles to relate a given representation to its source or origin, not as a thing-in-itself but as an appearance.[18] In a determinate object, understanding and image-forming capability work in tandem and it would not be incorrect to say that a "determinate object" is a product, in ideal conditions, of a genius who is imbued with a spirit which, in its purely aesthetic sense, can present in profusion or in its prodigality ("abundant material") aesthetical ideas that defy any logical analysis.[19] According to Kant, genius is a talent for art not science.[20]

Hirsch claims, in the context of his principle of sharability, that something exists in speech that surpasses meaning: "unencompassable areas of meaning."[21] This statement is best understood in relation to Kant's concept of genius whose expressive capability through his "sensuous incarnations" (Wordsworth's phrase) can be neither exhausted by the medium he chooses nor extended beyond the bounds of the medium.[22] The boundaries of the determinate object are neither fixed nor unfixed. Hirsch's answer to the second aspect of object-of-interpretation, namely "order," would be that the object-of-interpretation, insofar as an "intentional object" (on Krausz's testimony, pp. 119–120), is a willed object. "Will" here may be understood not in its narrower sense of "object of desire" but in its wider and more expansive sense in which Kant uses it in his *Critique of Practical Reason*—"Rational Will" (*Wille*)— where its determining ground is provided only by the form, its a priori principle.[23]

The only way to get around the problem of order is through "recognition."[24] This recognition, or "re-cognitive interpretation," as Hirsch calls it, in its Kantian formulation facilitates recapturing the order in which the act of synthesis is achieved in the representations.[25] Any other order would be an accidental order with no necessity following their connections.[26] Krausz's theory of multiplism, it may be remembered, is obliged to abandon causality.

Krausz says that self-identity is not limited to determinacy, but is extendable to indeterminacy of meaning (RR, p. 129). "Self" for Krausz is not the authorial or individual self but that of society. He endorses social intentionality of meaning in place of Hirsch's individual intentionality (RR, p. 130). Given the orientation of thought in *Rightness and Reasons* concerned largely with the interpretation of cultural practices, one wonders whether the phrase "social intentionality" purports to show that any significance and meaning found in social life may be attributed to culture than to some inaccessible antecedent cause. The notion of collectivity, implicit in "social intentionality," has an unmistakable public aspect to derive meanings from.

Perhaps for this reason, Krausz finds himself in agreement with Clifford Geertz (RR, pp. 107, 114), whose interpretive approach to culture makes meaning a public affair: "Culture is public because meaning is."[27] Geertz's appeal lies primarily in his distrust of scientism: an experimental science is in search of "law," whereas an interpretive one is in search of "meaning."[28] Law is associated with causality, which in turn involves the problematical antecedents and consequents. Cultural diversity cannot be reduced to a single cause and even if it were for simplification, it would still be deemed invalid: "our own constructions" are imposed on "other people's constructions."[29] Krausz's concepts of determinateness and identity ("indeterminate meanings may be sufficiently determinate and self-identical for requisite interpretive purposes") may be glossed this way. "Determinations" refer strictly to cultural determinations where the notion of culture eschews any primordial cause. "Identity" likewise is not relating oneself to some mythical "essential self": it springs from a general social mind and is incomplete without it, which perhaps is why contextualization is so crucial in Krausz.

"Identity" for Hirsch is what makes for sharability, and in this respect the concept is comparable to "identity" in Krausz where it originates in the public social mind. But here they part company, for Hirsch rules out the sharability of indeterminate meaning. Sharability presupposes commonality (in the sense of being "identical" and this has to be stable and unchanging for it to be sharable. This sharability requires no precision or clarity but determinacy, which is a capability for specifying and particularizing linguistic possibilities within a vast concourse of meaning.[30] Although "determinacy" is not to be confused with "determinate sequence of words," it does require on the one hand a determining subject for providing the normative principle in order to identify the intended meaning and on the other necessary connections— determinate connections—for the purposes of cognition.[31] Necessity of connections implies causation. Determinacy supplies subjective and objective grounds for self-identity. Causation, it may be remembered, has little or no place in Krausz's theory.

Let us examine the ineliminability of ethnocentrism in interpretation that dominates Krausz's theory of multiplism. Krausz asserts that his thesis of multiplism is not meant to establish object-of-interpretation as its interpretation but to undermine interpretation (RR, p. 130). His notion of multiplism questions authorial meaning and intention as an ideal basis for the interpretation of a text, while his notion of indeterminacy challenges, to borrow a phrase from Gerald Graff, "the traditional premises of literary study."[32] The issue is not as alarming as it appears because as Arnold Isenberg says "the importance or unimportance of a subject, its supposed rank in a hierarchy of eminence, has been settled perhaps long ago; opinions vary in accordance with our reflective preferences; only the idea of evaluating the aesthetic importance of a subject, as a quality, survives."[33]

Ethnocentrism has a surprising connection with the "present-mindedness" which is often cited as one of the most distinguishing features of the Enlightenment in its search for "hard, ascertained fact."[34] Such a quest must logically prefer in what is called "cultural posits" the myth of physical objects to the myths of Homeric gods because of the efficaciousness of the myth of physical objects, the factual component superseding the mythical component.[35] The next logical step is to proclaim that meaning is an affair of the "linguistic form" and that it resides in words and words alone, which renders on the whole definitions, synonymies, and translations an unreliable component of the cultural baggage. Scientific hypothesis will henceforth negotiate meanings.[36]

If meaning is to be sought in words and linguistic forms—anything else is unreliable for scientific scepticism—may not human institutions be subject to a similar rigorous analysis? Search for objective validity places strange obligations on man: to bring existence within the ambit of reason, Descartes had to ask himself whether he was the author of his thoughts.[37] This is what is meant by "language building positions of authority which language itself calls into question."[38] The classic Cartesian preoccupation with "foundations" resurfaces with a greater insistence and vigor in Thomas Kuhn.[39] Kuhn argues forcefully that the paradigm choice—which world to live in or which universe of discourse to participate in—is like making a choice between competing political institutions.[40]

One of the ominous implications of Kuhn's work is that scientific knowledge is shown to be the outcome of broad political processes and institutional arrangements. If knowledge exists not in its own right but as a form of socio-cognitive processes, owing its existence to social structures and institutions, and if no standard or process of evaluation is higher than the "assent of the relevant community" (Kuhn's phrase), interpretation will be at the mercy of "contexts" and without a normative criterion.[41] Claude Lévi-Strauss, for instance, characterizes the entire period between the sixteenth and nineteenth centuries as the period during which "direct or indirect destruction" was wrought by the western world upon non-western societies. The ostensible reason: to "found its own reality."[42] Here, and in the distinction he makes between "cold" and "hot" societies, Levi-Strauss emphasizes the structural necessity of history as a fabrication to effect change.[43] What we are witness to in such studies is that intentionality and subjectivity make way for structures and patterns with the result meaning is determined through cultural constructs and social structures. Krausz's theories of "social intentionality of meaning" and "ethnocentrism" acquire significance against this background as they express a deep longing for an idea of community on a sounder basis than on Kantian categories.

Hirsch's statement that meaning is an affair of "consciousness not of words" is a valiant defense of Kantian categories of thought and an attack on the "linguistic turn" of modern philosophy, but does not appreciate fully the nature of the problem faced in philosophy ever since Ludwig Wittgenstein.[44] What Bertrand Russell stated in general terms, ". . . the mistaken tendency among philosophers (since Kant and Berkeley) to allow the description of the world to be influenced unduly by considerations derived from the nature of human knowledge" had been taken far afield by Wittgenstein.[45] His oft-quoted words, "What we cannot speak about we must pass over in silence" sums up the logical necessity of "words" to make sense of existence when cognitive forms collapse. Any other articulation of the perception of existence will be explanatory and illusory. Kuhn understandably invokes Wittgenstein's authority to note that identifying and naming would have been simpler if not for the existence of natural families and that what goes for meaning is so only by virtue of convention.[46] The incommensurability of competing paradigms, Kuhn concludes, calls for a "new aesthetic" for its articulation.[47] You wonder whether there has not been an appropriate aesthetic already. Friedrich Nietzsche, developing Arthur Schopenhauer's ideas, accounts for the Dionysian principle in the Greek tragedy in the terrible awe that seizes upon man when he is unable to account for the cognitive forms of a phenomenon that reason cannot cope with.[48] Nietzsche with his descriptions of the collapse of the *principium individuationis* in the face of what may be seen only as a stupendous religious experience may have contributed not a little to Gadamer's rejection of the Cartesian "I" (what Hirsch identifies as Gadamer's "anti-intentional-ism").[49] Gadamer, it may be mentioned, like Nietzsche, resurrects some of these seminal Greek ideas.[50] A model for the kind of experience that Kuhn describes in his work does exist.

What is interesting for our purposes is what Gadamer does with this model. He rejects the "romantic hermeneutics" (associated with Kant and his followers) on grounds that in its interpretation of aesthetic and historical consciousness it surrenders itself to the writer's mind.[51] Understanding is not a matter of subjectivity but of communality and tradition.[52] Tradition in Gadamer is what is appropriated by the interpreter who "listens" to what "reaches" him from tradition as it works itself out.[53] In this way Gadamer seeks to overcome the subject-object distinction implicit in the "romantic hermeneutics" that ostensibly limits understanding. This line of thinking has affinity with Heidegger whose notion of "aletheia" or "unconcealment" carries with it the suggestion of a "self" that comes into its own after a long stupor or self-forgetfulness, a notion radically different from "self-consciousness" so meticulously developed by Kant in his *Critique of Pure Reason.*[54] This "aletheia" is not "truth."[55] Similarly, the interpreter is not a knower in Gadamer.[56] "Identity" in the traditional sense of correspondence or agreement between knowledge and its object or between knowledge and being has no relevance in a metaphysic that faces a challenge from the sciences and scientific theorizing.[57]

Heidegger asserts that the philosopher's method of "clearing" also concerns "matter"—"of the presence of what is present."[58] He is using the term "matter" in its double sense of "material substance" and "issue," but without the Aristotelian ontotheological implications.[59] Identity is the "eternal framework of our mind" as Emile Meyerson said.[60] But the identity where ontotheological thinking predominates can only engender "illusions."[61] Metaphysics is now required to cope with science whose business is to reinstate "reality in its rights."[62] Gadamer claims that "the hermeneutical experience is linguistic in nature."[63] With such claim, he is saying no more than that insofar as the philosopher is involved in "matter," in the Heideggerian sense, he can only give utterance to what he "encounters" and what he encounters is what is present or what "presents itself."[64] "Self-identity" would mean: being identical with a "presence," which is not open to interpretation in the old Kantian sense of the possibility of there being a "determinate object" and a "determinable self." Krausz's notion of ineliminability of ethnocentrism springs from a metaphysical need to redraw the map of cultures in the wake of scientific theorizing that subtly undermined the older concept of identity along with the concept of reality. When we assert that "it is not possible to eliminate time" because reversibility is unknown to nature, ethnocentrism must inevitably follow in which experiential content is open to recontextualization and reinterpretation.[65]

But to accept Krausz's formidable position is to concede his antifoundationalism and give up Kant's concepts of universality and necessity. To meet Krausz's challenge you are obliged to return to the central theme of *Rightness and Reasons.* Krausz contends that since no overarching standards exist, looking for a single right interpretation is fruitless. The crucial word here is "right." Krausz enlists Kuhn's concept of incommensurability to buttress his theory: the semantic code embedded in any cultural system makes its language untranslatable (RR, p. 106). Kuhn has argued for the articulation of a new paradigm because the old one initiated by Descartes and Newton has served its purpose.[66] Russell's dictum is instructive here: the notions of "right" or "wrong" do not apply in interpretation as a scientific concept, the choice between two interpretations, both satisfactory, is determined by taste and convenience.[67] The concept of right *(Recht)* in Kant is a concept in the understanding and it represents the moral property of actions.[68]

Interpretation at bottom is a moral idea or it has a moral significance. This is not surprising because according to Kant we know nothing about objects-in-themselves, only our mode of perceiving them and this is sharable universally: ". . . a mode which is peculiar to us, and not necessarily shared in by every being, though, certainly by every human being."[69] We may argue that as far as objects-of-representations are concerned what binds together diverse cultures is the content of their representations, whether the conceptions of these representations are crude or subtle, confused or clear.[70] Evidently some rule may be assumed in the act of synthesis by which the object is "given" in representations. But what distinguishes one culture from another culture is the power of abstraction. This capability for abstraction, often said to be the most arduous function of understanding, can present in representations the possibilities of a unity of a quite high order. If we assume that some kind of spontaneous morality is common to all cultures (irrespective of what brought this about: habit, custom or coercion) an "advanced" culture may show a remarkable propensity to investigate into the origins or springs of this moral impulse or principle.

Let me illustrate: the great insight of the nineteenth-century sociology, we are told, was into how the apparently irrational customs and practices in a society contributed not a little to the maintenance of the social order.[71] In the twentieth century, ethnographical studies, combined with psychology and cultural anthropology, demonstrate the significance of emotions in meaning-production.[72] Emotions, according to one theory, are grounded in mankind's biological endowment ("endogenous") and they are meaning-independent universals; according to another theory, emotions are constituted by culturally provided models and meaning-dependent ("exogenous").[73] According to Leo Leventhal, "emotional elements" in a child become "emotional experience" only through the "conceptualizations of affect," cognition is intimately bound up with emotion.[74] Paul Heelas who endorses these theories of emotion, argues that emotions are universal and culture-specific: emotional elements or perturbations "provide the inner or endogenous basis for what is universal or necessary to get emotional life underway; meanings, varying across cultures, provide the basis for what is culture-specific at the level of emotions themselves."[75]

My point is not that Kant's philosophical position finds confirmation or corroboration in these ethnographical studies, but that however much the rules informing the moral code differ from culture to culture, a common thread runs through them: an implicit acknowledgement of a relation between the "sensible" and the "intelligible" worlds. Only in the higher, more developed cultures, where appropriate cultural models are available, does the relation becomes explicit or recognizable in the cultural representations where the conceptualization of even the less accessible cognitive operations is made possible through the awareness of subjective emotion in the form of self-consciousness.

Krausz quotes with approval Kuhn's view that the concept of incommensurability does not rule out comparability (RR, p. 106). The moral relation that we have described above can be an adjudicating standard in "the reciprocal subjective purposiveness" (Kant's phrase) in the cultural representations. This standard can provide a solution to the problem of ethnocentrism.[76] Robert Hoopes brilliantly demonstrates in his *Right Reason in the English Renaissance* that right reason—*recta ratio*—has been formulated differently in different ages and that when the dignity of man, always associated with the concept of right reason, came to be equated with human power at the end of the seventeenth century, this ontology lost its relevance.[77] When Kant, who derives his concept of right from this older ontology, based on the notion of sinfulness of man, locates the concept in understanding, observing that we would be vainly looking for it in appearances—or representations—he is making human consciousness a snare and salvation.

Without prejudice to Krausz's thought, I will make one brief statement. A close reading of *Rightness and Reasons* will show that Krausz's theory of multiplism has a great deal in common with the postmodern thought in its concern with language, meaning, and even more crucially with difference instead of than identity. Yet, Krausz's work also leaves the impression that the author has glimpsed into the abyss of postmodernism and retreated. He is too humane to be comfortable in its "refusals" and negations. Consequently, he turns his attention to the concepts of "society" and "culture" which appear to be convenient resting places as he looks back wistfully on Kant from whom he had to distance himself to be himself.

NOTES

1. Michael Krausz, *Rightness and Reasons: Interpretations in Cultural Practices* (RR) (Ithaca: Cornell University Press, 1993).

2. Immanuel Kant, *Critique of Judgment*, trans. J. H. Bernard (New York: Hafner, 1951), p. 128.

3. E. D. Hirsch, Jr., *Validity in Interpretation* (New Haven: Yale University Press, 1967), p. 31.

4. *Ibid.*

5. *Ibid*, p. 26.

6. Louis Arnaud Reid, *Meaning in the Arts* (London: George Allen & Unwin, 1969), pp. 223–225.

7. Hirsch, *Validity*, pp. 245 *ff*.

8. *Ibid.*, p. 51.

9. *Ibid.*, pp. 50–51.

10. *Ibid.*, p. 31.

11. E. D. Hirsch, Jr., *The Aims of Interpretation* (Chicago: The University of Chicago Press, 1976), pp. 46–49.

12. Hirsch, *Validity*, p. 45.

13. *Ibid.*, p. 46.

14. *Ibid.,* p. 27.

15. *Ibid.*, p. 46.

16. *Ibid.*, p. 27.

17. Immanuel Kant, *Critique of Pure Reason*, trans. Norman Kemp Smith (London: Macmillan, 1933), p. 274.

18. *Ibid.*, pp. 82–83, 138, 274, 277.

19. Kant, *Judgment*, pp. 156–159.

20. *Ibid.*, p. 161.

21. Hirsch, *Validity*, p. 31.

22. Kant, *Pure Reason*, p. 272.

23. Immanuel Kant, *Critique of Practical Reason*, trans. Thomas Kingsmill Abbott (London: Longmans, Green, and Co., 1954), pp. 268–269, 16.

24. *Ibid.*, p. 146.

25. *Ibid.*, pp. 146–148.

26. *Ibid.*, p. 209.

27. Clifford Geertz, *The Interpretation of Cultures* (New York: Basic Books, 1973), p. 12.

28. *Ibid.*, p. 5.

29. *Ibid.*, p. 9.

30. Hirsch, *Validity*, pp. 47–48, 85.

31. *Ibid.*, p. 46.

32. Gerald Graff, "Determinacy/Indeterminacy," *Critical Terms for Literary Study*, eds. Frank Lentricchia and Thomas McLaughlin (Chicago: The University of Chicago Press, 1990), p. 170.

33. Arnold Isenberg, *Aesthetics and the Theory of Criticism*, ed. William Callaghan et al. (Chicago: The University of Chicago Press, 1973).

34. Ronald N. Stromberg, *Intellectual History of Modern Europe*, 2d ed (Englewood Cliffs, N. J.: Prentice Hall, 1975), pp. 174–175.

35. W. V. O. Quine, *From a Logical Point of View* (Cambridge: Harvard University Press, 1961), p. 44.

36. *Ibid.*, p. 22, 37–38, 45.

37. René Descartes, *Philosophical Writings*, trans. Norman Kemp Smith (London: Macmillan publishing Co., 1952), p. 203.

38. Graff, "Determinacy/Indeterminacy," p. 170.

39. Thomas S. Kuhn, *The Structure of Scientific Revolution* (Chicago: The University of Chicago Press, 1962), p. 84.

40. *Ibid*, pp. 92–93.

41. *Ibid.*, p. 93.

42. Claude Lévi-Strauss, *Structural Anthropology*, vol. 2, trans. Monique Layton (New York and London: Penguin Books, 1978), p. 315.

43. *Ibid.*, pp. 28–29.

44. Hirsch, *Validity*, p. 4.

45. Bertrand Russell, *Human Knowledge: Its Scope and Limits* (New York and London: George Allen and Unwin, 1948), p. 9.

46. Kuhn, *Scientific Revolutions*, p. 45.

47. *Ibid.*, pp. 154–157.

48. Friedrich Nietzsche, "The Birth of Tragedy," trans. Clifton P. Fadiman, *The Philosophy of Nietzsche* (New York: The Modern Library, 1972), pp. 171–172.

49. Hirsch, *Validity*, p. 246.

50. Hans-Georg Gadamer, *Truth and Method*, trans. William Glen-Doepel, ed. John Cumming and Garrett Barden (London: Sheed and Ward, 1975), p. 418.

51. *Ibid.*, p. 39.

52. *Ibid.*, p. 261.

53. *Ibid.*, pp. 419–420.

54. Martin Heidegger, "The End of Philosophy and the Task of Thinking (1964)," trans. Harper Collins Publishers, *Basic Writings*, ed. David Farrell Krell (London: Routledge, 1977), pp. 444–448.

55. Heidegger, "The End of Philosophy," p. 446.

56. Gadamer, *Truth and Method*, p. 449.

57. Robert S. Cohen and Marx W. Wartofsky, "Preface," *The Language of Philosophy*, ed. Morris Lazerowitz (Dordrecht: D. Reidel, 1977), p. vii.

58. Heidegger, "The End of Philosophy," p. 443.

59. *Ibid.*, p. 446.

60. Emile Meyerson, *Identity and Reality* (1908), trans. Kate Loewenberg (London: George Allen and Unwin, 1930), p. 284.

61. *Ibid.*, p. 440.

62. *Ibid.*, p. 284.

63. Gadamer, *Truth and Method*, p. 419.

64. *Ibid.*, p. 419.

65. Meyerson, *Identity and Reality*, p. 284.

66. Kuhn, *Scientific Revolutions*, pp. 120–121.

67. Russell, *Human Knowledge*, p. 256.

68. Kant, *Pure Reason*, p. 83.

69. *Ibid.,* p. 82.

70. *Ibid.,* pp. 134–135.

71. J. W. Burrow, *Evolution and Society* (Cambridge: Cambridge University Press, 1968), pp. 104–105.

72. Clare Armon-Jones, *Varieties of Affect* (New York: Harvester Whetsheaf, 1991).

73. Paul Heelas, "Emotions Across Cultures: Objectivity and Cultural Divergence," *Objectivity and Cultural Divergence,* ed. S. C. Brown (Cambridge: Cambridge University Press), pp. 25–26.

74. *Ibid.,* pp. 37–38.

75. *Ibid.,* p. 38.

76. Kant, *Judgment*, p. 128.

77. Robert Hoopes, *Right Reason in the English Renaissance* (Cambridge: Harvard University Press, 1962), pp. 1–2.

Fifteen

INTERPRETING HISTORICAL LEGACIES: THE ETHOS OF TRANSITION IN EASTERN EUROPE

Andreea Deciu Ritivoi

Throughout the years that followed the collapse of totalitarian regimes in southeastern and central Europe, "transition" has often been synonymous with economic fiasco, ideological confusion, political turmoil, violent ethnic conflict. And the list grows longer and more depressing with every uncovering of the compromised past of yet another leader, with the most recent case of undemocratic elections, or undemocratic forces winning the election on the tide of communist nostalgia. Troubled as it is by these many negative connotations, the word "transition" raises difficulties of reference, which then translate as normative impasse and analytical crisis. Does "transition" mean "change in a liberalizing direction?"[1] If so, how to account for its many setbacks and regressions? If what has been happening in most southeastern and central European countries over the past years is not yet a "transition" to democracy, then how to describe this turbulent shift in political orders?

An understanding of the challenges of transition, and its corresponding definitions and potential prescriptions, are ultimately dependent on how we conceptualize change. The analysis can focus (and has focused) on economic problems, debating whether a marketplace economy can succeed a centralized one. Or, it can tackle political issues regarding the type of democratic governmental structure that can most effectively replace socialist-communist regimes.

In this essay, I deal with social and cultural problems, in particular with the change of mentalities on the post-communist arena. I am interested in the impact of socio-political change on the identity rhetoric of the actors who experience the change. I discuss this impact along two dimensions: the opening to the West that marked the end of the Cold War, and the "trial" of communism as an interpretive process that mandates epistemic and axiological revisions. In my view, how we address the difficulties of transition is influenced by how we explain and interpret the conduct and discourse of post-communist social actors. The suffix "post" already gives away some of the assumptions we readily make about the nature of the gap between what was before and what came after 1989, signaling a departure, as well as a legacy.

But is such a departure the preamble, or the conclusion to larger, cultural and conceptual transformations? Shifts of political power are often, and sometimes hastily, associated with the modification of values, beliefs, and habits. Indeed, with the official disappearance from the public arena of certain *dramatis personae*—the much feared security officers, the omnipotent communist party secretaries, and their acolytes—the cast of characters on the Eastern European social scene has been modified. When individuals no longer have to censor their thinking, speaking, and acting, major behavioral and identity changes are not only possible, but in order. And yet, as the protagonist in one of Ivan Klima's post-1989 novels is forced to admit with much disappointment and surprise, although (or because?) many Eastern Europeans had become so adept at living in oppression, they are having significant difficulties in deciding how to best live in freedom, how to change, or even whether to change.[2]

Such difficulties can be explained as a consequence of the fact that freedom is no more a "natural" human condition than oppression. Both acquire meaning and significance within a cluster of influencing factors—political, social, historical, and political. Freedom does not involve a spontaneous awareness of adequate self-expression or ways of interacting with others. As Seyla Benhabib suggested, some of the problems involved in transplanting democracy onto the formerly communist soil can be explained as a conflict that emerges among different socio-historical opportunities and ideals— liberalism, socialism, market economy, state economy, individualism, communitarianism, and so on—as they are perceived by individuals with different experiences and expectations.[3] The actors who experience this conflict do so as victims and survivors, as well as redeemers and critics of competing ideals. Pulled between opposing roles, they are confronted with the task of redefining themselves, both in order to make sense of the new environment and be able to act meaningfully in it, and in order to learn how to influence opinions and decisions, to gain trust and build alliances.

With the disappearance of the Iron Curtain, Eastern Europe opened up to the West, not only by receiving support and joining its economic structures or political alliances, but also by adopting a lifestyle—attitudes and beliefs, behavioral norms and identity patterns. This adoption, a long and problematic process, began taking place at a difficult time for the region, a time of crisis described by Vaclav Havel as an existential revolution whose success depends not on isolated "mastery over one's ego or over the collective, but rather . . . (on) a . . . revolution within identity formation."[4] But while this "revolution" is still unfolding, many in the former communist countries avoid having to deal with the changes in the social fabric by investing in what political scientist Vladimir Tismaneanu calls "fantasies of salvation," instead of in critical examinations of potential roles and identification models.[5] With the ideological certainties of the previous regimes seriously compromised if not altogether defunct, dilemmas cropping up everywhere in public life are often addressed through recourse to "vindictive and messianic narratives," scapegoating strategies, and de-communization fanaticism.

Relying on Georges Sorel's concept of political myths as twisted representations designed to reify controversial and complex situations by reducing them to easily recognizable and Manichean patterns and characters, Tismaneanu reviews a series of a mythologies that make for a quite dark roster. He records numerous instances of synthesizing the responsibility for totalitarianism through transferring it onto a particular group of individuals, such as the Jewish minorities, blamed as the main culprits in the spread of communism throughout Eastern Europe. He finds economic hardship being explained as caused by the Roma minority, stereotyped as bums and thieves. Dubious nationalist past leaders, such as Romanian pro-Nazi marshal Ion Antonescu, executed as a war criminal in 1946, are remembered and honored as national heroes, while acts of diffidence against communist regimes are minimized or contested.

In Tismaneanu's opinion, shared by some but not all, the region's best hope for rehabilitation lies in its intellectuals, as engines of emancipation and as promoters of an underground liberal tradition they managed to maintain during communism. On such an account, people such as Havel, Adam Michnik, or Andrei Sacharov served as moral compasses during the dark years of communism, maintaining contact with the Western democratic world when Eastern Europe would have otherwise been completely incommunicado. No doubt, intellectuals were major actors during the events that brought about the collapse of communist throughout the region, but less sympathetic commentators have argued that, after 1989, they tried to impose their own agendas by "trading on their past credentials by promulgating their own salvation myths of market rationality, individualism, and liberalism."[6] By opting for solutions steeped in values and beliefs traditionally recognized as hallmarks of a Western mentality, intellectuals implicitly adopted, and tried to convince others to adopt, a certain framework for decision-making and problem solving in the context of transition.

Myths are not by default pernicious and dangerous, or redeeming and useful. They represent, in Claude Lévi-Strauss's terms, plausible models designed to overcome a contradiction, to explain especially problematic social and historical phenomena.[7] As a political myth, the Eastern European intellectual attracts both believers and opponents. Its relevance and effectiveness in the general socio-political context of transition depends on how the myth continues to satisfy and increase the numbers of believers by converting opponents. At the heart of the argument that intellectuals ought to have a major function in post-communist societies is the assumption that these societies are undergoing a transition from authoritarianism to democracy, with democracy seen as an order with readily available models in the Western world.

Jürgen Habermas, for example, sees the political and social changes of 1989 as a "rectifying revolution" (*nachholende Revolution*), and argues that the changes did not bring anything new, but simply allowed eastern and central Europe to join Western democracy in a long awaited epilogue to the French Revolution of 1789.[8] Habermas's reading of what happened in 1989 is also espoused (with various amendments or appendices) by other major figures in political science, such as Françoise Furet, Ernst Nolte, or Timothy Garton Ash.[9] An essential component of analyzing the myth's impact, then, is to see how the Eastern European intellectuals legitimize themselves to their Western colleagues, as a way of asserting their identity as intellectuals. Such a process of legitimization did not begin when communism collapsed: during the Cold War, mostly through émigré communities and specialized media institutions such as Radio Voice of America or Radio Free Europe, there were contacts between intellectuals on the two sides of the Iron Curtain. If a conversation existed, it is not entirely clear that a common language had been found or was being used in any systematic way.

In this paper I analyze the self-legitimization strategies employed by two Romanian intellectuals as they address the West in the aftermath of communism's collapse. My goal is to see how a shared discursive and mental space emerges by being problematized and actively sought, instead of taken for granted, and how these intellectuals adjust and interpret their own political responsibility in the past and in the present in order to inhabit this space. What interests me in particular is the extent to which the two choose self-defining strategies and expressions that articulate an intellectual identity designed to reach out to a Western audience. I coach my analytical findings and theoretical contribution using the key terms and distinctions proposed by Michael Krausz in his reflections on self-identity as an interpretive process.

1. Defining Identity Across Cultures

The question of how to define what we mean by the "identity" of an individual is an especially vexing one, because it is informed by seemingly contradictory efforts. The definition would have to provide a stable conceptual framework, in order to allow us not only to identify an individual upon encounter, but also to recognize her as the same one upon a second encounter. But the definition would also have to account for the change and variation that inevitably occur in a person's life, as a consequence of time. Some philosophical theories see identity as a constant located in individuals and revealed in assorted ways and contexts. Others deem it a variable that transcends individuals and is constituted by an interplay of social, political, cultural, and linguistic forces. Both have advantages and disadvantages that I have presented in more detail elsewhere.[10]

To define identity as sameness or preservation of some essential quality of a person is counterintuitive; yet the very meaning of the term "identity," as used in common discourse, assumes constancy, or the absence of change. This dilemma can be avoided by defining identity as the continuity of situations featuring the same actor, and thus by shifting the emphasis from identifying actors through characteristics to finding patterns that hold together the actions committed and events experienced by that actor in question. Krausz explains identity formation as a process designed to generate connectedness among the varied experiences of a person, as well as signal her responsiveness to the world around her and the afferent events and situations. This process is interpretive insofar as it is based on detecting patterns of coherence, matching responses with situations, and integrating disparate events into a consistent framework.

Unlike David Norton, who argues that individuals actualize their identities by discovering and living out their "innate potentialities," Krausz views identity formation as interpretation of lived experience and deliberation about how to best make sense of such experience.[11] How the interpretation should be fashioned, or the deliberation conceived allows, according to Krausz, for either one or several answers, depending on one's epistemic and ontological commitments, as they are defined or constrained by the cultural context. Norton, on the other hand, insists that each person has an identity-core that must be sought and actualized, as "living one's own truth constitutes integrity, the consummate virtue."[12] From his perspective, "the great enemy of integrity is not falsehood as such but . . . the attractiveness of foreign truths, truths that belong to others . . . . When an individual allows himself to be deflected from his own true course, he fails in that first responsibility from which all other genuine responsibilities follow."[13] Stated in such blunt philosophical terms, Norton's views are bound to repel many more relativistically inclined thinkers, including Krausz himself, who aligns himself more readily with perspectives that posit self-identity as derived from discursive (and hence, social and cultural) practices.

I do not wish to defend Norton's conception, because I disagree with it myself, but I want to point out that, translated in the concrete terms of the post-communist arena, such a conception deserves careful consideration. Should post-communist societies and their members embrace the Western mentality and lifestyle? The belief that communism's demise proves the validity of the Western model is highly controversial, and of those who reject it, some argue that the model simply clashes with the history and tradition of Eastern Europe (others argue that the Western model itself has flaws and problems). If we take Norton's notion of an "inner necessity" to represent, in a modified and significantly de-essentialized way, constraints imposed by historicized experience upon the assimilation of, and participation in assorted discursive practices, I believe we can do more justice to the complexities of identity formation and transformation in Eastern Europe.

Thus, I define identity as the narrative framework that structures lived experience into a coherent and meaningful configuration that makes individuals recognizable to themselves and to others, while also making them accountable for their past actions or decision. The narrative view of identity is widely espoused by theorists of different persuasions, for its capability of doing, in Fred Frohock's words, "that which appears to be exceedingly unlikely: define and interpret an organized self that may be yet distributed across social practices."[14] From a narrative perspective, change, no matter how radical, can be contained in a single framework provided that disparate or contradictory events can be connected in a plot. Plots are not linear or causal sequences, but complex interpretive patterns that function in accordance with a logic of motivation and relevance. To define the identity of post-communist actors in a narrative format is to allow for connections among the events they experienced under both political orders. Detecting such connections requires interpretive work that can establish plots that mediate between disparate components of action—chance occurrences, unfulfilled intentions, unknown causes, unexpected effects—and the temporal unity of the story recounted.

Krausz, too, resorts to the notion of an "inner necessity," defining it as constraints imposed on the actor once he or she has committed to a particular project or activity. Krausz explains the achievement of narrative focus through commitment to particular projects and activities. Projects, ranging from the writing of a book to nurturing the young (Krausz's examples), shape lives into life stories, and life paths into personal programs. In the social arena, personal programs impact one another, as the projects on which they are based can have ethical mandates and implications, and are subject to interpretation and evaluation. In Krausz's view, projects that continue to sustain a person's interest and commitment are the source of continuity across or despite change and transformation. But once a project has been adopted, he believes, "certain things must be done as mandated by the pertinent project, all the while bracketing the question whether those values are approbatory in a moral sense."[15] The "reasons offered in justification of a why a project has been adopted are internal to the standards implicated by the program as a whole which the project serves. Each operates according to different standards, and they are incongruent."[15]

What happens when actors who have formulated different personal programs under different historical and social circumstances meet and try to exchange rationales and motives, as a way of communicating and creating a shared discursive space? If each program operates according to its own standards, is such a task even possible, on Krausz's account? I want to introduce a rhetorical (in the disciplinary sense) perspective on identity formation, one that starts with the assumption that communicative situations represent occasions for community building.

Within a community, the perceived identity of the speaker (or actor) is seen as having a major persuasive impact on how the message is received. Under the rubric of *ethos*, rhetoric recognized as early as in Aristotle's time what twentieth century social psychology confirms with modern scientific evidence: that what a relevant community believes about a person (who they think she is, what they take her defining characteristics to be, how they evaluate her competence on a given matter, and how they locate her beliefs, values, and actions on their ethical scale) informs both the design and the reception of the person's communications and actions. Notice the context-bound aspect of this concept, its grounding in a particular locality, involving a particular community and its expectations, beliefs, norms, and values. Ethos, then, requires us to consider actors' identities in action and interaction, as reputations being formed and received, accepted or contested. Ethos marks the interface between rhetors and their audience, and represents a locus of identity formation controlled by both the first and the second. It is a source of identity and of identification. As "externalization of various aspects of the rhetor's self-structure . . . which affects, that is, contributes to the internalization of the [community's] self-structure," ethos directly and actively shapes a community, in which the speaker and the audience come together.[17]

The concept of ethos has dialectical elasticity, and presents us with the advantage of not having to worry about the "authentic" or "constructed" selfhood. Ethos is predicated on a dialectical and mutual reinforcement of an "authentic" and a "constructed" identity, aligning the effects an actor's perceived identity has on others with concrete strategies that allow these effects to match the actor's intentions. But such reinforcement and aligning is possible through recourse to some shared element—values or models, features or commitments. Krausz's notion of a project can constitute such needed shared element, especially in the case of intellectuals. For what distinguishes them more readily and generally from other professional groups and social actors, if not a commitment to the study of written texts recorded in a tradition of thought? I am aware that I am offering a quite general definition of intellectuals here—one that I scrutinize more closely later on in the paper—but I do so as a way of connecting an ethos-based view of identity formation with a narrative perspective that capitalizes on projects as the focus of emplotment. Also, since ethos develops over time, and is not strictly emergent from one particular interaction, its ultimate expression is bound to incorporate a more comprehensive image of the rhetor—one informed by his or her narrative.

As I mentioned earlier, a narrative view of identity incorporates a theory of interpretation, insofar as plots result from the interpretation of disconnected events and situations. Krausz offers theoretical distinctions that can qualify our understanding of interpretation by asking that we explain our notion of interpretive aims. Thus, in developing a narrative framework that establishes the identity of a particular person, do we feel constrained by accuracy? According to Krausz, interpretation in general can respond to two aims: elucidation or edification. To elucidate is to clarify an issue, while to edify is to incorporate elucidatory insights into different types of problem solving, such as, for example, self-improvement (using the elucidation of tendencies a person has manifested throughout her life in order to help her improve and change). In the case of transition, interpretation can elucidate the role played by assorted individuals within the communist power apparatus, and then use the elucidation to provide edification regarding redemptive measures. Krausz favors elucidation as the primary aim of interpretation, but I suspect many scholars will find his distinction tenuous. What does it mean to elucidate, as long as we do not allow for a purpose of the elucidation in question? As we have learned from philosophers of history and historians themselves, elucidation slips easily into edification, even in the case of the interpretation of historical events, where the accuracy constraint is especially crucial.[18]

But I think the distinction is worth preserving as a heuristic tool, instead of an epistemic differentiation. To want to render clear a set of circumstances, motives, and actions that define one's life story, all along knowing that such rendition serves some goal or purpose (like putting that person in a certain light), is one thing. To provide a deliberately distorted interpretation in order to serve that goal or purpose is a different thing. In the case of controversial projects, such a heuristic distinction becomes fundamentally crucial. It is also fundamental when the interpretive process operates across cultures and seeks to build a common ground, drawing from elucidatory insights. Clearly, however, elucidation is also crucial, especially when the cross-cultural ventures involves overcoming stereotypes, as is the case in an encounter between the parties formerly separated by the Iron Curtain. In the analysis that follows, my focus is on the edificatory aim of interpretive processes at work in creating identity narratives.

2. Reaching Behind the Iron Curtain

In the 2002 April newsletter of the Modern Language Association, the president, Stephen Greenblatt, announced the creation of a new forum for scholarly communication and intellectual exchange (via email communication) designed to bring academics from historically underprivileged countries in Eastern Europe or Africa in contact with their more fortunate Western counterparts for the purpose of discussing common topics of interest, offering bibliographical suggestions (if not more concrete bibliographical help in the form of photocopied articles or even book donations), and facilitating contact with publishers and academic communities of like-minded individuals.[19] On his own admission, Greenblatt was inspired to organize this forum after he was pleasantly surprised, but still surprised, to encounter a lively audience of well-educated and sophisticated scholars when he delivered a paper at the New Europe Institute for Advanced Studies in the Humanities, in Bucharest, Romania, in the fall of 1999. One can hardly reproach Greenblatt his apprehensions prior to the trip to Romania: for many Western academics, the former communist countries are still immersed in the darkness of history, and the profiles of those who live there are accordingly hard to make out. The Iron Curtain blocked physical as well as interpretive access, letting certain things in and keeping others out, and more importantly, twisting the ones that got in so as to make them fit a stereotype, a particular profile or program assumed to be characteristic of those who lived on the other side.

More than a decade before western academics would have had the opportunity to consider a conferencing appointment beyond the Yalta border, art historian Andrei Plesu, director of the New Europe Institute during Greenblatt's visit, signed along with other six Romanian intellectuals a protest letter addressed to Ceausescu. In response, Plesu lost his job on the faculty of the Art History Institute, and was forced to accept employment outside the capital city of Bucharest.

The initiative and signing of the protest letter was one of the few overtly dissident acts performed in a country with anemic (compared to Poland or Czechoslovakia) opposition efforts. The act remained singular in Plesu's career, for the most part the career of an academic and writer interested in the history of religion and aesthetics, but nevertheless consecrated him as an official opponent of communism. After 1989, he was appointed minister of culture under the first postcommunist regime led by president Ion Iliescu; in 1996, he became minister of external affairs in the second postcommunist government led by president Emil Constantinescu. In 2000, Plesu took a third public office as head of the Romanian commission investigating the surveillance files of the former security police. He founded the New Europe Institute for Advanced Studies in 1993, using the funds he had won as a McCarthur Fellow. The New Europe Institute is affiliated with the Wissenschaftskolleg zu Berlin and the Collegium Budapest, and it represents one of the most prestigious post-1989 forums for humanistic and social scientific research in eastern and central Europe.

In an article published in the UC Berkeley-based journal "Representations," and hence primarily addressed to an American audience, Plesu talks about what it means to be an intellectual and a dissident in communist Romania. He uses as a springboard for his reflections the reaction he had when political scientist and Yale professor Bruce Ackerman, with whom in 1990 Plesu had spent six months in residence at the Institute for Advanced Studies in Berlin, asked him how he had managed to remain intellectually fit in a communist country. "To a certain extent," reflects Plesu, "the question flattered me. It meant that I hadn't met his gloomy expectations: I was not inarticulate, I had read other writers besides Marx and Engels, I was perhaps more cosmopolitan than narrowly tribal, I could be accepted as a plausible partner in discussion."[20]

Plesu clearly reads Ackerman's question as an assumption that communist regimes cannot produce or even tolerate intellectuals, as long as to be an intellectual involves an ability to think freely, eloquence, freedom to choose to read and free access to information, and the possibility to move around the world and communicate with other like-minded people—luxuries still partly lacking in eastern European countries, as Greenblatt's initiative recognizes.

Awareness of such an assumption is what also compels Gabriel Liiceanu to attempt to deconstruct the stereotype of the inarticulate, indoctrinated, and tribal Eastern European intellectual, in his 1992 address to the European College of Cultural Co-operation in Luxembourg. A philosopher and publisher, close friend and associate of Plesu both during and after communism, Liiceanu has been a civil rights activist since 1990, but he made no explicitly dissident interventions under Ceausescu.

In his Luxembourg speech, Liiceanu introduces himself to the Western audience via a reflection on the historical and rhetorical situation of his address: "An intellectual coming from the post-war East who has to address a forum of western cultures . . . has . . . the essential pride that, at the other end of a history which had proposed to transform him into a new species of man (the 'new man'), *he has remained a European.* 'Look at me,' this intellectual is saying to you. 'I can write, and on occasion even speak, in three or four modern languages; I learnt Latin and Greek on my own, in order to have access to the ancient philosophical texts in the original. I can discuss Homer, Plato, Saint Augustine, Shakespeare, and Goethe with you; or equally Flaubert, Thomas Mann, Kafka, Yourcenar, and Umberto Eco. I can talk about Derrida too."[21]

Confronted with the task to explain the similarity between intellectuals east of west of the Iron Curtain, both Plesu and Liiceanu proceed by focusing on "technical" competence—a shared commitment to, and familiarity with a body of knowledge, as well as linguistic competence in the idioms of the west. Yet by simply being so wiling to justify or detail the nature of such similarity, they give more than just a nod to the assumption of difference. Their introductory statements reflect an effort to gain acceptance in their audience's community by stressing compatibility with what they presume to be the defining features of the Western academic and intellectual. Recognizing the gap between audience and speaker, or "you-in-the-West/we-in-the-East," they try to bridge it instead of eliminate it.

At this point in my argument, I feel both pressed to offer a definition of the term "intellectual," as well as reluctant to limit its scope by attempting to pin down a precise meaning. As Jeffrey Goldfarb aptly put it, "intellectuals are ambiguous characters. In societies with strong democratic traditions, such as the United States, they are the objects of popular and elite suspicions. In societies with stronger aristocratic traditions, such as those of Central Europe, they are often the objects of veneration and high hopes."[22] Instead of defining the term, allow me to ponder some of the paradoxes and dilemmas that make it so notoriously controversial and fraught with ambiguity.

The history of how the term "intellectuals" has been attributed to assorted social groups, although no less disputed or complicated, sheds some light on these dilemmas and paradoxes. While some historians are trying to extend the origin of "intellectuals" all the way to Socrates or to the Medieval vagrant scholars, it is more commonly assumed that in the modern sense the concept becomes operative in the nineteenth century in France during the Dreyfus Affair, when writers such as Marcel Proust, Paul Valery, or Emile Zola intervened in the political scandal surrounding the case of captain Dreyfus, to demand his release. "It was therefore the action of intervening in politics by intellectuals," note Jeremy Jennings and Tony Kemp-Welch, "that was constitutive of the definition of the noun."[23]

At the same time, however, "intellectual" was deployed in that context also as a term of abuse, to condemn political action taken by individuals whose role was seen as limited to the sphere of theoretical reflection, contemplation, and "disinterested" pursuit of ideas. What makes the meaning of the word "intellectual" especially difficult to pin down is the network of oppositions in which the concept is entangled: opposition to "manual" labor, opposition to political institutions with decisional and executive power (like the State), and even a more diffuse opposition to the average citizen insofar as we deem the intellectuals an elite. If, as we have been repeatedly told, intellectuals' defining characteristic is their concern with ideas instead of action (Julien Benda), or the universal instead of the local (Havel), or the durable instead of the ephemeral (Timothy Garton Ash), should they be involved in public life?[24] Should intellectuals be allowed or asked to make decisions on public matters, or only to critique them?

More than questions, these are dilemmas that shape the intellectual's identity at its core. Benda famously argued, in his *Trahison des clercs*, that intellectuals who offer their specialized competence to support or further political goals more often than not contribute to the wrong goals, because their type of expertise is not a reliable source of political wisdom.[25] Pleading for a strict separation between intellectual or contemplative, and political or active life, Benda made a series of dark prophesies that have been in part confirmed, about what would happen once the separation is not maintained. Traitors in Benda's sense were the French intellectuals who supported the Nazi politics of the Vichy government, or those who championed Stalin. It is such errors of judgment that throw a negative light on intellectuals' involvement in social and political decisions. But on a different account that receives equal confirmation from history, "intellectuals are central democratic actors, and when they leave the political stage, democratic performance ends in failure."[26]

Antonio Gramsci's concept of intellectuals promises to bypass such dilemmas of involvement or aloofness.[27] By acknowledging that intellectuals are products of an ideology, whether they reject or sponsor it, Gramsci pleaded for the intellectuals' participation in public life. On his description, the intellectual's mission is virtually indistinguishable from that of a civic activist. Gramsci wanted to expand the scope of the term "intellectual," to also include other professional groups. He argued that such an expansion would occur naturally as societies progressed toward socialism. The socialist order, more than liberal democracies, relied on intellectuals for operation and legitimization.

The result was that, as Goldfarb observes, in the socialist countries of Eastern Europe, "intellectuals (Party and state officials along with creative artists, scholars, and scientists) enjoyed privileges unknown to the general population."[28] While social and political involvement was more of an opportunity or option in the West, it became an obligation in the East, and it came both with rewards and penalties. More importantly, under communism intellectuals lost their cultural freedom. Reflecting on their peculiar position, Goldfarb tries to explain: "(their) lives . . . were filled with ironies: characterized by honor and shame, grand hopes and illusions, petty opportunism and unacknowledged acts of bravery . . . . When we think about the experience of the intellectual in previously existing socialist societies, privilege is usually not the first condition that comes to mind. Instead, political repression of culture and the struggle for cultural freedom seem to have been the definitive characteristic of 'socialist' intellectual life. Aleksander Solzhenitsyn, Andrei Sakharov, Vaclav Havel, Adam Michnik, George Konrad et al. . . . against the repressive Party-state. . . . The intellectual struggle for autonomy came to be at the center of resistance to the communist system. It was indeed the worst of times, as well as the best of times, for intellectuals."[29]

On such a reading, the intellectuals' opposition to communism would appear at least in part self-serving. Whether they influenced or brought about the collapse of communism, intellectuals certainly benefited from it, not only by regaining cultural freedom, but also by being in the spotlight on the political arena. In the dichotomous logic that opposed intellectuals to workers, and as a regime predicated on proletarian values—even if in name only—communism victimized its intellectuals (or at least those who refused to support or further its agenda), deploying them as parasitic, arrogant, and retrograde.

When the regime fell, its victims (re)gained authority precisely because they were the victims. In 1989, intellectuals had moral capital and suasive power as public speakers, as historians and sociologists, as political philosophers and writers, a combination uniquely suited for public office in societies aspiring to become democratic. In a 1991 epilogue to the *Intellectuals to Road Power*, Ivan Szeleniy contended that in the power vacuum created in Eastern Europe after 1989, and "in the absence of a domestic propertied bourgeoisie, the only serious contender for the role of the elite is the intelligentsia."[30] Szeleniy's prediction, that the newly forming political class would recruit its members exclusively from the intelligentsia, has been partly confirmed, especially in Poland and in the former Czechoslovakia. Havel, the president of Czechoslovakia between 1989 and 1993, is the paradigmatic example of the major political role played by intellectuals immediately after communist regimes collapsed.

But even Havel's success, more glamorous that any other intellectual's in the East, was short lived (he resigned after the breaking of Czechoslovakia). His limited political effectiveness has been explained in unflattering terms by Western commentators, as attributable to the lack of viable alternatives at that particular point in time, much more so than Havel's own merit. "At a time when personalities rather than political institutions dominated political life, his reputation gave him political resources unmatched by other leaders."[31] If immediately after the Velvet Revolution Havel had little competition, he was ousted as soon as democratic political institutions matured and competitive rivals rose to the challenge. Such an unflattering perspective on the political careers of Eastern European intellectuals after communism reflects a more general tendency among commentators and analysts in the West, who have grown "tired of their old protégés, whose current performances has not lived up to a speculative belief in the great promise of the velvet (or kind, or gentle) revolution." Tismaneanu finds "a sense of exasperation, the equivalent of a too quickly requited love, evident in the harsh criticism heaped onto the once lionized resistance."[32]

While the disenchantment of Western intellectuals with their Eastern colleagues only goes back to the second half of the first post-communist decade, in the case of those from countries such as Hungary or the Czech republic, the Romanian intelligentsia "failed" from the start. The first free elections held in the country after 1989 were won by the Front for National Salvation, a political organization widely recognized in the West as led by the reformed communist elite. After the elections in May 1990, members of the opposition gathered in the University Square in Bucharest and launched a long series of protests that extended over a period of several weeks until June 12. It ended when the downtown area of the capital city was virtually occupied by coalminers deployed as a special intervention force by president Iliescu, who was getting increasingly worried about the riots turning into a new *coup d'etat*.

The miners vandalized the buildings of the University of Bucharest and the headquarters of opposition parties, and attacked violently, not only leaders of the political opposition, but also college students and people recognized as intellectuals. The coal miners' slogan—"We are workers, not thinkers!"—plugged directly into a dichotomy favored by the communist ideology, and resuscitated the concept of intellectuals as idle and parasitic, thus attempting to de-legitimize their involvement in politics and public life. Literally and figuratively beaten down, the Romanian post-communist intellectual faced the daunting task of gaining credibility in the West, as agent of change and promoter of democracy, despite lack of credibility and effectiveness at home.

3. Intellectuals as Agents of Change: From Myth to Ethos

Credibility is not just a direct function of confirmed abilities and concrete accomplishments, but is also predicated on evidence of shared values and beliefs. In the communicative realm, to gain credibility, speakers enter the axiological and epistemological space of their audience and try to act naturally and compellingly in it. Through appropriate discursive strategies and behavioral characteristics, they establish a commonness of beliefs, values, and attitudes with the audience. In the encounter between Eastern European and Western intellectuals, the euphoria created on both sides after the collapse of communism may well have obscured precisely the epistemic and axiological differences between the two categories. To be sure, these differences can be easy to miss if the focus is on a shared technical competence— the familiarity with canonical names and titles displayed by Plesu and Liiceanu.

It may be tempting to presume that if we subscribe to a common tradition of thought, we also have the same values, beliefs, and norms naturally associated with the tradition in question. But such an assumption would be predicated on the naïve notion of a direct, uninterpreted, unfiltered, unmediated access to texts and ideas. The Western tradition of thought is list of names and titles acting symbolically as a repository of beliefs and values that are constantly interpreted, evaluated, and then assumed. Un-interpreted, the list does not constitute a discursive arena. If it offers a vocabulary, it does not also automatically and unambiguously offer what Kenneth Burke called a "terministic screen," an interpretive grid for making sense of ideas and their contexts.[33]

Historically, the political and social role of the Eastern European intellectuals has been markedly different from that of intellectuals in the West, even when they were educated at the same universities, studied the same curricula, and relied on similar taxonomies or bibliographical references. The network of oppositions defining the identity of the Eastern European intellectual is especially difficult to grasp, because each opposition is in its turn stacked upon its own network of oppositions, explainable only through recourse to the unique history of the region. I cannot offer an extensive analysis of such differences, but I will focus on particular instances, which are relevant for the cases I am investigating.

Eastern European intellectuals have always espoused some type of nationalist ideals. When intellectuals in France or England were striving to secure an autonomous (that is, uncontrolled by the state) space of reflection and action, by contrast, "East Europeans would construct programs that would discuss how state power could be won to empower their oppressed nations."[34] In this sense, the Eastern Europeans would have more in common with the anti-imperialist intellectuals in the colonized countries of the twentieth century. This historical dimension of Eastern European intellectuals is especially problematic and potentially disturbing to a Western observer in light of nationalism escalating into violent conflicts in several parts in the region. Are intellectual politics in Eastern Europe now rooted in the nationalist legacy? This question is difficult not only to answer, but also to ask. To ask it is to insinuate a condemnable continuity. To not ask it, however, is to potentially ignore historical chains of causation.

Eastern European intellectuals have responded to different historical and social realities, and hence their mission and role have often been decided and defined in a framework different from that of their Western counterparts. The stakes in Eastern Europe were different, and even when they appeared similar, as they might when we compare the Leftist intellectuals in the West to those in the East, ideological credos and metaphysical beliefs were interpreted in distinct keys and for distinct edificatory purposes. I think Polish writer Adam Zagajewski neatly summarized this difference in stakes, goals, and values. "The first, second, and third time I was in the West," Zagajewski confesses, "I was struck by the subtle difference in *sensibilities* of Western and Eastern intellectuals, which was not reduced to the political cleavage between the left and the non-Communist stance. No, I would define the difference as the opposition between a more epistemological and a more ontological stance, between asking 'Is truth possible at all?' and asking 'Where is truth?'"[35] Translated as "habits of the heart" and of the mind, the epistemic stance described by Zagajewski commits the Western intellectual to a more flexible rationality, comfortable with uncertainty and willing to entertain multiple interpretive scenarios. The ontological stance, on the other hand, makes the intellectual in the East feel burdened by dilemmas and hence prone to seeking their resolution, often by insisting on unambiguous diagnoses and verdicts.

Obviously, a trenchant dichotomy such as Zagajeweski's risks amassing many different kinds of Eastern European and Western intellectuals in reductive categories. It is a risk worth taking, however (especially if we are careful to verify the assumption in a close reading of particular people's beliefs and statements, as I will in the next section), if we want to understand better the challenges involved in a cross-cultural self-definition. We should be careful to avoid caricaturizing the ontological propensities of intellectuals in the East, and suggesting that their commitment to truth was naïve and their approach to finding it rigid. Conversely, we must resist the stereotype of the relativist Western academic (there are plenty of foundationalist ones!). But the difference noticed by Zagajewski indicates a crucial potential point of disjuncture between intellectuals east and west of the Yalta border.

Such a disjuncture is reflected in the Eastern Europeans' engagement with their past—the way in which the communist experience is assumed and analyzed. In retrospect, communism had a uniformizing and totalizing effect on the past, disguising its many nuances and obscuring its internal conflicts, its diverse reception even within one country, and its cohabitation with many other ideologies and sub-ideologies (like anti-Semitism, sexism, ethnocentrism, and so on).

Assuming that non-communists were anti-communists is tempting. But the communist experience had many layers of significance, which makes "the conundrums of East-Central European memory seem twisted," according to Richard Esbenhade, "even in the global context of the struggle over memories of World War II, the Holocaust, colonialism, and the cold war."[36] As Esbenhade warned, a "totalizing view" of the communist experience is bound to result (and has resulted) in more problems than solutions. In Poland, when the Solidarity leaders insisted on achieving an agreed upon collective view of the past, the result was a nationalist ideology that brought to the fore diffuse anti-Semitic inclinations. In Czechoslovakia, when the emphasis on individual rights and memory encouraged by former dissident intellectuals led to fragmentation and contributed, Esbenhade opined, to the separation of Slovakia and the Czech republic. If intellectuals are to facilitate an understanding of the 1989 events and their positive potential for social emancipation and economic welfare, their theoretical observations and active involvement require a willingness to probe the many stories the past has to tell.

If credibility derives from shared values and assumptions, beliefs and aspirations, it can be established between Eastern European and Western intellectuals if the points of rupture I have just mentioned are addressed. Thus, the challenge lies in articulating a self-identity and a personal program that can reconcile the epistemic and the ontological stances, by reckoning with the nationalist legacy and with the totalizing impulses in interpreting the communist past. Such reconciliation, furthermore, takes place in the context of transition, on the occasion of the opening to the West, and is inextricably associated with the idea of change.

4. Interpreting Change: Gap or Shift?

So far, I have taken at face value statements such as Havel's, that the collapse of communism meant an existential revolution that triggered major identity revolutions. It is time to ponder the issue of the change that occurred in 1989 more critically. Consider, then, the nature of the social upheavals that led to the collapse of totalitarian regimes in southeastern and central European countries. From the Velvet Revolution in Czechoslovakia, to the fall of the Berlin Wall, euphorically celebrated on both sides, and finally to the violence and bloodshed that devastated Romania, political change took many forms and shapes. Partly based on how they occurred, the 1989 transformations have been described as "revolutions," as well as simply "events," in an effort to precisely withhold, or at least postpone an interpretation until more clarification of those circumstances is provided.

Ethnographic studies of transition to post-communism in eastern and central Europe proceed by trying to explain the apparently chaotic nature of the transition process by systematically paying attention to remnants of a communist ideology and mentality as a *legacy*, instead of an extinct political order.[37] This move allows researchers to see that "what may appear as 'restorations' of patterns familiar from socialism are something quite different: direct *responses* to the new market initiatives, produced *by* them, rather than remnants of an older mentality."[38] Such an argument effectively counters the thesis that the non-revolutionary nature of 1989 is confirmed by the fact that many former communist countries have been slipping back into their old habits and reinstating some of the communist structures of power.

Documenting genuine change and departure from the previous political order does not imply that we cannot also acknowledge that "people's responses to a situation may often appear as holdovers precisely because they employ a language and symbols adapted from previous orders," yet this "means only that action employs symbols and words that are not created *de novo* but develop using the forms already known, even if with new senses and to new ends."[39] The studies collected by Michael Buroway and Katherine Verdery all argue for an approach concerned with understanding the consequences of communism instead of celebrating its extinction, as well as capable of providing insights into the incubation of a new order instead of its genesis.

But regardless of our eagerness or reluctance to declare the demise of communism, the survival of those who lived under it is a different question. How do we locate the actors on the post-communist scene in comparison to their instantiations in the previous order? Prima facie at least, these are the same individuals, even when the change in the political and social environment was abrupt enough to appear radical. On December 21, 1989, most Romanians (living inside the country) were fearful and obedient members of a totalitarian society. On December 22, 1989, many of the same people were fearless protestors against the regime, gathered in the main square of Bucharest to demand Ceausescu's resignation. Tragically, some of them did not survive, shot and killed in the public riots that extended into the next two or three days.

Later that month, Ceausescu was apprehended and his execution broadcast on public television. The broadcast marked the public recognition of a radical change in the political system of Romania. But I suspect most viewers, ecstatic as they were about their newly proclaimed freedom, paid little attention, if any, to a change at the level of some deeper forum of their selves. I do not mean to imply that people did not discover new potentials of self-realization, as careers or interests formerly taboo became readily available to them, or that they could not have changed without an awareness of change. There were, to be sure, new offers in precisely what Krausz calls projects. The question is: how does the transition to new personal programs and projects take place, if the change is supposed to be radical and if indeed incommensurable standards of evaluation make programs incongruent?

To assume that the collapse of communism generated automatically identity transformations is not only unwarranted and to some extent even counterintuitive, but also dangerous. Such an assumption can have an all-exculpatory function: if with the change of the political order came a change of identity, why hold anyone accountable for the wrongdoings of that order? And especially in those cases in which we see clear indications of communist structures being restored, would such an approach not lead to the paradox identified by some political commentators under the rubric of "communism without communists"?

To avoid such pitfalls, I argue that political and social transformation are accompanied by changes in personal programs, but do not necessarily mandate replacement. A narrative perspective on identity formation tells us that even if a replacement is in order, it, too, will be made drawing from existing resources, using patterns of thought and discursive strategies based on an experience that is inextricably connected to what was before the change. Whether we are talking about replacement or alteration, neither is automatic, or guaranteed successful. Actors must want to change, recognize the opportunity for change, and consider particular approaches to change. What can both help decide and orient the change is the discursive encounter with an audience that must be won over, or persuaded.

The view I am proposing deploys the transition to modified personal programs as an interpretive task with two exigencies, along temporal and cultural axes. In the following sections I document two ways in which such a task is performed, by Plesu and Liiceanu, and I argue that the successful performance is predicated on an edificatory interpretation of models and values inherited from the past and refashioned to correspond to the exigencies imposed by the encounter with a western audience. In the spirit of a reconciliation of the ontological stance defining the Eastern European intellectual with the epistemic stance characteristic of the Western counterpart, such an edificatory interpretation of models and values must also be alert to potentially controversial issues, and capable of navigating among them without deliberately distorting events or situations and with an awareness of multiple scenarios.

Finally, then, let me sum up the main distinctions based on which I seek to articulate a theoretical and analytical framework for discussing how post-communist intellectuals define themselves as potential members of a larger, intellectual community associated with democracy as a political order and with the Western tradition of thought as a body of knowledge. I started with Tismaneanu's concept of political myths as representations of problematic social realities, embodied in, or identified with representations of particular (groups of) actors. In Eastern Europe, intellectuals constitute a political myth founded on the ideal of democratic emancipation and Westernization. Yet this particular myth is eroded by dwindling belief in it by the Western intelligentsia and by political setbacks taking place in most former communist countries.

To be revitalized, the myth requires an active (re)construction of credibility on the part of Eastern European intellectuals. We can understand how such credibility might be gained if we approach the interactions between intellectuals from the West and those from the former communist bloc as negotiations of ethos via the creation of a shared epistemic and axiological space. But the task of building such credibility also involves a temporal dimension, insofar as those who tackle it do so in a period of deep transformation and crisis, when private and public values are challenged, when the boundaries between "authentic self" and "perceived self," intention and effect are blurred. How I will further analyze and explain ethos takes into account two variables, the cultural aspect of an encounter East-West, as well as an exploration of the communist legacy.

5. Ethos Through Identification: A Controversial Role Model

To the question "how can an intellectual survive communism," both Plesu and Liiceanu respond in the first person singular, but what follows is not an autobiographical account. Perhaps justifiably so, since the survival in question cannot be their own survival, inasmuch as such notion only makes sense if the person who survives exists prior to the threat. Plesu and Liiceanu were born in the first decade after World War II; they were too young to have experienced the pre-communist period, but they came to know about it, and to see themselves as its continuers, thanks to their common mentor, Constantin Noica.

A philosopher trained before the war in both Paris and Heidelberg, a contemporary and friend of Mircea Eliade and Eugene Ionesco, and an illustrious representative of pre-communist intellectual life in Romania, Noica was more than an individual. He was an institution, and the engine, or inspiration, of many exercises in mythology. Unlike other prewar intellectuals who either emigrated or died prematurely (executed after quick show trials, in long prison sentences, or under the harsh conditions of labor camps), Noica stayed in Romania until his death in a hospital shortly after he had a suffered stroke in 1987, at age 75. During his life and afterwards, he was and remains a highly controversial character. His philosophical career began in the troubled intellectual and political atmosphere of interwar Romania, influenced, like so many members of his generation, by Nae Ionescu, an extreme rightwing leader and academic whose philosophical ideas were designed to match the political ideals of the Iron Guard, the fascist organization responsible for the Romanian Holocaust. After the communist takeover, Noica was first detained in his home in the small town of Cimpulung, and then served an eight-year prison sentence.

Upon release in 1964, he was employed as researcher in the Center for Logic of the Romanian Academy; the appointment was a sinecure, as Noica spent most of his time reading, writing, and later hunting young men (no women) in different parts of the country to offer them what he called a "serious cultural couching" designed to turn them into high-powered intellectuals. Traveling from one city to another, interviewing high school and college students, Noica chose his underlings based on their speculative aptitudes and talent for languages, especially German, Latin, and Greek—the consecrated idioms (in his view) of a philosophical education. His goal was to bring together twenty-two individuals, the future geniuses of Romania, each of them literally one in a million in a country of twenty-two million people. When the teacher retired to the small mountain resort of Paltinis, in 1977, where he lived for the rest of his life in a small room furnished with a bed, a table, and a wood stove, the "students" would pay him regular visits to receive tutoring in the fundamental works of Western philosophy.

The Paltinis "school," as it came to be known, in effect offered a personal program, one grounded in the project of reading major books and discussing philosophical ideas. Noica envisioned the creation of a Socratic elite society whose members would dedicate their existence to reading and discussing the canonical texts in the history of (primarily Western) philosophy and religion, translating some of them in Romanian, learning foreign languages in order to be able to read even more texts in their original idiom, and developing original philosophical projects. This unorthodox educational system did indeed produce some of the leading intellectual figures of post-communist Romania, with Liiceanu and Plesu as especially well respected and accomplished representatives.

The idea of developing an ideal school that would train young people in the philosophical tradition of the West dated all the way back to the war period. Noica first outlined his pedagogical vision in an entry in his 1944 *Philosophical Diary*, in which he describes a school at the outskirts of a city, hence eccentric to the *polis*, a school where no one would teach and no one would be assigned homework, a place liberated from the "tyranny of teachers" and hence open to the free exchange of ideas, the sharing of interests and expertise.[40] The founding assumption of this educational project was that all aspects of the human experience and all compartments of human life should be subsumed to high culture, by which Noica meant philosophy. He convinced his pupils that high culture represents the medium of an individual's existence, as water is for fish and air for birds.

While the emphasis on high culture in a social system predicated on proletarian values can be read subversively, the Paltinis school was not explicitly intended as a political movement: nowhere did Noica or his students indicate that they were leaving the capital in protest, as a way of turning their back on a world inhabited and controlled by communism. Nor did they engage in any particular way the communist dogma. In stead, their rhetoric of seclusion and ex-centricity can be and has been read in connection to the generic conventions of philosophy as a knowledge producing practice. What Noica left behind is not necessarily substantially different from what René Descartes abandoned upon retiring to the small, unheated room where he was to write *Discourse on Method*, or Martin Heidegger before moving into his mountain cabin. But that is not to say that a program founded upon the negation of contingency, of politics and history, cannot acquire a political significance contingent upon the circumstances of its emergence, no matter how hard it might try to bracket the notion of circumstantial.

It may be ironic that this political significance has also been turned against Noica and his group by those who chose to interpret the retreat as failure to take responsibility for the country's sufferings, or even worse, as a tacit acceptance of the communist ruling, if not downright the sign of a pact with the officials who were much happier with a recluse than with a civically active intelligentsia. In Romania, one and the same project has been seen by different commentators as (1) non-political by intention, (2) political and more especially anti-communist by design, and (3) political and especially pro-communist by implications.

This is the paradox that underlines the legacy of Noica's Paltinis school. How can such widely distinct interpretations be either reconciled in what would count as a singularist response, or maintained and distinguished in an order of preference and admissibility in what would constitute a multiplist response? More importantly, how would we know whether a singularist or a multiplist response is in order? Put differently and in more general terms: how to justify a particular reading of a past that is so fraught with ambiguity and ambivalence?

6. Dealing With Contested Symbols: An Attempt at Elucidation

Conducts of inquiry are shaped, according to Krausz, by how one answers the following question: must there be a single admissible interpretation of a given object or situation? Those who answer affirmatively are singularists. In contrast, multiplists allow for competing interpretations of the same thing, even though they do not deem all accepted interpretations equally admissible. If we wish to narrow the range of admissible interpretations, Krausz recommends providing "thick descriptions of pertinent interpretive contexts."[41]

The description of the context I offer in my presentation of Noica's legacy is indebted to two radically opposed analyses by American sociologist Katherine Verdery, and French philosopher Alexandra Lavaigne-Lastignel.[42] Their work both summarizes and expands the corpus of studies of this topic produced in Romania, which I have also consulted. Both Verdery and Lavaigne-Lastignel provide thick descriptions of the context in question, but focus on different features of the context: Verdery looks at the larger context of public and intellectual life in Romania during the 1980s decade, when the Paltinis school became a social phenomenon, while Lavaigne-Lastignel does a close reading of Noica's philosophy and situates it in the much larger intellectual and political context of eastern Europe, comparing Noica to Jan Patocka, Czech dissident and philosopher.

Both researchers marshal an impressive array of evidence to support opposing views, and even though in both cases alternative interpretations are allowed "on the table" for the sake of generating a robust argumentation, in the end Lavaigne-Lastignel allows for only one interpretation, while Verdery is willing to tolerate more than one. Concluding her brief but revelatory biographical sketch, Verdery recognizes that "Noica was rich in ambiguities, making him an excellent prospect for symbolic manipulation and competing genealogical appropriations."[43] In her reading, "Noica was directly continuous with the interwar arguments on the national essence."[44]

Indeed, one of Noica's most popular books, *The Romanian Feeling of Being*, echoed the title of a text published before the war by philosopher Mircea Vulcanescu, *The Romanian Dimension of Existence*: although writing decades apart, both authors advocate ethno-national ideas in an attempt to articulate the particularity of a Romanian national identity. In the precommunist milieu, debates over the national character constituted the hegemonic discourse of public life, whether that discourse was incorporated in an abstract body of knowledge such as philosophy, theology, literature, even in the more scientific areas relying on fieldwork and hard data, such as psychology, ethnography, or history, or in political and social agendas. In at least some aspects, the theoretical interest in discovering a "national specificity" was the counterpart of a more explicitly political nationalism.

In postwar Romania, especially after Ceausescu became the general secretary of the Romanian communist party, a similar type of hegemonic discourse began to form in response to a new version of nationalism at the social and political level. Especially after the Soviet invasion of Czechoslovakia, Ceausescu decided to break free from the Soviet tutelage by replacing the Marxist-Leninist communist doctrine with a homegrown version named *protochronism*—a nationalist ideology that claimed the priority of Romanians in almost all domains, from " the theory of relativity to psychoanalysis, from cybernetics to aesthetics, from literature to engineering."[45] As one critic aptly put it, *protochronists* systematically found Romanians among "the first to invent, discover, initiate, or imagine most things human."[46] Protochronism created a blending of the prewar preoccupation with national specificity and its communist revival by bringing them to "their lowest common denominator, anti-Western sentiment. At its most vulgar and vehement, protochronism openly blamed the West for robbing Romania of its greatest intellectual and artistic achievements, and for mounting a vicious plot against everything Romanian."[47]

On Lavaigne-Lastignel's reading, Noica's philosophy grew directly out of protochronism. She traces his concern with ontological questions about national identity as it surreptitiously turned into an ontic obsession with Romanian-ness as an essentialized and superior identity, as the philosopher moved closer to espousing a critique of modernity from an anti-democratic nationalist perspective. According to Lavaigne-Lastignel, Noica eventually elided the distinction between the Romanian dimension of being and Being in more general, strong ontological terms. Indeed, on several occasions Noica was critical of the West in a way that lent itself fairly easily to an appropriation by the protochronist anti-Western sentiment. He rejected what he called the "scientism" and "technocracy" reigning over Western Europe, holding them responsible for creating an "ethos of neutrality" hostile to difference and individuality. He frequently insisted that only through recourse to national identity can one resist a future in which variation would be erased by modernization, and individuality lost in translation to the Esperanto of technology and marketing.

While to Lavaigne-Lastignel such claims sound helplessly retrograde and prone to fetishizing difference in a narrow, tribal, sense, what counts for Verdery is less the beliefs proposed at Paltinis and more the people who advanced them. She focuses on the communicators, instead of the message, namely, on a re-empowered intelligentsia who thus acquired the needed "platform from which to influence the democratization of Romanian society after Ceausescu."[48] Probing the past and seeking to understand its lessons for the transition to post-communism, Lavaigne-Lastignel worries about the nationalist legacy. This legacy Verdery certainly acknowledges, but she sees it as part of the process that engendered political credibility for the intellectuals, who were able to propose political agendas after the communist regime was no longer in place.

So far, neither of these two readings has been definitively proven wrong: while the nationalist legacy in Romania, as in other eastern European countries, cannot be denied or ignored, the intellectuals associated with the Paltinis school do have a political platform from which to launch a campaign in support of democracy. Plesu, who has served in two governments and is at the time I am writing the director of the national committee in charge of the former archives of the political police, is a case in point. The incompatibility between the interpretations offered by Verdery and Lavaigne-Lastignel indicates that thick descriptions do not necessarily provide an unproblematic path to one particular interpretation, and that the context of interpretation does not always hold sufficient discriminatory value to sway us in one particular direction. Both researchers make primarily bold elucidatory efforts, by positing the relevant links between the past and the present and the future from a totalizing perspective concerned with the global legacy of history, instead of its concrete incorporation(s) in identity programs. Half-heartedly recognizing the shortcomings of Noica's school, by calling its disregard for the workers and peasants, and anyone not interested in philosophy "unfortunate," Verdery insists on the "moral standing" Noica's group gained in the 1980s. What moral standing?—Lavaigne-Lastignel replies, showing instead precisely how ethically and morally pernicious the intellectualist stance in communist Romania was. Yet both pay less attention to post-1989 attempts to come to terms with this particular legacy in the articulation of a revised personal program defining the intellectual ethos. Their work is tremendously valuable because of the rich detail it produces, but in the end neither approach manages, in my opinion, to unseat the conclusions of the other.

7. Using the Past as Source of Edification: A Singularist Interpretation

In his last interview, Noica explicitly linked the personal program proposed by his pedagogy and philosophy to the western ethos, describing his program as "the protest of a marginalized European in support of the true Europe, which no longer knows itself." The "true" European spirit, according to Noica, would be able to promote universal values without repressing the individual, an enterprise possible, in his view, only through recourse to the traditional philosophical ideas promoted by the pillars of the West, from Plato to Hegel, Aristotle to Kant, and Descartes to Heidegger. The same names were included in the curriculum of the Paltinis school, along with the others mentioned by Liiceanu in the opening paragraph of his Luxembourg address. The link between Liiceanu and his former mentor is in the form of a shared intellectual tradition, that of Western philosophy. How can such a generic link mandate a shared personal program?

After the collapse of Ceausescu's regime, some of Noica's pupils were among the founding members of the Romanian Group for Social Dialogue, a forum for political analysis and reflection intended to protect the newly formed civil society. Since its creation, the Group has played a major role in the country's political life, and had a significant contribution to the result of the 1996 elections, which were widely acclaimed by many as the first true victory of a democratic party. But is there a direct inheritance by the political- and civic-minded class founded after 1989 of the intellectualist agenda of Noica's elitist program? Put differently: was Noica's philosophical commitment the legacy for contemporary civic movements?

On Liiceanu's account, the Paltinis school had a political significance that must be understood in its particular context. He explains: "Paradoxically, totalitarian societies are de-politicized societies *par excellence*. Politics, that is to say the activity through which you participate in the destiny of a group of people and take decisions concerning it, is, in a totalitarian society, the monopoly of a tiny minority (sometimes of one individual), and is limited to the expression of decrees. The rest of the population is infantilized: they are told what to think, what to say and what to do. In this closed world, in which the mind above all is under threat, culture becomes a means of transgression, and so, by this fact, takes on a political significance. It is not only an alternative view of the world, but also a barely perceptible resistance to total isolation, rupture, discontinuity and absorption in the mass. *It is the memory of destroyed values, and the possibility of their future reconstruction.* When all means of participating in the destiny of the community are suppressed, culture remains a way of continuing to participate from the shadows and of preparing for regeneration. It is thus in the highest degree subversive."[49]

By articulating a notion of resistance through culture, Liiceanu is able to identify for his western audience a connection between Noica's school and the exit from communism, and the connection is justified by the post-1989 civic involvement of the author himself and of other intellectuals associated with Noica, most importantly, Plesu. But this link could just as well be viewed as a posit, or a post-factum rationalization of a non-political agenda. What would ultimately unseat either one of these interpretations is contingent upon whether the audience accepts Liiceanu's interpretation. And their acceptance is determined by how inclined they are to understand high culture as a form of political dissidence.

Such an understanding, in its turn, hangs on two additional premises: (1) that a totalitarian regime can effectively disable agency, and hence cannot be broken through any kind of direct intervention, protest, dissent, and (2) that the regeneration necessary after the regime collapses involves a rehabilitation of at least some pre-communist, bracketed values. The second assumption is problematic insofar as it eliminates the need or even the possibility of a critical appraisal of the pre-communist legacy, which, as I have shown in the previous section, is in some aspects highly controversial. For the first premise, Liiceanu invokes historical support, although his historical account, too, is susceptible of alternative interpretations: Romania had no overt, organized dissident movement similar to the Czech Charter 77 or the Polish Solidarity, whether because of a more effective political repression, or because of some other cultural particularity.

Liiceanu's reliance on an ethos of the weak, virtually non-existent initiative or intentionality (disabled or repressed by totalitarianism) is consistent, for he even describes the collapse of communism as a "rendezvous that history had prepared for (Romania's intellectuals)," instead of as a response or intervention of actors. But how could there have been any resistance at all, including through culture, if it was history—an impersonal force, the same one that used to "threaten" the country under communism—that brought about the end of the totalitarian regime? Is Liiceanu simply being inconsistent in his use of the words "resistance" and "history"?

The way I read it, his account takes on two interpretive tasks, or two rhetorical exigencies, and winds up conflating them into a single one. Such conflation amounts to what Krausz would call a shift from multiplism to singularism. The two interpretive tasks are (1) to articulate a credible intellectual identity, an ethos based on a technical notion of competence, as familiarity with a certain canon, fluency in a certain type of conversation, ability to operate with certain arguments, and (2) to also defend this ethos based on a moral and ethical notion of competence, as in responsibility for the welfare of the society. One is a task of accreditation, the other is a task of justification, and both are crucial maneuvers in the process of transition.

The need for both accreditation and justification is directly connected to the dual nature of his rhetorical exigency: for an audience of Western intellectuals who might think of eastern Europe as a cultural desert, Liiceanu wants to document the richness of intellectual life in communist Romania (accreditation). But how to account for the fact that intellectual life under communism could unfold normally, without also admitting that the regime allowed for that? This is how accreditation and justification fuse: the intellectual who can discuss Homer, Plato, Saint Augustine, Shakespeare and Goethe with his Western counterpart has not spent the communist decades simply polishing his conversational skills or rehearsing arguments from Plato or Goethe. Instead, such habits and aptitudes were also political instruments that make possible the occasion for the current conversation. What Liiceanu points out to his audience is that it is not only *what* the East European or Romanian intellectual can discuss, but also *that he can discuss.*

Notice, however, that this interpretation of what it means to be an intellectual does not require an ethos that accords much importance to motives or intentions, and deliberation. Instead, by postdictively positing a personal program with political impact (the rationalization part), it gestures toward an ethos conceived as locus of reflection and critical scrutiny (that are still limited to a certain period in the past). These two kinds of ethos cannot be fruitfully incorporated into one, without also compromising the quite interpretive work that has led to them. More importantly, they do not match an epistemic stance, and hence the expectations of a Western audience.

In the final analysis, Liiceanu can only account for partial survival in a "world asphyxiated by lies, ideology and vulgarity." Alongside intellectuals, he is forced to acknowledge the existence of "the deteriorated minds and souls of those . . . who were not fortunate enough to be able to resist through culture," those for whom there was no Latin, Greek, German, and "the pious reading of the great books of humanity" to make the "nightmare at once . . . bearable."[50] These unaccounted many are the reason, according to him, the exit from communism did not happen in a few days or a few months, and the reason it is not clear whether it will ever happen in Romania: "What they (Romanian intellectuals) are experiencing now is the . . . drama of the doctor killed by his patients. Our minds are again prey to the thought that history is being made over our heads."[51] Agency, again, threatens to slip into history, and in the face of such perils, Liiceanu can only hypothesize about the future.

The last two paragraphs of his essay, which analyze "what is to be done," sound hesitant and pessimistic, in contrast to the triumphant voice that narrated the past, confidently asserting accomplishments and registering victories. All last eight sentences begin with the phrase "it may be," and the final one with "let us hope." This hovering, a stylistic as well as surely cognitive mark, is instructive insofar as it is the correlate of an ethos that involves an ability reflect but not deliberate, or to exercise its deliberative faculty only as part of a narrative retrospect.

Liiceanu's is an elitist argument for the political relevance of intellectual activity in a totalitarian regime. His is a singularist reading of a particular aspect of the past (the philosophical project of Constantin Noica's school), which tries to capitalize on its alleged political consequences. Whether this reading is admissible at all is not the question I want to ask. I am not concerned with its elucidatory power, but with its edificatory resources: what does this reading entail for the way in which transition is understood and experienced? Does it articulate a revised personal program, compatible with Western standards? Does it propose a coherent vision for the future? The answer is, on Liiceanu's own reading negative: seen through his eyes, the future looks dim. Further, the ethos he defines excludes, in order to exist, a large segment of the population and is thus conducive to social and political cleavage, exactly the kind of cleavage that renders dubious the social and political role of the intellectual. I find more edificatory force in Plesu's multiplist interpretation of the role played by Noica and his students in the public arena of communist Romania.

8. Inheriting the Past: A Multiplist Interpretation

At the heart of Plesu's reconstruction is the notion of survival: the philosophical mentoring offered by Noica kept him and others intellectually alive under a regime that sought to destroy intellectual values and to replace ideas with dogma. But the concept of survival poses some problems, not just in this context but also in theoretical terms. Survival implies a sense of acknowledged continuity despite perceived threats against that continuity. Yet the maintenance of continuity is ascertained retrospectively, and can be considered dubious. Further, survival implies less intentionality than resistance, at least on a common understanding of resistance: while resistance involves deliberate effort, conscious intention, strategic intervention, and (perhaps even) explicit opposition, survival can simply be an accident, a happy coincidence, a welcome, but not planned effect.

Plesu's account is predicated on this non-heroic, almost passive notion of survival. In some instances, he points out, what allowed intellectuals to survive under communism was the sheer ineptitude of the communist officials, who sometimes simply "failed" to censor more promptly different cultural initiatives, or did not understand them well enough to anticipate their impact, or to discern their implications and assumptions. More important, survival was also inevitable because the danger, or the source of threat was bound to be in part inefficient or at least not always as efficient. The case mounted by Plesu in support of this thesis is entirely philosophical (instead of historical or political). "Ontologically—and theologically" claims Plesu, "evil is imperfect, which means it always leaves . . . a chance for maneuvering to those under its influence. Even the worst of all worlds is—I would say— *cosmotic;* that is, it illustrates an order within which all the ingredients of the normal world are present. . . . If the Communist world had been a world of consistent evil, the numerous mechanisms of survival concretized in scientific and artistic performances . . . would never have occurred within its bounds."[52] Plesu thus introduces the concept of "interstices" of evil, hiatuses in the fabric of an oppressive political order, which lead to a peculiar simultaneity of

"normal" life (read, free of political manipulation) and life under the conditions of dictatorship (read, thoroughly controlled). Survival, in this context, is
tantamount to the simultaneity of two kinds of life; its locus is the "interstice," and as such, it is no longer predicated on conflict or opposition, but on
bivalence and parallelism.

A consequence of this "imperfection" of the Communist evil, or an associated trait, is arbitrariness. Plesu contests the idea that dictatorships create
"an atmosphere of hysterical necessity, of absolute rigor." The "interstices"
that punctuate the oppressive order make unexpected relaxations possible, as
"the law can suddenly become lax for no apparent reason." This is how
"normative abuse" becomes at the same time sporadic. A translation of Heidegger is published in 1983 (when "capitalist" writing is forbidden) not because there is no rule or systematic prohibition of such things, but because the
existing rule happens to not be applied to this particular case.

Oddly, this interpretation says that the initial question—how could an
intellectual survive communism—does not require an answer, insofar as survival is rendered inevitable and thus not especially interesting, or is unan-
swerable because an answer would also be a logical investigation intended to
find causal connections that are simply defied by arbitrariness. It is in this
context—of a subtly deconstructed premise, the one of survival, which already de-emphasized intentions and deliberation, that Plesu introduces the
figure of his mentor, Noica.

The deconstruction of the premise may sound odd, but it fulfils a necessary function in structuring the interpretation: it suspends further assumptions
of bravery or resistance, and thus promises to create a space of investigation
free of bias. And in this interpretive context, we also no longer expect hero-
ism, acts of deliberate rejection or courageous opposition. Noica is himself
the embodiment of this concept of "survival": a former political prisoner, he
is one of the representatives of the Romanian prewar intelligentsia, most of
them killed, forced to emigrate, or incarcerated by the communists, and few
lucky enough to be present again in the public arena after 1964, thanks to an
unexpected or circumstantial relaxation of the totalitarian fist, a pardoning act
applicable to political prisoners. As one of the many, Noica was the conduit
to an extant tradition; as one of the few, he was a precious reminder, if not
perhaps the desired proof that such a tradition did exist, that there were good
times, if not a "golden age" when people were free to say and to do whatever
they chose. "The world around us was talking only about fracture, about the
new that must do away with the old, about "the bright future" of Communism," Plesu reminds us. As a response to this exigency, "we felt all the more
a need for legitimacy which only contact with the previous generation could
give us. We needed to feel, *therapeutically*, that although we were in a waste-
land, we were not feeble creatures living in a desert. And this feeling was
consolidated by the *pedagogical* presence of those who had been in prison."[53]

The conflation of therapy and pedagogy, on this rendering, is informative. It allows Plesu to merge trauma with enlightenment, the specter of the past with the challenge of the future. To feel that one is not a feeble creature is obviously not necessarily the same as not being a feeble creature, or as being a strong creature. But insofar as such a feeling enables certain behaviors, commitments, and accomplishments that would typically be associated with not being feeble and perhaps even with being strong, the distinction is rendered irrelevant.

The commitments and behaviors encouraged, or indeed made possible by Noica's "pedagogical presence" all fell under the rubric of "cultural performance," with the word "performance" used both in the sense of "remarkable achievement" and "acting out." Cultural performance thus creates a semblance of reality, a possible universe of reference or realm without concrete empirical presence. Noica demanded that his pupils dedicate all their energy to intellectual pursuits, learning Greek and German, and reading Plato, Hegel, Plotinus and Descartes, and that they do not become invested in contingency, in ephemeral circumstances. Plesu quotes his mentor's favorite formulas: "Don't pay attention to the immediate circumstances. Consider history to be pure meteorology: you don't change your destiny and your ideas depending on the weather. History needs circus horses. I ask you to be racehorses."[54]

Noica himself had learnt to disregard history and contingency while in prison, where he managed not only to ignore the inevitable vicissitudes, but also to use them as an incentive for intellectual activity. Plesu recounts: "He had somehow managed to harmoniously integrate the episode of detention, claiming that his arrest had happened at the right time, when his own ideas had entered a vicious circle and needed a vital infusion—no matter how dramatic."[55] Later in life, Noica succeeded again in bypassing contingency, when he retired to the mountain resort Paltinis. And Plesu explicitly connects these topoi (the prisoner's cell and the philosopher's room) analogically, describing Noica's departure from Bucharest to Paltinis as a "*return* to an atmosphere of seclusion." (To speak of a return makes sense only insofar as we admit that he had been there before, not to the actual place, Paltinis, but to a symbolic location.) The structure of the analogy, however, is ambiguous in this case, as is its function by consequence: is the mountain cabin indeed like a prison cell—which would implicitly politicize the retirement—or was the prison cell like a mountain cabin—which would inevitably romanticize imprisonment, as some have feared. In Plesu's reading (or instead, in my reading of Plesu), the ambiguity of the analogy is deliberate and not designed to be easily resolvable.

I do not mean to insinuate that Plesu would espouse a romanticized view of communist prisons. If he did, he would not have acknowledged, which he does, Cioran's objection to this analogy as irreverent to those who suffered in the communist Gulag. The mechanism at work in this analogy is precisely in line with multiplism, because it assumes that one is willing to tolerate more than one interpretation, by agreeing to equate the mountain resort with the prison while still understanding the extent to which they are distinct. It is a bold move on Plesu's part to propose the topos of political imprisonment as "out-of-the-world," instead of "critical of the world" and thus fundamentally "part of the world." And whether the move is historically accurate or justified is not a question I will venture to explore in this paper.

But as an interpretive move, Plesu's account is meaningful and crucial. What connects the prison cell and the mountain resort is only at a superficial level the idea of seclusion; the strong link is the element of separation, or removal from the world. By reading intellectual survival—in prison and at Paltinis—in disconnection from contingency, he is simultaneously suggesting that (1) intellectual activity was socially and politically aloof, and that (2) intellectual activity under communism operated a breach in the existing order. What makes these interpretations distinct and incongruent, so that they can count as a multiplist reading? The condition of incongruence requires that they be opposed, yet not exclusive. , There must be opposition but not mutual exclusiveness between the ideas of aloofness and subversion in the case of intellectual activity under communism.

It is obvious why intellectual survival in prison was concurrently aloof in a political and social sense, and disruptive of the existing order. The intellectual activity produced in prison was also confined to prison, and virtually inexistent for those who lived outside, in the social and political arena. On a different level, its sheer existence under conditions supposed to inhibit it was an implicit victory, a form of protest. The analogy of the mountain cabin as prison cell only functions effectively if we understand the argumentation strategy at work, one that depicts Noica, the recluse incarcerated, as symbol of pre-communist Romania.

This argumentation strategy is carried out in the trope of synecdoche, in which the part is used for the whole: Noica, only one among others who lived and worked in Romania before the communist takeover, becomes coeval with the entire epoch, and by extension, with the idea of an alternative plane, something other than communism. After communism collapsed, referentiality can be assigned to that plane of representation inaugurated by Noica's program with its emphasis on cultural performance. This kind of representation is made possible through a rhetorical move (by which I mean both argumentative and stylistic). Especially, two tropes are at work here: synecdoche, insofar as Noica, as part of a bygone era is seen as the whole era, and metonymy insofar as an effect, the free world of post-communism, is presented as cause, the free world of intellectual activity carried out at Paltinis. Rhetorical scholars have argued that synecdoche is the master trope of representation because it has the ability "to affect perception, to abbreviate a situation or context, and to sum up its essence."[56] But by deliberately putting the part and the whole on a par, synecdoche becomes the vehicle for a totalizing impulse, the impulse I have criticized in Liiceanu's reading.

Metonymy works more subtly. Even though predicated on a linear logic that connects effects to causes, it has a loose grip on what is between effects and causes, and is quite liberal in regard to the nature or content of the connections. Metonymy does not commit one to the past even as it may mythologize some of its aspects by seeking plausible effects on the present. Liiceanu's most problematic assumption—that the recovery from communism ought to be based on a regeneration of pre-communist values and ideals—is not entailed by Plesu's idea of the breach as an alternative reality. Their rhetorics are different as they match different interpretive ideals: Liiceanu's singularism is put into practice via synecdoche, while Plesu's multiplism is carried out through recourse to metonymy.

What are the implications of this difference in rhetoric for an ethos informed by an edificatory understanding of the legacy of communism? First, although arguing for the political relevance of the Paltinis school, Plesu's reading does not require a heroic notion of resistance or dissidence. His interpretation is less likely to slip into dangerous mythologies. Nor does it rely on an ethos defined only by retrospective reflection, but not efficient deliberation. In practical terms, such an ethos is severely impoverished for periods of transition, when there are so many deliberative exigencies.

Second, Plesu's reading identifies an alternative realm of representation, partly coextensive with the prewar tradition and partly created parallel to the communist order, which can provide at least provisional ontological support for transition. A skeptic could ask: is Plesu's notion of a "breach" in the communist order fundamentally different from the notion of "interstice" in the fabric of evil? While the interstice is empty of meaning, or at the best dormant, the breach comes much closer to representing a conscious affirmation of alternatives. Let me further unpack this claim by pondering the meaning of Plesu's unexpected and misleadingly pessimistic or skeptical final paragraph: "Many of us, I myself, survived thanks to the 'ob-nubilation' which his (Noica's) way of thinking conveyed to us. I don't understand well, even now, what the real price of this survival is, to what extent it created irreversible mental and psychic distortions. Sometimes I am inclined to believe that the right answer to Bruce Ackerman's question 'How could you possibly survive under Communist dictatorship?" should be: 'Did I?'"[57]

Is Plesu refuting his own argument in the end? Is he giving in to the same kind of analytical and deliberative impasse that Liiceanu was forced to acknowledge? I read this final skepticism as the confirmation of the successful shift from an ontological to an epistemic stance, as well as the ultimate expression of a multiplist stance, a kind of exercise in analytical reasoning that considers alternatives and ponders dilemmas in order to reassure itself that it considers all the possibilities. A dilemma is not an admission to deliberative deficiency, but a starting point for further investigation. As a metadiscursive reflex—"Did I survive" can be read as "Have I given admissible interpretation(s) of the past"—Plesu's question is not meant to challenge the validity of his conclusion.

This question does not insinuate that perhaps intellectual activity under communism was not genuinely intellectual, or that it did not successfully create an alternative representation. Instead, by raising new questions, such as the "real price of this survival," it already signals new topics of inquiry and types of analyses. Thus, Plesu resists giving an approach, or sounding as if he were, that would "totalize" the past or "essentialize" its features. His account is a narrative, and as such, it has a two-pronged structure: an experiential level, where particular events and actions are located, and a level of commentary, at which the events are incorporated into a meaningful plot. Between these two levels, the final dilemma-question "opens" a space in which the narrator, Plesu, can "converse" with himself, scrutinize the interpretation and consider potential alternatives, and in so doing, take hold of experiences and assume responsibility for the past, as well as choose life paths and make decisions for the future.

In this critical space Plesu articulates an "internal rhetoric" that can differentiate opportune from opportunistic moves, as understanding and responding to the particularity and significance of a situation "does not mean only satisfying immediate interests, which a . . . short-term thinker is likely to do. It means grasping the larger significance of the situation—its possible consequences and moral import."[58] This "internal rhetoric" is grounded in the existence and awareness of reasons adduced in support of multiple interpretations. As Krausz says, "the point of adopting the nomenclature of singularism/multiplism . . . is to allow for good reasons for one's preferred interpretations."[59] Granted, in multiplist cases such reasons should not be so strong as to unseat all alternatives as inadmissible, but that does not mean that multiplism is some-how ethically indecisive or argumentatively feeble. When situations demand it, multiplism can express a rigorous ethical and argumentative stance, because it does not allow for hasty decisions.

9. Conclusion

Let me briefly recapitulate my claims and consider what, if anything, they can help us to accomplish. Pondering the difficult case of transition to post-totalitarian societies, I have proposed a reading of the task of renegotiating personal programs in the aftermath of a major social and political change from a multiplist perspective and with an edificatory aim. In order to present such a reading I had to consider the following issues: how radical was the change that took place in eastern and central Europe in the 1990s? Can one still talk about continuity in that context, and if so, what kind of continuity would that be? I offered my response in the form of a close reading of the ethos of post-communist intellectuals as instantiated in two narratives of the same personal program. At a theoretical level, my analysis hopes to flesh out the distinction between ideals of interpretation by approaching them as rhetorical stances shaped by exigencies and informed by different epistemic commitments. I also try to show how muddled this distinction becomes, without losing its relevance or making it impossible to choose one perspective over the other, in the interpretive practices at work in our reading and writing of history, politics, and social life.

What is the relevance of my analysis? I believe it teaches us a needed lesson about how to think about transition periods—in the post-communist societies of eastern and central Europe in particular, but also in more general terms—and both the way in which they constrain the identity of the actors affected, and the way in which these actors engage in processes of identity formation that can ultimately complete the transition and define the newly created order. Elsewhere I have looked at a different instance of transition, immigrants entering and adjusting to a new culture, and found a similar interpretive stance responsible for some of the most successful adaptations.[60] Do immigrants "reinvent" themselves in the new country? Do their personal programs "transfer" from one culture to another, without schism or tension?

For some, the answer to both previous questions can be affirmative. But then there are also cases of adaptation involving a fusion of the self shaped in and by one culture and the self inspired or produced in response to the other culture. This fusion is predicated on establishing a coherent narrative pattern in the immigrant's life story, instead of on finding a strict continuity between "the one from before" and the "one after" immigration. Similarly, the transition from one historical period to another, especially when its abruptness resembles the experience of immigration, requires a dynamic engagement with the past, a concern for its multifaceted nature, awareness of and patience with its contested legacies, and ability to take stock of both its achievements and failures. The ethos of post-communist intellectuals in Romania illustrates a way of making sense of the diverse and fragmented experience of transition by problematizing the past as it is embodied in a personal program. At a concrete level, the impact the interpretive work involved in defining this ethos can have on particular policies involving the present and the future is significant. This impact can translate as urban planning, in the form of a decision to restore buildings in the architectural style characteristic of prewar Romania, or to adopt a new, different style; it can translate as educational policy, in the form of textbooks that associate or dissociate communist nationalism with or from prewar extreme right ideologies; it can translate as political decision per se, by restoring monarchy (Romania's form of government before communist takeover) or advocating republicanism.

Finally, notice that neither Plesu, nor Liiceanu leaves us with a clear, black-and-white image of who Noica was: a hero or a villain. Neither settles the controversy surrounding this historical figure. But while one tries to argue, if only implicitly, for a reenactment of the past and is forced to accept its impossibility with nothing to propose instead, the other ponders the lessons of the past and refuses to give easy answers.

NOTES

1. Ruti G. Teitel, *Transitional Justice* (Oxford: Oxford University Press, 2000), p. 3.
2. Ivan Kilma, *The Ultimate Intimacy*, trans. A. G. Brain (New York: Grove Press, 1997).
3. Seyla Benhabib, "Response," *Political Theory*, 23:4 (1998), pp. 677–678.
4. M. J. Matustik, "Havel and Habermas on Identity and Revolution," in *Praxis International* 10:3 (1990–1991), pp. 261–277.
5. Vladimir Tismaneanu, *Fantasies of Salvation* (Princeton, N.J.: Princeton University Press, 1998).
6. Denise Powers, "Review of *Fantasies of Salvation*," *Comparative Political Studies*, 8 (2000), pp. 107–109.
7. Claude Lévi-Strauss, *Structural Anthropology* (New York: Basic Books, (1963), p. 229.
8. Jürgen Habermas, "The Rectifying Revolution," *New Left Review,* 183 (1990), p. 5.
9. Ernst Nolte, "Die unvollständige Revolution. Die Rehabilitierung des Bürgertums und des defensiven Nationalismus," *Frankfurter Allgemeine Zeitung*: (24 January 1991), p. 27. Françoise Furet, "L'enigme de la désagrégation communiste," *Le Débat*: (November-December 1990), p. 168. Timothy Garton Ash, "Revolution," *The Uses of Adversity: Essays on the Fate of Central Europe* (New York: Vintage, 1990), pp. 309–324.
10. Andreea Deciu Ritivoi, *Yesterday's Self: Nostalgia and the Immigrant Experience* (Lanham, Md.: Rowman and Littlefield, 2002), pp. 43–72.
11. Michael Krausz, *Limits of Rightness* (LR) (Lanham, Md: Rowman and Littlefield, 2000), p. 113.
12. David Norton, *Personal Destinies: A Philosophy of Ethical Individualism* (Princeton: Princeton University Press, 1976), p. 9.
13. *Ibid.*
14. Fred Frohock, *Public Reason. Mediated Authority in the Liberal State* (Ithaca, N. Y.: Cornell University Press, 1999), p. 101.
15. Krausz, *Limits of Rightness*, p. 145.
16. *Ibid.*, p. 146.
17. Marshall W. Alcorn, Jr., "Self-Structure as a Rhetorical Device: Modern Ethos and the Divisiveness of the Self," in *Ethos: New Essays in Rhetorical and Critical Theory*, ed. James S. Baumlin and Tita French Baumlin (Dallas, Tx.: Southern Methodist University Press, 1994), p. 21.

18. Steven Knapp, "Collective Memory and the Actual Past," *Representations*, 10:26 (1989), pp. 123–149.

19. Stephen Greenblatt, *Modern Languages Association Newsletter* (April 2002), p. 35.

20. Andrei Plesu, "Intellectual Life under Dictatorship," *Representations*, 49: (1995), pp. 61–71.

21. Gabriel Liiceanu, *Paltinis Diary* (Budapest: Central European University Press, 2000), p. 3.

22. Jeffrey Goldfarb, *Civility and Subversion: The Intellectual in Democratic Society* (Cambridge: Cambridge University Press, 1998), p. 76.

23. Jeremy Jennings and Tony Kemp-Welch, "The Century of the Intellectual: From the Dreyfus Affair to Salman Rushdie," *Intellectuals in Politics: From the Dreyfus Affair to Salman Rushdie*, ed. Tony Kemp-Welch and Jeremy Jennings (London: Routldge, 1997), p. 7.

24. *Ibid.*, pp. 11–12.

25. Julien Benda, *Trahison des clercs* Paris: B. Grasset, 1927).

26. Goldfarb, *Civility and Subversion*, p. 1.

27. Antonio Gramsci, *Gli intellettuali e l'organizzazione della cultura* (Roma: Editori Riuniti, 1997).

28. Goldfarb, *Civility and Subversion*, p. 84.

29. *Ibid.*, p. 85.

30. Ivan Szeleniy, "Postscript 1990," in Ivan Szelenyi and Bill Martin, "The Three Waves of New Class Theories and a Postscript, *Intellectuals and Politics. Social Theory in a Changing World*, ed. Charles S. Lemert (Newbury Park, London: Sage Publications, 1991).

31. Ray Taras, *Postcommunist Presidents* Cambridge: Cambridge University Press, 1997), p. 181).

32. Tismaneanu, *Fantasies of Salvation*, p. 142.

33. Kenneth Burke, *A Rhetoric of Motives* (Berkeley: University of California Press, 1969).

34. Zygmunt Bauman, "Intellectuals in East-Central Europe," in *Eastern European Politics and Societies*, 1 (1987), pp. 33–48.

35. Adam Zagajewski, "Intellectuals and Social Change in Central and Eastern Europe," in *Partisan Review*: (Fall 1992), p. 273.

36. Richard Esbenhade, "Remembering to Forget: Memory, History, National Identity in Postwar East-Central Europe," in *Representations*, 49:10 (1995), pp. 72–96.

37. Michael Buroway and Katherine Verdery, *Uncertain Transition: Ethnographies of Change in the Postsocialist World* (Lanham, Md.: Rowman and Littlefield, 1998).

38. *Ibid.*, p. 3.

39. *Ibid.*

40. Constantin Noica, *Jurnal filozofic* (Bucuresti: Editura Fundatiilor Regale, 1944), p. 15.

41. Krausz, *Limits of Rightness*, p. 8.

42. Katherine Verdery, *National Ideology under Socialism: Identity and Cultural Politics in Ceausescu's Romania* (Berkeley: University of California Press, 1995); Alexandra Lavaigne-Lastignel, *Philosophie et nationalisme: le paradox Noica* (Paris: Presses Universitaire, 1995).

43. *National Ideology*, p. 266.

44. *Ibid.*, p. 257.

45. Sorin Antohi, "Foreword to *Paltinis Diary,*" p. xvii.

46. *Ibid,*. p. xviii.

47. *Ibid.*, p. xx.

48. Verdery, *National Ideology*, p. 301.

49. Liiceanu, *Paltinis Diary*, p. 13, my emphasis.

50. *Ibid.*, p. 14.

51. *Ibid.*, p. 15.

52. Plesu, "Intellectual Life under Dictatorship," p. 65.

53. *Ibid.*, p. 67.

54. *Ibid.*, p. 69.

55. *Ibid.*, p. 69.

56. Burke, *A Grammar of Motives*, p. 82.

57. Plesu, "Intellectual Life under Dictatorship," p. 72.

58. Jean Nienkamp, *Internal Rhetoric: Toward a History and Theory of Self-Persuasion* (Carbondale, Ill.: Southern Illinois University Press, 2001),p. 134.

59. Krausz, *Limits of Rightness*, p. 7.

60. Ritivoi, *Yesterday's Self.*

Sixteen

MORAL UNIVERSALISM AND CULTURAL ANTI-ESSENTIALISM: AN EXTENSION OF KRAUSZ'S THEORY OF INTERPRETATION

Krassimir Stojanov

Perhaps the best way to evaluate a philosophical work is to apply to it the criterion of the extent that work puts traditional assumptions into question, which have been understood as self-evident truths within the philosophical discourse or within the realm of common sense. According to this criterion, Michael Krausz's work is of highest philosophical quality.[1] His work develops the argument of the detachability of ideality and ontology with regard to interpretive knowledge and deconstructs the common presumption that singularism is necessarily connected with realism and that multiplism is necessarily connected with constructivism.

We can generalize this argument by formulating the claim that ideals of interpretive practices are independent from any concrete assumptions about the ontological status of their objects, yet they obviously are always connected with assumptions of some kind, insofar as "there is a larger 'metaphysical' context implicated in the very idea of singularism and multiplism," a context that "includes the existential claims made by singularism and multiplism as well as the intentional considerations that help make particular objects of interpretation and interpretations intelligible" (LR, p. 15). We need ontology (otherwise we will not have objects of interpretation) but the kind of ontology we use here is contingent, because it depends upon the kind of practice in question.

Interpreting Krausz's philosophy in this way enables us to recognize that the innovative contribution of his philosophy goes far beyond traditional epistemological topics in the narrow sense—such as the question of the relationship between concepts of truth and ontological premises. Krausz offers an original theory of interpretation that necessarily has an anti-essentialist metaphysical background, because the metaphysical assumptions are not prior to and independent of that practice, but are constructed within it and as a necessary moment of it.

In this essay I will discuss this claim in the terms of a praxiological turn of epistemological matters regarding cultural objects; locate the question of validity of moral norms within that turn and work out the problem of justifying universal moral principles, a problem which in my view requires a revision of Krausz's praxiological framework; and finally sketch a way this revision could be done by accommodating the deontological approach of discourse ethics .

In many places, Krausz points out that his purpose is to develop an anti-essentialist philosophy, which in part emphasizes an "anti-essentialist view of human nature." Krausz describes his understanding of essentialism in the following way: "In brief, the doctrine of essentialism holds that a thing is . . . what it is in virtue of its embodying an essence whose properties are inherent and invariant" (LR, p. 118). And further: "I take essentialism in its orthodox sense to hold that a thing is what it is inherently and invariantly, irrespective of its relation to other things or interests" (LR, p. 137). The point here is, that from an anti-essentialist perspective the objects of interpretation are relational. The meanings of these objects are constituted by their links to other objects and to intentions, norms, and worldviews of interpreters. Objects-of-interpretation are always context-situated, given in a social setting, in a *Lebenswelt* (LR, p. 14).

Whether these objects have been seen as real or as constructed entities depends on the features of this *Lebenswelt*: the scientific ones should display themselves as real, as given outside and independent of the mind, yet within the life-world of the arts these objects occurs as created by human activities (RR, pp. 163, 166). It becomes evident why the detachability thesis is so crucial for Krausz. For example, if we assume that realism presupposes singularism, then we would probably tend to interpret realism in an essentialist way—in such a way that each object exists in itself (*an sich*). Here the right interpretation would be a proposition that captures an object's essence. The detachability thesis implies instead that both the ontological and the epistemological status of the object are constructed within the *Lebenswelt*. This raises the possibility that there could also be an anti-essentialist version of realism—a possibility that I investigate in the last part of this paper. From the anti-essentialist view follows the thesis of the "praxial ideality of cultural entities," a thesis that should be seen as a background of a "praxial constructionism" (RR, p. 163).

Krausz's praxial constructionism leads directly to a cultural relativism: The object-of-interpretation is constructed from the home culture, including a self-differentiation of a home culture's "us" and alien "them." The constructionist practice depends upon the consensus of informed practitioners who share common traditions from which the pertinent objects-of-interpretation arise (RR, pp. 164 f.).

The problem with this view is that it allows no logical space for ideal entities or for "intentional objects," "endowed with meaning or significance within a field of cultural codes and norms" (LR, p. 13), still claiming universal, cross-cultural validity. I have in mind here entities such as universal moral principles. My purpose is to show that precisely a praxiological antiessentialist approach can offer the best argumentative ground for defending such principles and for reconstructing the mechanisms of their constitution.

Remarkably, Krausz has not thematized moral norms and values in his works, despite these values and norms being typical intentional objects-of-interpretation (LR, p. 13f.). They become meaningful only when they are situated within a cultural field. Some of them—like the notion of human rights—claim universal validity. Taking this claim seriously and examining its legitimacy is valuable.

The ideality of such moral entities is shaped by a (dialectic) contradiction between their contextual situating and their claim to universal, context-independent validity. Two strategies present themselves to avoid this contradiction, yet both of them are reductionist. The first strategy accommodates an ontological essentialism, usually combined with an epistemological singularism. Here moral norms appear as Platonic ideas that embody timeless essences that always remain identical in themselves, regardless of their relations to different settings of social action and ways these ideas have been interpreted. Here there can be only one right way of seeing an idea, of accommodating a moral norm. This way requires transcending your cultural embeddedness, your *Lebenswelt*.

Arguing for universalistic human rights in this way is tempting. But doing so will ignore that the moral norms are moral norms insofar as they are meaningful entities. And "meaningful" means—as Krausz convincingly demonstrates—to be relational, to be constituted within a horizon of references, within a *Lebenswelt*. The first strategy does not imply that moral entities are necessarily particularist, as the second strategy suggests. Proponents of the second strategy argue that universal claims of the human rights cannot be legitimated, that finally they are a form of Western cultural imperialism. This cultural-relativist conclusion, which Krausz—if I understand him correctly—shares, ignores the difference between aesthetic and moral "objects," respectively. It ignores differences in the constitution of both kinds of "objects" within the *Lebenswelt*. We must not interpret universal moral norms as Platonic essences. Instead we can hypothesize that the *practice* of constituting moral norms provides them with universal validity.

Unlike aesthetic objects, which are unique, moral norms tend to be universal: moral agents normally claim that what they hold for right is right in itself and applies to all human beings. Consequently there arises a tension in moral argumentation under multicultural conditions, where alternative ethical notions co-exist.

When I say "moral argumentation" I assume the distinction between moral norms or principles and ethical values introduced by Jürgen Habermas.[2] While ethical values are notions about the good life, moral norms are content-neutral, they focus on the form of the communication about relevant ethical issues, on the way validity claims regarding such issues can be legitimately raised, discussed, and eventually transformed. And this kind of argumentative communication guided by the impartial moral point of view implies formal normative principles—such as reciprocity, equal access of all potentially concerned by ethically relevant decisions persons to the moral discourse, equal opportunity of every participant to articulate free by his or her positions and concerns, recognizing the dialogical partner as a reasonably acting free agent, and so forth.

We can conclude that (1) this kind of speech-grounded moral theory covers the basic principles of human rights and that (2) moral norms appear here not as "objects-of-interpretation" but as "by-products" of the reflection on the interpretation of ethical objects, by-products that are content-neutral and context-invariant—or compatible with different worldviews and, broadly speaking, cultural fields. Remember that the character of this reflection is conditioned by the inescapable contradiction between contextual situating of ethical beliefs and their claims for universal validity. The handling of this contradiction under multicultural conditions leads to the distinction between content and form of the interpretation of ethical objects.

Habermas names the paradigm that arises from this distinction "formal pragmatics." I think that a reception of Habermas's formal pragmatics within the framework of Krausz's philosophy would result in a quite interesting radicalization of the praxiological turn that this philosophy is carrying out, namely in an opportunity to interpret universalities in a praxial anti-essentialist way. Perhaps with Krausz we can call this kind of interpretation "praxial singularism." I would also argue that this "praxial singularism" should be combined with a kind of anti-essentialist, deontological realism.

In order to explain the term "praxial singularism" we have to discuss the formal-pragmatic concept of moral deliberation in more detail. This deliberation occurs in the moment in which ethical considerations about the good life become self-reflexive. This is the normal case under multicultural conditions. For Immanuel Kant, moral thinking focuses on the question of the universality of the maxim of ethically relevant action. To act morally means not to hurt interests and values of others, or, in the case of conflict, to give proof that your maxim is closer to the ideal of impartiality than the maxims of opponents, or to initiate a process of deliberation between all parties in order to reach a consensus, to elaborate a common maxim that satisfies the ideal of impartiality. This implies that moral deliberations and actions entail the recognition of real and virtual communicative partners and potentially of all persons as "ends-in-themselves," as noumens, as "Dinge an sich." Moral action and moral deliberation imply the understanding of others not as phenomena that are constructed in our mind on the ground of our worldviews and interests, but as sovereign and independent entities, as sources of (other) worldviews, as other "zero-points" (as Edmund Husserl called them) of distinguished perceptional frames of reality.

My claim is that the necessary implications of moral action and deliberation embody a kind of realism, which (1) is reflexive and reconstructive, which (2) is discourse-dependent, which (3) is developed on a primordial level, and which (4) grounds a kind of anti-essentialist singularism. I would like to develop these four points.

We distinguish between naive and axiomatic epistemological realism of the everyday attitude toward the world and moral realism that is a product of our reflection about our ethical practice. At the first level I believe that mind-independent objects exist. At the second level I discover myself reflexively as an "itself-existence," as source of sovereign interests and worldviews that exist among other such "itself-noumens." Discovering myself as a noumen and recognizing others as noumens are two aspects of the one and the same process. And, with Husserl, this recognition is fundamental for constituting the general meaning of the term "real world."

Krausz accommodates a view according to which realism postulates dis-course-independent objects while the constructivism understands all objects as discourse-dependent. In contrast, the realism of moral reflection displays "objects" of moral consideration (the other subjects) as being-itself-entities precisely because they are sites of the discourse. In that sense we can speak here of a discourse-dependent realism. For Habermas discourse is a meta-communication that is needed when the self-evidences of everyday life be-comes problematic. As I said, this is the normal situation in the case of inter-cultural communication. This kind of reflexive meta-communication is em-bodied in every form of speech practice oriented toward reaching under-standing. Every speech act necessarily has a reflexive dimension consisting in the I–awareness of the speaker and of the receiver, and awareness of each Ego of its difference with the Alter Ego. Moral discourse makes this implicit dimension of every speech act explicit and initiates the development of self-understanding of the actor as "being-itself-entity" by recognizing his or her communicative partners as "being-itself-entities" and by claiming to be rec-ognized as him or herself by them as "being-itself-entity."

With Axel Honneth we can interpret this dialectic between the constitu-tion of self and his or her relationship of mutual recognition to the others as selves as a main feature of intersubjective communication in general, not only of the practice of the moral deliberation.[3] The constitution of the self still requires a realistic concept of the existence of other persons—not necessarily about objects of the world.

This last statement indicates that this kind of realism is primordial. To recognize a person as a person means to recognize her or him as a "Ding-an-sich," as a noumen. A *Ding-an-sich* is not a part of the objective world, merely a condition for its constitution. That means that Ego meets and per-ceives Alter Ego not in the way that it deals with things in the world. Instead, the communication between Egos is located, so to speak, beyond the world of things, and this communication should be seen as the source of the constitu-tion of the world. This communication has a transcendental, or better, a "quasi-transcendental" status, as Habermas says.

Calling moral norms "objects" is perhaps misleading, for the term "ob-ject" usually concerns things in the world, phenomena. Moral norms are em-bodiments of the understanding of your self and of others as subjects, as noumena, as ends-in-themselves. As such these norms are not objects in the sense that physical things or even works of art are. Correspondently, it would probably be better to explain the broad metaphysical context of interpretation, of the grasping the meaning of moral norms, not in the terms of ontology but in those of deontology. This choice would underpin the conclusion that follows the model of formal pragmatics, namely, that moral realism is a consequence of the way in which validity of moral norms is constituted. This realism does not follow from, and has nothing in common with, assumptions about the existence of the phenomenal world.

One consequence of formal pragmatics is that only one way exists to interpret persons morally—namely as ends-in-themselves. This is an inescapable singularism. This singularism is praxial and anti-essentialist because, first, this singularism is embodied in the practice of the moral argumentation and, second, within its frame, persons are interpreted as existing only through their relations to other persons. Selves are constituted as ends-in-themselves in relations of intersubjective recognition. Every such end-in-itself exists only as a point on the intersubjective net. It occurs within the process of moral deliberation.

This idea of every person being an end-in-her- or himself is at the core of the idea of human rights. Many critiques claim that this understanding is not universal but Western-specific, that many cultures do not share it and that the attempt to present human rights as a universal regulative principle is nothing but a form of Western cultural imperialism.

These critiques are incorrect. The domain of the grounding principle of human rights is not represented by cultural groups, but by individuals. This principle has been deduced not from ethical notions about the good life but from the form of moral discourse, finally from the reflexivity of speech practice as an intersubjective enterprise. As I said, this reflexivity becomes explicit especially in the situation of intercultural communication. Societies that are open to this communication are likely to develop acceptance of human rights, and vice versa. This acceptance does not depend on ideologically constructed substantialist group values, such as "Asian values" or "Balkan mentality," but on the inner communicative structure of a concrete society, and in the processes of global international communication. Correspondingly, parts of the international community ignoring human rights claims of dissidents of particular countries, with the argument that the cultures in which they live are not compatible with the principles of human rights and so those principles should not be imposed on those cultures, is an expression of highest cynicism. If we take the anti-essentialist lesson about ethical and moral issues seriously, we will recognize that this argument is based on false premises.

This paper is inspired largely by Krausz's theory of interpretation, especially by the outcomes of his deconstructive work. These outcomes make it possible to avoid automatically associating (ontological) realism and (epistemological) singularism with essentialist premises, and to modify your ontological and epistemological presumptions in dependence on the domains of interpretive practice. Krausz's philosophy made it possible for me to argue without scruples for a praxiological-reflexive realism and singularism on the level of moral practice, rejecting at the same time the naive realism of the everyday attitude and of the classical natural sciences, and still remaining a convinced anti-essentialist. In the concept of reflexive intersubjective realism that results in a praxiological moral singularism I see a way to develop a strong argument for the validity of moral universalities and against substantialist cultural relativism.

NOTES

1. Michael Krausz, *Rightness and Reason: Interpretation in Cultural Practices* (RR) (Ithaca: Cornell University Press, 1993); Michael Krausz, *Limits of Rightness* (LR) (Lanham, Md.: Rowman and Littlefield, 2000).

2. Jürgen Habermas, *Erläuterungen zur Diskursethik* (Frankfurt am Main: Suhrkamp, 1991).

3. Axel Honneth, *Kampf um Anerkennung: Zur moralischen Grammatik sozialer Konflikte* (Frankfurt am Main: Suhrkamp, 1992.

Seventeen

RELATIVISM AND THE LIMITS
OF HUMAN CONSCIOUSNESS

D. P. Chattopadhyaya

1. Toward Krausz

Until recently relativism, like skepticism, was a handy whipping boy to nearly all realists, idealists and scientific philosophers. Among the writers who have recently made significant contributions to secure a philosophically respectable place for relativism, Michael Krausz deserves special mention. His works, authored and edited, have broadened and deepened our understanding of the different aspects of the relations among relativism, realism, constructivism, interpretation, and truth.[1] This is an extremely difficult area of philosophy because of the complexity of the issues involved and the competing and competent views on the issues and their interrelationships. Krausz has taken immense pains and shown admirable analytic acumen and ingenuity in assessing the views and arguments of others and in offering his own conclusions on the pro-relativistic ideas of interpretations and indicating their limits. His studies in different types of realism and their relation with constructivism have helped him to arrive at his own carefully worked out conclusion. Where his views and mine agree and where they differ will be clear from what follows.

Criticism or acceptance of relativism is not of much philosophical interest. Unless why you criticize or reject relativism is spelled out, the issue remains uninstructive. Somewhat similarly, speaking in support of relativism without indicating its proclaimed reasons does not mean much either. Without detailing the kind of relativism that you proposes to attack or defend if an attempt is undertaken to state the case for or against relativism in a very general way, that does not enlighten about the problematic or the thematic character of it. I do not intend to suggest that no general formulation of relativism is possible. Instead, the critic's uneasiness lies mainly in the abundance of general formulations. Unfortunately, most of those formulations of relativism are found to be too weak or indefinite or vague to be pointedly criticized or substantiated. Who will care to waste time and labor to rebut a weak global or all-encompassing relativism? What is the point in trying to achieve a pyrrhic victory against a weak opponent?

We learn from historical and contemporary philosophy of science that there have been and still are too many scientific theories addressed to the same set of problems, physical, biological, psychological, or socio-logical. The issues of what Krausz calls singularist and multiplist interpretations are encountered at every level of epistemic inquiry, from the natural to the cultural, from the empirical to the transcendental. Every singular object, even at the physical level, has its multiple facets; but every multifaceted cultural object has its referential singularity and identity. Besides the levels explicitly mentioned as a matter of convention in epistemological discourse, many objects that are candidates for interpretation exist in other borderline levels. In fact, the gradualist tells us, within each of these levels we find several sub-levels of objects. Careful scrutiny shows that what is pre-analytically called object and the synthetic-epistemic act of objectification, though analytically distinguishable, cannot be epistemologically disentangled. Even the distinction between levels is partly a matter of construction. The emergence of disciplines such as biophysics, biochemistry, physiological psychology, and socio-linguistics makes the point evident. It may sound unbelievable today that alchemy and chemistry, astrology and astronomy were not demarcated for many centuries. Before the days of Antoine-Laurent Lavoisier (1743–1794), Humphry Davy (1778–1829), and Michael Faraday (1791–1867), even chemistry did not have the dignity of independent existence as a scientific discipline.

2. Finding and Fabricating or Fictionalizing Fact

To move from the metaphysical ways of discussing relativism to the pro-scientific approaches to relativism that are currently influential is instructive. Many writers, formerly committed to full-blooded realism marked by essentialism, have recently been coming round to "internal realism," if not a cautious version of pragmatism. In this connection, the name that comes readily to my mind is Hilary Putnam. Another very insightful version of relativism is found in Nelson Goodman's later works, such as *Ways of Worldmaking*. In spite of its distance from Goodman's earlier works, such as *The Structure of Appearance,* their affinity and continuity are unmistakable to the discerning reader. His views and arguments purport to show, in brief, that nominalism and realism, mythic, scientific, and metaphysical worldviews are not necessarily antagonistic. In other words, the supposed unity of "the real world" and its multiple versions are not always incompatible. Intriguingly enough, neo-Kantians like Ernst Cassirer, naturalist-cum-phenomenalists like Goodman, and internal realists like Putnam are often found to sail in the same boat carrying the cargoes of different varieties of realism and relativism. The fact that Richard Rorty, who has been often accused of defending one of the most radical versions of relativism, never disowns his indebtedness to Putnam's version of realism and the (Tarskian correspondence-mediated) version of objectivism of Donald Davidson, is even more intriguing.

"Fact," "object," "thing," and other similar words are interesting and problematic. We often hear some utterances such as "scientists are concerned with hard facts." What is left unsaid but clearly indicated is this: fiction, fictitious objects and things have no place in science. Those scientists and philosophers of science who believe in the primacy of theory are never tired of speaking of the theory-ladenness of all facts, scientific or artistic. In the arena of science two very extreme approaches, fact-fetishism and theory-intoxication, easily meet without entering into conflict. We might rightly affirm that fact is theory-laden and theory is fact-laden. Theories or hypotheses or fictions, like myths and metaphysics, are intended to relate and interpret facts and make them intelligible (and even repeatable in a way). Well-established hypotheses are said to be fact and are accorded the dignity of proven truth. In ordinary discourse fiction is given a low status. But in the legal discourse, for example, fiction has operational significance creating concrete rights. When, after the passage of a stipulated period of time, the ripening of *de facto* into *de jure* rights is explained in terms of one or another fiction, the practical importance of the latter becomes clear.

When we speak of ways of finding fact, we often remain unaware of how easily we interpret the concerned fact or facts. If interpretation is believed to be inherent in our fact-finding operations, denying that these operations are destined to fabricate the concerned facts in some way is difficult. The supposed distinction between finding facts and fabricating them, on scrutiny, is found to be untenable. This so-called faithful representation of fact in the human mind can hardly be free from the varying effects of fabrication, interpretation, and construction. We may safely say that physical fact, perceptual fact, and linguistic fact are various versions, variously interpreted versions, of the "same" identifiable facts.

The supposed gap between "the actual" and "the possible" may also be substantially narrowed down. The spatio-temporal segment of the world in which I am now actually situated was very much in the realm of possibility an hour before. "The possible" transcends in a way the "actual" but remains also traceably related to it. If we break or deny this relation, the world of possibility will unbelievably inflate and the entities, objects, and the like will propagate endlessly in an epistemologically unmanageable manner. The actualist's position and the possibilist's position do not differ in kind but only in degree of cognitive availability or in terms of relative transcendence. Also the specific identity of the cognizer is centrally relevant to the issue. The point has been argued by Goodman, among others, in many of his works.[2] Modal realists such as Saul Kripke also emphasize the non-mysterious close relation between the actual worlds and the possible ones.[3] Philosophers of language such as Ludwig Wittgeinstein, W. V. O. Quine, Goodman, and Davidson, have shown why the supposed distinction between "relations of ideas" and "matters of fact," between "questions of language" and "questions of fact," on analysis, turn out to be thin, if not nonexistent. Excessive attention to natural science and little or no attention to fine arts have made many philosophers forgetful of the importance of ordinary language, personal communication, and roles of analogy and metaphor in all kinds of discourse, from mathematical and physical to poetic and musical. Most of us are unconscious of various and subtle ways that physical and even mathematical objects are filtered by our ordinary language.[4] Many aspects of this important point have been brought to our notice, for example, by Wittgenstein.[5]

Whether relativism and realism, actualism and possibilism, and the comparable cognates are compatible or not depends much upon how we take and spell them out. Goodman takes pains to show that realism and relativism go together and are not incompatible with the idea of possible world. The "real world," to him, is without kinds or patterns in it. To the physicist it appears in one way. To the artist it does appear differently. Even different kinds of artists "represent" the world in different ways. Pressing them to tell us definitely which of these versions are "really true" is idle. Goodman thinks that

> For the man-in-the-street, most versions from science, art and perception depart in some ways from the familiar serviceable world . . . this world, indeed, is the one most often taken as real; for reality in a world, like realism in a picture, is largely a matter of habit. . . . [O]ur passion for *one* world is satisfied, at different times and for different purposes, in many different ways.[6]

These liberal and alternative versions of relativism are not necessarily antagonistic to the spirit of realism. This important point may be illustrated by referring to the writings of William James, Goodman himself, and Putnam who has traveled a long way from his early (pro-Kripkean) essentialism to the later pro-Jamesian pragmatism. For the proper understanding of a particular philosopher's version of the relation between realism and relativism we are required to know his changing identity and traditional (philosophically traditional) affiliation. Recognizing the limits of "fabrication" of facts, the bounds of interpretation, and the difference between a right interpretation and a wrong interpretation within a given discourse, is crucial. Goodman writes: "My outline of the facts concerning the fabrication of facts is of course itself a fabrication; but as I have cautioned more than once, recognition of multiple alternative world-versions betokens no policy of laissez-faire."[7] Recognition of the limitations of versions are due to no unique concept of truth—correspondence, coherence, or pragmatism. For each one of these concepts has lent itself to numerous interpretations. This is clearly illustrated from the departure of Wittgenstein's later view on truth from Wittgenstein's early view on the subject, Popper's retreat from his early Tarskian commitment to correspondence (as truth) to the notion of verisimilitude or truth-likeness, and Davidson's late leanings toward coherence, a marked departure from his early pro-Tarskian position.[8] A comparable trend is evident in the later writings of Putnam.[9] My reference to these writings is not intended to underrate their repeatedly professed commitment to realism or (its old but weaker ally) objectivism.

I emphasize: no grand project of a universal methodology or epistemology ensuring cognitive availability of unquestionable truth seems workable. In a way it summarizes the changing history of Euro-American epistemology during the second half of the twentieth century. If Immanuel Kant has brought down metaphysics from the height of heavens to the depth of the earth, from things-in-themselves to the metaphysic of experience, the strongly pro-scientific theorists of knowledge, in their self-critical and reflective mood, have been increasingly realizing the necessity of austere relativism, alternative versions of what is "really there," and unarrestable (but limited) multiplicity of interpretations. For example, in *The Many Faces of Realism*, Putnam rejects the dichotomies between "things-in-themselves" and "things-as-they appear" and between "truth-conditional semantics" and "assertibility-conditional semantics" and tells us that the division of the mundane reality into a "scientific image" and the "manifest image" is untenable. He rightly recognizes that our "real world" has in it sensible objects such as tables and chairs and theoretical objects such as quarks and gravitational fields. You can easily add music and painting to this-worldly population. In our description of the world, our interests and choices enter silently but in an unmistakable manner.[10]

Relativism is no longer a tolerated enemy but, surprisingly enough, a respected ally to many of us. Those who have followed Rorty's line of thought and reasoning since the 1970s have never been in doubt about the depth of his main thesis that scientific knowledge is not really going to discover a "true" and "objective reality," independent of mind and language. He has been painstakingly arguing that independently of our mind and language we cannot have a view of reality that is out there in space and time and available only to the privileged scientist and robust (epistemological) realist. In effect our ways of knowing the world, manifest or scientific, are unavoidably interwoven with our habits and actions and means of coping with the same. Thought, detached from practice, does not provide a reliable access to the world we live in. Our situatedness in the world, affiliation to this or that culture, and its web of beliefs invariably enter into our world-view. Rorty's understanding of objectivity, relativism, and truth, though admittedly anti-representationist, is not definitely hostile to the spirit of realism. If we remember that several varieties of representationist and anti-representationist realism exist, showing that Rorty's ethnocentric or (what I call) anthropological objectivism is compatible with sober realism is not difficult.[11] The proclaimed affinity of his epistemological ideas with those of Davidson and Putnam deserve to be taken and studied seriously.

Fortunately, the blind and unstudied anti-relativism of yesteryear has, of late, become so weak and empty that the robust anti-relativists have to invent a straw man called "metaphysical realist" or "uncritical defender of things-in-themselves." Since finding a practicing philosopher who defends "metaphysical realism" is difficult, some imaginary Rortys, Kuhns, and Feyerabends are singled out for unstudied denunciation and summary rejection. When a serious philosopher of science and erudite scholar such as Paul Feyerabend writes *Against Method* or speaks of "anything goes," he should be studied in his own proclaimed context, for he is rightly against making scientific method or epistemology a fetish against serious self-critical examination that is the avowed aim of philosophy. In fact Feyerabend, initially influenced by Karl Popper, has been trying to point out that science has no special and magic method of its own in terms of which a sharp line of demarcation between science and non-science could be drawn. It was a frontal attack against Popper's doctrine of falsifiability as a criterion of demarcation between the so-called science and so-called metaphysics. He rightly observes: "[I]f we want to understand nature, if we master our physical surroundings, then we must use *all* ideas, *all* methods, and not just a small selection of them."[12] Neither Feyerabend, nor Imre Lakatos is anti-scientific or subjectivist in their temper and approach. Their strong criticism against methodological and ideological tyranny of a particular variety earned for them the highly questionable tag of bad relativism. Both of them have persuasively argued in favor of their chosen versions of realism, objectivism and relativism.[13] Sadly, F. A. von Hayek's early warning against the counter-revolutionary role of science or "abuse of reason" went largely unstudied and unheeded.[14]

3. Return to Krausz

It will be perhaps advisable to turn our attention to the sort of relativism defended by Krausz and some other like-minded writers. Remarkably free from traditional varieties of realism and idealism, perceptively responsive to different cultures and disciplines, and studiously committed to hermeneutics, Krausz has worked out his critical version of relativism. His central thesis as it appears to me is that before we try to discuss and criticize relativism we must situate the discourse within a field of identifiable objects—scientific, cultural, aesthetic, or religious. To speak of relativism *in abstracto* is likely to mislead us to the extremes of indefensible singularism and unjustifiable multiplism. Singularism and multiplism may each be right in their legitimate areas. When the limits of those areas are transgressed, wittingly or unwittingly, relativism turns out to be misleading, if not totally directionless and pointless.

While in the light of many-valued logic Krausz may grudgingly tolerate incongruence between different interpretations of an identifiably same object, he insists on the condition of their non-exclusivity.[15] On this issue he is likely to remind us of the Jain Logic of anekîntavîda, many-sidedness of truth, referred to before. The cautious variety of relativism he defends is compatible with realism and constructivism and takes due note of Putnam's internal realism and its Popperian variant espoused by Chhanda Gupta. A streak of neo-Kantian metaphysics appears to be necessary in his scheme of thought, particularly in the context of explication of cultural objects.[16] A relatively stronger streak of realism also seems to be acceptable to him on the ground that, unless we metaphysically assume that our natural environment has law-like structures and substructures hidden or discoverable within it, our scientific investigation as a serious undertaking will appear without even its prima facie justification. To say that science has its own aim or even to recognize the definite aim of a particular practicing scientist does not entail that that aim will be necessarily realizable or that (hypothetically) aimed-at structures or substructures are essential furniture or constitute unalterable features of nature. That the supposedly same structures of nature lend themselves to different, not necessarily alternative in all respects, constructions and interpretations is evident from the history of revolutionary and normal science. Nature is not always obliging and does not fulfill many of our aims, including the scientist's ones. And that accounts for, among other things, endless modification or refutation of scientific theories. It has to be recognized that nature always nests within its (hitherto) known structures many unknown but (in principle) knowable substructures, which are not necessarily replicative or isomorphic. The working scientist experiences an element of surprise during the course of an investigation. In other words, nature is not marked by uniformity or by limited variety. The man in the street and the professional scientist, notwithstanding his or her long experience, are open to negative experience or evidence.

Fallibilism is a part of singularist and also of multiplist relativism. This important point has not apparently received due attention from Krausz. Though I am raising the question in the context of natural sciences, the question is relevant to the context of cultural studies as well. The bridge that can, and in fact, continuously does connect natural sciences with such other sciences as anthropology, history, law, and even literature is language, the language of interpretation.

The classical scientists such as Isaac Newton, taking cues from Francis Bacon, wrongly concluded that the sure way to scientific truth lies in disengagement of the knowing human mind from its study of the text of nature. The book of nature, contrary to Bacon's belief, is closed (not open), and for "reading" or disclosing its hidden truths, to purge the human mind of all the so-called idols is not easy. Thinkers such as Wilhelm Dilthey have critically tried to point out the mistake of this proclaimed detached or purely objective study of nature. They wanted to point out that the true interpretation of nature and that of culture are both required to be drawn out of the matrix of the lived life. Phenomenologists such as Edmund Husserl and Martin Heidegger tried to highlight the importance of history and language to broaden and deepen the horizon of the lifeworld referred to by Dilthey, trying to make it play the role of connecting cultural sciences with natural sciences.[17]

This large and ambitious project could not be successful without assigning a central role to the language of interpretation. The words "language" and "interpretation" are to be taken in right earnest. Neither interpretation nor language knows any terminal point of its journey of ceaseless disclosure of truth. No text, scientific, cultural, legal, or religious, can unilaterally foreclose its future and multiple interpretability. This truth-seeking force is inherent in the very nature of language, be it Sanskrit or Greek or their various modern descendants. Language is endlessly (and yet questionably) expressive and disclosive. This quality accounts for the perpetual open-endedness and many-sidedness of possible interpretations of a text.

Central to this issue is the presence of the human being situated within language and using it to express his or her understanding of nature and culture as texts presented by the creative (and occasionally destructive) course of history. Human beings are in effect simultaneously consumer and producer of history and language. By assimilating history they create history and by using language they create language. Questionability, fallibility, and incompleteness of human interpretation of nature and culture are no indication of interpretation's estrangement from truth. On the contrary, the very fact that every text, natural or cultural, lends itself to many interpretations, singular or multiple, shows its ability to enlarge the truth and inexhaustible many-sidedness. Our pressing practical or pragmatic inclinations lead us to concentrate our attention only on the few selective views of these possible interpretations, depending on our time, station, and aim in life.

While I focus my attention on the enlarging and many-sided characteristics of truth and allow our aim of life and pragmatic considerations to have a very important say on the issue of relativism, several other relativists, in addition to Krausz, highlight the necessity of limiting the bounds of different versions of relativism. In the process they are required to introduce concepts, including singularism and multiplism, constructivism and realism, ascription and description and their cognates, which narrow down their widely supposed differences. The achievement of Krausz lies particularly in pointing out finely graded varieties of singularism, multiplism, realism, and constructivism.

Much of the logical space for these fine differentiations has been secured by his notion of singularism as "the view that which is interpreted should always answer to one and only one ideally admissible interpretation" and that of multiplism as "the view that which is interpreted need not always answer to one and only one fully congruent ideally admissible interpretation." The singularist position is apparently weakened and made unduly vulnerable by this restrictive definition. But the insertion of the "ideally admissible" condition, a rear-guard action, cancels much of the initially suggested restriction put on "singularism." Every singular object lends itself to many, but not an infinite number of, ideally admissible interpretations. To make the case of singular object logically plausible its ascertainable identity has to be secured. In his bid to detach his version of singularism and multiplism from the contest between realism and (even) constructivism, Krausz is obliged to fall back upon some kind of metaphysics. But the very notion of the contest between singularism and multiplism makes no sense in his scheme of thought unless they are addressed to common objects. The establishment of common identity of the object is sought in terms of some properties of familial resemblance.

From a careful perusal of Krausz's impressive survey of literature on the subject, referring pointedly to the views of Rom Harré (external constructivism), Joseph Margolis (internal constructivism), Paul Thom, Bernard Harrison and Patricia Hanna (on practice-independent materia), Putnam and Chhanda Gupta (descriptive language-relative notions of dependence and independence) you get the clear impression that he is unwilling to tie his boat of singular objective interpretation to any one of these cited versions of relativism. Yet his relativistic sympathy objectively gives him an appreciative proximity to each one of these views. At times the said proximity amounts to affinity.

Krausz's strong orientation toward multiplism is evident from (a) his rejection of David Norton's insistence that cultural objects answer singularist condition, (b) the proclaimed detachability of singularism and multiplism from the contest between realism and constructivism, and (c) special emphasis on the relation between ideals of interpretation of pertinent objects with ideals of life, paths, and objects. Even if you bear his caveats and refinements of the central notions deployed to demarcate the hermeneutic domain of singularism from that of multiplism and to delimit their myriad scopes, you are likely to end up with the conclusion that he associates singularism primarily with the scientific discourse and pluralism with the humanistic discourse. I can well imagine that Krausz, passionately attached to the ideal of endless refinement, may not accept my reading of his liberal and rational theory of interpretation.

Krausz's perceptive program to bring singularism and multiplism, constructivism, and realism and other such paired views of interpretation, indicating simultaneously their range and limits of admissibility, reminds me of what I have called elsewhere anthropological rationalism detached from essentialism and a God's-eye-view of the World. That the changing acts of human interpretations are deeply rooted in an "inner necessity" or, to vary the term, anthropological rationality, is clearly admitted by Krausz. This changing of inner necessity accounts for and accords well with the changing values and projects of our life.

NOTES

1. Michael Krausz, ed., *Relativism: Interpretation and Confrontation* (Notre Dame: Notre Dame University Press, 1989); Michael Krausz, *Rightness and Reasons: Interpretation in Cultural Practices* (Ithaca, N. Y.: Cornell University Press, 1993); Michael Krausz, *Limits of Rightness* (LR) (Lanham, Md: Rowman & Littlefield, 2000).

2. Nelson Goodman, *Ways of Worldmaking* (Indianapolis and Cambridge: Hackett, 1978), pp. 93–97.

3. Saul Kripke, *Naming and Necessity* (Cambridge, Mass: Harvard University Press, 1980); see also David Lewis, *On the Plurality of Worlds* (Oxford: Basil Blackwell, 1986), pp. 92–93.

4. D. P. Chattopadhyaya, "Models and Metaphors in Arts, Science and Mathematics" in *Mind, Language and Necessity*, eds. P. K. Sen and D. P. Chattopadhyaya (Delhi: Macmillan, 1981).

5. Ludwig Wittgenstein, *Remarks on the Foundations of Mathematics*, trans. G. E. M. Anscombe (London: Basil Blackwell, 1967), pp. 49–53.

6. Goodman, *Ways of Worldmaking*, p. 20.

7. *Ibid.*, p. 107.

8. Ludwig Wittgenstein, *Philosophical Investigations*, trans. G. E. M. Anscombe. New York: Macmillan, 1953), pp. 135, 136, 223, 226; Ludwig Wittgenstein, *Tractatus Logico-Philosophicus*, trans. D. F. Pears and B. F. McGuinness (New York: Routledge & Kegan Paul, 1961), 2.1, 2.12, 2.15, 2.1511, 2.1514; Karl R. Popper, *Conjectures and Refutations* (London: Routledge and Kegan Paul, 1963), pp. 232 ff, 391 ff, and 399–404; Donald Davidson, "The Folly of Trying to Define Truth" *Realism: Responses and Reactions*, ed. D. P. Chattopadhyaya (New Delhi: Indian Council of Philosophical Research, 2000), pp. 170–186; Hilary Putnam, *Representation and Reality* (Cambridge, Mass.: MIT Press, 1991),chapters 4, 7.

9. Hilary Putnam, *The Many Faces of Realism* (LaSalle, Ill.: Open Court, 1987), pp. 34–38.

10. D. P. Chattopadhyaya, *Individuals and Worlds: Essays in Anthropological Rationalism* (Delhi: Oxford University Press, 1976); D. P. Chattopadhyaya, *Knowledge Freedom and Language* (Delhi: Motilal Banarsidass, 1989).

11. Richard Rorty, *Objectivity, Relativism, and Truth* (Cambridge: Cambridge University Press, 1991), pp. 1–17.

12. Paul Feyerabend, *Against Method* (London: New Left Books (NLB), 1975), p. 306.

13. P. K. Feyerabend, *Realism, Rationalism and Scientific Method: Philosophical Papers*, Vol. 1 (Cambridge: Cambridge University Press, 1986); Imre Lakatos, *The Methodology of Scientific Research Programmes: Philosophical Papers*, Vol. 1 (Cambridge: Cambridge University Press, 1978).

14. F. A. von Hayek, *The Counter-Revolution of Science: Or Abuse of Reason* (Glencoe, Ill.: Free Press, 1952).

15. Krausz, *Limits of Rightness*, p. 149.

16. *Ibid.*, p. 150.

17. Hans-Georg Gadamer, *Truth and Method* (New York: Crossroad, 1982), pp. 210 ff, 297 ff, 411 ff.

EXTENSIONS AND APPLICATIONS

Eighteen

RIGHTNESS, ONTOLOGY, AND THE ADJUDICATION OF TRUTH: ADUMBRATIONS FROM THE LAW'S TRIAL

Nancy A. Weston

In his 1993 *Rightness and Reasons* and now again in *Limits of Rightness*, Michael Krausz has given us a thoughtful and thorough account of interpretation, in which he explores the idea of an interpretation's possible rightness and questions the singularity that such rightness is often taken to entail.[1] Concluding that rightness is instead to be understood as multiple, Krausz holds its determination to be independent of—"detachable" from—considerations of ontology, in particular from any necessity of choosing among the various currently contending ontological theories classed under the banners of "realism" or "constructivism," with respect to which Krausz, accordingly, declares himself agnostic. Intriguingly, then, in unfolding his account of interpretation, Krausz invites us to contemplate both rightness and ontology, as well as the relation between them, two vast domains of philosophical interest and inquiry that are usually approached separately.

I come to the issues of rightness and ontology from a background and set of concerns different from those of other contributors to and readers of these essays. My field is the philosophy of law, with law taken in the first instance not, as it is generally, as a set of posited and rationalized rules and their effectuating institutions, but as the understanding of obligation and right action without which such rules and institutions lack—and must endeavor, then, always to gain—authority and legitimacy. I am concerned with how we come to address questions of rightness, and I understand these questions and ways of addressing them to arise similarly in connection with law and in determinations of right and truth more generally. I do not, then, undertake to engage with the particulars of the account of interpretation Krausz offers, or to debate its theoretical sufficiency. Instead I take the occasion to explore some questions I find implicitly raised by the project of determining rightness generally, the project that Krausz explores in the context of interpretation.

First, I offer an account of the ways in which the distinctions and issues Krausz raises appear in, and present strains upon, familiar institutions of legal adjudication. I then use the occasion of these strains to inquire further into those issues themselves. Legal thought may be seen to have taken the same course, and taken up the same premises, problems, and solutions, as has thought on questions of the determination of truth and right in general. It is my hope that addressing the implications of the analogous legal thought may

therefore be informative or illuminating for those interested in questions surrounding the determination of rightness more generally. As a result of this
convergence of developments, the discussion will increasingly concern itself
with questions of the determination of truth and right in general. Finally, this
course will bring us, in conclusion, once more before questions of rightness
and ontology, the questions from which, with Krausz, we began.

Let us first consider the Krauszian ideas of singularism and multiplism
as they appear in the context of a trial at law—a situation in which "adjudication among competing truth claims" is not a mere metaphor but is the institution's explicit mission. In a standard court case, only one judgment, endorsing one interpretation of the events at issue, is possible: a criminal defendant
is either found guilty or is acquitted; a civil suit is decided either for the plaintiff or for the civil defendant. Viewed in the light of the inquiry Krausz has
undertaken, this state of affairs appears to constitute an institutional constraint
that mandates singularism.

The trial court issues its singular judgment despite encountering a lack
of conclusiveness in the reasons offered to support the interpretation of the
case given by one side or the other of the dispute. This lack of conclusiveness, such as follows from ambiguities and incompleteness in the process of
proof, may be understood as contingent and regrettable, if chronic, compatibly with singularism; or as intrinsic and appropriate, compatibly with multiplism, although it will then appear incongruous and insupportable that multiplism is abandoned for singularism in the court's final judgment.

There exists another, time-honored way in which to understand a court
trial as intrinsically incapable of reaching its judgment with conclusiveness
while yet remaining a singularist. That is the position implicit in the canonical
distinction between the *forum internum* of the defendant's conscience and the
forum externum of the court. That the court is necessarily incapable of conclusively ascertaining the quality of the will with which the criminal defendant acted (his *mens rea*) is not in itself an obstacle to its reaching its (singular) judgment, nor to the idea that there is a single right answer to the question of the defendant's guilt, even if the court, as *forum externum*, cannot ever
be in a position to ascertain it. Krausz would, I expect, see in this distinction
an instance of "pluralization," which he describes as the singularist strategic
move of separating an object-of-interpretation into plural distinct objects-of-
interpretation—here, the defendant's legal guilt and his actual or moral
guilt—to each of which may then correspond a singular right answer.

Alternatively, we may understand the distinction between the *fora internum* and *externum* as presenting the law's implicit acknowledgement of (to
borrow Krausz's intriguing title) the "limits of rightness" to which it might
aspire. Yet there are two very different ways to understand such a limitation
and the conclusion to be drawn from it: The traditional distinction between
the *fora* points, much like Immanuel Kant's first *Critique*, to the idea that the
farther truth (here, moral guilt) is unreachable by the court. In contrast, con-

temporary thought, following Friedrich Nietzsche, sees no reason to assume that such an unreachable truth exists; rather, *because* it cannot be ascertained and proven by us, it ceases to be truth at all. In the case of law, it eventuates that the only guilt that exists is legal guilt: The guilty are those the court declares to be guilty. As we shall see, this is a development of more than legal-historical interest and one that touches far more than this single doctrine, but instead goes to the heart of contemporary understandings of truth and right and the perceived necessity of the grounds of their determination.

Everyday procedures of case administration afford ingenious mechanisms by which the law may be seen to manage the discrepancy between the multiple interpretations it confronts and the demand that the case eventuate in a single, conclusive result. By far the most commonly encountered of these is settlement. Because it pre-empts trial, settlement spares the court from having to reach a defensible determination of its singular result. The costs of doing so, if not its philosophical difficulties, are salient to court observers, for the practice accounts for the disposition of approximately ninety percent of all cases, and is so prevalent that the legal system depends upon it for its capacity to function efficiently. Although the court may order the parties to meet to explore settlement, it does not, in a standard civil case, speak to the result. The court enters a dismissal of the case pursuant to the request of the claimant (who is possessed of discretion as to whether to proceed), but gives no endorsement to the settlement itself.

What occurs in settlement is not understood as the reaching of any conclusion, not even a multiplist one, on the questions of truth or right at issue, but instead as a strategic compromise of the parties' material demands. The parties reach agreement not on the underlying questions but only on a division of the benefit each had hoped to gain (or retain) by winning the case at trial. Because the usual remedy sought is money—value already abstracted from principle—it is peculiarly available to being so divided. The result is negotiated strategically, and is determined by the parties' perceptions of their relative strength in persisting to trial as well as prevailing there. The possible truth or rightness of their underlying claims is of merely strategic bearing, or none. Thus a civil plaintiff may bring a novel or unlikely claim that is settled for what is bluntly called "nuisance value," the price a defendant is willing to pay to avoid the larger expense of a trial he expects he would win. Conversely, civil defendants can extract favorable settlement terms by outlasting less affluent opponents whose cases may well have warranted success at trial.

This process, which candidly abandons concern with truth and right to a contest of strategic power, is more decorously framed when the matter to be settled is criminal, where the settlement procedure is known as "plea-bargaining." There the prosecutor—representing the people, and not the victim, for it is the *law* that is offended by crime—will agree to refrain from prosecuting a serious charge, such as burglary, instead "settling" for a lesser included offense, such as criminal trespass or possessing stolen goods. The standard plea bargain procedure requires the defendant to appear in court and enter a plea of guilty to that offense—and to declare that he does so freely, not out of coercion or inducement—as a condition of the settlement. This step could be understood simply as the defendant's part of the "bargain," and all that he is in a position to offer. It may also be viewed as the court's way of achieving a singularist resolution of the matter despite a lack of conclusiveness so severe as to discourage the parties from pressing their interpretations at trial. Yet it may instead manifest the law's discomfiture, born of repugnance to the idea that case resolution is simply a matter of bargaining. If so, it bespeaks a concern less to uphold the singularism of the court's determinations than to uphold the law as that from which strategic considerations of advantage are properly absent. We may wonder if this aspiration can endure within contemporary accounts of law, a matter to which we shall return.

This conjecture is supported by the cold reception given another practice, seemingly indistinguishable from settlement, but one that threatens to bring bargaining, with its disregard for questions of truth and right, into the sanctum of the court itself: the "splitting" of a verdict by a jury, whereby it avoids reaching an all-or-nothing verdict by dividing the amount at issue between the parties. Although it is sometimes assumed that juries frequently split verdicts (the inviolability of the jury's deliberations makes it impossible to know), doing so is forbidden, as it violates the jury's duty to determine the truth of the facts presented to it and apply the law accordingly. In splitting its verdict, the jury may be understood to decline its singularist mandate; yet the means by which it may do so directly—as by confessing itself to be unable to reach a decision (a "hung" jury), or by determining different counts, charges, or claims for different parties (on the account Krausz offers, perhaps an instance of singularist pluralism)—are perfectly acceptable. It would appear that, although the parties understand settlement as undertaken to gain a maximally advantageous position, the law refuses openly to countenance this understanding; rather, like other instances of advantage seeking, bargaining is implicitly understood to be *extra-legal*.

Yet bargaining is coming, now, to overtake our understanding of the law—as manifested, for instance, in the extraordinary currency within the contemporary legal academy of the economic account of law, to which bargaining is native; as a result, to those imbued with that understanding such abstention comes increasingly to appear as artificial and indefensible. On the economic account, rightness at law is identified with the resolution prescribed by considerations of efficiency or maximal net gain (a point determinable by bargaining and buying power and, thanks to the mechanics of differential calculus and of markets, always determinable). Rightness in any sense independent of this being unavailable to capture by the theoretic model, it is proclaimed unintelligible and, finally, ruled out of existence as nothing at all, although, as later discussion will reveal, this is in fact the premise of such thought instead of its conclusion. As it will also show, dismissal of non-economic rightness is not a phenomenon isolated to law (though the implications of this development are perhaps more dramatic there), but is a development inextricable from how we have come to understand truth and right to be determined and determinable more generally. Before turning to that discussion, let us first consider several more specifically legal illustrations.

When a case does proceed to trial, the law again makes use of a number of procedures by which it may be understood to accommodate the multiplicity and incommensurability of the accounts of legally significant facts and events with which it is presented, and the inconclusiveness of the methods of proof by which it may adjudicate among them, while yet remaining within the strictures that require it to issue only a single judgment in each case. Such accommodation may be discerned in such familiar doctrines as the burden of proof, whereby the moving party must advance substantial evidence for an issue to be triable at all; the presumption of innocence of a criminal defendant, which prescribes a judgment of acquittal where the evidence is equivocal; and the standard of proof—the preponderance of the evidence in civil cases and beyond a reasonable doubt in criminal cases—which sets a threshold for sufficient evidence for judgment that is well below conclusiveness.

These are doctrines and procedures generally regarded as expressive of substantive legal rights and of the basic requirements of a fair and orderly trial. Alternatively, we can see them as yielding decision-making rules and procedures that effectively take multiplist inputs across a chasm of inconclusiveness that they cannot themselves bridge, to yield a singular result notwithstanding. So viewed, it appears that the law cunningly employs multiplist strategies—in particular, those of separating admissibility from conclusiveness, and of forgoing aspirations to conclusiveness—to reach its singularist end, even to mitigate the strictures of its singularism. In so proceeding it does not openly relinquish the claim to provide singular resolution that is a prominent feature of its constitution and a principal source of its authority and legitimacy and of the importance of its public and political role.

And yet, maintaining such a credibility-straining amalgam of avowed singularism and practical multiplism is now becoming untenable. A fulfilled singularism has come to be acknowledged among certain legal constituencies as beyond the limits of what the law is able to undertake. For it has become transparent that the court does not have available to it any grounds that would warrant its determination to be unique and conclusive, rendering it right (as distinct from dispositive) in the manner singularism requires.

The course of this breakdown is of the highest significance for our understanding of the possibilities of rightness, for in law it does not appear to be the case that anything that could be considered a multiplist sense of rightness has come into play in lieu of the singularist one, but only contention among the multiple contestants that now remain. In the current situation of law the only possibilities available are an exhausted and implausible singularism on the one hand, and unsatisfyingly unprincipled multiplist skirmishes on the other. Yet these are not alternatives after all but two sides of the same thin coin: Just as in a lawsuit, either a single claimant's singular account of the truth and right in issue prevails; or, if it cannot—and *because* it cannot—then there is no resolution of these matters, but only a draw between the multiple claimants and, on the basis of might instead of right, a division of spoils between them. This, writ large, is the situation of the entire field of law as it appears to us now, because contemporary thought on the nature of law leaves us without a way in which we may understand law as a matter of rightness.

Further, the "alternatives" that are sometimes offered to this situation—ones that would have us resolve legal questions by resort to conventional practice, to politics, to empirical data, or to the satisfaction of selected aims and purposes—also partake of the same standard strand of modern legal thought, woven into these few variations. These proposed resolutions share a decisive tenet, according to which law is, and can only be, a contest of preference—the only understanding of law that is seen, now, to be available—for it is only on the basis of that tenet, and its inability to yield rightness, that these resolutions emerge to invite us to turn to them instead. All of these purported alternatives therefore compound our abdication of the duty to decide legal questions *as* questions of truth or right, the task that singularism cannot solve for us. Yet, as we shall see, singularism is not on that account given up. It still governs our legal decision-making, bringing us to make that abdication whenever it cannot be satisfied, thus remaining decisively in charge. As a result, it has come increasingly to be concluded that, if law is not to be conclusively determined— either by the programs, sources, and methods that have been tried or by any that can be imagined—then its determination *can only be* a matter of competition among proffered outcomes.

Those contending outcomes, in turn, owe their origin and character to their having been advanced by an advocate, each of whom devises an account (the "theory of the case"), culminating in the outcome preferred by the advocate's client, so as to appeal to the court and gain its preferment. On this understanding, the court is the arbiter of the law, but not its defender, for *there is no law to defend* apart from its production in the court's performative declaration of it. Since the substance of this declaration plainly can—and, in the frequent event of credible dissent or appellate reversal, does—admit of multiple "right answers," the court's pronouncement of a singular answer comes to appear illegitimate, an insupportably excessive status bestowed willfully upon one resolution selected by the court from among the class of equally admissible and inconclusive alternatives. (Krausz has characterized such a discrepancy between claimed and deliverable status as "overshooting" on the part of singularism.) The determination of law by the court and the resolution of a case on its basis thus come to be understood as merely an exercise of power instead of as the discernment and pronouncement of right.

The understanding of rightness as having anything to do with the law or with the court's undertaking increasingly appears dispensable and superfluous, readily ignored unless it can be turned to one's legal advantage. Rightness as such—that is, rightness understood other than already as a tool for the promotion of utility, including the utility of reaching a resolution on inconclusive evidence—drops out of consideration. Among the legal cognoscenti (though not yet, or not yet consciously and consistently, among the legal public), it is widely conceded that rightness is of only tangential and occasional concern to the court, and of no concern at all to the lawyers and clients unless it should fortuitously coincide with their preferred objectives.

Thus our ways of proceeding to determine right at law—and, before that, the peculiar demands of determinability we put upon it, as we do upon questions of truth and right more generally—relegate the appearance of right to an occasional and fortuitous luxury, so that it comes to appear to much of the legal profession to be wholly dispensable. At least, this is so if rightness is understood in the broadly moral sense of uprightness, as in the phrase "the right thing to do" or, here, "the right decision." To be sure, it very often is not; rather, rightness at law is conventionally understood among these legal constituencies as conformity to statute or precedent, independent of (up)rightness; to imagine otherwise belongs to the naïveté of the legally untrained, and a beginning law student learns, before learning anything else, to banish such thoughts under penalty of scorn. This eclipse of (up)rightness by conformity to the positive law of statute and precedent is, however, not a matter of legal idiom, nor of professional sophistication, and it is not a contingent fact of twentieth-century legal culture—interesting to note, perhaps, but ultimately without philosophical significance.

Instead, the ascendancy of positive law, with its concomitant eclipse of right, to its contemporary position of exclusive and exhaustive occupation of the field of law is a highly significant development in the history of our search for ways of determining questions of truth and right, and richly suggestive for our consideration of the matters Krausz has brought before us. Tracing the path of positivism's ascendancy invites us to encounter and contemplate the claim, central to the account Krausz offers of the turn from singularism to multiplism, of the absence of a "single overarching standard" with which we might conclusively determine questions of truth and right. Doing so, we come to see the ground and unity of what otherwise appear to be separate episodes and theoretical developments, in legal theory as well as in such seemingly tangential fields as moral theory and epistemology. For the mainspring of this finally single history, of which all these relatively recent steps are undertaken on behalf and in fulfillment, is the drive, begun far earlier, to achieve mastery over the determination of questions of truth and right.

The loss of right from law, as evidenced by its apparent dispensability in the resolution of a dispute at law, reflects the profound repercussions that follow upon our having come in the modern West to understand law in a single, distinctive, and dominant way: as the product of our invention and imposition, dependent for its existence upon our choosing to posit, promulgate, and enforce it, and located exhaustively in the aggregated products of these enterprises. So dominant is this understanding of law that it does not even appear to us, now, to be distinctive or questionable; indeed, it does not appear at all, but is rather taken for granted as the sole, necessary, and "obvious" understanding of law—as what law simply *is*, and must be.

Because law, on this understanding, is and must be posited, or put in place, in order to be law, the understanding (generally mistaken for a theory) is denominated legal positivism, and the law it describes positive law. It is conventionally contrasted with natural law, an understanding of much older origin—and of lesser intelligibility to modern minds, in large measure because it too is commonly presented as a theory: an intellectual invention constructed and presented for appeal and optional adoption, should one be so persuaded. Yet this is an understanding of thinking and what it requires that belongs squarely within positivism; it is the positive account of thought.

In addition, natural law is often construed as inextricable from the Christian religious doctrine with which it is historically intertwined, such that law, on this account, is presented as the ordinance of God. When, however, we fail to attend to the relation of God (that is, of any god, *qua* god) to right necessary to make this account intelligible—a matter impeded not merely by religious skepticism and secularism but much more so by our (absent) understanding of right—natural law too reduces to a kind of divine positivism. When so viewed, the debate between natural law and positive law becomes but another instance of the debate, perennial within positivism, over "Who gets to say?" what the law is. That question is devoted to locating—in the king, the judge, the electorate, or, here, God—the power to invent and enforce what will then gain power's prize: being in force and effective, hence law; for, on this account, from the outset, that is all that law is or can be. So understood, it should be apparent, we have not taken a single step outside of positivism. Yet this way of thinking is so pervasive in modern thought, not only on law but, as we shall see, on matters of truth and right more generally, that it is by no means clear that we can now comprehend any alternative to it.

The other challenge routinely pressed upon natural law theorists (of whom there are now very few, so that the position comes to be in the main a straw man, silent and antique) is, "But how can we *know* this natural law?" Various answers, including divine revelation and nature understood as teleological, have traditionally been proposed; in the wake of their diminished plausibility, natural law, like morality more generally, is taken to be doomed. Thus threatened, theories of law and morality typically turn, as a last resort, to empirical sources of support, including the utility and prevalence of the moral and legal practices they would preserve, although the promise of refuge thereby grasped is false and recourse to it is a fatal mistake.

Seldom, however, is the question that has produced this flight of law and morals itself brought into the light of question. Like its correlate in morals, "But how can we *know* the natural law?" asks for a way or method by which we can ascertain what law or morality requires of us in a given situation. But this demand for a method of ascertaining that answer—that is, of determining it with certainty—charges that determination with too high a level of stringency; in the terms offered by Krausz, it is a demand belonging to singularism that, as such, asks too much of the methods of determination available to us. I suggest, however, that the fundamental problem posed by this demand lies deeper than does a dispute of degree, which might be satisfactorily addressed by a moderated demand for stringency, perhaps one that recognized the ability of multiple contending answers to meet it. For the further problem with this demand is one that remains, no matter where the bar of proof is set or how many answers it may then validate.

This persistent demand for a way or method by which we can determine what law or morality requires directs us to look away from the legal or moral situation that lies before us, and instead to the rule, yardstick, or method that will determine the question with finality—and so which we are eager to find, challenge, and defend. That guidance might instead be found in the matter before us, attention to which might well reveal what resolution is called for, perhaps even obviating the recourse to rule and method, is a possibility that does not reside within the compass of the question (much as "But I didn't beat it!" lies outside the range of immediately available answers to "So, did you stop beating your dog yet?"). We exclude this possibility from the outset, for the "might" or maybe with which we may expect a resolution from attending to the situation is too iffy; it refuses us the certainty we crave and require. Moreover, it contravenes our presumption, shared by both those who ask the question and those who respond to its demand (whether or not that response turns out to be adequate), that we are to look anywhere *but* to the situation before us for a determination of what is required. For the question asks for something *else*, some sign or determinant or proxy or yardstick or rule or authority, by which we may dispose of the question of right. For this search to be understood as necessary, or even possible, it must be presumed that rightness and its determination are extraneous to the situation itself and the possible resolutions attending it, as well as no enduring concern of ours.

When we demand such a yardstick or authority as a "single overarching standard that will adjudicate between claims to rightness," what we crave and require is, above all, disposition: We wish, not merely for an answer to the question of rightness, still less for "mere" rightness if it is other than dispositive, but instead for an answer of a quite particular sort, namely one that will *dispose* of the question, answering it conclusively so that we may be done with it and with any duty to attend to it further. We want relief from the question, and from the responsibility for determining right; paradoxically, we make this demand even as we claim to be "in charge" of such questions, as under a constructivist or consensualist view of what truth or right require. The paradox is merely apparent, however, for we can make that claim only because our demand for authoritative determinability and disposition presumes rightness to be extraneous to the matter itself. There thus arises an apparent vacuum of rightness, into which we step as its creators, though we have created only this "opportunity"—and not rightness, as we suppose.

Stripped in advance of the possibility of possessing any intrinsic rightness, these potential resolutions can only appear, as they now do, as items taken from the agendas of interested parties, preferred by one or another of them, then by the court, and ultimately by the electorate. Though the question is often raised as to whose preferences should prevail, gaining preferment and, with it, ascendancy, it is largely undisputed that preference, governed by considerations of advantage, exhausts the possibilities for determining legal and political questions. The spectacular ascendancy in recent decades of the economic account of law, as of politics openly given over to the promotion of interest, owes its success to this largely unexamined development.

Accordingly, what takes the place of consideration of rightness in the court's resolution is understood to be the expression of the preferences of the court, the parties, or other legal constituencies, determined in each case by considerations of advantage. Any suggestion of an alternative ground of decision or an alternative understanding of the judicial enterprise is dismissed as merely mendacious cover for an advancement of interest—as indeed it must appear, given the presuppositions from which modern legal thought begins. In sum, the judicial decision, like the litigants' actions and the lawyers' arguments, is now understood to have the character of a choice among preferences, to be determined by the consultation and comparison of advantages yielded by different resolutions for the satisfaction of desire. That such desire may be altruistic, as with public interest advocacy, or responsive to collective or social preference instead of to the judge's personal preference, does not alter this preferential character or diminish its pervasiveness, for even the selection of such a ground as determinative of one's actions is itself understood to be a matter of preference.

Much legal scholarship of the last several decades has adopted this explicitly and exhaustively political view of adjudication. It has come to be the prevailing view not only on the left, where it is the matter-of-fact starting premise of such schools of legal scholarship as critical legal studies and critical race theory, but also on the right and within the legal and political mainstream. It has become widely routine, for example, to advert to the political affiliations of judicial nominees, on the implicit supposition that such affiliations are germane and decisive to the decision of cases. Such a supposition appears to be the upshot of the loss of singularist faith in the judicial task.

Yet this widespread supposition is the upshot only of that faith's impairment and removal to the status of an impossible dream. It does not reflect any loss of, or a cessation of subscription to, the singularist ideal. On the contrary, we continue tacitly to hold to the singularist model of determinations of right and truth—in particular, to the idea that, in order to *be* a determination of right or truth, it must be made on conclusive grounds and with exclusive efficacy. On that basis we conclude that, when satisfaction of that model is not to be had, we are left instead with only the competition of power, desire, and advantage from which considerations of right and truth are absent. For it is only those requirements of the determination of right or truth that are now in question, and (it is increasingly conceded) unavailable, or at least not uniformly and reliably available, which amounts to the same fatal impairment. The "limits of rightness," as these now come to be understood, are not limitations inhering in *our* attempt to determine right, but *right's* limitations in failing to offer itself up to our conclusive determination, as we continue to hold it must—a failing that, we thereby conclude, is fatal to right.

That determinations of law *must* be only the outcome of competitions of preference and power, rather than—still, somehow—a matter of right or truth, follows, however, only if those requirements, belonging to singularism, continue to demand satisfaction and receive our allegiance in any determination of rightness or truth. We no longer think it possible that the singularist conditions we suppose must be met by a court's determination of truth or right—specifically, that it be made on conclusive grounds and with the power to exclude as wrong any alternative—can be met; but we continue notwithstanding to subscribe to the necessity of those same conditions, which in this way continue to prevail, undisturbed, as they dictate what an adequate determination of truth or right must be, and would be were it possible to satisfy them.

That this satisfaction is not possible is taken, in the case of law, to follow inexorably upon the discovery that what appear to be legally similar cases often eventuate in divergent results. The initial discovery of this variance by the legal profession owed much to the work of publishers who began in the second half of the nineteenth century to collect and systematize what had been an incomplete and ad hoc system of case reportage—an undertaking that, as might be expected, has now evolved into a searchable electronic database. The conclusion became increasingly irresistible that the evidence of legal variation that thereby came to light precluded the law from continuing to profess singularism. As a result, the lawyer's stock in trade increasingly came to be, as it remains, marshalling and managing rules and precedents—that is, finding rulings and decided cases that support one's position, and arguing away those that do not. (This "arguing away" is called "distinguishing the case," and it provides another illustration of the strategy Krausz identifies as "pluralizing.") Again, what the quarried cases are sought to support is the client's, and so the lawyer's, preferred outcome; arguments as to what the court ought to do as a matter of right are but lucky makeweights, invoked only when they aid a client's cause and not for their own sake.

In these developments, we may find an illuminating analogue of developments pertinent to the issues to which Krausz has drawn our attention. In the discovery of legal variation we have an echo of the similar discovery, fostered by anthropological and historical research in the nineteenth century and since, of variations in cultural practices, a discovery that is taken to have irredeemably impaired claims of universal standards of right or truth. Such claims are, accordingly, understood now to be at best provincial, and, worse, offensively ethnocentric and culturally imperialistic. The late modern discovery of cultural variation has generated the conclusion Krausz highlights, that there is "no single overarching standard" that will adjudicate among claims to rightness.

Yet in order for such a "discovery" of legal or other variation to generate this conclusion—in order for it even to be sought—it must already be presumed to be collectible. It must, accordingly, be presumed that the legal or other decisions are susceptible, without fatal loss of intelligibility, to being abstracted, arrayed, and compared, and that their content and significance are accessible through these activities. Further, it is necessarily presumed as well that the decisions so abstracted must, in order to be defensible, be uniform across cases raising similar claims. Both assumptions accomplish the severance of the decision from the immediacy and particularity of the case in which it was reached, and so cut the analyst of decisions off from a possible understanding of what, in the matter then at hand, may have called for it. Whenever we proceed so, we necessarily jettison attention to the particularity of decision-making for the sake of the power the method of uniformity promises.

That power would be considerable. Armed with a uniform method of making decisions on questions of truth and right, we would at last be in a position to render those decisions with finality, and so to be rid of the duty to attend to what truth and right might require in each or any case. Oliver Wendell Holmes anticipated with approval that the number of questions requiring adjudication would rapidly diminish if undertaken in this fashion, inasmuch as situations would cease, except rarely, to be novel and so not already settled. More is driving this development, however, than just the temptation to gain the utility that the prospect of wholesale adjudication excites. A power arises with the presumption that decisions are to be uniform—a power not merely to make those decisions with greater efficiency, but to require those making them to accede to our demands for predictability and for equivalence. In the case of law, the demand is for an exact equivalence in the justice meted out: Justice, the rightness of the decision reached, is required to be—and so, is presumed to be—translatable without residue into terms susceptible to prediction and comparison. Quantification and social scientific methodology accordingly become attractively useful instruments for the pursuit of these demands, which remain unquestioned and unthought. Legal decisions are thereby rendered accessible to scrutiny, and then to challenge, for any deviation from equivalence, either to whatever had been published, and so predicted, or to whatever others before the law had received.

These demands for equivalence and predictability have, in turn, still further sources of interest. The demand that the law and legal decision-making be predictable is born of the desire to maximize our gains from our activities and to secure them against being diminished by our being "overly compliant" with the law, as we might well be were it less than fully explicit and predictable. This understanding of the law (as Holmes, its first expositor, expressly noted) characterizes a "bad man," one who is not concerned to obey the law but only to exploit his opportunities to avoid its strictures, which he understands as costs. The law is here frankly understood as a matter of arbitrary imposition—as, consistent with positivism, it is—and as something merely to be complied with, or not; this, too, is consistent with positivism, for, inasmuch as the law's connection to right is severed by positivism, obedience to it for its own sake is not a possibility.

The demand for equivalence in determinations at law—a demand we are accustomed to exacting as well from determinations of truth and right more generally—also emerges from sources that warrant further thought. We come to see that, just as with the demand for predictability, our usual supposition— that the demand for equivalence is a requirement of justice, or attention to right—is highly questionable. For what is it we are seeking when we demand that judgments at law exhibit equivalence or uniformity in result across cases? We may find such a demand voiced, for example, by a convicted criminal defendant objecting that his sentence is not equivalent to that received by another, apparently similar defendant. As this example suggests, a demand for uniformity typically arises out of jealousy over others' gains (or avoidance of loss) at the hands of the law, the fear that others might be gaining more (or losing less) than oneself. As such, it is a demand born of envy, competition, and a desire for gain, and not of a regard for right; to object to one's sentence on the grounds of its justice, its appropriateness to one's *own* crime, circumstances, and character, is a wholly different matter.

When the demand for equivalence and uniformity is raised more generally, and not by those with an immediate interest in a particular judgment challenged on that basis, it is harder to see, at first, that a similar spring is at work. Yet whenever we raise this demand, invoking equivalence and uniformity as the criteria of rightness, we, like the criminal defendant, look *away* from the possible rightness of the decision at hand, toward its conformity with *another* decision, for it is only such conformity, and not its own rightness, that is thereby demanded of the present decision. Further, the prior decision's rightness is not the reason for its invocation as a standard to be matched; for, in that event, we would be seeking to emulate, not its outcome abstracted from its circumstances—which is all that can be matched across cases—but its rightness. And that would bring us to attend to the rightness of the present decision in the present case. This we do not do, having tacitly ruled out the possibility that there is rightness there to be found.

Even though it is here invoked disinterestedly, the demand for uniformity promises highly desirable benefits to be gained from diverting attention from questions of right to questions of equivalence, a prospect that may well be a significant attraction of this way of thinking: As their susceptibility to quantification suggests, questions of equivalence are readily resolved. Simple comparison of abstracted, accessible data yields a definitive, dispositive resolution. Similarly, equivalence, taken to be the end and standard of justice, is readily satisfied: we are merely to conform our decision to the standard without needing to concern ourselves with the rightness of either the standard or the decision before us. This procedure is, above all, efficient; it yields great advantages to our determinations of justice (or would, if they could remain determinations of justice under this procedure). These include not only the ease with which we would thereby be able to reach those determinations, but also the immunity from criticism they would thereby gain. Such ease and immunity turn out to be of paramount importance to our adopting these ways of proceeding. For once it has been determined that the results are equivalent—and, before that, that equivalence will substitute for justice—then no other thought or consideration is needed, and no challenge on grounds of justice is possible.

On questions of truth and right more generally, too, our insistence upon uniformity and equivalence in the determination of answers reveals that we are more concerned to be immunized from error and criticism than we are to be right, if being right is not to be accompanied by security against such vulnerability. These attractions, which bring us so readily to substitute uniformity for truth or right, similarly bring us to crave answers that are dispositive, that will free us from having to attend further to those who would challenge our determination—or, indeed, from having to attend further to the question, to giving further (or any) consideration to what truth and right, as distinct from uniformity, might require. The security and utility of immunity from criticism, and from any need for further thought, are powerful inducements to adopting requirements, such as equivalence and uniformity across determinations, that promise those benefits. As we shall see, other requirements we are accustomed to supposing necessary to the determination of truth and right, such as conclusive and exclusive grounds for determination, the setting and meeting of standards, and the gaining of consensus, hold out the promise of attaining those same benefits. We should, however, be more candid with ourselves before concluding, as we so often do, that these are requirements arising from truth and right themselves. For it is just these that we look away from, and are enabled to look away from, so long as we attend to and argue over such matters as the uniformity of determinations, the meeting of standards, or the supplying of conclusive grounds instead.

Sometimes we acknowledge that we do look to such matters *instead* of to whatever truth and right might require, as when we claim that this resort is justified because "really, there isn't any" truth or right of the matter to look to. This baldly nihilistic assertion—infamously self-refuting, but, it seems, no less appealing on that account—is, in turn, claimed to be justified by the difficulty of finding truth or right with ease in the places and by the means that we continue to insist upon. It thereby confesses its failure to come to grips with, or even to consider, the questionability of this demand, which endures undiminished despite its unsatisfiability. This demand—that truth and right accede to our demands for accessibility and determinability, or be dismissed as nothing—links modernism, which holds fast to the demand and hopes to see it satisfied, and the postmodern conclusion that there "is no" truth or right, which holds fast to the demand though no longer expecting to see it satisfied. The enduring demand finally gains its Pyrrhic triumph in that conclusion; postmodern dismissal of the possibility of truth and right merely carries out the threat that was implicit in modernism all along.

Variants of this conclusion—paths leading to the same destination—include the epistemological dodge, "But how can we *know* what is true or right, except by such means?" (which, along with certitude, thus continue to be required); and, as still another attempt to supply them, the simultaneous invocation and disparagement of authority: "Well, who gets to *say* what is true or right?" This last maneuver is especially revealing inasmuch as it abandons judgment for the decree of an authority—a step both fallacious and irresponsible—at the same time conceding, not these serious faults, but only the unlikelihood of satisfying the demand for an authoritatively designated authority with unchallengeable finality.

Legal thought has rung the identical changes on the isomorphic question of the determinability of law, with the same outcome: *Because* law has been found to be insufficiently determinable—that is, determinable with insufficient predictability or uniformity or conclusiveness—by such methods as formalism or empiricism, and because no alternative way has been found (or, as it increasingly appears, may yet be found) of providing the certitude, ease, and finality we continue to insist upon, it comes to be concluded that there "is no" law, in any sense related to right, but only the sheer play of power. In the stark bleakness of this conclusion concerning law we may see presaged what is now coming to pass as well for truth and right more generally.

For here, too, it is power that occupies the field, power that has come to seize, exhaust, and rule the determination of questions of truth and right, just as has come to be the case (as is conceded, though without astonishment) in law. The desire for advantage that brings us to insist upon uniformity, equivalence, ease of determination, and predictability are but a few manifestations of this dominance. It is for the sake of our power, utility, and convenience that we seek these things, demanding them from determinations of truth and right—on pain of dismissing the possibility of determining truth and right at all and with it any need on our part to continue to attend to them. We thereby throw over the field of inquiry into truth and right, and their determinations, to considerations of power—here, the power we seek in advantage—which are to govern the matter. Although it may seem that we are thereby secured as "in charge" of the inquiry, it is instead the inherently insatiable claim of power that reigns (as Nietzsche recognized), for that is what we here defer to and serve.

Another manifestation of the way in which considerations of power come to dominance here appears in the strength and persistence of our desire and demand, throughout all the ways we attempt to determine questions of truth and right, that the means of determination be such as to confer upon those determinations immunity from criticism. This requirement has an affinity with the demand for conclusiveness and finality, and in that company we can see that immunity from criticism is, like conclusiveness and finality, a feature of considerable utility and sought on that basis. In particular, these features all afford the great advantage of closing off questions of truth and right from any need for further consideration; they thus confer the benefit of efficiency upon such determinations, the gain of being able to be done with these matters so as to move on to others (a desideratum that presumes that there *are* "other" matters, and so that truth and right are but incidental and occasional). But immunity from criticism offers more than just efficient closure, for that could be gained from the sheer efficacy of an enforced fiat. What would be missing in that event would be the acknowledgement of the result as right or true, for fiat concededly lacks any nexus to these. If, declining nihilism, we yet shrink from taking this step of identifying truth and right with whatever fiat ordains, it is because we see in too bold relief the destiny promised for the determination of truth and right on grounds of power, a destiny at which the law has already arrived.

Although it may seem that the desire to be immune from criticism bespeaks modesty, a consciousness of fallibility, a desire to avoid error, that is not at all what brings us to demand this immunity—for, in that event, we would be concerned with continuing to address right (or truth), not with closing off the inquiry. Far from manifesting humility or a concern to avoid error, the desire for immunity from criticism is a desire to vanquish opposition and remove the opportunity for others to challenge our determinations (or to point out our errors so that they may be rectified). What we seek is to win the contest over truth or right so decisively that the matter is closed, and we are released from having to attend to it further or to brook opposition to our contentions, now entrenched as victorious. More than mere closure, we seek victory—and, as increasing its value, enduring victory. The determination of truth or right is undertaken by means that promise immunity from criticism so that the victor may secure his winnings.

This character is not mitigated or altered by resorting to a model of decision-making that, in lieu of singularism's all-or-nothing determination, issues in a multiplicity of "right answers" instead. Without more, this merely enlarges the number of victors, perhaps removing the occasion for their competition with each other as they nonetheless continue, now in league with their fellow "winners," to strive to defeat still other challengers. The desire for vindication on questions of right—for being determined and *declared* right, hence victorious—need not be exclusive but can allow for confederates, group advancement, or other forms of complicity with non-threatening allies without diminishing its essentially competitive nature.

It is, in sum, conquest and victory—and, before that, the gain such victory promises—that we seek, and have long sought, when we claim to be seeking the determination of truth or right. It is for this reason that we do not in the first instance inquire into what is, or may be, right or true in connection with the matter before us. Instead, we turn straightaway to the pursuit of arguments, grounds, and answers that will dispose of the question, ending our involvement with it. In fact, we have come unquestioningly to conflate the two and to identify the true or right answer as that which is dispositive, that for which conclusive grounds can be shown, or that on which we can gain the alliance of agreement and thereby foreclose challenge and opposition. As Martin Heidegger has shown, this ascendancy of combat and conquest, eclipsing our consideration of any truth that might belong to the matter at hand, has come to prevail as the distinctive understanding of truth in the West.[2]

It is in accordance with this ascendancy of combat over truth (understood other than, already, as the prize of combat) that we have come to demand grounds for the determination of questions of right and truth that are conclusive, closing the question off from further thought, as well as exclusive, ruling out all but a single victorious answer. That is the answer that, being thus victorious over all others, is, on that account, thereafter to be acclaimed as right and entitled to the spoils of that victory, which include the banishment of all rivals. Thus we have come to equate being right with being in a position to demand such banishment, that is, with being sole victor; this is the position Krausz identifies as "singularism." As we may now see, however, the claim to exclusiveness that singularism expresses is not an isolable and detachable requirement (and not a requirement of merely theoretical provenance and standing in any event) for it belongs to the history of how we have come to understand truth. As part of the history that constitutes how we have come to think and who we have thereby become that we do so, the demand for exclusiveness is no more readily expunged than is our rationalism.

Seeing this, we may come to view in a different light the central place held in discussions of truth and right by the issue Krausz rightly identifies as pivotal: the lack of a decisive standard of adjudication by which such questions may be determined. As Krausz explains, the late modern discovery that there is "no single overarching standard" that will adjudicate among claims to rightness has brought in its wake the conclusion that multiplism is, accordingly, inescapable. Multiplism is endorsed because, as he relates, there is ample reason to question the stringency of singularism, with its demands for conclusiveness and exclusivity; waiving or relaxing those demands, we may find ourselves in a position to entertain multiple answers instead, each of which may be preferred by a relevant constituency or authority, may satisfy several of their aims, or may comport with their preferred or accustomed practices. This, he suggests, is ample rightness, and there is no reason—as these criteria do not require it—to limit in advance the number of the successful candidates for rightness to a maximum of one.

All of this is presented with such genial reasonableness that it would be churlish, as well as foolish, to disagree. Certainly Krausz is right that singularism is excessive, perhaps particularly so in connection with the interpretation of art works, and unnecessary. As we have already seen, it invokes and provokes a kind of combativeness that is extraneous to the question of right or truth at hand, and a distraction from it. The question remains, however, as to how we are to understand the movement away from singularism. Is singularism rejected because of this extraneousness, that is, on grounds of its irrelation to truth and right, or because it is unsatisfiable or otherwise unworkable or unserviceable? And what are we to understand to take singularism's place?

Krausz says at a number of points that the motivation for abandoning singularism is the absence of the "single overarching standard" by which a singular right answer may be determined. It thus appears that it is this methodological failing—the failure of singularism to deliver up the method of exclusive determinacy it requires and implicitly promises—that dooms it. This suggests the possibility that, were such a standard to be discovered tomorrow, singularism would perhaps be reinstated and upheld after all, for its infirmity, the ground for its present discard, is merely the unfortunate but contingent fact that the standard is not now in evidence. In that event, we may see that we would not at all have given up our dependence upon the standard, but only our expectation (which may later be revised or reinstated) that it will be presently realized.

Alternatively, it may be argued that there *can be* no such standard, for the irreducible multiplicity of the world's practices and practitioners by which and by whom right answers are determined precludes it. Such a conclusion would depend in the first instance, however, not on the fact of that multiplicity, which may be conceded, but on a prior decision that we are to look to such practices and practitioners for the determination of rightness. In proceeding on that basis, we appoint these empirically variable and multiple sites and ways of decision-making to the position of governing the understanding of how we are to determine rightness. Thus the argument does not do away with the requirement of a standard that will determine the question—the same requirement that motivated and promised to justify singularism—but instead relocates that standard to an irreducibly multiple assortment of sites, fracturing and distributing the standard's authority without questioning or diminishing its sway or our reliance upon it.

The argument raises further questions as well: Why should we look, as the argument requires, to empirical instances of decision-making on questions of rightness at all? It would seem that, in doing so, we have already presumed that that is where rightness is to be found, thus that it is an empirical matter. This, however, is open to question (as Kant and David Hume, for different reasons, would concur). In addition, it is not clear why we should follow such empirical practices and practitioners in determining rightness in any event unless we had reason to believe that their determinations are, indeed, *right*— as distinct from effective or widely conformed to—unless we are tacitly equating these. But that, too, appears a questionable step requiring careful and explicit attention.

More promising, perhaps, would be the idea that the "single overarching standard" we have sought is needless. In that event, singularism, which required and justified itself on the basis of that standard, would be dispensable as well. On this account, singularism, the idea that there is and must be a single right answer, has been a mistake born of an excess of zeal, for we have no need to so restrict ourselves, but can, on many questions, entertain multiple right answers. Doing so will often be useful and productive (much as John Stuart Mill envisioned), far more than will our continuing to wage disputes over which of several serviceable answers is the single right one. Needing no single answer to proceed with our activities, we need no single overarching standard by which it may be selected and designated. The fruitless search for it may be abandoned, owing not to the fruitlessness of the search but to the uselessness of the standard, even were it to be found. In this light, it becomes puzzling why anyone would continue to hold to singularism, inasmuch as that is not the path that will lead us to multiplism and its evident advantages.

This is a temptingly reasonable rationale. Yet it is worth noting, and reflecting upon, the evident fact that our thinking here is governed by what we "need," what we find serviceable and thus congenial. For it thus appears that it is still our search for what will be of utility that is at work, directing our decision as to how to think about what questions of truth or right call for, and our "need," or estimation of that utility, that determines what answer—and how many—will "count as" right or true. As we are coming to see, however, this elevation of utility over right and truth, whereby it dictates their determination, is precisely the same way of thinking that brought singularism to the fore. It still prevails, unquestioned, on this rationale for discarding singularism in favor of what is ostensibly an alternative to it.

Finally, we encounter the question of what we are left with in singularism's wake. Later discussion will attend in more detail to some possibilities that may be thought to serve as replacement grounds or criteria of rightness, taking the place of the single overarching standard that is not to be had. Yet we can see already that if singularism is to be discarded because it is not "working," that is, not delivering us with efficiency to goals of our choosing (in particular, those associated with determinability), then any alternative we embrace, on account of and in completion of this rejection, would be warranted only by its enhanced likelihood of delivering such utility, the same ground as that underlying singularism. And, indeed, we shall see that it is just those grounds and criteria that confer utility and advance the satisfaction of preference that come to the fore and offer themselves as alternative determinants of right, though in their preference-character they do not present an alternative to the prior grounds after all. Similarly, if it is the fruitlessness of the search for the singularist standard that motivates the switch from singularism to multiplism, then the standard, directing that switch on the grounds and in the event of its unavailability, continues to govern our thinking.

The ways of thinking that have brought us to seek for so long a single, decisive standard for the determination of questions of truth and right are not, perhaps, so readily dislodged as by simply switching from singularism to multiplism. In the end, multiplism may not be opposed to or even fundamentally distinct from singularism and its search for a single overarching standard after all, insofar as multiplism relaxes the strictures of that standard, broadening their reach so as to include more qualifiers, but without calling our reliance upon it into question or fundamentally challenging or departing from it. It thus appears that the "single overarching standard" *remains* every bit as decisive an issue as Krausz suggests it was previously, when it delivered us to singularism. For in switching to multiplism, we have not come to give it up; instead, we continue to show our allegiance to it, quite undiminished by our present acknowledgement of its impossibility, for it is on the ground of its supposed absence—and continuing necessity—that we are, now, to turn to utility and preference to determine questions of rightness. Sometimes, as in law, this turn to utility and preference is recognized as a substitution for right; in other contexts it is not, but maintained that this is still rightness, or rightness enough; and in still others it is regarded as rightness *faute de mieux*, for (it is averred) there "really is no" right or truth other than this. All of these essentially indistinguishable positions are taken to follow from the "discovery" that "there is no single overarching standard" for determining rightness; in truth, they follow only from our continuing demand that there be just that.

The recent history of how we think to determine questions of law, truth, and right illustrates with unsettling clarity the stranglehold that has been held on all these questions by this single issue. That history, indeed, has been largely generated by this single demand, now seen to be unsatisfiable—though not on that account given up—for a "single right answer" to questions of rightness, yielded by a "single overarching standard." As we may now see, this demand is not merely futile in fact but deeply, disturbingly questionable. And it is not dislodged but instead confirmed and complied with by concluding that resort to the pursuit of utility and the satisfaction of preferences is the only remaining possibility for an account of what is to be determined on questions of right or truth.

It is worth considering the nature and source of our allegiance to this demand, which we uphold despite concluding, now, that it is impossible to satisfy, and despite being led thereby to abandon the search for right or truth in any sense other than that of the satisfaction of preferences. Why do we suppose that such a single overarching standard, one that could adjudicate between multiple interpretations, is necessary to an adequate account of truth or right—so necessary that its necessity persists and governs the recognition of all possible truth and right despite the impossibility of satisfying it? Let us pause to acknowledge the astonishing tribute exacted by this conceit: On its basis we have concluded—and so may today hear it averred matter-of-factly among academic sophisticates—that *there is no* truth or right, but only a competition of preference and power that passes under those names. Truth and right, in any sense other than this, *are not.* And what is the reason, the ground on which we have reached (or claimed to) this extraordinary, literally inconceivable conclusion? Only this: that truth and right have failed to make themselves accessible to our conclusive determination, as by a single over-arching standard that is itself accessible and conclusively determinable. Since the discovery of such a standard now appears implausible, truth and right are ruled out of existence altogether—or collapsed into matters of preference and power, which accomplishes the identical relegation.

We have come to jettison the possibility of right and truth (or purport to), in deference to—what? To a conclusive standard by which we may determine them, even though holding to it has rendered truth and right themselves impossible. Dwelling on the strangeness of this state of affairs, perhaps we may finally come to see that this standard, and the demand that it be satisfied, are *nothing belonging to truth and right themselves.* Instead, it is *we* who have insisted on such a standard and its satisfaction, *we* who have demanded that questions of truth and right be determined conclusively, with authority and finality. And we continue to demand this, on threat of their being openly relegated to service as the instrument and product of our preferences and desires.

And yet, on this account, that is what they have been all along: For the reason we make this demand, and invest it with the power to govern questions of truth and right and finally their very possibility, is the expedience it affords us in reaching such determinations and the utility it promises in making those determinations uniform and effective. In this way, truth and right are *already* understood as in service to our desires; that they are our disposable invention follows, in time, as a matter of course. This truth is, however, incompletely understood when it is taken to entail, or affirm, that truth and right are and must be just such creatures of our invention. For whether this is so depends upon whether their existence and possibility are properly governed by our demand for a method by which they may be conclusively determined, and that is the matter in issue.

The utility such conclusive determination would afford would be impressive. It would be very useful to have a way of determining right or truth that was ironclad, precluding all challenge, dispute, and uncertainty; one that would entitle me to insist upon your submission to my answer and to banish yours thereafter as that of a fool, fraud, or infidel; one that would establish, once and for all, that just *this* is truth and right, or what the law requires, so that we would not have to remain engaged with such questions. With them well and firmly put behind us, we could turn our attention back to our (other) aims and programs, and finally make some real progress. After all, it is our desire to advance those aims, programs, and preferences that has been our guiding desideratum all along. It is for the sake of the ease and efficiency a determinative yardstick or "single overarching standard" might afford that we have long sought it; to conclude, now, that truth and right are not to be had because such a yardstick is unavailable is to continue to demand that truth and right offer us such determinability, on pain of being dismissed as non-existent.

Alternatively, we may purport not to dismiss them, but instead to aver that they are "really" just the upshot of determinations of utility "after all." This occurs when, for instance, we conclude that these questions are to be governed by convention, the answers' satisfaction of selected aims or purposes, or their efficacy in practice ("what works"). In all these ways, we continue to hold truth and right hostage to their capacity to deliver a payoff and advance us to goals of our choosing. The constant that endures through all these developments (which thus represent only changes on a single theme and not any alternative) is the elevation of our desires and utility as the measure and warrant—the standard—of truth and of right. Insofar as these are the alternatives we turn to following the loss of the "single overarching standard," we have not, in fact, lost our fundamental standard or our continuing allegiance to it, but only turned to a new device for achieving it.

All this is evident enough in the last case, where truth and right are equated with "what works"—with what is efficacious, what delivers the payoff we have already determined to be their ground and warrant. (This resort is not, incidentally, compelled by the skeptic's ready question, "Well, what *else* would they be?" for that, too, already installs as the ground and warrant of any candidate for truth or right something that would answer to the demand for immediate accessibility and determinability—insisting, straightaway, upon another efficacious answer, if the first is to be denied—and so does not at all dislodge or question efficacy itself as the criterion of truth and of right.) Similarly, it is no change at all from our current understanding of truth and right, whereby we demand that they be determinable by a single overarching standard, to propose, as the new ground of truth or right, their capacity to satisfy the aims, goals, or purposes we may elect to pursue. For it was the advancement and satisfaction of our aims and purposes that motivated, and purported to justify, the demand for a single overarching standard of truth, and of right, in the first place.

When we subject truth and right to determination by our aims and purposes—thus adopting the analogue, in theories of truth and right, to legal positivism—we have already ruled out, as insufficiently serviceable to our preferences, the possibility that the determination will be governed by truth or right instead (a conclusion not avoided by assimilating these at the outset to whatever is so serviceable). Nor is it avoided by suggesting that these decisive preferences will only be held or indulged "for good reasons," for it is not clear what would remain on this account by virtue of which our reasons could be understood as good—as distinct, once again, from useful to the satisfaction of our preferred aims.

Krausz gives occasional hints of another way in which we might understand rightness when he speaks of an interpretation's appropriateness. Because, he suggests, appropriateness is not a necessarily exclusive concept—more than one answer or way of proceeding may be appropriate in any given case—adopting appropriateness as the standard of rightness would not commit us to singularism but is instead compatible with multiplism. It is true that appropriateness is not exclusive, and it may well be that appropriateness does offer us a way of understanding rightness that avoids the excessive strictures of exclusive determinacy we have come to demand of truth and right. It would be tempting to adopt it for those theoretical advantages. Yet if we were to do so we would not, in fact, have departed after all from what has been consistently decisive in modern thought about rightness—namely, the concern to advance our theoretical and practical aims and the demands we place upon truth and right to do so. Thus the questions remain: How are we to understand appropriateness here, and on what grounds is it proposed? In particular, what is it that an interpretation is to be understood as appropriate *to*? If to the fulfillment of an interpreter's or relevant group's aims, then the proposal does not appear to offer an alternative to the prevailing way of understanding rightness as a matter of advancing the fulfillment of aims but continues to partake of all the troubling implications of that familiar way of thinking. Appropriateness may yet be understood in a manner that does not lead us to replicate the resort to elevation of our aims and preferences as the determinant of rightness; we shall return to this intriguing possibility shortly.

The remaining avenue, which suggests that the standard of truth or rightness is, in lieu of the absent single overarching standard, to be found in convention (or "practices") instead, may seem to be more promising. Certainly a great deal of academic attention has been given in recent years to the idea that truth and right are a matter of convention, to be located in and determined by prevailing social practices, from which they must, accordingly, take as well whatever warrant they may be thought to have. Sometimes the implication is that this resort to convention—or its equivalent, consensus or agreement—is justified by its functional advantages: Looking to conventional practice on a question of truth or right would, no doubt, allow us to determine the matter straightforwardly, with relatively little difficulty; such promised ease and mastery is always the lure when we turn to empirical determinations of such questions. And because, *ex hypothesi*, the determination reached is one that is, in fact, agreed upon within the relevant community, this method has the added bonus of affording our determination insulation from challenge—the deliverance we sought from the single overarching standard as well. In this light, the proposal is revealed as a close cousin of the other two, sharing their project of subjecting truth and right to accessible and efficacious determination, the better to advance the aims, and reap the utility, that continue to hold dominion instead.

On this account, truth and right, as conventional, are whatever is taken to be true or right by the relevant constituencies. Significantly, there is already in play here a tacitly acknowledged distinction between what is, in truth, true or right (whatever that may be, if indeed it is still intelligible) and what is taken *as* true or right, passes for it, and will suffice, it is hoped, in its stead—but is not it. In this distinction we may see an intimation, even an involuntary confession, of the difficulty this proposal faces: It seeks to determine a question of truth or right by looking to empirical facts concerning what people—various, variable, and fallible—say, opine, accept, prefer, endorse, believe, or otherwise hold to be true or right. There is simply no necessary nexus between whatever such a poll, however conducted, might reveal to be held, however sincerely, and the question of what the truth or right of the matter in question is—unless we rule out in advance the possibility of any discordance by conflating the two at the outset.

Nor will it do to attempt to meet this difficulty by confining the range of admissible responses, and thus the possible determinations of the question, to the opinions of a select or elite portion of the relevant community that agree among themselves—that is, to an *authoritative* convention. For that simply returns us to the problem of authority, which is to say the problem of its relation to rightness: In what does the authority of such an authoritative group, and therewith of its determinations, consist? If the answer is the group's sheer dominance or efficacy ("success"), then, again, we have no reason to understand its determinations as possessed of *rightness*, as distinct from the dominance and efficacy that enable these opinions to be promulgated and enforced. If, however, the authoritative group is rightfully ascendant and authoritative, then it owes its authority to the rightness with which it has come to make its determinations, and it is to that rightness—not its expression in authoritative pronouncements, which will be occasionally wrong and always derivative—that we ought to attend. Though this is a task we continually try to avoid, resorting instead to such substitutes, we can now see that in doing so we persist in, rather than depart from, the thinking that has brought us to singularism.

What might we conclude from this discussion of how we have come to understand law, truth, right, and their determination as it bears upon the issues presented by Krausz?

First, we see that the history of this understanding, sketched here, does not offer us a resolution of our theoretical problems. In its myriad forms, the understanding of law, truth, and right as necessarily of ready, ideally exclusive determinability is thoroughly familiar to us in the modern West. As perhaps we can appreciate, that understanding is distinctive and troubling as well. Yet, precisely because it is so distinctively and characteristically *our* way of understanding these matters, it is not something merely to be jettisoned, so as to provide a solution as to a theoretical problem. On the contrary, the supposed availability of such an easy exchange of ways of thinking, already understood as tools at our disposal, belongs wholly within the ways of thinking in question. In seeing this history as our own, we may come to see that it offers not a pesky problem to be solved but an invitation to pause before doing so yet again, that we may give thought to what that undertaking requires us to presuppose and with what warrant.

I have suggested, following Heidegger, that the unexamined demands for ready determinability we place upon truth and right have generated not only that history as a whole but also its theories, both those ensconced as standard and those rejected as inadequate, as well as the controversies over these theories that continue to percolate and the alternatives they entertain and over which they contend. Seeing the scope of this history and its prevailing exhaustiveness, we can grasp as well the reason these are not issues susceptible to theoretical resolution: It is because the understanding of truth and right and what they require by way of determination are not theoretical problems in the first instance, but instead ways in which the world presents itself to our understanding. There is thus no suprahistorical position to which we might retreat for authoritative or final determination of these matters, as theory envisions, and no ready comparison as with other times and cultures (already regarded as available to our inspection) from which we might extract a theoretical diagnosis or cure.

There are nevertheless implications to be drawn from this history for the issues Krausz puts before us. Foremost is that these familiar ways of proceeding bring us to lose sight of just what we had thought we were seeking—namely, truth and right. Our methods have instead been devoted to seeking certainty, exclusivity, finality, and other desirable features we have presumed truth or right must have, albeit in their name. But, just as has happened in law, we find that giving over the determination of questions of truth and right to methods that promise the power of conclusive determination—and, later, to sheer power itself—has had the result that truth and right themselves have vanished; most recently, they have been dismissed as impossibilities based on the growing consensus that there exists no "single overarching standard" to adjudicate between claimants to that title. This astonishing outcome suggests that something in the desire to master truth and right by such methods is profoundly and fundamentally antithetical to whatever it is or may be that truth and right, like law, require.

This conclusion would appear to support a position of multiplism, inasmuch as that drive for mastery on questions of truth and right has reached farthest, perhaps, in singularism's demand for exclusivity, for the banishment as wrong of all but the sole victorious claimant to rightness. Much depends, however, on how multiplism, and the grounds of its adoption, are to be understood. For, just as singularism's insistence upon exclusivity is not a discrete or adventitious requirement but instead grows out of an entire way of thinking about truth and right and the determinability we require of them, so too is multiplism perfectly capable of drawing nourishment from that same soil. Thus, a multiplism that retained the same demands for conclusiveness, authoritative determination, and finality, only moderating the demand for exclusiveness so as to leave several "winners" standing at the end instead of just one, would not be a multiplism that took to heart the difficulties of singularism and their ground. Similarly, a multiplism adopted out of the realization that there is no "single overarching standard" of rightness such as would satisfy singularism would be a multiplism that still held to the decisive necessity of just such a standard.

In short, singularism, like its rejection for multiplism when these are taken as equally available theoretical alternatives, depends on a further, deeper ground which we have by no means necessarily seen or come to grips with, still less given up, in choosing between them. We have maintained singularism, with its demand for exclusivity in determinations of right and truth, owing to the advantages of security and power such exclusivity confers. We may well endorse multiplism for its equivalent advantages—including the utility of being able to reach determinations of rightness without need for exclusiveness—distributed among its several victors. Such a result would, however, question few of our assumptions concerning right and truth and address few of the deeper problems our ingrained singularism presents.

Yet multiplism could well be endorsed—or rather: we could come to understand that rightness can be multiple—for other reasons. As Krausz suggests, multiple right interpretations may be called for by the richness of the thing before us, a possibility that is especially salient in the case of artworks but not confined there. More broadly, we could realize that exclusivity is nothing truth and right require, but merely what we have demanded of their determinations. Realizing this, we would be brought to give up as well the other demands we are accustomed to making upon truth and right, all of which partake of the same demanding disposition toward them, a disposition that has long been decisive on such questions. In that event, we would understand any demand for ready determinability, for the security of authoritativeness, or for such determinations and criteria as advance our aims—demands which can readily persist under multiplism—to be appropriately relinquished as well.

But what, it might be asked, is left, then, to *rightness*? Are we not to understand it as determinable at all? Having followed the question this far, we find ourselves as though at sea, bereft of our usual planks of support and resolution: If all of those usual ways of proceeding are now to be understood as in question—then whither rightness? *By virtue of what* is a judgment or interpretation to be understood as *right*? It seems we have disabled ourselves from employing any of the usual answers to this question, precisely as we have come to understand all extraneous considerations, such as the utility of come to understand all extraneous considerations, such as the utility of reaching authoritative or exclusive determinations, as likewise unavailable.

The only remaining possibility, following on these exclusions and our appreciation of their necessity, lies in attending to the matter at hand, so that we understand rightness to obtain in relation to *it*. When we do so, we return to a consideration of the thing before us—the work of art, the dispute at law, the question of truth or of right—and ask whether the interpretation, judgment, or answer under consideration is right with respect to *it*. In fact, only such a conception of rightness can release multiplism from the bogey of interpretive anarchy—a prime motivator toward singularism, as Krausz recounts—without abandoning it to its Charybdis, the arbitrary fiat of preference.

It is worth emphasizing, given the nature of the concerns raised by Krausz,that nothing in this inquiry requires selection of a single right answer, nor even the comparison of one proposed answer with another that such a selection would require. Instead, each is to be judged in relation to the matter at hand, which may well call for many right interpretations, judgments, or answers, a general univocity being but our restriction, imposed upon the matter from without. We have likewise no reason to suppose that this inquiry entails or requires anything like the "absolute first principles," either "self-evident, or . . . [embodying] an absolute order of reality or real essences or real human nature" that Krausz imagines a singularist might invoke but which he quite rightly declines to support. The familiar supposition that some such principles are necessary similarly owes its origin to our traditional demands for univocity and conclusive determination, forit is these demands that provision of such principles would satisfy and on the basis of which they are sought.

Finally relinquishing these demands, we may come to understand rightness simply as the right relation between what we say about a thing, in an interpretation or judgment of it, and the thing itself. The name that suggests itself for this right relation is appropriateness, which speaks of the belonging together of the two: What makes an interpretation, judgment, or answer appropriate is its fit—which is to say, its fittingness—to the matter at hand. As was discussed earlier, Krausz has himself proposed appropriateness as one among his multiplist criteria. It is not clear, however, whether he would endorse an understanding of appropriateness that, as here, is to be expressly removed from consideration of our aims and preferences as determinants of rightness, or that he would allow appropriateness, as suggested here, to constitute the entirety of the consideration of rightness, obviating resort to the array of other grounds and criteria to which we have become accustomed to look.

Finally, it is not clear how such an understanding could be reconciled with the ontological agnosticism to which Krausz subscribes. Appropriateness, understood as the ground, content, and criterion of rightness, requires us to attend to the matter before us to see if an interpretation or judgment befits it. Further, it requires us to attend to the matter before us in arriving at the interpretation or judgment in question, that which will thereafter be a candidate for rightness. It is not at all clear how, on either of these occasions, one could attend to the matter at hand without attending as well to its being, to what and how it is. Any interpretation or judgment (including a judgment of an interpretation's rightness) that failed to do so could not itself manifest appropriateness, or even conscientiously attempt it. Instead, it would be condemned to the self-contradictory position of a judgmental or interpretive solipsism. Though the judgments professedly made from that position may be readily multiplied, questions of rightness among them can be resolved only by the arbitrary fiat of preference or else by abdication in interpretive anarchy, for they bear no relation to the matter at hand, and can bear none, so long as we decline to contemplate it in its being before us.

We must, in short, understand the matter as having an existence to which the fidelity of appropriateness is possible. The rightness of an interpretation or judgment, understood as its appropriateness or fittingness, lies in its fitting *to*—something. The matter at hand must be understood to *be*, in such a way that such fittingness is a possibility. This is an ontological understanding—that is, an understanding of the being of the matter in issue, specifically of its being such as can elicit and countenance the judgments and interpretations in question. For this to be possible, the matter cannot owe its being to our aims and purposes, including those of ready determinability or theoretical power, for then it would be only to these that our interpretations and judgments can or need conform. We have seen the difficulties for understanding the possibility of rightness that attend that course. Instead, the matter's being must be such as to escape such demands for subjection if it is to be capable of calling for the interpretations and judgments we offer and sanctioning their possible rightness.

This is, perhaps, a more robust and substantial existence than Krausz or other contemporary theorists are prepared to entertain. In fact, it does not appear to be of the sort of ontological theory that, on his account, they do entertain, the varieties of which he lays out and among which he declines to choose to subscribe. Plainly, it is not an account of constructivism, or the understanding of entities as but the products of cultural practices of construction and interpretation (itself understood as construction). Neither, however, is it realism, if realism is taken, as it appears it is, as a theory about reality and its criteria—a theory that, as such, requires argument, defense, revision, strategic reformulation, and the other familiar activities of theory building. When we proceed so in connection with ontology, we have presumed that it is up to us whether and how entities are, that they require a theory from us, whose conditions they must then show they satisfy, to justify their existence.

A realism so understood, holding that "objects are autonomous and independent of interpretive practices," is, in fact, but a variety of constructivism: The purported distinction between them is the presence or absence of *our construction*; in either its positive or its negative valence, our construction remains decisively in charge, channeling the possibilities of understanding the entity's being (as, plainly, it does under such variants as "constructive realism" as well). Like legal positivism, its cousin in the realm of law, constructivism subjects all possibility of understanding the being of entities to our aims and purposes. It is for the sake of advancing these aims and purposes that construction of theories and, through them, of entities is undertaken. But it is not only in the event of that construction being carried out that this subjection takes place. Before that, the elevation of those aims and purposes makes such construction appear both possible (whether or not actualized in a given case), and necessary when it is so actualized, it having been determined to be "necessary"—that is, useful—to their satisfaction to do so. More fundamentally, it is, throughout, our aims and purposes that we require entities to satisfy in propounding and relying upon the theories of their being that we do: When entities satisfy our demands that they reveal themselves in accord with those theories, we pronounce them "real"; when they fail to, we proceed to construction. Either way, the enduring demand for the advancement of our aims, including those of ready determinability and theoretical power, persists and prevails. Either way, we subject the being of entities to determination by our theoretical and evaluative activities, denying the possibility of their being otherwise—the essential premise of constructivism.

Perhaps this subjection explains why, as Krausz has found, none of the varieties of ontological theory he describes has distinctive or determinative bearing upon an interpretation's possible rightness: Insofar as these ontological accounts all begin from the essentially constructivist understanding that being is a matter requiring theoretical foundation and defense, there is no entity understood as in being already to which we must or can attend. On the understanding of rightness as appropriateness to such an entity, there is then no possibility of reaching or comprehending rightness, to which such theories are from the outset, and remain, essentially—and equivalently—indifferent. If ontology so understood appears to be "detachable" from rightness, perhaps it is because it was never "attached" to the being of the entity that makes rightness comprehensible in the first place. Alternatively, if we were to regard an interpretation's rightness as lying in its compatibility with the advancement of our aims and purposes, we would again find such ontological theories equivalently compatible with that undertaking, for constructivism in all its varieties (including the one here called "realism," the abeyance of a construction still understood as fundamental) begins from a similar privileging of such aims and purposes, for it is these that construction is undertaken to serve.

We have seen such pursuit of advantage to be at work all along the modern course of the determination of rightness, on questions of law as well as on those of truth and right more generally, recurrently commandeering that determination and prescribing its methods, theories, and conclusions. We may now see as well that it is precisely such determination by advantage that has closed us off from a possible understanding of rightness all along. For it seems that rightness itself requires that not only the determination of truth and right, but before that, the being of the matter of which interpretations and judgments are offered, be preserved from just such subjection to advantage, if it is to be capable of calling for the interpretations and judgments we offer and granting their aspirations to rightness.

In the end, then, we return to the central, paired concerns Krausz has brought into view: rightness and ontology. But we are brought to consider, now, not how the two might be severed (the case for which Krausz makes at length) but how, if we are to grasp a significant possibility for the understanding of rightness, they cannot be. With the help of Krausz, we can see the difficulty in understanding rightness as a matter resolved, or even touched, by the various contemporary theories of ontology; and we can also see now, perhaps, why just these present themselves as available. Krausz is quite right to conclude that these contemporary ontological theories do not bear upon the undertaking of understanding rightness. Yet it is not the case that ontological considerations may simply be dispensed with and dismissed. Instead, it appears to be of paramount importance to the prospect of understanding rightness that we attend, not perhaps to those contemporary theories, but to the being of the matter before us, if we are to be able either to make an interpretation or judgment of it that is a candidate for rightness or to judge that candidacy. This difficulty and this importance accruing to the relation of rightness and ontology only come to light, however, from a contemplation of the possibility of understanding rightness. For bringing these issues forward and inviting us into that contemplation, we are indebted to Michael Krausz and his explorations.

NOTES

1. Michael Krausz, *Rightness and Reasons* (Ithaca, N. Y.: Cornell University Press, 1993); Michael Krausz, *Limits of Rightness* (Lanham, Md.: Rowman and Littlefield, 2000).

2. Martin Heidegger, *Parmenides.* Frankfurt am Main: Vittorio Klostermann, trans. A. Schuwer and R. Rojcewicz (Bloomington: Indiana University Press, 1982); Martin Heidegger, *Der Satz vom Grund* (Pfullingen: Verlag Gunther Neske, trans. as *The Principle of Reason,* by R. Lilli [Bloomington: Indiana University Press, 1957]).

Nineteen

ART AS ITS OWN INTERPRETATION

Nicholas Maxwell

Contributing to this volume dedicated to Michael Krausz gives me enormous pleasure. But I find the occasion also extremely intimidating, for I propose to respond to Krausz's two most recent books, *Rightness and Reason* (RR) and *Limits of Rightness* (LR).[1] What Krausz has to say in these two volumes is so cogent, so lucid, so masterly, that you are left wondering what could be added, questioned, or challenged. Krausz is in an especially good position to speak on these issues of interpretation as, in addition to being a philosopher, he is also an artist and conductor. Problems of interpretation arise for him not just as philosophical problems to be reflected on, but as practical problems that need to be dealt with during the process of creation and recreation, in art and music. My only hope, I have decided, is to be provocative, no doubt foolishly provocative. In this essay I will defend a version of what Krausz calls "singularism." The version that I defend makes what may well appear outrageous claims. Not only does it assert that works of art have one correct interpretation, it has the audacity to specify, in each case, what this one correct interpretation is. This view, you might think, exhibits all the overarching ambitiousness, the hubris, in the field of hermeneutics, that claims to propound the one and only true "theory-of-everything" have in theoretical physics.

As those who have read RR and LR will know, Krausz distinguishes two views, which he calls singularism and multiplism. Singularism asserts, as I have already indicated, that each work of art (or cultural artifacts more generally) has just one admissible, correct interpretation, while multiplism allows that some works of art may have several different admissible interpretations. According to multiplism, Vincent van Gogh's *Potato Eaters* (to take one of Krausz's examples) may admissibly be interpreted along formalist, psychoanalytic, Marxist or feminist lines. It may be possible to give reasons as to why one of these interpretations is better than another, but these reasons are likely to be inconclusive, and it need not be the case that just one correct interpretation exists. Two or more incompatible interpretations may be equally correct.

The version of singularism that I wish to defend holds that the work of art itself is the correct interpretation of itself. *King Lear* is the correct interpretation of William Shakespeare's play *King Lear*; the *Mona Lisa* is itself the correct interpretation of Leonardo da Vinci's picture; and Johann S. Bach's *St. Matthew Passion* is the correct interpretation of itself. "This is nonsense," the cry may go up. "How can a work of art be its own interpretation, let alone the correct interpretation?" An interpretation is, by definition, something quite distinct from the work of art itself. A work of art may be a picture, a piece of music, a dance, a play, a novel or poem, a film, a sculpture. An interpretation, by contrast, is a piece of discursive prose that sets forth a particular view about the meaning of the work of art in question. Its function is to illuminate the work of art. An interpretation is not a work of art in its own right. An interpretation is a text that expounds, questions, criticizes, and argues. Apart from those rare cases where a work of art is itself just such a text (Plato's dialogues, perhaps), an interpretation cannot itself be a picture, piece of music, etc. No interpretive scholar paints, chisels or composes to write his text: he or she writes. The thesis is refuted.

Krausz would not, I think, agree with this objection. RR opens with a discussion of musical interpretation, during the course of which Krausz makes the thoroughly reasonable point that several performances may give the same interpretation of a quartet or symphony. We cannot identify an interpretation with a performance, but a performance (if any good) nevertheless yields, or is an example of, an interpretation. Here, an interpretation of a piece of music is itself a performance of that piece of music. And even when rival interpretations are being discussed, on the radio for example, to compare and contrast pieces of recorded rival performances, to indicate different interpretations, is normal practice. Art historians sometimes do something similar. They give sketches of a work of art under discussion to indicate structural patterns, geometrical forms implicit in a group of figures. Sometimes a crossover from one art form to another occurs: conductors, in order to indicate how they wish a passage to be phrased or interpreted, may do so with gestures, with sweeps of the hand in the air, even with grimaces. And this may be far more graphic and effective than anything they could say. Conducting is perhaps, in part, the art of indicating an interpretation by means of a kind of restricted dance.

Nothing here precludes the possibility of an interpretation being in the same medium as the work being interpreted, and nothing precludes the work from being its own best interpretation. In many circumstances, to take the form of a text, perhaps with illustrations, is more useful for an adjunct interpretation—as we may call an interpretation that is not the work of art itself— than for it to take the form of another work of art in the same medium. This will be the case whenever the adjunct work of art would be just as opaque, as incomprehensible, to the audience, as the original work. But this will by no means be always true. And in any case, no deep principle exists here: just a practical question as to what kind of adjunct interpretation will do the job best, in the given context, given the nature of the work of art, and the level of expertise of the audience.

Let us concede that an interpretation can take the form of a performance, a drawing, a gesture, and does not need to be a text. This does not establish that a work of art can be its interpretation. An interpretation, it may be argued, is distinct from that which is interpreted. No work of art can be its interpretation.

This question can be settled by fiat, by just defining "interpretation" as non-reflexive, incapable of applying to itself. But does this follow from the ordinary meaning of "interpretation"? Krausz refers to the *English Oxford Dictionary* definitions of interpretation as "explanation" and "exposition" (LR, p. 16). Why should these not be interpretable reflexively? Why should not something be self-explanatory, the best exposition of itself? Krausz goes on to quote the *Oxford Dictionary* as explicating interpretation in such terms as "construction put upon" or "representation"; and in terms of such prepositional phrases as "to expound," "to render clear or explicit," "to elucidate," "to bring out the meaning of," "to obtain significant information from," "to take in a manner," "to construe," and "to signify." Nothing here makes it impossible to construe interpretation in such a way that it can be reflexive, that a work of art can be an interpretation of itself. What could "represent," "expound," "render clear and explicit," "elucidate," "bring out the meaning of" "construe," and "signify" a work of art better than the work of art itself? If something other than the work of art represents, expounds, and so on, the work of art better than the work of art itself, is not this other thing, whatever it may be, a better work of art in its right? No conceptual or definitional objection has been found to holding that a work of art is its correct interpretation. But this does not make it true. Is it ever true? Is it always true?

One way of construing the matter would make it only infrequently true. Conceivably, a work of art, a novel or poem, might contain within itself an interpretation of itself. The author, using his authorial voice, tells us in no uncertain terms what the overall meaning of the novel is; the poet provides a stanza, which provides an interpretation of the rest of the poem. That is not what I mean when I declare that a work of art is its correct interpretation. That is a case of a work of art containing an (adjunct) interpretation of itself; it does not amount to the work of art, in its entirety, being the correct interpretation of itself.

So far I have considered objections to the thesis that a work of art is its correct interpretation. What positive grounds are there for adopting this view?

One great advantage of holding that the work of art is its correct interpretation is that this view automatically ensures that, in the world of interpretive activity, the work of art has pride of place. One danger that besets interpretive work (as usually understood) is that interpretation may come to appear almost more important than that which is being interpreted, the second being no more than the raw material for the first. Scholarly literary studies sometimes appear to exalt themselves above literature, and poor students, instead of absorbing literature at first hand, absorb diverse opinions of scholarly academic experts about literature. Scholarly debates between the experts can come to appear more important than the literature that gives rise to the debates in the first place. Likewise, history of art can appear to become a distinct, almost autonomous discipline, with its arcane rituals, remote from the art that art history is intended to illuminate.

The view I am defending implies that, even in the world of interpretation, the work of art itself is supreme. Adjunct interpretations can only be, at most, ad hoc additions to the correct interpretation, the work of art itself. Given this view, in seeking to improve our understanding and appreciation of works of art, to these works of art we must return, interpretive studies being used only as adjuncts. Music criticism is secondary to music, literary criticism secondary to literature, history of art secondary to art, and so on.

Many artists are reluctant to pronounce on the meaning of the works of art they have created. This reluctance can be construed as a manifestation of the view I am defending. For such an artist, the work of art says just what needs to be said, and is complete in itself. Its meaning is contained within itself. If the work of art could be summed up in a sentence, it would be redundant and the sentence would do instead. If the work needed additional remarks to be understood and appreciated, then it would be incomplete and defective as a work of art. Attitudes such as these, often implicit in artists' refusals to comment on their work, can be regarded as expressions of the view that the work contains its interpretation, its meaning; it expounds itself; and, if any good, does not need the prop of adjunct interpretations and explanations.

Holding that the work of art is its correct interpretation presents another advantage, which in some ways works in the opposite direction to the above: the line between art and its interpretation becomes much less divisive, much less a line of demarcation. If the correct interpretation is the work of art itself, then adjunct interpretations can, and perhaps ought to, aspire to being works of art in their right. Studies of literature that are not turgid, indigestible tracts of academic prose but are literature in their right are worth having. All good adjunct interpretations ought to embody good aesthetic standards that do not obstruct the job of being a good adjunct interpretation.

Let us concede it legitimate to construe "interpret" reflexively, so that a work of art is an interpretation of itself. Does it follow that a work of art is always, and necessarily, the correct interpretation of itself? Some years ago I read Simone de Beauvoir's novel *L'invitée* in translation, with the title *She Came To Stay*. It struck me then to be a novel that embodied a radically false interpretation of itself. The novel is based on Jean-Paul Sartre's and de Beauvoir's life together. In the novel the Sartre figure has an affair with a younger woman. Sartre and de Beauvoir—in real life, and in the novel— have agreed that possessiveness and jealousy are bad, bourgeois attitudes and emotions, to be banished from their lives. Love affairs with others are entirely acceptable, and can be accommodated within their relationship. In the novel, officially, the de Beauvoir figure dislikes the younger woman, not because she is jealous of her, but because she thinks she is shallow, and because she sees her as scheming against her. That, at any rate, is how I remember the novel. My overpowering impression on reading the novel was that the Simone de Beauvoir character was furiously and passionately jealous of the younger woman, trembling and faint, at times, with rage and jealousy. This was depicted in the novel, but the author, the real Simone de Beauvoir, did not officially recognize these symptoms as jealousy, and it was not a part of the official plot and meaning of the novel that the heroine suffered from jealousy, even unacknowledged jealousy. The novel embodied a radically false interpretation of itself.

My interpretation of the novel may have been quite wrong. Simone de Beauvoir may, all along, have been writing a novel about repressed jealousy, about the hypocrisy that can result from deciding that an emotion does not exist because it has been judged to be deplorable. Quite conceivably, my interpretation of the novel is correct—or another novel misinterprets itself along the lines I have indicated. The conclusion is evident: a work of art can misinterpret itself. But if a work of art does misinterpret itself in this sort of way, then this is a serious artistic flaw. What may appear to be a misinterpretation might be nothing of the kind; a misinterpretation might be a quite deliberate, perhaps ironically intended perspective on the work of art, woven quite consciously and artistically into the fabric of the work, a vital dimension of the work, enriching its meaning.

Once we concede that a work of art can be a fallacious interpretation of itself, in the kind of way I have indicated, we have to conclude that all works of art are self-interpretations. The Simone de Beauvoir novel (as I remember it) is not a case of a work that contains, within itself, a false adjunct interpretation, a paragraph that declares, firmly and falsely, that this is not a novel about unacknowledged jealousy. The false interpretation is built into the whole structure of the novel as a feature of the novel itself, and is not confined to an adjunct interpretation contained within the novel.

We have given a strong argument in favor of holding that works of art do embody interpretations of themselves. That works of art do embody self-interpretations is the case for works of art that have a literary character associated with them: the novel, the poem, the opera, and even perhaps the ballet or picture that tells a story. But how a piece of music could embody a misinterpretation of itself is not evident. Some of Mozart's music, even when apparently sprightly and cheerful, has an underlying mood of immense sadness. But this is not misinterpretation, but great art. Nevertheless, if literary art can misinterpret itself, and thus invariably interpret itself, all art interprets itself.

Art is its interpretation and, apart from scattered cases of flawed literary works that misinterpret themselves, works of art embody the correct interpretation of themselves. Great works of art do that. I wish to defend this version of singularism.

But I can anticipate an objection that stems from Krausz's writings on interpretation. In LR Krausz declares that singularism and multiplism are parasitic upon the idea of "an end of inquiry," in the pragmatic sense that "informed practitioners may agree that all pertinent evidence or argumentation is available to make a suitably informed determination as to whether a given object of interpretation answers to one or more than one interpretation" (p. 9-10). But the work of art itself stands, not at the end of inquiry, but at the beginning of inquiry (apart, perhaps, for the artist herself). Notoriously, the work of art does not itself answer all questions. If it did, there would be no need for critics, art historians, musicologists, and other professional interpreters to produce their mass of adjunct interpretations. If the correct interpretation, or the correct batch of interpretations (granted multiplism), presuppose that, in some pragmatic sense, all the relevant features have been covered, all the relevant questions answered, then the work of art cannot possibly itself be the correct interpretation.

And I can also foresee another, related objection. In RR, Krausz characterizes the singularist as holding "his or her preferred interpretation to be conclusively right" (p. 2). But this is hardly something that the work of art can itself accomplish. Perhaps in some, and probably quite uninteresting, cases just one conceivable interpretation exists, no discussion whatsoever being required to identify it. But in most cases, and in most cases of great art, this is by no means true. Only after sustained imaginative critical exploration of diverse possible interpretations of the work of art may some agreed interpretation (or batch of acceptable interpretations) emerge; and even then it may be that no such agreement is reached. The work of art cannot supply this sustained exploration of possibilities; it cannot, of itself, establish that its interpretation of itself is "conclusively right." Singularism, as understood above, is untenable.

But neither of these objections is valid against the version of singularism I am defending here. To begin with, "correct" is not the same thing as "complete" in the sense that all interpretive questions that can be asked about the work are answered in a manner available instantly to everyone. In the first place, the work of art may contain within itself answers to questions about what the work of art means or says, but these answers are by no means obvious, even to those who enjoy and understand the work of art. The value of a work may be unperceived, even by experts. It took about a century for the grandeur and profundity of Bach's music to be perceived and enjoyed generally by the music-loving public. (In connection with this point, I have defended a version of realism about value in general, and aesthetic value in particular, to make room for the possibility of learning about what is of value, including learning about the aesthetic value of works of art.[2]) Second, there may be all sorts of historical, cultural, linguistic, or factual matters alluded to by the work of art, which need to be known and understood for a proper appreciation and understanding of the work, but which the work does not itself answer. In order to be able to understand a poem or novel you have to understand the language; in order to understand and appreciate a picture, you may need to know about a mythological story depicted by the picture. In order to understand a piece of music you need to know something about, or to have had some experience of, the musical tradition within which the piece exists. Third, the artist may have left some matters of interpretation obscure; private references or allusions exist in the piece which no amount of knowledge about traditions, history, culture, and other publicly available matters can reveal. In this sort of case, it needs the artist (or someone who knows the artist well) to provide the necessary information.

In these sorts of ways, then, the correct interpretation of the work of art, namely the work of art itself, though correct, is unlikely of itself instantly to answer all interpretive questions for everyone. Diverse adjunct interpretations are needed to answer diverse questions that different people ask, perhaps because of different educational, cultural or historical backgrounds, or different interests. But this diversity of equally good adjunct interpretations does not mean that multiplism holds. The adjunct interpretations differ not because they contradict one another, but because they address different audiences, and tackle different questions about the work of art.

As far as the second objection is concerned, if singularism as understood here is correct, and known to be correct, then we do know what the correct interpretation is: the work of art itself. But because this interpretation is not complete, any number of crucial questions about the work may remain to be answered. And even if we concede that singularism, as understood here, is known to be correct, this does not mean that we know for certain which of several conflicting adjunct interpretations is correct. Because an adjunct interpretation, even if correct, will remain more or less conjectural in character, a range of conflicting interpretations may need to be put forward, to increase our chances of choosing the correct one. Just this situation obtains in science. In order to increase our chances of discovering the truth we need to put forward a range of conflicting theories, which then suggest crucial experiments that may be performed in attempts to weed out the false theories. In LR, Krausz acknowledges that fallibilist versions of singularism are possible, and that singularists may encourage the development of alternative (adjunct) interpretations for the kind of reasons just indicated (LR, p.10-11).

Singularism, as understood here, can do justice to a point emphasized by Krausz, that a work of art may be inherently ambiguous. Consider, for example, Leonardo's *Last Supper*. Following a famous essay on the *Last Supper* by Goethe, the tendency has been, in modern times, to interpret the fresco as depicting the moment at which Jesus announces, "One of you shall betray me . . . ." This interpretation explains the reactions of astonishment, horror and disbelief from the disciples. Leo Steinberg has argued that the real meaning of the painting is the Eucharist, marked by the words "Take, eat: this is my body."[3] Jesus' outstretched arms indicate bread and wine on the table before him: his central position in the picture, his stillness in such marked contrast to the disciples, the way the whole picture radiates outwards from him, all indicate that what is depicted is Jesus giving himself to the world. For Steinberg, the announcement of the betrayal is absorbed into this greater meaning of the

Eucharist. In a fascinating review of Steinberg's book, Michael Podro suggests a different emphasis: perhaps "the sacramental aspect can work effectively only if the astonishment at the prophecy of betrayal is highlighted, if the transcendent significance of the event is allowed to emerge understated, to radiate through the overall structure."[4] The true meaning of the *Last Supper*, in short, is bound up, not just with the existence of two, equally valid, different interpretations (betrayal and Eucharist), but with the way in which these two readings interact with one another, or are related to each other, in the form of the picture. The correct adjunct interpretation will incorporate all these meanings.

Something similar can perhaps be said of Anselm Kiefer's paintings, much discussed by Krausz as a typical case of incongruence. Kiefer's paintings incorporate Nazi symbolism, and can be seen as "celebrating or exorcising the world's unresolved memories of that terrible past," as Joseph Margolis puts it in a passage quoted by Krausz (LR, p. 21). But here, perhaps the element of celebration, of fascination, is essential to the exorcism; if something of the ghastly appeal of Nazism is not depicted and appreciated, the exorcism will be perfunctory and incomplete. We have here, in short, not two incompatible interpretations ambiguously presented to us, but a coherent meaning which emerges out of the dissonance of the two interpretations indicated by Margolis. Krausz suggests something along these lines himself (LR, p. 23).

So far I have defended a version of singularism that declares that the work of art is its correct interpretation. Krausz, in defending multiplism, tends to write of different equally "admissible" interpretations, instead of different equally "correct" interpretations. "Admissible" is a much looser term than "correct." We might well want to hold that there can be many different, mutually incompatible, but equally admissible (adjunct) interpretations, even though only one correct interpretation can be found.

One way this state of affairs can come about is because of ignorance. We do not know enough to be able to decide which of two or more incompatible interpretations is correct; in order to be "admissible," an interpretation must be good enough to be a candidate for being the correct interpretation, given the knowledge available to us. We may need to put forward a variety of conflicting interpretations that are admissible, in this sense, in order to increase our chances of discovering the correct interpretation. As we have already seen, just this happens in science, where conflicting hypotheses are put forward as part of the attempt to discover the truth, all the hypotheses being "admissible," in the sense that they are candidates for the truth. Multiplicity of conflicting adjunct interpretations that are all equally "admissible," in this sense, far from contradicting singularism, is required by singularism.

An interpretation might be "admissible" in other ways, even though not correct—and even though known not to be correct. What is admissible may well depend on context. Something inadmissible in one context may be admissible in another. In the context of satire, or the jokes of a stand-up come-dian, interpretations of politicians, political parties, institutions, even works of art, may be entirely "admissible," because hilarious, utterly absurd, and yet containing a tiny germ of truth (exaggerated to the point of absurdity), even though, in another context, such an interpretation would be shockingly and appallingly inadmissible. Political cartoons, jokes, and satirical comment depend for their effect on distortion and exaggeration: this kind of diversity of admissible interpretations is, again, compatible with singularism.

Another kind of context is closer to Krausz's concerns, where the exis-tence of diverse, conflicting equally admissible interpretations appears unde-niable, and more of a challenge to singularism. I have in mind the context of the performing arts. In Chapter One of RR, Krausz makes what is, to me, a convincing case for acknowledging that there can be equally admissible, even equally correct, different interpretations of one and the same piece of music. And in the theatre, opera, and ballet too, we would say that the same thing holds. How can singularism, as I am defending the doctrine here, accommo-date this point?

To some extent singularism can accommodate a variety of conflicting admissible interpretations of performing arts in ways already indicated. A range of interpretations of a symphony or play may be admissible in part be-cause we want to discover what works, what most successfully brings out the inherent aesthetic value of the piece. Again, a range of different interpreta-tions may be admissible because, when it comes to the performing arts, per-formers have aims other than to discover the "correct" interpretation. Direc-tors of plays and operas may set out to shock, to provoke, or to win attention, a critical outcry, and an audience. Conductors, singers, actors, directors and other performers may want to highlight some aspect of a well-known work that they feel has been neglected, at the expense, perhaps, of more obvious and, in the end, more important, features. Mere fashion plays a major role in influencing how music and plays are performed. How odd that, as far as mu-sic is concerned, authentic performances are all the rage, but when it comes to theater, just the opposite fashion prevails, it being almost *de rigueur* that a production of *Hamlet* for today should be set in a modern corporation, the King, the Queen, and the courtiers being business executives wearing suits and name tags, and shooting each other with machine guns (as depicted by a 2001, "much admired," production of *Hamlet* by The Royal Shakespeare Company).

Putting aside such examples of diverse admissible interpretations as these, which can be dealt with by singularism in ways indicated above, there appears to be a residue of cases which pose much more of a challenge to sin-gularism. Symphonies can be performed in several different but equally le-gitimate, authentic, correct ways; and the same goes for plays, operas, and ballet. In some of these cases, the range of different interpretations might be narrowed down if we knew more. The composer or playwright might emphatically dismiss some interpretations as doing violence to his or her intentions. I do not want to suggest that the artist's verdict is decisive. Artists can change their mind, grow old, and forget what they originally intended, or just misjudge some performance matters, so that if their instructions are followed to the letter, the resulting performance fails to do justice to what is of most value in the work. There may be more than one creative artist involved, and these may not agree. Nevertheless, what the intentions of an artist were in creating a work of art is a factor in determining what constitutes a correct interpretation of the work. Discovering what these intentions are is difficult in many cases, the artist being long dead.

But even if we were able to consult the composer or playwright, thinking that the response would be sufficient to determine just one way of performing or producing the work as the correct one (in all cases) is implausible. When the artist still lives, he or she may be undecided, or even fallible, about crucial interpretive issues. A composer or playwright may be delighted that a symphony or play can be performed in a variety of different ways, different interpretations emphasizing different aspects of the work, several different interpretations being equally correct. If this is the case, what becomes of singularism?

One way to defend singularism against this apparently lethal objection is to argue that the performing arts are in a different category from other art forms. In the case of the performing arts, the work of art only comes to life, only exists, through performance. The score, the text of the play, or the choreographic score is not a work of art in its right, but is a set of instructions for the creation of a work of art, which comes to fruition in a performance. The work of art is not the score or text but the clutch of ideal kinds of performance, which realize the "set of instructions" in different, but equally valid, equally correct ways. What is peculiar about performing art is that the work of art—the clutch of ideal kinds of performance—is inherently multifaceted. In referring to Shakespeare's *Hamlet* or Ludwig von Beethoven's *Ninth* we are referring to several distinct works of art with some common features, a family resemblance, and a common inheritance: namely the distinct kinds of ideal performance, all engendered by, made possible by, Shakespeare's text, or Beethoven's score. Actors and musicians are creative artists aided and abetted by words and notes of the works they perform. And this way of viewing the matter is supported by our honoring great actors and performers as creative artists, along with the artists who create the works they perform.

That singularism breaks down in the case of the performing arts is due not to any inadequacy in singularism, but to the strange, "hydra-headed" character of a performed work of art. When a performer "interprets" a play or musical score, he or she does something quite different from what an art historian does in providing an adjunct interpretation of a picture, and quite different, again, from what a musicologist or music critic does in writing about music. The performer recreates—or co-creates—the work of art. In performing Franz Schubert's *Moments musicaux*, a pianist brings into full reality, into our common, public world, something that, before, was only a potentiality, a set of instructions for the work of art the pianist (with the assistance of Schubert's instructions) creates. The art historian or music critic does nothing of the kind. Their adjunct interpretations are not realizations of the works of art under discussion. What we have, in short, in the case of the performing arts, is not one work of art and many different equally correct adjunct interpretations, but many different works of art, all sharing common features, and stemming from a common source, a common set of instructions, each having just one correct adjunct interpretation (apart from the qualifications to this that have been discussed above).

A mischievous interlocutor might at this point take up the above argument and, pushing it to the limit, argue that all art is performing art, there being no evident dividing line between performing art, and art that is not performed. Poetry can be performed, just like plays. Novels can be read out loud to audiences, and thus performed. Charles Dickens went on tours reading his novels. These days one can buy cassettes and CDs of actors reading works of literature. How a painting, or a sculpture can become a set of instructions for a performance is not quite evident (although some visual artists are "performance artists").

On the other hand, pushing the dividing line between performance and non-performance art in the other direction, it might be argued that performances are just the result of tradition and custom, and are never essential, because we can understand, enjoy and appreciate all art without them. We do not have to go to the theatre to enjoy Shakespeare; we can pick up a book and read one of his plays. Even a musician can read a musical score, so that the music of the score is heard with the mind's ear.

Or, put another way, it might be argued that all art involves performance in that we, in experiencing, enjoying and understanding the work recreate it in our imagination. We read a musical score and, if we have the skill, create in our mind the sounds of a quartet playing. We read a play, and in our imagination put on a production, complete with actors, makeup, scenery, entrances and exits. We read a novel, and create in our imagination the landscape, the people, and the action. And when we look at a picture, we co-create the work of art, the forms, the landscape, the atmosphere, the mood and meaning of the picture. We are all artists, and works of art are all, without exception, sets of instructions for the creation of the works of art we see, hear, read, and enjoy. And since we are all different, with different past experiences, imaginations, knowledge, and skills, we all create different works of art from any one set of instructions: *Lear, The Mona Lisa, St. Matthew Passion*. Art is hydra-headed. The version of singularism I have been defending here, which begins with the claim that the work of art is its interpretation, has vanished without trace. A work of art is much too multifaceted a thing to be capable of being "the correct interpretation of itself." No such object exists, only a set of instructions, and as many distinct works of art as people who have used the "set of instructions" to co-create, for themselves, their particular, personal, performed work of art. Singularism is nonsense. It drowns in this ocean of multifaceted works of art.

This extreme subjectivist view can be resisted, and ought to be resisted. One way to do this would be to take the argument further, until it becomes a *reductio ad absurdum*. Not just works of art are created by the performances we stage in our imagination. The same applies to trees, houses, people, cars, to "middle-sized objects," as Krausz would say, quite generally. What we appear to experience, is not out there, in the physical world, but is the outcome of the perceptual and interpretive machinery of our minds, or brains, getting to work on physical stimuli that we absorb via our sense organs. The world external to us is, roughly, what modern physics says it is, quite different from what we ordinarily experience and suppose it to be, or something unknown, unknowable, and unimaginable.

The quasi-Kantian view just outlined deserves to be rejected. It constitutes a false solution to what is, in my view, the fundamental problem of philosophy which, elsewhere, I have formulated like this: "How can we understand our human world, embedded within the physical universe, in such a way that justice is done to the richness, meaning, and value of human life on the one hand, and to what modern science tells us about the physical universe on the other hand?"[5] This problem is to be solved by appreciating that physics is concerned only with a highly selected aspect of all that exists, that "causally efficacious" aspect, which determines the way events unfold. In addition to the physical is the experiential: colors, sounds, smells, tactile qualities, as we experience them, and moral and value qualities of people and works of art. These exist out there in the world around us, compatible with, but not reducible to, the physical. In particular, then, works of art exist out there in the world around us, imbued with the kind of aesthetic features we attribute to them.[6] The world as we experience it is not, as René Descartes thought, and as Immanuel Kant thought in a different way, in the mind.

In particular, then, the usual distinction that we would make between a performed work of art, and one not performed, continues to hold. A performance is something that takes place in the public world, music played in a concert hall, or a play performed in a theatre. When we read a play, we may, in some sense, create a production of the play in our imagination; but this creation, being private, taking place only in our imagination, is not a performance. Even if we accepted the quasi-Cartesian or Kantian view, there would still be an analogous distinction between "public performances," and "private imaginings."

I have admitted above that a work of art, even though being (in most cases) the correct interpretation of itself, is nevertheless unlikely to be complete, in the sense that it answers all questions about how the work is to be understood. The question arises: can we be sure that always one correct answer to such questions exists, even in the case of non-performing art, and even if you allow that we may never know what the correct answer (if it exists) is? May not some works of art be inherently loosely specified, even be quite consciously designed to carry two or more incompatible adjunct interpretations? Is it beyond the wit of any artist to create such a work of art, perhaps with the deliberate intention of falsifying singularism? Consider William Wordsworth's Lucy poem "A Slumber Did My Spirit Seal," discussed by Krausz (RR, p. 77-79). Here is the poem:

> A slumber did my spirit seal;
> I had no human fears:
> She seemed a thing that could not feel
> The touch of earthly years.
> No motion has she now, no force;
> She neither hears nor sees;
> Rolled round in earth's diurnal course,
> With rocks, and stones, and trees.

Krausz considers two conflicting interpretations of this poem, by Cleanth Brooks and by F. W. Bateson. Brooks sees the poem as expressing the lover's agonized shock at the inertness, the dead lifelessness, of the loved one, depicted in the second stanza. Bateson, by contrast, sees the poem as expressing the pantheistic grandeur of the dead—Lucy becoming a part of the sublime processes of nature. These readings are incompatible; but nothing in the poem allows us to favor one over the other. Is this not a case of multiplism?

Wordsworth himself might have favored one interpretation over the other, as doing better justice to his intentions in writing the poem. But even the author's intention might not be judged conclusive. It could always be argued that, even if Wordsworth did intend the poem to be understood in one way instead of the other, nothing in the poem itself supports this judgment. If this was Wordsworth's intention, then he failed to realize it adequately in his poem. Wordsworth might point to other poems and writings of his where, perhaps, the pantheistic theme is pronounced, to support Bateson's reading, but he would then be proceeding in the same kind of way that a literary critic would proceed.

My view is that this case does not refute singularism. I think the poem—the correct interpretation of the poem—incorporates elements of the two readings, Brooks's and Bateson's. The poem expresses the shock and horror associated with Lucy's inert state of death, her body being reduced to being rolled round with earth, stones, rocks, and trees. But a kind of consolation arises from Lucy's participation in the grandeur of nature, as Bateson points out. The poem itself—the correct interpretation of the poem—includes the horror and the grandeur.

Singularism can be regarded as a blinkered, single-minded view, which insists that works of art have just one definite interpretation—a view that cannot tolerate ambiguity, richness, and contradictory emotional responses to things. But it could be argued that just the reverse is the case. The multiplist cannot tolerate ambiguity, richness, apparently contradictory emotional responses in a single interpretation, and feels obliged to postulate many different interpretations (each interpretation doing justice just to one aspect of the work). The multiplist is blinkered and single-minded, intolerant of ambiguity, richness, and the complexity of our emotional responses to things.

But what of the artist who sets out to create a work that has two contradictory interpretations built into it, in order to refute singularism? Even this would not refute singularism; for the correct interpretation would be that a single, coherent, artistic intention was to create a work with two contradictory interpretations.

To conclude, the view expounded here has features more characteristic of multiplism, although the view is a version of singularism that I have defended throughout. First, my view acknowledges that we may never know which of two or more conflicting interpretations is the correct one. Second, it emphasizes the importance of developing a variety of different, and possibly equally admissible, interpretations, in part in order to help discover the correct interpretation. Third, incongruence is recognized as a crucial feature of some works of art. Incongruence, when it exits, is incorporated within the single correct interpretation, and is not distributed between different interpretations, as multiplism might have it, none being able to do justice to the real meaning of the work as a result. Fourth, my view emphasizes that the whole point of adjunct interpretations is to help an audience all the better experience, know, understand, appreciate, and enjoy what is of most value in a work of art—or, possibly, see through what is fraudulent, shabby, dishonest, and third-rate. Adjunct interpretations, in order to be good, need to be appropriate to their audience, its education, the times it lives in, the experience it has of comparable works of art, and so on. There may be many different adjunct interpretations, at different levels, tackling different questions. None is complete; but all might be correct. Fifth, my view argues that in different contexts, especially in connection with the performing arts, a variety of interpretations may be admissible, even though not correct. Finally, the view recognizes the multifaceted character of performed works of art.

NOTES

1. Michael Krausz, *Rightness and Reasons: Interpretation in Cultural Practices* (RR) (Ithaca, N. Y.: Cornell University Press, 1993); Michael Krausz, *Limits of Rightness* (LR) (Lanham, Md: Rowman and Littlefield, 2000).

2. Nicholas Maxwell, "Are There Objective Values?" *The Dalhousie Review* 79: (1999), pp 301–317; Nicholas Maxwell, *The Human World in the Physical Uni-*

verse (Lanham, Md.: Rowman and Littlefield, 1984), ch. 2; Nicholas Maxwell, *From Knowledge to Wisdom* (Oxford: Blackwell, 1984), ch. 10.

3. Leo Steinberg, *Leonardo's Incessant Last Supper* (New York: Zone Books, 1993).

4. Michael Podro, "Space, Time, and Leonardo," *Times Literary Supplement*, no. 5153: (4 January 2002), p. 17.

5. Maxwell, *The Human World.*

6. *Ibid.*, ch. 2; Maxwell, *From Knowledge to Wisdom*, ch. 10.

Twenty

VERSIONS, DUBS, AND REMIXES: REALISM AND RIGHTNESS IN AESTHETIC INTERPRETATION

Christoph Cox

"Rightness" has been the watchword of Michael Krausz's work over the past decade. Across two books and a range of articles, Krausz has asked: which interpretation of a cultural text, if any, is the single *right* one? Resisting any simple or quick answer, Krausz has tried instead to sort out the methodological presuppositions of possible answers to this question, notably to detach ontological commitments ("realism" and "constructionism") from interpretive ideals ("singularism"/"multiplism").[1]

Krausz's subtle and illuminating analyses go a long way toward clarifying the real differences between competing interpretations. In the musical context that will mostly concern me here, his work also presents serious challenges to realist conceptions of the musical work and singularist conceptions of musical interpretation. At the close of his essay "Rightness and Reasons in Musical Interpretation," Krausz writes: "the understanding of musical interpretation should begin not with a realist view of works of music, but rather with an understanding of musical practice. Whichever posture one favors regarding the ontology of works of music, one cannot make musical phenomena intelligible independent of the historically constituted practices in which they are found and fostered."[2]

Taking these words to heart, I want to extend Krausz's examination of musical ontology and interpretation by drawing attention to the historical conditions of classical music practice (the practice of European art music since around 1750) and by situating this practice in relation to non-classical musical practices. If we look at music in this broader context, we will see that the firm distinction between "work" and "interpretation" breaks down, and that the realist conception of the work and the singularist criterion for interpretive "rightness" lose their footing. I take my remarks here to provide an extension of multiplist and constructionist themes in Krausz's work, to spin these themes into a kind of *remix*—a notion central to the view I develop here.

The questions I ask are basic ontological and epistemological ones. What *is* an interpretation? What *is* a text? What is the relationship between an interpretation and a text? How might your answers to these questions differ depending on whether your ontology is realist or constructionist? Alongside these, I want to press a set of broader cultural and historical questions. How might focusing on the small class of artworks on which philosophers of art overwhelmingly tend to focus (namely, the "high art" of post-Renaissance Europe) implicitly lend credence to some hermeneutic and ontological claims? How might a focus on other sorts of artworks lend support to a different set of claims?

First, consider the question: what is an interpretation? The ordinary answer to this question is implicitly realist and singularist. It runs something like the following: Some primary object out there is called a text. Some secondary thing is called an interpretation. And the aim of interpretation is "to get the text right." This aesthetic view is analogous to the traditional epistemological picture, according to which there is a world out there and, as inquirers, our aim is "to get it right." Nonetheless, if we examine these epistemological and aesthetic scenarios together, we find some intriguing differences and similarities.

In the epistemological case, "getting the world right" is never a matter of simple mirroring; instead, it always involves translation and transformation: that of physical objects or states of affairs into beliefs or sentences. Insisting upon the *aesthetic* character of this epistemological translation from one domain to another, Friedrich Nietzsche asserts that knowledge and language are inherently "metaphorical" in the etymological sense of this term: to carry over or across.[3] On the other hand, the case of aesthetic interpretation would appear to allow for a more direct and literal way of "getting right" its object or text. If the object is a photograph, you might re-photograph it, as the artist Sherrie Levine has done with the photographs of Walker Evans, Alexander Rodchenko, and others. If a literary text, you might rewrite it word for word, a practice that Jorge Luis Borges describes in his well-known story "Pierre Menard, Author of the *Quixote*," which tells the tale of an early twentieth-century author who sets out to write "a few pages which would coincide—word for word and line for line—with those of Miguel de Cervantes."[4] As the narrator and Menard himself acknowledge, given the temporal and contextual differences that separate "text" and "interpretation," even such repetition never quite manages "to get the text right."[5] "To compose the *Quixote* at the beginning of the seventeenth century," remarks Menard, "was a reasonable undertaking, necessary and perhaps even unavoidable; at the beginning of the twentieth, it is almost impossible. It is not in vain that three hundred years have gone by, filled with exceedingly complex events. Amongst them, to mention only one, is the *Quixote* itself."[6]

It would be a mistake to dismiss such examples as mere pranks, for they exemplify fundamental features of the work of art in the age of mechanical and digital production and reproduction, and raise important issues concerning the original and originality, recording and repetition, and so forth. More to the point, they help us to see that interpretation never is or can be a matter of "getting the text right," that even the most faithful interpretation will involve something other than simple repetition.[7] Interpretation always involves transformation—or, as Nietzsche polemically puts it "forcing, adjusting, abbreviating, omitting, padding, inventing, falsifying, and whatever else is of the *es-*

sence of interpreting."[8] To put it another way, no interpreter of a text (with the possible exception of the classical music performer, whose practice we will examine in a moment) ever cares to reproduce the original, which, after all, already exists. Instead, he or she cares to bring something new into the world, namely a new text that transforms (by selecting, highlighting, rendering in a different medium, etc.) the original text. And I think that this basic fact puts realism and singularism under strain.

The focus, in philosophical aesthetics, on works of "high art" in the modern European canon lends undue credence to the realist, singularist view. For complex historical, political, and economic reasons, modern European works of high art are extraordinarily and unusually fixed and stable. In literature and music, for example, the modern work is fixed in writing, signed by an author, and protected by copyright. Some stable and bounded *thing* is called *the* work. And for another complex set of reasons, the modern European tradition has separated and hierarchized the practices of creation and of criticism. Parasitical on the work of the creative genius, a class of literary critics or musical performers exists whose interpretive productions are secondary and beholden to the original work of art.

Contemporary musical aesthetics has largely taken for granted these conceptions of the work and of interpretation. Despite their differences, nominalists and Platonists alike take the musical work to be a kind of thing or object—for the nominalist a score, for the Platonist an ideal type—and "interpretation" to be a matter of fidelity to this object. Yet the notion of music as embodied in fixed objects is an anomaly in the history of music. The notion is characteristic only of about two hundred years of Western art music—a tiny slice of musical history and geography that in no way exemplifies music in general.[9] Throughout most of human history, music has existed without reference to a fixed object; and throughout most of the world (the West included), it still does.[10] That the *thinghood* of music is merely a contingent byproduct of the economics of musical life in modern Europe is arguable: music became a thing only when composers and musicians were forced to sell their wares on the market, which favors fixed and exchangeable objects that are the legally protected private property of an author. The concept of "the musical work" would appear to be an exemplary instance of what Karl Marx calls "the fetishism of commodities" and what Georg Lukács calls "reification": the process by which the products of human, social activity take on a life of their own and confront their producers as autonomous objects with a "phantom objectivity."[11] This characteristic of modern life is facilitated by the division of labor (for example, between composer, conductor, and performer) and by the elevation of the product over the process, the abstract over the concrete, and the objective over the subjective (for example, the score over performance).

The "reification" of musical practice—the transformation of a process into a thing—has its philosophical analog in musical Platonism and score-nominalism. Faced with the obvious sensuous facts that (1) music is a temporal art, (2) musical performances are ephemeral, and (3) no two performances are alike, modern musicians and philosophers have sought the identity of the musical work in a conceptual abstraction outside of and beyond the irreducibly physical, sensuous, temporal, and individual character of musical performances. What began as a mnemonic aid for performance—the score—became an autonomous entity that governed performances and to which they were held accountable.[12] This is precisely the Platonist move that Nietzsche and Wittgenstein warn us against: the preposterous inversion by which the concept "leaf" becomes the cause of particular leaves—or, in the musical case, an abstract non-musical entity becomes the cause of musical performances.[13] But the inversion will be seen for a conception of music standing on its head. Only musical performances exist, each one different from the next to a greater or lesser degree. Only a "family resemblance" among performances allows us to identify anything like a musical "work," a designation that will only ever be a conceptual abstraction.[14] Music is a becoming, not a being, a process, not a thing. We can try to halt this process by producing an abstract, transcendent object that serves as the model for performances; and "interpretation" can be taken as a matter of performing in fidelity to this model. But performances will always reassert process and becoming by introducing variations; and "interpretations" will always be—whether desired or not—creative.

This becomes more evident once we consider pre- and postmodern works of art. Take, for example, the *Iliad*—not the written text attributed to Homer but the fluid and anonymous oral poem that—over centuries, was continuously added to, subtracted from, and reworked.[15] In this case, no single text, no "original," exists. And interpreters (the successive poets) are not "getting right" some original text but inheriting a version and reworking it in performance. In the twentieth century, this is more or less the way the jazz canon works. The jazz "standard" is merely a rudimentary chart or prompt for improvisation; and improvisations respond to other improvisations instead of to any "original." Not one "Body and Soul" exists, but thousands. The original (written by the comparatively obscure team of Edward Heyman, John Green, Rob Sour, and Frank Eyton, and debuted by Gertrude Lawrence and Jack Hylton's Orchestra) is buried under stronger versions (for example, those by Billie Holiday, Louis Armstrong, Thelonious Monk, or John Coltrane); and the "interpreters" are the authors of new texts.

These examples begin to suggest a constructionist answer to the questions "what is an interpretation?" and "what is the relationship between interpretation and text?" In the epistemological and ontological context, the constructionist dissolves the firm distinction between self and world, subject and object. The world is not some independent given thing out there that our job as knowers is to represent adequately. Instead, subject and object, self and world are terms in a symbol system (Nelson Goodman), web (Richard Rorty), text (Jacques Derrida), or discursive field (Michel Foucault). Similarly, in the aesthetic context, the constructionist undermines any firm distinction between interpretation and text. For the constructionist (Nietzsche or Derrida, for example), the text is always itself an interpretation, a reworking of materials already on hand; and any new interpretation is an interpretation of an interpretation, with no ultimate or final *Ur*-text underlying this process. On this model, then, the question about interpretation is not the realist question "is it right (in the sense of 'faithful')?" but the pragmatic, constructionist questions "is it interesting?" "is it new?" "is it useful?" "is it important?"

When we survey the practice of what we ordinarily call aesthetic "interpretation," I think we find that this is precisely what "interpretations" do and precisely what we want from them. What does the literary scholar do? Via a host of conventions, he or she mixes literary with analytical prose to produce a new text. What does the art critic do? He or she translates the visual into the verbal and supplements descriptive with evaluative prose to produce a new text. And these "interpretations" are judged not according to how faithfully they reproduce the original but according to whether they show us something new, interesting, or important.

In this regard, I want to take up and extend Goodman's notion of the "version." For Goodman, all knowledge and inquiry (scientific, aesthetic, etc.) is a matter of inhabiting and producing "worlds" or "versions," which have the peculiar characteristic of being without an original, singular, or common base. According to Goodman, no single, given World exists but only ever different "worlds" or "versions," which are themselves constructed from other "worlds" or "versions."[16] Among other virtues, Goodman's notion of the "version" is felicitous here because it links with an important musical use of this term. In Jamaican dancehall reggae during the late 1960s, the term "version" referred to the instrumental B-side of a reggae single. These B-sides were to be played by a DJ in a dancehall as the backing tracks for a "toaster" who would rap (or "toast") over them. It did not take long before producers such as King Tubby, Errol Thompson, and Lee "Scratch" Perry began to think of the "version" (or "dub") as its own entity. Their "dubs" drastically reworked the original tracks, fragmenting the vocals or dropping them out entirely, foregrounding a single element (such as a bass line or a hi-hat rhythm), splicing in portions of other tracks, or highlighting studio effects (such as echo and delay).

In contemporary electronic music, this practice has been considerably extended via the notion of the remix. In the early 1980s, remixes maintained a fairly strict fidelity to their original tracks, and served primarily to make them more dance-friendly by extending them and foregrounding the rhythmic elements. In the past decade or so, the practice of remixing has become much more radical and creative. Remixes often radically overhaul the original material such that only select bits are maintained in the new versions. Some remixes bear no audible relationship whatsoever to the original (for example, Oval's 1996 remixes of tracks by Tortoise).[17]

Why deem such tracks "remixes" or "interpretations?" Why not call them new "originals" or "texts?" In the first place, these tracks come with the designation "remix," which, like any title, sets up audience expectations—in this case, that one track (the "remix") will be heard in relation to another (the "original"). Secondly, regardless of its sonic properties, the remix is economically and legally tied to the "original," for, in current practice, the remixer is paid a flat fee, while the original artist maintains the copyright (and collects royalties) on the remix.[18] Finally, such extreme cases call attention to that fact that, in the age of recording and digital sampling, so much of contemporary music is a matter of sonic recycling that every track is a sort of remix.[19] As the producer Kevin Martin puts it "neither the artist nor the remixer are 'creators' in the traditional sense"; rather, both "act as 'filters' for a sort of cultural flow."[20] In the digital age, notes Brian Eno, "the artist is more curator than creator. An artist is now much more seen as a connector of things, a person who scans the enormous field of possible places for artistic attention, and says, 'What I am going to do is draw your attention to *this* sequence of things.'"[21] In short, the artist is an interpreter and the interpreter an artist.

Within electronic music culture, the measure of a remix is not "is it faithful to the original?" (Nobody wants that, for the original already exists. Why repeat it?) Instead, a remix is evaluated by answering the questions "where does it take the original?" "what's left of the original?" "is it interesting?" Again, I suggest that this is what any interpretation does and always has done. If this is the case, then the focus of interpretation will be shifted away from the realist, singularist aim of "getting the text right" to the constructionist, multiplist aim of transforming a text itself an interpretation.

To the classical music aficionado and the traditional philosopher of music, the musical practices of versioning, dubbing, and remixing may appear exotic and exceptional. My contention is that these are contemporary instances of the age-old practice of music making, a practice obscured by a focus on the classical aesthetic. From Homer through John Coltrane, Grandmaster Flash, and Oval, music has always been a matter of transformative performance, of reinterpreting texts that are themselves interpretations. Theodor Adorno and Jacques Attali argued that musical recording reifies and commodifies music to an even greater degree than does the classical score.[22] Yet sampling and remix practice demonstrate the contrary: that recording makes possible a new kind of musical practice, a new *musica practica* that anyone with rudimentary playback technology can engage in. As Chris Cutler and Mark Poster have argued, art in the digital age recapitulates (albeit via different technology) the folk mode of production exemplified by oral poetry, with its focus on performance and the continual transformation of inherited, all but anonymous, public texts.[23] If this is what music is and means, then philosophers of music have been asking the wrong questions about music and coming to the wrong conclusions about it. At best, they have been "philosophers of classical music" who have taken the exception to be the rule.

To conclude, I have tried to argue for the following claims. Realism and constructionism differ significantly about what they take a work of art and an interpretation to be. Interpretation never is what the realist takes it to be, namely, a faithful rendering of an original text. Instead, interpretation always transforms the text via translation, selection, supplementation, and deformation. Interpretation is always a constructive, artistic, project that challenges the firm distinction between the work and the interpretation, and challenges the hierarchy that places the first above the second. On the constructionist model, the question about interpretation is not "Does it get the original right?" but "How does it render the original otherwise?" and "Is this interesting? New? Significant?" Along the way, I have insisted that the exclusive focus on European high art, with its unusually fixed and stable works, has given undue credence to realism and singularism and that a focus on different aesthetic objects and practices can begin to lend credence to the constructionist conception of what a work of art is and what an interpretation is. Finally, I have suggested that a "philosophy of music" worthy of the name would come to see classical music as the exception instead of the rule. It would begin to examine music more broadly and to take as primary not fixed abstract objects but the fluid process of physical, temporal music-making and remaking.

NOTES

1. Michael Krausz, *Rightness and Reasons: Interpretation in Cultural Practices* (RR) (Ithaca, N. Y.: Cornell University Press, 1993); Michael Krausz, *Limits of Rightness* (Lanham, Md.: Rowman & Littlefield, 2000).

2. RR, p. 37.

3. Friedrich Nietzsche, "On Truth and Lies in a Nonmoral Sense," *Philosophy and Truth: Selections from Nietzsche's Notebooks of the Early 1870's*, ed. and trans. Daniel Breazeale (Atlantic Highlands, N. J.: Humanities Press International, 1979), p. 82.

4. Jorge Luis Borges, "Pierre Menard, Author of the *Quixote*," *Labyrinths: Selected Stories and Other Writings*, ed. Donald A. Yates and James E. Irby (New York: New Directions, 1962), p. 39; Jorge Luis Borges, "Of Exactitude in Science," *A Universal History of Infamy*, trans. Norman Thomas di Giovanni (New York: E.P. Dutton, 1972), p. 141.

5. Hans-Georg Gadamer, *Truth and Method*, 2d edition, trans. Garrett Barden and John Cumming, revised by Joel Weinsheimer and Donald G. Marshall (New York: Continuum, 1993); Jacques Derrida, "Signature Event Context," *Margins of Philosophy*, trans. Alan Bass (Chicago: University of Chicago Press, 1982), pp. 307–330.

6. "Pierre Menard, Author of the *Quixote*," p. 41.

7. Krausz, *Rightness and Reasons*, p. 17.

8. Friedrich Nietzsche, *On the Genealogy of Morals*, Essay 3, §24, in *Basic Writings of Nietzsche*, ed. and trans. Walter Kaufmann (New York: Modern Library, 1966), p. 587.

9. Carl Dahlhaus, *Esthetics of Music*, trans. William Austin (Cambridge: Cambridge University Press, 1982), pp. 9ff; Lydia Goehr, *The Imaginary Museum of Musical Works* (Oxford: Clarendon Press, 1992); Michael Chanan, *Musica Practica: The Social Practice of Western Music from Gregorian Chant to Postmodernism* (London: Verso, 1994); Jacques Attali, *Noise: The Political Economy of Music*, trans. Brian Massumi (Minneapolis: University of Minnesota Press, 1985).

10. Christopher Small, *Musicking* (Hanover, N. H.: Wesleyan University Press, 1998); Christopher Small, *Music of the Common Tongue* (New York: Riverrun Press, 1987); Kathleen Higgins, *The Music of Our Lives* (Philadelphia: Temple University Press, 1991).

11. Karl Marx, *Capital*, Vol. 1, *The Marx-Engels Reader*, 2d edition, ed. Robert C. Tucker (New York: W.W. Norton and Co., 1978), pp. 319 ff; Georg Lukács, "Reification and the Consciousness of the Proletariat," *History and Class Consciousness: Studies in Marxist Dialectics*, trans. Rodney Livingstone (Cambridge: MIT Press, 1971), pp. 83 ff.

12. Jacques Charpentier, quoted by Derek Bailey, *Improvisation: Its Nature and Practice in Music* (New York: Da Capo, 1992), p. 59; Small, *Music of the Common Tongue*, pp. 231 ff, 281 ff; Chanan, *Musica Practica*, pp. 54 ff.

13. Nietzsche, "On Truth and Lies," p. 83; Ludwig Wittgenstein, *The Blue and Brown Books* (New York: Harper and Row, 1958), pp. 17–18.

14. Higgens, *The Music of Our Lives*, p. 31.

15. Seth Schein, *The Mortal Hero: An Introduction to Homer's Iliad* (Berkeley: University of California Press, 1984), ch. 1.

16. Nelson Goodman, "The Way the World Is," *Problems and Projects* (Indianapolis: Bobbs-Merrill, 1972), pp. 24–32.

17. Simon Reynolds, *Generation Ecstasy: Into the World of Techno and Rave Culture* (New York: Little, Brown, and Company, 1998), p. 279.

18. *Ibid.*, p. 280.

19. David Sanjek, "'Don't Have to DJ No More': Sampling and the Autonomous Creator," *The Construction of Authorship: Textual Appropriation in Law and Literature*, eds. Martha Woodmansee and Peter Jaszi (Durham: Duke University Press, 1994), pp. 343–360; John Oswald, "Plunderphonics, or Audio Piracy as Compositional Prerogative," *Negativland et al., Fair Use: The Story of the Letter U and the Number 2* (Concord, Calif.: Seeland, 1995); John Mowitt, "The Sound of Music in the Era of Its Electronic Reproducibility," *Music and Society: The Politics of Composition, Performance, and Reception*, eds., Richard Leppert and Susan McClary (Cambridge: Cambridge University Press, 1987), pp. 173–197; Andrew Goodwin, "Sample and Hold: Pop Music in the Digital Age of Reproduction," *On Record: Rock, Pop, and the Written Word*, ed. Simon Frith and Andrew Goodwin (New York: Pantheon, 1990), pp. 258–273.

20. Reynolds, *Generation Ecstasy*, p. 280.

21. Brian Eno, "Gossip is Philosophy," in *Wired* 3.05: (May 1995), p. 207.

22. Theodor Adorno, "Musical Life," *Introduction to the Sociology of Music*, trans. E. B. Ashton (New York: Continuum, 1989); Attali, *Noise*, chapter 4.

23. Chris Cutler, "Necessity and Choice in Musical Forms," *File Under Popular: Theoretical and Critical Writings on Music* (New York: Autonomedia, 1993); Chris Cutler, "A History of Plunderphonics," *Resonance* 3:2 and 4:1 (1995); Mark Poster, *What's the Matter with the Internet?* (Minneapolis: University of Minnesota Press, 2001).

Twenty-one

THE WORK AND THE PILGRIMS OF MUSIC

Giridhari Lal Pandit

Dedicated by the author to Hans Günter Dosch, Institut für Theoretische Physik, Universität Heidelberg, on the occasion of his 65th birthday.

1. Disentanglement and the Detachability Question

If we take the work of music and its performances as correlative concepts, just as a text and its interpretations are correlative concepts, then how do the indefinitely many performances of a work of music relate to it, and to one another? The same question arises regarding the text and its interpretations, where these interpretations appear in the *language-scapes* of a given language. (The language-scapes of a language are akin to the landscapes of a country. Think of an original text in German that has different translations in English by different authors. I regard a particular translation of it as a co-text, and several translations of it, in the same language or across different languages, as co-texts in different language-scapes.) There may be a close similarity between the two kinds of cases, the one dealing with the work of music and the other with the works of art, literature and science, or with cultural entities generally. But we should not close our eyes to crucial differences. To borrow Karl R. Popper's terminology, while cultural entities, including scientific theories, generally belong to World 3, which is itself interactively embedded in World 1, the realm of physical entities, and World 2 of minds or states of consciousness, I think that works of music belong to a different realm, a World 4, if because of their unique character.[1] I have in mind especially that scientific theories change and develop over time, some of them being always superseded by others. This type of "progress" is entirely alien to the works of music. Hence, I propose to locate them in World 4 instead of World 3. And yet, in the context of a work of music—think, for example, of any composition by Wolfgang Amadeus Mozart—as also in the context of art generally, or of the forms and beauties of nature, sooner or later one must raise, with Michael Krausz, some fundamental questions regarding what it is to understand, or interpret, such work, given that there may be more than one possibility of achieving our interpretive aims.

We can ask what is the place, range and reach of an interpretation, how far can alternative interpretations compete with one another, and with what kind of legitimacy is it possible to claim for a particular interpretation as the correct one, or the best of all possible interpretations? Are the aims of interpretation, or of performances in the case of music, and their rightness and authenticity, strongly correlated in some way? Do not the categories themselves, to which the objects of interpretation may belong, diverge from one another sufficiently enough to warrant different theories of interpretation and ontological entanglement for the different categorial contexts? Assuming that the objects of interpretation are themselves indeterminate, how does this indeterminacy correlate with their multiple interpretability?

If the distinction between that which is interpreted and its interpretation has metaphysical import, as Krausz has suggested, then this complicates the scenario for interpretational possibilities. As he points out, "the intentionality of that which is interpreted also involves metaphysical considerations. Intentionality concerns the cultural settings—rules, norms, and the like—in terms of which any cultural entity must be made intelligible. The thicker the intentional context, the narrower the range of admissible interpretations may become."[2] Krausz implies that there cannot be any denial regarding the place of metaphysical entanglements in the discussion on interpretation, if the claims of existence and intentionality (of objects of interpretation) are recognized as metaphysical. This naturally raises the question whether, and how far, disentangling this aspect of interpretation from other aspects is possible.

Whether there also arises here a further question of interpretation's detachability from other aspects is debatable. The task of identifying the ontological aspect of interpretation is as important as distinguishing between the question of its disentanglement (Ordnung) and the question of its detachability (Entfernung). While we must admire the attention Krausz pays to the second question, the former question is not even raised for discussion. Does he assume that the disentanglement question is already included in the detachability question? Krausz's implicit assumption, that the task of disentangling the metaphysical aspect entails the task of detaching that aspect from other aspects, is incorrect. Any demand for detachability would signal a requirement or a condition which is far stronger than disentanglement.

2. Essentialism

I have some reservations about the quite general approach to the theory of interpretation and ontology formulated by Krausz. I formulate them by raising questions concerning the relation between music and performance as if performances were what interpretations are to the object of interpretation. The approach in question concerns the possibility of a general theory of interpretation and ontology embracing the cultural entities and practices generally, including the works of art, literature, music, or other culturally crucial creative pursuits such as science. Particular assumptions made by him lead quite directly to this kind of approach.

First, Krausz thinks that no aims could be considered intrinsic to interpretive activity, although every interpretation may have an aim, or several aims, depending upon different kinds of interest. Second, Krausz also holds that metaphysical essentialism, as the claim that a thing is what it is because of possessing an invariant essence as the object of interpretation, is dispensable. This is a view with which we can readily agree. But while doing so, we should not forget the crucial task of making evident exactly what can be regarded as an appropriate successor for metaphysical essentialism. I have argued elsewhere that essentialism denied at one level of analysis raises its head at other levels.[3] I would like to ask whether, when the assumptions made by Krausz build up a scenario for the search for a fairly general theory of interpretation and ontology that applies to all the above entities, called cultural entities, we have essentialism in another form, irrespective of the categorial differences between them, or of the disciplinary boundaries between their categories.

I fear that Krausz's quite forceful and crucial distinction between singularism and multiplism might not address one crucial issue. How heterogenous, or type-distinct, can the objects of interpretation be, warranting or making it quite likely that a theory of interpretation applicable in the context of cultural entities generally in his sense might not be applicable, or relevant, in another context, namely in the context of music.

In what follows, I raise this problem, thereby inviting his response. But I will limit myself to a brief discussion of the work of music as it lives through its performances, which may be regarded as indefinitely many forms of life that never become identical with music and never lose their identity as an origin and as a destination. My criticism here, it must be noted, is directed at the general framework within which Krausz's analysis and argument concerning interpretation proceed. I don't at all intend this criticism to apply to his arguments about the philosophy of music. I am suggesting that while appreciating his claim that an essentialist theory of musical interpretation must be implausible simply because music itself is not of a natural kind, our concept of musical interpretation fluctuating within the history of music itself, his more general claims about a theory of interpretation and ontology cannot possibly escape the charge of essentialism in some form or the other.

The idea of interpretation in general plays a central role in Krausz's worldview of interpretation. From the outset, interpretation is inclusive enough with respect to method and range of application. I am not questioning its legitimacy as a multiplist philosophy. I am only pointing out the fundamental problem of inconsistency, which creeps in as soon as Krausz claims it possible to develop an all-embracing theory of interpretation free from all forms of essentialism. Krausz's approach is characterized by an excessive preoccupation with cultural entities and practices including music. And following Popper, he places music in World 3 alongside science and mathematics. In what follows, it will be my main aim to explore the possibility of how far music can be freed not only from the tyranny of causality and historical time but also from World 3.

3. Musical Consciousness

Living on the edge of a Guadeloupe volcano in 1859, pianist Louis Moreau
Gottschalk (born in New Orleans in 1829) gave piano recitals to the universe
breaking the silence over Guadeloupe. He wrote: "Every evening I moved my
piano out upon the terrace, and there, in view of the most beautiful scenery in
the world, which was bathed in the serene and limpid atmosphere of the trop-
ics, I played, *for myself alone*, everything that the scene open before me inspired—and what a scene! Imagine a gigantic amphitheater, such as army of
Titans might have carved out in the mountains; to the right and left virgin
forests filled with wild and distant harmonies . . . farther on, the green savan-
nas (and) the immensity of the ocean, whose line of deep blue forms the horizon. . . . I let my fingers run over the keyboard, wrapped up in the contemplation of these marvels."[4] The experience of the pianist-audience in this case
raises many deep questions. In so far as we are interested in relating different
aspects of musical experience to one another and the work of music itself to
its performances, is not the piano, or the string instrument, the performer,
indeed the composer himself or herself, each the ideal listener? Is music a
matter of creation, or discovery? Or is it something we can call a dynamic
passage of internal time, between the origin and the destination? Is there music in the universe that the musical experience in the composer and the performer approximates? Does "Good," or "Great," or "Universal" Music exist
or subsist beyond the space and time of this world, free of form, as the famous composer Ferrucio Busoni thought when he was still a young pianist?

What the composer, the performer, and the instrument as a whole aim
at, is to meet the challenge of "hearing" this music more and more distinctly,
and to give it a form of life as approximately beautiful as possible. A search
for music begins in a process of our disentanglement from the redundancy
and ambiguity of our day-to-day empirical world. And the search ends with
the creation of a new form of life, which we call composition and performance, or which we can just call the play of the instruments. Insofar as a composer's notation is only an approximation of the ideal, which is pure music
itself, a composition is as much a form of life of the original text (*Urtext*),
music in an absolute sense, as its performances are.

But what is there in the universe of music that brings all of them together, the composer, the performer, and the musical instrument? Is there
music out there, which the style of a composer might miss? Is there music out
there, which only the rule-breaking or rule-enriching creativity of a great
composer can seek by capturing it in a revolutionary notation or style? How
do the musical instruments follow the composer and the performer into the
rule-breaking or rule-enriching zones of creativity? Can we say, in the final
analysis, that the composer and the performer share a kind of form of life, a
form of existence, which resembles, or which imitates, the life of the musical
instrument itself? I myself do not know the correct answer.

In the ancient Hindu worldview, a creative artist such as a poet-seer is likened to a musical instrument, to the play of the instrument as an effective medium of creation. The poet-seer Rabindranath Tagore spoke of the poet's life as if it was the string instrument Veena. What he meant by this was that the life of the poet is the life of the musical instrument Veena, which sings. We can generalize this idea and say the same thing about the composer's and the performer's musical consciousness.

Let us assume that in musical experience the performers themselves are the ideal listeners. What is the difference between the listener's consciousness of the internal time in which the performance of a work of music develops with a beginning and an ending, and our consciousness of the external clock-time in which external events appear as an objective world, that science aims to tell us more and more about? In order to be in a state of receptivity towards the internal (audible) time of a musical performance, one must walk into that zone of silence, also a zone of timelessness, which we know by the familiar name of the Concert Hall. One must do so, as if plunging into a deep state of meditation. Meditative state and timelessness make for a useful metaphor in this context, since they convey an understanding of the dissolution of external time in which the external world appears to us as an object.

A theorist interested in understanding music must presuppose the existence of musical consciousness in the composer and the performer alike. For example, we can think of an ideal listener, in the performer himself or herself, as one who is expected to understand and experience the beauty and harmony of the melodies, their form and the art of orchestration. The listener should have the ability to get into the heart of the intentions of the composer. In the presence of the musical instruments and in the midst of performances, the listener's world is translated from the external time to the internal time of the composition, concurrently with the dissolution of the external world in favor of the musical experience structured in internal time. Think of those women and men who sit together in the audience, in a meditative state of timelessness, listening to their still and calm minds. Similarly, think of the performer-listener in the field of music. With the musical instruments and musical scores waiting for him or her to play, the performer-listener generates the internal time of musical experience, as if in a concerted bid to build a cathedral of great beauty and sublimity. L. Rowell has eloquently described this aspect of the musical experience: "It seems to me that this period of no-time is extremely useful as a preparation for the new time which is to be audibly created and sustained. It is a highly artificial, tensed silence—a way of erasing our previous consciousness of time and of external events, a period of intense focus, concentration, and pure expectation during which we are poised on the brink of time, as it were, and made ready to process the rapid succession of temporal clues we are about to receive."[5] Being an artist-composer is being engaged in the work of dissolution and creation, and also being in search of a spiritual unity with the *Urtext*, absolute music itself, or pure music as the *Urtext* is sometimes called. Writing on the sublime, the Greek author Longinus spoke of a harmonious arrangement of sounds as a marvelous instrument of grandeur and passion in the following words: "For does not the flute instill certain emotions into those that hear it, seeming to carry them away and fill them with a divine frenzy? Does it not give rhythmic movement, and compel the hearer to conform to the melody and adapt his movements to this rhythm, even if he is not in the least musical? Then the tones of the harp, in themselves meaningless, often cast a wonderful spell, as you know, by their variations in sound and the throbbing interplay and harmonious blending of the notes struck."[6]

In ancient Indian mythology, which is traceable in the *Puranas* (notably the *Visnu Purana*), we find the notion of the universe as a grand play, akin to a musical performance, which is subject to beginnings and endings in time, to creation and destruction in a cyclical order, as though the world were an instrument with a form of life that comes to an end in order to begin its cycle again. In this mythical conception, we come across the most beautiful imagery of the immensity of the time-scales on which the final dissolution of the time-cycles of the empirical world of phenomena can be calculated. Interestingly enough, the imagery carries reference to the dreams of the sleeping god Visnu. Imagine Visnu as a divine instrument of creation, who creates only in a dream as soon as his wife Laksmi strokes his leg and he falls asleep. The mythological scenario of creation then shows itself up as an endless cosmic ocean where god Brahma sitting on a lotus emerges from the body (navel) of the sleeping god Visnu. First, sitting there at the feet of Visnu is his wife Laksmi. Brahma, Visnu and Laksmi are all of them floating on a raft-like couch, which is the body of the multi-headed mythical snake, suspended in the center of the cosmic ocean. As Laksmi strokes her husband's leg, he falls asleep and starts dreaming. From his dream state there emerges the lotus from which god Brahma appears. The creation and the dissolution (*pralaya*) of a universe, of four declining cosmic forms of its life, are correlated with the opening and the closing of Brahma's eyes. The lifetime of a universe is determined by the lifetime of Brahma, at the end of which everything including god Brahma himself and the lotus dissolve again into the body of the divine dreamer Visnu.

What do we learn from the Visnu Purana regarding musical consciousness? Where do we place then the composer, his or her work, the artist-listener and the musical instrument? Are they not closely akin to the manifest contents of Visnu's dream? Is not the composer's work like the divine dream of Visnu, with Brahma and Laksmi as the main performers? In any case, independent of this mythological variation on musical consciousness and the creation of the song of the universe, as we might call it, how can we explain or understand this puzzle? Musical experiences, in their beginnings and endings and in their creative internal time-structures, have a greater similarity to dreams than to the experiences of our normal daily lives. Without the external world dissolving itself into a zone of silence, neither the composer nor the performer-listener could generate that energy which is necessary for creating the internal time-structure differently called composition and music. Just as, without the external world dissolving itself into a zone of sleep, the human subject could not let dreams come of their accord. The human unconscious lets dreams be what they are, without a direct hint of their deep structure, or of the original text of their latent content as we might call it. In a letter, which most authorities believe to have been written c.1789, Mozart probably hints at such dissolution while telling us about the different aspects of his creativity in music. For his creativity, which is, on his account, inexplicable as to "whence and how" it came, he remains thankful to his Divine creator: "When I am, as it were, completely myself, entirely alone, and of good cheer—say, traveling in a carriage, or walking after a good meal, or during the night when I cannot sleep; it is on such occasions that my ideas flow the best and most abundantly. Whence and how they come, I know not; nor can I force them . . ." And, as he then goes on to tell us more: "All this fires my soul, ... All this inventing, this production, takes place in a pleasing lively dream. Still the hearing of the *tout ensemble* is after all the best. What has been thus produced I do not easily forget and this is perhaps the best gift I have my Divine Maker to thank for."[7] Much later, the composer Felix Mendelssohn-Bartholdy said something of profound significance and closely similar to this. According to him, so much has been talked about music and yet so little said. He argued against an attempt to understand and respond to music the same way we understand and respond to spoken communication, and when asked what his "Lieder ohne Wörte" (songs without words) mean, he defined them as sounds whose significance cannot be rendered in words, and insisted on the separation between music and language.[8] In order to let music be what it is, the external world, including the world of speech, must be dissolved in favor of that another world where all words fail.

How far are then the work of music, the artist-listener and the musical instrument, taken as *tout ensemble*, akin to the manifest contents of a dream? Do not our musical experiences in the zone of silence (the Concert Hall, the Opera, and so forth) closely resemble our dream experiences during our sleep? Do not the work of music, the artist-listener and the musical instrument—*tout ensemble*—again and again remind us of the original text, to which all music approximates but which is authorless, or too deep and unfathomable for words? Dream experiences become possible, as we have seen, only as and when we fall asleep, as if to let the world we are born in be dissolved into a zone of silence. They start then unfolding into an encoded structure in the internal time of the sleeping subject himself/herself. Good and bad dreams will always occur, depending on how the individual subject is affected by them. And this is mainly true of those dreams that are puzzling but pleasant in their manifest contents. My hypothesis that there exists an interesting similarity, or parallelism, between musical experiences and dreams—

what I would like to call a similarity in dynamic passage of internal time between two kinds of ensembles—is here intended to underline the need for
researching their deep structures and their manifest structures. Unlike our
pleasant dreams, musical experiences are informed by a sense of continuity, a
goal-directed structure with a definite beginning and an ending in internal
time, or a definite origin and destination. But we can also argue in the terms
of Freudian psychoanalysis as follows: Who can say that our dreams do not
have a deep structure, similarly "oriented and proportioned" in internal time,
which makes them such a befitting subject of scientific and comparative
study? There has been a renewed interest among philosophers and
psychoanalysts in a hermeneutic search for the meaning-connections as
against the causal connections in the field of psychoanalysis.[9] Reading from
the art objects as it were backwards to artists themselves is, according to
Ellen Eve Frank, "what we have seen in this century as psychoanalytic
criticism."[10] Just think of dreams as if they were unique art objects. How do
we recover and reconstruct the latent content of a dream from its 'translation
into the manifest content'? Similar questions of interpretation can be asked
about the Freudian unconscious—that turbulent mind which is hidden and
manifest at one and the same time.

4. A Pilgrimage Constantly Renewed

A concluding word about the metaphor of a "form of life" is here in order.
The metaphor is most appropriate in the context of a work of music, and its
performance, and in the context of an original text and its interpretations or
translations in the discourse of particular languages. Musical interpretation
and translation also share much deeper questions. We can ask of either of
them whether it embodies in some sense a timeless conversation. Whether it
has a being not at all restricted by the limitations of the discourses of a given
language? I myself do not know how to answer these questions. But if the
answer is in the affirmative, what could one expect, or look for, while translating the original text on the one hand and performing the work of musical
composition on the other? Given a class of interpretations and performances,
we could say that the original text relates the interpreted or translated text as
its co-text across a rich diversity of language-scapes, while the work of music
relates itself to its performance in different places and at different times.
Since there could not be an interpretation or translation which provides the
last co-text, in the last language-scape, or a performance which is the definitive performance, in either case we have timeless conversations taking place,
which may even have an origin but which are never able to reach a final destination. The tension of being and not being original, of being and not being
interpretable, of being and not being capable of a performance at one and the
same time can only belong to such timeless conversation. Did not Mendelssohn-Bartholdy remind us how much has been discussed about music but

how little has been said? The words have hardly the ability to speak about music. If they had the ability to do so, it would be no more necessary for the composer to compose a musical work.

Against Krausz's generalizations about cultural entities including music, I began this discussion on a quite skeptical note, suggesting that a work of music can be best located only in the World 4 instead of the World 3. If we admit, with Mendelssohn-Bartholdy, that the World 4 of musical compositions is a world where our words and our many languages, with their variable language-scapes, fail to reach, we can no longer ignore the serious limitations which a general theory of interpretation and ontology in Krausz's sense encounters as soon as we think of the work of music, and especially of its indefinitely many performances which unfold within its implicate order. The questions I have posed here for consideration are then these: how far does interpretational multiplism, as defined by Krausz, address these limitations? Is it adequate enough to recognize musical works as abstract objects while including them among other cultural entities for the purpose of building a general theory of interpretation and ontology? Is it not instead wiser to recognize musical works from the outset as being a glaring exception to any general theory of interpretation and ontology, entailing an implicate order of musical consciousness and demanding an understanding in terms of its structures, movements, and categories? Is it not appropriate to take a more dynamic view of music as a passage of time from the origin to the destination and from the destination back to the origin?

I think that a work of music is not just an abstract object among other abstract objects in the realm of cultural entities. Along with its performances, a work of music is akin to a pilgrimage that must be constantly remade. It generates its implicate order, its space and time of internal evolution, in which what comes after, shapes or affects what has come before. Already in this image an asymmetry between the internal structural temporality of music and the external temporal frame in which the events in the world occur in a causal sequence is to be found, even a deeper asymmetry between the performances of a work of music and the interpretations or translations of an original text. Music is like several pilgrims joining the one pilgrim who is already on the way to individual emergence. The pilgrims of music are none other than the composer, the work of musical composition, the performances, the musical instruments and the participating audiences, all of them together making an implicate order of musical consciousness. Different groups of pilgrims of music may choose to follow different trajectories to perform the same kind of pilgrimage, with all of them finally converging on the same point. Which trajectories they follow will depend largely upon the participants, their background, their location, their experiences and their imagination. In a nutshell, musical works are not mere abstract entities in the World 3 waiting for interpretation. They belong to a higher plane of life, or of con-

sciousness, making an implicate order, which I have called musical consciousness.

NOTES

1. Karl R. Popper, *Objective Knowledge. An Evolutionary Approach* (Oxford: Clarendon Press, 1972).

2. Michael Krausz, *Limits of Rightness* (Lanham, Md.: Rowman and Littlefield, 2000), p. 4.

3. G. L. Pandit, *Methodological Variance: Essays in Epistemological Ontology and the Methodology of Science* (Dordrecht: Kluwer Academic Publishers, 1991).

4. Louis Moreau Gottschalk, *Notes of a Pianist*, ed. Jeanne Behrend (New York: A.A. Knopf, 1964).

5. L. Rowell, "The Creation of Audible Time," *The Study of Time IV*, ed. J. T. Fraser, Nathaniel Morris Lawrence, and David Allen Parks (Berlin: Springer Verlag, 1981), pp. 198–210.

6. Longinus, "On the Sublime," *Classical Literary Criticism*, ed. T. S. Dorsch, (Penguin Books, 1965), p. 150.

7. Edward Holmes, *The Life of Mozart, Including his Correspondence* (London: Chapman and Hall, 1878), p. 211–213.

8. Harold Kupferberg, *Die Mendelssohns* (Tübingen and Stuttgart: Rainer Wunderlich Verlag, 1972), p. 182–183.

9. Adolf Grünbaum, *The Foundations of Psychoanalysis* (Berkeley: University of California Press, 1984).

10. Ellen Eve Frank, *Literary Architecture* (Berkeley: University of California Press, 1979), p. 240.

Twenty-two

REFLECTIONS ON THE INTERPRETATION OF RELIGIOUS TEXTS

Vibha Chaturvedi

Something that appears truly undeniable in contemporary times is the presence of differences and diversity in outlooks. The modern mind finds it difficult to rest content with the smug assertion that his way of thinking and living is the right way and all others are wrong. Singularism—which maintains that for any object of interpretation there can be only one ideally admissible interpretation of it—no more remains an unproblematic and attractive option for the liberal mind. Multiplism, the view that there can be more than one ideally admissible interpretation of some objects of interpretation, is obviously better suited to our cognizance of differences. Sometimes the differing interpretations may be opposed to each other substantially and significantly. A necessary condition of real opposition of interpretations is that the object being interpreted by these different views is in reality the same and identifiable as such.

Given that this condition of sameness is satisfied, we are faced with the question whether all different interpretations can be said to be equally correct at the same time. There can be several responses to the phenomenon of multiplicity or diversity of available interpretations of the same object. The singularist approach would be to accept only one of the several interpretations as correct or true. An approach that Michael Krausz calls "critical pluralism" would treat all admissible interpretations as equally true or acceptable or correct. In contrast, a multiplist approach, in the sense given to it by Krausz, would be to maintain that while some different interpretations are admissible, good reasons exist for preferring one over others. I address some issues involved in the debate between singularism on the one hand and critical pluralism and multiplism on the other hand as regards the question of interpretation of revealed or authoritative religious texts. In particular I show that given the assumptions that every reading or understanding of such a text involves interpretation by the reader, and further that more than one interpretation of the same text are possible and admissible, serious doubts can be raised regarding the plausibility of the multiplist approach.

I assume that a revealed or authoritative religious text is a proper object for interpretation. It can be regarded as an intentional object in the sense given to the term by Jitendra Mohanty, namely an object, which is endowed with meaning or significance within a field of cultural codes and norms; an object as represented within a framework of cultural representations.[1] A scripture or an authoritative religious text is to be understood within a form of life (*Lebenswelt*) and it concerns a social setting of shared norms, procedures and values. Plurality or diversity of interpretations is easier to cope with in case of works of art and literature because in general they do not claim to put forward ontological claims or statements of fact. This is not to deny that serious differences can arise regarding an adequate interpretation of a literary work or a work of art. Wherever the object of interpretation makes ontological commitments about how things are in the real, shared world, such diversity becomes much more problematic. If you are confronted with diametrically opposite interpretations, such diversity becomes even more problematic. Significantly different claims about the same object, which have different ontological implications, cannot be admitted as equally true at the same time without giving up altogether the idea of truth representing reality in some sense. Doctrinal and other statements in a scripture are ontologically loaded and have significant implications about how things are in the real world.

In my view, any attempt to treat religious language in its entirety as purely non-cognitive is unsatisfactory. No doubt religious uses of language have a lot to do with feelings, emotions, and commitment to lead your life in a particular way, and symbolic and metaphorical use of language also remains integral to them. Yet putative assertions about God, creation, and so forth, cannot be said to be merely expressions of feelings or commitments to particular moral principles or to a particular way of life. Nor can they be said to be cases of purely symbolic or metaphorical use of language. If we do not acknowledge the ontological import of scriptural sayings, several religious practices and the absolute commitment to your faith demanded of a sincere believer are extremely difficult to understand. From the point of view of a descriptive analysis of religious language, to deny that several scriptural sayings make ontological commitments is not plausible.

In cases of a revealed or authoritative religious text interpretation enters at two levels. First are cases when people try to articulate their revelatory or mystical experiences, which provide the foundation for the text. Second are cases when people, who read or hear the text try to understand what is written in the text. There can be interpretation at other levels also, wherever a third person's understanding of an already available interpretation of a text by a reader or hearer is involved.

One possible objection to my contention could be that at the first level no interpretation exists, only faithful recording or describing of your experiences, which yields the scriptural sayings. Let me take the case of claims of revelation first. The traditional view of revelation in Christianity, dominant in the medieval ages and supported at present by Roman Catholicism and also by conservative Protestantism, holds that the content of divine revelation is a body of truths expressed in statements or propositions. The Bible is regarded as an authoritative record of such revealed truths. Faith on this view consists in the obedient acceptance of revealed truths, which must be accepted literally. This revealed text is not regarded as a human and fallible record of revealed truths. This view has been challenged within the Christian tradition itself, especially by the Protestant standpoint. The second holds that God himself is the object of revelation and reveals Himself by acting in human history and thereby coming within the orbit of human experience. Scriptural propositions on this view represent attempts by some persons to understand and articulate their religious experiences, when confronted with particular events in human history. Interpretation becomes a crucial factor here and the possibility of interpreting the same events in different and even in completely secular ways is granted.

The element of interpretation by human persons cannot be disregarded even in the propositional view, since understanding and articulation of experiential data invariably involves interpretation by the human mind. The non-propositional view gives greater consideration to this element of interpretation at the level of the recipient of the revelation and at the level of the reader or hearer of the linguistic articulation by the recipient of his experience. Since the scripture is believed to be a fallible record of people's attempt to understand particular special events, it remains possible that those who read it may interpret it in different ways. In this view, the element of interpretation by the reader can be more easily accommodated. In the case of mystical or religious experiences also, the element of interpretation by the person, who has particular special and uncommon experiences, cannot be ruled out. The articulation and communication of the nature and content of such experiences in ordinary language is extremely difficult and even impossible, when mystical experiences are said to be ineffable. This quality makes religious interpretations even more problematic. A great diversity of religious views exists with regard to claims of divine revelation and claims derived from religious or mystical experiences.

I would at this point like to address the question whether factors exist that act as effective impediments to the possibility of diversity of ontological views. Supporters of a naive form of empiricism might say that what you experience and know is determined by how things are. The knowing mind receives the input from experience. On this view there cannot be significantly different, much less conflicting complete accounts of the same object at the same time. This picture of human mind does not appear to be satisfactory. We must acknowledge the significant contribution of the knowing mind in how things are understood or interpreted. To argue that constraints exist on admissibility of different interpretations still remains possible. David Hume tried to show that principles of human nature determine what beliefs we have.[2] Even when we realize that particular fundamental beliefs that we all share cannot be rationally defended, we cannot give up these beliefs, given the way human understanding functions. As examples he mentions belief in the continued and independent existence of bodies, in personal identity and in uniformity of nature, among others. Hume does suggest that the nature of human understanding is the same for all human persons and consequently all of them would share similar fundamental beliefs. Similarly, Immanuel Kant maintains that the forms of sensibility and the categories of understanding determine our knowledge of objects, and these are common in all human beings.[3] On both these views, for people to think in particular ways and have particular beliefs is inevitable. The possibility of different ontological interpretations is ruled out beyond a point. Hume comes close to saying that belief in polytheism is a natural belief having its roots in fear of the unknown and he also admits that all of us share a feeling for attributing design in the world. This commonality does not imply that the nature of human understanding determines us to have particular religious beliefs appropriate to doctrines of a developed religion. Kant implies that human reason in a way makes it necessary for us to have a belief in a divine dispenser of justice and immortality of the soul. If these are presuppositions of morality and all human beings possess practical reason, then all human beings as moral agents would have to accept them. The difficulties in Hume's and Kant's views need not be discussed here. That the interpretive apparatus of all human beings must be the same is by no means evident. To allow the possibility that different people may interpret the same kind of experiences differently is reasonable: more so in the case of religious experiences. W. T. Stace acknowledges this possibility in his discussion of mystical experiences, when he says that the same experience of undifferentiated unity comes to be interpreted in different ways depending on the culture and religion to which the interpreter belongs.[4] It would be pertinent to mention here that in the case of religious experiences you can challenge the contention that different people had the same kind of experiences.

With regard to interpretation of divine revelation, we come across diversity at two levels, at the level of inter-religious differences, and at the level of intra-religious differences. In the first case quite often the events regarded as revelatory or the texts supposed to be recording revealed truths are different. Here we may say that the objects of interpretation are different and no opposition of interpretations results. This is not always the case, since the texts in question may sometimes put forward conflicting claims about the same event or historical character.[5] If a particular event is given a religious interpretation by you and an atheistic or secular interpretation by me, it may be said to yield opposite interpretations. Similarly in cases of mystical or religious experiences, the possibility of diversity would arise only when it can be shown that the same kind of experiences lie behind different religious traditions. If the objects of interpretation were taken to be different, a crucial consequence of this admission would be that no religious tradition would be able to claim universal validity.

Besides inter-religious differences, we are also confronted with intra-religious differences, which pertain to differences in interpretation of the same revealed or sacred text. No religion is immune from these, be it Christianity, Islam, Buddhism, or Hinduism. Sometimes inter-religious differences also involve different interpretations of the same text. For example, the Bible remains the sacred text for Jews and Christians and yet they have serious differences among them. Differences regarding interpretation of the Bible occur among Catholics and Protestants. Sometimes these differences pertain to the question as to which parts are to be treated as containing authentic revelation. Here the object of interpretation is under dispute. But wherever the object is the same we are confronted with real multiplism. Within the Hindu tradition an example of diversity of interpretations of the same object can be seen with regard to different viewpoints of *Vedanta*.[6] The term "Vedānta" means "the final portions of the *Vedas,*" namely the *Upanisads.* It has come to signify "the settled conclusions of the *Vedas* taken as a whole." As far as the *Pūrva-Mimāmsā* school is concerned, it can be said that it addresses a different object, namely a different part of the *Veda.* But the different schools of Vedanta refer to the same *śruti.* Other orthodox systems of Indian Philosophy also in general owe allegiance to, and accept the authority of the *Vedas* and yet give quite different views about the nature of reality and the ultimate aim of human life. These schools do not claim to derive their doctrines directly from the *Vedas.* The different schools of Vedanta, on the other hand, claim to interpret the same text, but their interpretations present great divergence. The chief schools of Vedanta are three, known as Advaita, Visistadvaita and Dvaita and these are associated with Sankara, Ramanuja and Madhva. The Advaita Vedānta of Sankara and Dvaita Vedānta of Madhvācārya are diametrically opposed in their interpretation of the nature of reality. Scholars generally accept that the Hindu tradition believes that the same truth can be viewed, stated or interpreted differently.

Given that this diversity and divergence is an undeniable fact, the question is how to account for it in a plausible way? The issue of ontological commitments of a religious point of view becomes relevant at this point. If religious language is treated as non-cognitive, the difference and divergence can be explained as pertaining to differences in attitudes, feelings, moral commitments, and so on. But if religious language is said to involve assertions about the nature of reality, this diversity becomes greatly problematic, especially when we are confronted with diametrically opposed interpretations of the same object. An exclusivist approach to such diversity is to disallow the rival interpretations as true or correct. You cannot give any justification for this position without presupposing the validity of your interpretive framework. This move begs the question. An inclusivist approach may claim that its view includes what is presented as the other. An example would be the view that Christianity gives us the truth but salvation is available even to those who adhere to some other religion, since Jesus Christ has atoned for the sins of all human beings. A "critical pluralist" approach would be to accept all religious viewpoints as equally valid. This sort of acceptance though is hardly ever available. Even when some truth is granted to views other than yours, this admission is generally qualified by the claim that your view is superior to others or is the best. The only case I can think of where a religion allows that the modes of prayer or worship of all religions are equally efficacious and you are free to follow any of them is the Bahai faith. But then Bahai is a quite unusual kind of religion where doctrines and rituals are minimal.

The Indian philosophical tradition is by and large sympathetic to diversity. It grants that the truth may admit of different interpretations. Different strategies are adopted to create room for diversity. The Jaina *Anekāntavāda* admits that truth may have several aspects and each claim should be seen as giving partial truth.[7] A different approach is available in the Buddhist doctrine of *Sūnyavāda* of Nāgārjuna, which claims that the validity of each view is dependent on its context.[8] No view can be said to be valid independently of its context. If validity is taken to demand that a view should not be context dependent, then it follows that no view is valid. Nāgārjuna denies absolute being to the world and the soul on the basis of the principle of dependent causation.[9] Within the Hindu tradition several different approaches are available to account for diversity of metaphysical or religious views. Sometimes Hindus say that the same reality may be considered or addressed differently as in the *Rig-Vedic* saying that truth is one but the learned talk about it differently. The reference here is to different *Vedic* gods. Swāmi Vivekānanda outlines different models to understand the diversity of religious views in his Chicago addresses.[10] One suggestion is that the same truth appears differently when people with different intellectual and emotional constitutions try to understand it, just as the same light is reflected differently in glasses of different colors. The other is that all religions constitute different paths to the same goal. From his discussions he evidently takes the Advaita Vedāntic doctrine of oneness of the ultimate reality as "The Truth" and all other views of reality as admissible approximations to it. In his view the ultimate aim of life is the realization of the *Brahman* where all consciousness of diversity and multiplicity is negated. Radhakrishnan adopts a similar approach while talking of the transcendental unity of all religions. This sort of approach does not constitute a full-blooded acceptance of diversity. It may appear a condescending way of accepting the validity of different views up to a point, since ultimately all are to be transcended to reach something higher. Each of the above-mentioned approaches faces serious difficulties. Discussing these approaches in detail is not within the purview of this paper.

When faced with diversity of interpretations, what would be a plausible approach? Once we grant that factors such as the social, cultural, and linguistic background or the conceptual structure of the interpreter have a significant role in understanding the meaning of an object or text, and that these may vary, we must admit the possibility of different interpretations of the same object. Does it remain possible to adjudicate between different interpretations? Can we say that good reasons exist for preferring one interpretation to others as implied by multiplism? Let me take the case of different interpretations of the same sacred text. You might say that if an interpretation can competently explain or account for the whole text or most of the text, that interpretation is preferable to others that fail to do so.[11] But to expect that the preferred interpretation must account for the essential or more significant parts of the text is reasonable, even if it fails to do so with respect to large sections of the not so essential parts. There can be difference of opinion about what constitutes essential or most crucial parts. So long as the differing interpretations are outcomes of the same interpretive apparatus, we can give reasons for favoring one over others. But these reasons in most cases may reflect the purpose or the preference of the person giving the reasons and cannot be said to be objective. What is regarded as a good reason by you may not be so regarded by me. We find that even people who share the same socio-cultural and linguistic background may come up with different interpretations of the same text. Different schools of Vedānta would be a good example here. In this case, no neutral, presupposition-free point of view is available that can be made the basis of judging and evaluating the different views presented. A "view from no where" is not possible.[12] And yet the reluctance to give up considerations of realism and correspondence with how things are do not allow us to rest content with the diversity of significantly different, often opposite views, which have different ontological commitments about a shared world. To admit all the different, even opposing interpretations to be equally valid is not possible so long as we retain a non-relativist conception of truth. A relativistic conception of truth would allow us to accept the diversity of interpretations wholeheartedly, but whether religions can accommodate such a conception without sacrificing vital aspects of religious life and faith is quite doubtful. In the case of the divergence of doctrines of different religious traditions, no good reasons exist to prefer one to others. Such differences can be accounted for by means of differences in social, cultural, and linguistic frameworks. You would be evaluating a view different from yours in the light of your interpretive apparatus. This effort would fail to provide any objective basis or a good reason for regarding a particular interpretation as better or more adequate.

You may question whether different religious viewpoints, those pertaining to different religions and those pertaining to the same religion, should be seen as competing hypotheses or theories about a common, shared reality or world. Ludwig Wittgenstein's views in his later works provide an argument against this line of thinking. He repeatedly warns against treating a religious belief as a scientific hypothesis.[13] In his view, "believing" in religious contexts is a matter of having particular "pictures" that guide and regulate the thinking and life of the believer. The belief is a firm and unshakable belief not based on supporting evidence. Even where believers cite historical or other kinds of evidence, they treat this evidence quite differently and do not subject it to the kinds of checks to which they subject scientific and historical evidence. He goes to the extent of saying that if there were evidence it would destroy the whole business.[14] Believing here is a matter of living your life according to particular pictures inherent in religious beliefs. It involves submitting to authority and passionately seizing hold of the interpretation offered by religion. This acceptance of authority is a matter of all or none; you accept it wholeheartedly or not at all. Having once accepted it, your whole life is regulated by it. Wittgenstein observes: "It strikes me that a religious belief could only be something like a passionate commitment to a system of reference. Hence although it is belief, it is really a way of living or a way of assessing life. It is passionately seizing hold of this interpretation."[15] For Wittgenstein believing in the context of religion is a matter of adopting particular practices and living in a particular way. The acceptance of religious interpretation is not a matter of weighing rational reasons in its favor. But once a person has submitted to authority his thinking and life are regulated by that belief.

Wittgenstein points out that a nonbeliever does not contradict a believer. The believer does not accept something to be true that the nonbeliever contradicts. They are on different planes, they live differently and the pictures that regulate the believer's life have no role in the nonbeliever's life. Wittgenstein means by nonbeliever an atheist and by believer a practicing Christian. The relevant point is that theism and atheism are not to be seen as rival hypotheses or theories. We may extend this point to cover inter-religious and intra-religious differences in interpretation. We may say that different religious views should not be treated as rival theories about the same reality. Once this view is accepted, all that you can do is to note the differences and study and analyze each interpretation on its terms. Whether this analysis can be accepted as an adequate description of religious faith is debatable.[16]

The admission that interpretive activity is inseparable from knowing or judging any object leaves no scope for objective grounds for evaluating different interpretations or preferring one to others. This is a one-way road that ultimately leads to relativism. The dilemma faced by the modern mind is that taking cognizance of the diversity of interpretations of the same object or reality cannot be escaped. And yet, you can not accept that significantly different interpretations of the same reality or object, such that these interpretations cannot be conjoined to yield a total or comprehensive picture, or contradictory interpretations can be admissible as right at the same time. The admission of diversity raises problems regarding the possibility of understanding interpretations different from yours. Wittgenstein said that the rules of one language-game cannot be applied to another language-game and what is a right move in one is not a guide to what is a right move in another. In a similar vein we may say that one interpretation cannot be judged in terms of another. So the diversity with all its epistemological and ontological implications and complications has to be accepted.

And yet it cannot be denied that human beings share a common form of life. It makes sense to talk of a human way of life, which involves shared patterns of acting and being in a shared natural environment in which they live. This human form of life at the same time admits of differences within it, which refer to different particular ways of conceptualizing human experience and associated behavior patterns and actions. How to reconcile the recognition of this commonality and sharing of environment and a way of life with the diversity of interpretations along with their varying ontological commitments is a question that eludes an easy answer. I am reminded of the story of Abhimanyu from the Indian epic *Mahābhārata.* Abhimanyu was the son of the great warrior Arjuna. One day during the war between Pāndavas and Kauravas he had to take the responsibility of countering a circular formation of the opponent's army referred to as *cakravyūha.* Abhimanyu knew how to enter this formation but did not know how to come out of it. The modern mind is caught in a similar situation. We know how to proceed toward diversity of interpretations but do not know how to go beyond it to have a common ground in our interpretations of a shared world and life.

NOTES

1. Michael Krausz, *Limits of Rightness* (LR) (Lanham, Md.: Rowman & Littlefield, 2000), p. 13.

2. David Hume, *Enquiry Concerning Human Understanding,* ed. L. A. Selby-Bigge (Oxford: Clarendon Press, 1975, 3d ed.).

3. Immanuel Kant, *Critique of Pure Reason,* trans. Norman Kemp Smith (London: Macmillan, 1978).

4. Walter T. Stace, "The Teachings of the Mystics," *Readings in the Philosophy of Religion,* ed. Baruch A. Brody (New York: Prentice Hall, 1974).

5. William A. Christian, *Meaning and Truth in Religion* (Princeton: Princeton University Press, 1964); William A. Christian, *Oppositions of Religious Doctrines: A Study in the Logic of Dialogue Among Religions* (London, New York: Macmillan, 1972).

6. Mysore Hiriyanna, *Essentials of Indian Philosophy* (London: George Allen and Unwin, 1949), pp. 151–199. Also Savarepalli Radhakrishnan, *Indian Philosophy* (London: George Allen and Unwin, 1923 [rep. in India: Blackie & Son, 1940]), vol. 2, pp. 430–765.

7. Sarvepalli Radhakrishnan, *Indian Philosophy,* vol. 1, pp. 298–304.

8. Kamaleswar Bhattacharya, Edward Hamilton Johnson, and Arnold Kunst, *The Dialectical Method of Nāgārjuna* (Delhi: Vigraha vyāvartani, Motilal Banarasidas, 1978).

9. Radhakrishnan, *Indian Philosophy,* vol. 1, pp. 645–657.

10. Swami Vivekānānda, *Chicago Addresses,* (Calcutta: Advaita Ashrama Publication Department, 1990).

11. Krausz, *Limits of Rightness,* p. 9.

12. Thomas Nagel, *The View From Nowhere* (New York: Oxford University Press, 1986).

13. Ludwig Wittgenstein and Cyril Barrett, *Lectures and Conversations on Aesthetics, Psychology, and Religious Belief* (Oxford: Basil Blackwell, 1966).

14. *Ibid,* p. 56.

15. G. H. von Wright, *Culture and Value*, trans. Peter Winch (Oxford: Basil Blackwell, 1980), p. 46e.

16. Vibha Chaturvedi, "Believer versus Unbeliever: Reflections on the Wittgensteinian Perspective," *Indian Philosophical Quarterly* (April 1993).

REPLIES AND REFLECTIONS

Twenty-three

REPLIES AND REFLECTIONS

Michael Krausz

In *Rightness and Reasons* (RR) and *Limits of Rightness* (LR), I restricted my claims to a discernibly narrow range. One overarching concern of both these works is with the thesis of the logical detachability of singularism and multiplism from realism, constructivism, and constructive realism. At the same time, in my development of the narrow detachability thesis I propounded neither realism, constructivism, nor constructive realism. In light of the range of issues upon which the detachability thesis bears, and the rich discussions by contributors to this volume, I have been drawn into larger issues. I do here situate myself in the ontological landscape and, with particular qualifications, I associate myself with the kind of practice-centered ontology offered by Bernard Harrison and Patricia Hanna.

Further, when considering cultural entities I concentrated on musical cases, visual artistic cases, literary cases, and cross-cultural cases. I have not concentrated on moral cases—except by implication—in my work on cultural relativism. Yet some of the presuppositions of my work on the theory of interpretation bear on desiderata for a moral theory. So when contributors draw me out about ontology and morality, my present replies on these matters amount to desiderata instead of fully developed theories.

1. Assumptions and Motivations

I offer here a ramified tally of background assumptions. First, I begin with two central theses: 1) the Detachability Thesis: realism, constructivism, and constructive realism entail neither singularism nor multiplism, and vice versa. And 2) the Relationality Thesis: whether a given object of interpretation answers to singularism or multiplism depends upon its identity (i.e., numerical) conditions, set within the context of the practice in which it nests. Whether singularist or multiplist conditions obtain in a given case depends on the number of object(s) of interpretation and the number of its corresponding interpretation(s). The applicability of singularism and multiplism is a relational matter. You find no necessity in counting an object of interpretation as such or an interpretation as such in one way or another. The mere inspection of an object of interpretation will not establish whether it answers to singularism or multiplism.

Further, 3) I broadly assume an anti-essentialism that rejects the thought that one should seek ultimate explanations in terms of inherent essences; that in every thing is an essence of an inherent nature which necessarily causes it to be what it is. This anti-essentialism rejects explanations in terms of inherent, timeless, immutable or invariantly necessary natures. My anti-essentialism is global instead of piecemeal. Accordingly, essentialism may not be distributed over some domains while anti-essentialism is distributed over other domains. Consequently, I adopt a broadly non-foundationalist stance, one that resists a "God's eye" point of view that would seek an Archimedian ground for pertinent claims. Accordingly, all would-be claims of necessity, intrinsicality or essentiality are subtended under a general historicist rubric. And that includes the historicist claim in question. 4) The inventoried ontologies themselves provide no resources for sorting among distributive claims. These are not methodologies for the "triage" of knowledge. Yet they do provide terms in which such triage is made intelligible. So I do not thereby embrace the pragmatist assertion that we should retire ontology. In addition, 5) the notion of an "ultimate nature of reality" should be retired, and with it any attempt to ground individuals there. The temptation to place "nature" in contrast to "culture" in the "ultimate nature of reality" should be rejected. The distinction between nature and culture cannot be presumed to reflect distinct kinds at an "ultimate level of reality." 6) The distinction between nature and culture cannot be made to fit the distinction between realism and constructivism. Neither of these distinctions is exclusive, and the two distinctions are not coextensive. We cannot withhold realist commitments from the cultural, nor can we withhold constructivist commitments from the natural. The distinction between the natural and the cultural is mixed. 7) All cognitive claims are fallible. No one claim is immune from the in-principle possibility that it might be mistaken. Rather, the current state of knowledge amounts to a tentative report about our best conjectures. Finally, 8) interpretation characteristically aims to elucidate its objects of interpretation, although it may be "used" for ancillary edificatory purposes.

While the center of gravity of RR and LR concerns the ideals of interpretation, its objects, and its characteristic elucidatory aim, Ronald Moore, for example, regards the main portions of LR as a prolegomenon to the edificatory uses to which interpretation might be put. He wishes I had identified the focus of my work to have been on edification. While edification may sometimes be a significant use of interpretation, I see no reason to privilege it as the primary or core aim of interpretive activity. Nor—as Moore suggests it should—need edification be taken as the motivation or the culmination of my work on interpretation. Although crucial the connection between the ideals of interpretation and edification turns out to be more indirect than Moore takes it to be.

Moore favors multiplism because he thinks it less oppressive. Multiplism is more "tolerant" than singularism in the logical sense that singularism, as a universal claim, disallows any multiplist cases, and multiplism allows some singularist cases. But Moore has something else in mind. He thinks that multiplism enhances worthwhile, meaningful lives. He thinks the ability to understand people who understand things differently from us helps overcome conflict and dissonance. Moore calls this ability "cognitive dexterity." I agree that cognitive dexterity contributes to the betterment of life. Cognitive dexterity is critical for "reconciliation, compromise, conciliation, and tolerance" as he puts it. Yet such cognitive dexterity does not entail multiplism. A singularist could be as cognitively dexterous as a multiplist. A singularist could well agree that to develop the imaginative ability to see how different interpretations might be plausibly advanced is crucial, but still insist that one and only one interpretation is ideally admissible. At the same time, a singularist might encourage the formulation and pursuit of many alternative interpretations, not as finally admissible but because they might be interesting, or suggestive, or because pursuit of alternatives is healthy for critical discourse in general. In LR I dubbed this attitude "liberal singularism" (LR, p. 10). Nicholas Maxwell concurs that to uniquely associate intolerance or oppression with singularism, and tolerance or liberation with multiplism, is a mistake. Closed-mindedness and open-mindedness are not coextensive with singularism and multiplism respectively. Yet to say that no entailment relation exists between singularism and multiplism on the one hand and intolerance and tolerance on the other hand, is not to say that no connection exists at all. I hope to make headway in articulating that connection as I proceed with the review of pertinent articles.

I have ordered my following remarks to reflect a progression of issues—from the distinction between singularism and multiplism, to aims of interpretation, to interpretation and its relation to its objects, to the detachability thesis and its relation to pertinent ontologies, and finally to the application of these issues to the representative cases of morality, trans-cultural experience, religion, and music. Yet any pair of these issues is integrally related. I will respond to selected points in each of the contributions. Further points await treatment on another occasion.

2. Ideals of Interpretation

Let us consider the distinction between singularism and multiplism. David Crocker correctly notes that the distinction between singularism and multiplism is asymmetrical, i.e. that multiplism allows that some cases may answer to a single admissible interpretation but singularism disallows any cases, which answer to more than one admissible interpretation. He proposes that we should substitute the distinction with an alternative pair of symmetrical definitions. We should designate singularism as the view that for any object of interpretation, only one admissible interpretation of it is to be found. This accords with my usage. But, he urges, we should re-define multiplism as the view that with respect to any object of interpretation more than one admissible interpretation is possible. The original definition of multiplism (that some objects of interpretation may answer to more than one admissible interpretation) would fall somewhere between the two "pure" (as he says) poles of Crocker's continuum.

Whether Crocker's way of re-drawing the distinction is more perspicuous (as he says) than mine is an open question. At an early stage in writing RR, I considered the possibility of defining multiplism as Crocker proposes and decided not to do so because one of his pure poles is not a live option in the face of such singularist examples as, "*Hamlet* is about a Danish prince." No one would seriously entertain the thought that this is one of several admissible interpretations, perhaps allowing that *Hamlet* might be about a Bulgarian prince and a Danish prince, for example. I chose to chart the philosophical landscape in terms of live options between which we should choose. Crocker's proposal sets a "dead" option at the one end of his continuum, leaving the further task of identifying the live option of multiplism as originally defined somewhere in the middle of his continuum. Either way, the same substantive questions remain. How should we distinguish between admissible and inadmissible interpretations, and what sorts of cases answer to one and to more than one admissible interpretation? Accordingly, redrawing the distinction would not amount to a significant philosophical difference as regards substantive instead of definitional issues, and so there would be no palpable advantage in changing the matrix of the central themes of my work.

For the sake of clarity, we should note that Nirmalangshu Mukherji mistakenly characterizes singularism and multiplism when he says that, "Singularism is the thesis that a given 'cultural entity' admits of exactly one interpretation; multiplism is the thesis that cultural entities admit of more than one interpretation" (p. 40). More accurately, singularism is the thesis that any object of interpretation—including cultural entities—admits of one and only one interpretation. Multiplism holds that some objects of interpretation—cultural or not cultural—may admit of more than one interpretation. Cultural entities are not the only ones that may answer to more than one admissible interpretation.

Bernard Harrison and Patricia Hanna rightly characterize my view as holding that, where the interpretive ideals apply at all, either singularism or multiplism exclusively obtain. In contrast, Harrison and Hanna hold that, "One and the same object of interpretation may answer to singularism or to multiplism, because (roughly speaking) the choice depends not on the type of object whose nature we are concerned to interpret, but on the structure of the linguistic practice through which our interrogation of the object under interpretation is conducted" (p. 94).

Harrison and Hanna's observation that whether an object of interpretation answers to singularism or to multiplism depends upon more than its nature, accords with and extends what I have called the thesis of relationality. Whether a given object of interpretation answers to singularism or multiplism depends upon the relation between it (counted as one) and its proffered interpretation(s) (counted as one or more). And, whether pertinent objects and interpretations are to be counted as one or more depends not (only) upon the nature of the object in question but upon how they are construed in pertinent practices. No mere inspection of the object of interpretation will determine this matter. I endorse Harrison and Hanna's effort to feature the praxial settings in which questions of identity and countability are to be couched.

But their correct practice-centered thesis does not countenance their separate claim that singularism and multiplism need not be exclusive. Once, within the context of the pertinent practice a given object of interpretation has been fixed, it can answer to one or (exclusively) to more than one interpretation as so counted within that practice. That an object of interpretation is nested within a practice does not allow that both "one" and "more than one" may be admitted in an inclusive way. Either one or (exclusively) more than one admissible interpretation is to be found within the terms of the practice.

But Harrison and Hanna argue that singularism and multiplism may be conjoinable in some cases. They hold that singularism and multiplism may obtain simultaneously, as in the case of measuring. Measuring, they hold, must be understood in terms of some modulus. Measuring as such does not exist, only measuring in inches or in microns or in some other modulus. They argue that one's ability to measure in inches or in microns shows that more than one admissible interpretations of the length of a physical object exist. Hence, multiplism. They also hold that, for a given modulus, there may be one and only one admissible interpretation regarding the length of a physical object. Hence, singularism. Hence, both multiplism and singularism.

We must ask, though, whether the plurality of moduli does entail a multiplist condition. If pertinent moduli were inter-translatable without residue, they would not be incongruent. There would be no "opposition-without-contradiction." The fact is that inches and microns are mutually translatable without residue. A formula does exist that translates between inches and microns without the residue of any irrational numbers. An inch is defined as 2.54 centimeters exactly, and a micron is 1/10000 of a centimeter exactly. An inch is 25,400 microns exactly. No irrational numbers are involved. No "incongruence" holds between the two moduli. But then the example would amount to a case of singularism and not multiplism. So it would fail to exemplify one of Harrison and Hanna's joint claims that singularism and multiplism obtain simultaneously.

In private correspondence (5, 10, and 12 April 2002) Hanna replies that an inch being translatable into microns is irrelevant. What is crucial is the propriety of invoking one or another modulus on different occasions. On some occasions to invoke inches is appropriate and to invoke microns inappropriate. And on other occasions to invoke microns is appropriate and to invoke inches inappropriate. When measuring a picture frame, for example, to describe its length in terms of microns would be inappropriate, even if its inches were fully translatable into microns. And on other occasions as in subatomic physics to invoke microns and not inches is appropriate. Incongruence obtains at the level of the propriety of use of these moduli, not at the level of the translatability of moduli. When that incongruence does obtain, we do have a case of multiplism. Yet, according to Hanna, a single right measurement in inches exists, and a single right measurement in microns also exists.

But the question arises whether, as between the practice of measuring in inches and microns, the same object is being measured. Is there perhaps a shift in the referent of what is being measured as between inches and microns? Is that which is described in inches the same thing as that described in microns? A shift in the object of interpretation would entail the failure of multiplism. The object of interpretation would have been pluralized, such that a one-to-one relation would obtain between interpretation and object of interpretation—thus fulfilling the singularist requirement. Accordingly, the putative conjunction of multiplism and singularism would fail. Under these circumstances, it would be more accurate to say that each of the admissible interpretations is keyed to a modulus in a singularist way. The diversity of moduli or levels of description do not entail multiplism. In any event, Harrison and Hanna have not shown that for a given self-identical object of interpretation, it can answer to both a singularist and a multiplist condition.

By observing that the question of the sameness of the object arises I am not asserting that the object cannot be the same as described by different moduli. Rather, for such sameness to obtain a pertinent account needs to be offered. To anticipate, in the spirit of Harrison and Hanna's practice-centered idea I will suggest that the question of sameness for candidate cases can be answered only within the context of pertinent practices and not in virtue of some would-be object independent of practices. Accordingly, no presumption can be made that sameness obtains where different moduli operate. No general practice-independent answer to the question of sameness can be found.

Note that Harrison and Hanna's practice-centered ontology is an ontology, a constructive realist ontology. And that ontology is relevant to interpretation theory insofar as it provides the terms in which, on a practice by practice basis, a candidate is to be taken as one or more than one object. Taking it one way or another is not determinative of singularism or multiplism, but is a necessary condition for the application of singularism or multiplism.

Harrison and Hanna's concerns about "levels of interpretation" are worth pursuing. D. P. Chattopadhyaya suggests that for every level of description, yet a further level is to be found. He affirms that the description of a given entity at a given level cannot exhaust all of its levels. A further level of description always may be unearthed. I will refer to this phenomenon as "infimacy." There being innumerable levels of description does not mandate multiplism, for it is an open question whether innumerable levels of description exist with respect to a given object of interpretation. When regarding, say, a table as a middle-sized object or as a collection of molecules, are we talking about the same "object?" Without the commonality of an object of interpretation multiplism would not obtain. Multiplism requires that a common object of interpretation subsist throughout pertinent levels of interpretations.

Chattopadhyaya draws our attention to the further fact that any given object of interpretation (at a given level) is multi-faceted. Notice that difficulties in specifying all of its facets at a given level do not mandate multiplism. For the possibility is open that at a given level there may be one comprehensive overarching single interpretation. The possibility is open that along with singularism at each level there may be one comprehensive overarching single interpretation of the common object at all levels, so long as no incongruence holds between levels, and so long as the levels are denumerable. Yet Chattopadhyaya effectively argues that there can be no fact of the matter as to the nature and number of levels, for they themselves are constructed achievements. He says: "Even the distinction between levels is partly a matter of construction. The emergence of disciplines such as biophysics, biochemistry, physiological psychology, and sociolinguistics makes the point evident" (p. 226).

The number of levels is conventional and open, undercutting the denumerability required for a comprehensive single interpretation of a would-be given object common at all possible levels. And if no fact of the matter exists about the number of all possible levels, then there can be no fact of the matter as to whether, between all levels, a common object is to be found. I agree with Chattopadhyaya's rejection of a grand universal methodology, in this case for settling upon the would-be complete list of all possible levels and for settling upon the would-be common object that would subsist through them (p. 229).

I have suggested that the application of singularism and multiplism requires that all pertinent arguments and evidence are taken to be "in." This might wrongly suggest that I embrace the thought that inquiry has an end, a point at which I find conclusive closure. No such thing as an end of inquiry exists. Yet we can still use a serviceable notion of "ideal" of interpretation where that notion is nested within pertinent practices. Where qualified practitioners agree that for their purposes, where all necessary information is effectively in, they can reasonably judge whether one or more than one admissible interpretations exist.

My lead article in this volume ("Interpretation and Its Objects: A Synoptic View") introduces the notion of *Grenzbegriff* or a "limiting concept," to capture the idea of such a pragmatic notion of the end of inquiry. Richard Rorty uses the term, and I reference him. Unfortunately, Joseph Margolis takes my mention of Rorty to amount to an endorsement of Rorty's entire program, which dispenses with methodology and ontology. Margolis wrongly imputes to me Rorty's anti-ontological and anti-methodological attitude.

As I have said, multiplism is the view that some objects of interpretation answer to more than one incongruent admissible interpretation. And incongruent interpretations—being incongruent—are not conjoinable into one interpretation. Yet Maxwell urges us to conjoin incongruent interpretations. We can understand Maxwell to be a "pan-aggregator" of admissible interpretations, holding that any pairs of admissible interpretations—congruent or not—may be aggregated into a single hyphenated interpretation. He observes that the multiplist is needlessly more "demanding" than the singularist, in that the multiplist rules out such a conjunction. Instead, Maxwell favors the thought that a singularist should tolerate incongruence within a given interpretation. Yet notice that the multiplist tolerates tensions between admissible interpretations and the singularist does not. Who is the more demanding in these respects is not clear.

In affirming his singularism, Maxwell tolerates incongruence within a single interpretation instead of between interpretations. Consider his "aggregating" handling of the *Lucy* poem of Wordsworth. He says: "Brooks sees the poem as expressing the lover's agonizing shock at the inertness, the dead lifelessness, of the loved one, depicted in the second stanza. Bateson, by contrast, sees the poem as expressing the pantheistic grandeur of the dead—Lucy becoming a part of the sublime processes of nature. These readings are incompatible. . . . I think the poem—the correct interpretation of the poem—incorporates elements of both of the two readings" (p. 281). If Maxwell incorporates incongruent elements within a single (hyphenated) admissible interpretation he would be as permissive or undemanding as the multiplist who would admit separate incongruent interpretations.

In turn, Ken-ichi Sasaki pursues the sub-distinction between existential versus regulative singularism on the one hand, and existential versus regulative multiplism on the other hand. The existential singularist holds that for any object of interpretation a single admissible interpretation exists. The existential multiplist holds that for some objects of interpretation more admissible interpretations than one exist. In contrast, the regulative singularist holds that you should conduct your inquiry as if only one admissible interpretation exists for any object of interpretation. And the regulative multiplist holds that you should conduct your inquiry as if more than one admissible interpretation exists for some objects of interpretation.

Sasaki claims that existential singularism is self-refuting. Of the existential possibilities, existential multiplism is the only coherently adoptable ideal. One could be a singularist only from a regulative point of view. Sasaki's argument depends upon his claim that the notion of interpretation entails existential multiplism. He says, "Interpretation implies the existence of different interpretations: conflict is an essential feature of interpretation" (p. 70). The notion of singularism—being parasitic of the notion of interpretation—cannot be sustained. Thus, there can be no debate between (existential) singularism and multiplism. Sasaki says: "In my opinion interpretation implies multiplism and the opposition between singularism and multiplism is only apparent" (p. 78).

But Sasaki provides no independent argument why interpretation as such entails existential multiplism, so I see no reason why (at least on his account) existential singularism should not be coherently adoptable. Yet we should note that the distinction between existential and regulative ideals does provide interesting possibilities for "mixed ideals." Singularism and multiplism would be contradictory if both were taken in their existential sense. Yet the conjunction of an existential ideal with a regulative ideal does not result in contradiction. The regulative suggestion that one should behave as if any object of interpretation answers to a single admissible interpretation, or the regulative suggestion that you should behave as if some cases answer to more than one admissible interpretation contradicts neither existential multiplism nor existential singularism respectively. You could well mix existential and regulative senses of singularism and multiplism. You might argue that in particular cases it might be useful to behave as if there were a single admissible interpretation even though you disbelieved it. (See Maxwell.) Obversely, it might be useful to behave as if, for a given case, more than one admissible interpretation existed, even though you disbelieved it. (See Crocker.)

Crocker asks whether a difference in kind holds between singularism and multiplism. If we understand multiplism in terms of incongruence, and if we understand incongruence in terms of preferability with good reasons, and if, further, the offering of good reasons allows one to rank preferred interpretations, then, on Crocker's account, the distinction between singularism and multiplism appears to dissipate. What Crocker leaves out of his inference is that preference with good reason is characteristically inconclusive, for it carries no univocal standard for adjudication.

Vibha Chaturvedi provides an excellent way to see that preference with good reasons does not amount to singularism when she asks,

> Can we say that good reasons exist for preferring one interpretation to others as implied by multiplism? Let me take the case of different interpretations of the same sacred text. You might say that if an interpretation can competently explain or account for the whole text or most of the text, that interpretation is preferable to others that fail to do so. But to expect that the preferred interpretation must account for the essential or more significant parts of the text is reasonable, even if it fails to do so with respect to large sections of the not so essential parts. There can be difference of opinion about what constitutes essential or most crucial parts (pp. 308–309).

In short, an interpretation may be justified with good reasons as more preferable over another because it accounts for "the essential or more significant parts" of the text. And there may be a "difference of opinion about what constitutes essential or most important parts" as Chaturvedi says. But further, what is "essential" of "significant" is characteristically contestable. For this reason, conclusivity need not obtain in such cases.

But Crocker suggests that preferred interpretations based on good reasons do disqualify alternative interpretations as inadmissible. Consequently, no difference in kind is to be found between multiplism and singularism. He says, "Perhaps the singularist's one admissible interpretation comes to no more than the multiplist's most preferable interpretation. In short, Krausz's sharp distinction might collapse into two points on a continuum (determined by degree of preferability supplied by reasons)" (p. 58).

In short, how is the difference between singularism and multiplism not reducible to a difference in degree only? Consider an object of interpretation some of whose properties have been identified as salient or significant or meaningful in contrast with others. A good reason for one interpretation might be that it amounts to an illuminating story about the identified properties holistically presented. Yet different people of different interests and values may identify different properties as salient or significant or meaningful, prompting not just another story but another story about a different set of identified properties configured in a different holistic pattern of significance. So the disagreements about salience or significance or meaningfulness result not in competition between two stories about a fully common object of interpretation but a difference about what are assumed or should be assumed to be the object of interpretation. That difference further disallows the possibility of a univocal standard for adjudication between interpretations. Yet, again, it remains that one may have good reasons for preferring one interpretation over another based on considerations that do not amount to univocal standards for adjudication.

Consider Hanna's suggestion that incongruence should be understood in terms of "appropriateness in use." Returning to Harrison and Hanna's previous example, it would be inappropriate (under usual circumstances) to measure a picture frame in microns, for example, even though inches are translatable (commensurable) into microns. One may have good reasons for measuring the picture frame in inches instead of microns. It would be appropriate to do so. But such appropriateness does not amount to a univocal standard that disallows measurement in microns as inadmissible. The absence of such a conclusive standard distinguishes the difference in kind between singularism and multiplism.

Crocker also asks the further question whether the distinction between singularism and multiplism amounts to a practical difference. Not all philosophical accounts need issue in a practical difference. But consider whether the distinction might make a practical difference in the conduct of inquiry. The multiplist interpreter who says, "I prefer this interpretation over others and I have good reasons for doing so, but I allow that certain others are also admis-

sible," might display an attitude different than that of the singularist interpreter who says, "There is only one admissible interpretation. I think mine is
it." On first glance, it might appear that the multiplist is more conciliatory,
more tolerant, more open to reconciliation, more flexible, or the like. But
must this be so?

Consider the case of a singularist mediator in a dispute such as that between Israelis and Palestinians, or between Protestants and Catholics in Ire-
land, or between Hindus and Moslems in India. Alternatively, consider the
case of a singularist counselor who seeks to help reconcile two estranged
partners. Presumably, a singularist mediator or therapist would guide discussions toward eliciting all pertinent facts in the service of arriving at the single
right interpretation and to chart a course of dialogue or action in accord with
it. In contrast, presumably a multiplist would seek to reveal the reasonableness, appropriateness or aptness of each party's story, and to suggest to each
party that they consider the reasonableness of the other's story—without assuming that there must be one and only one admissible story.

The mediator or counselor could be an existential singularist but embrace a regulative multiplism, holding that existential singularism is not helpful in reconciliationist or therapeutic contexts. He or she could hold that in
such contexts, the issue of existential singularism versus existential multiplism should not arise. It would sidetrack the immediate aim of reconciliation.

But a regulative multiplist might counter that the embrace of existential
multiplism is part and parcel of the way in which one should pursue reconciliationist or therapeutic processes themselves; that not embracing existential
multiplism would amount to bad faith; that in the long run the suppression of
the mediator's or therapist's disbelief of existential multiplism would become
manifest and undercut the reconciliationist or therapeutic process. I find that
while singularism does not preclude the sort of empathetic understanding that
is conducive to reconciliationist or therapeutic efforts, multiplism is more
conducive to such efforts.

In contrast to Crocker, Nancy Weston thinks a practical difference does
exist between singularism and multiplism. And she cleaves to singularism for
fear that its abandonment to multiplism results in interpretive anarchy. At the
same time, Weston holds that singularism licenses legislation by fiat or the
sheer exercise of power. In the legal case one typically "overshoots" justifying grounds to a singular verdict. In such a space power is exercised. Weston
says: "In a standard court case, only one judgment, endorsing one interpretation of the events at issue, is possible: a criminal defendant is either found
guilty or is acquitted; a civil suit is decided either for the plaintiff or for the
civil defendant. Viewed in the light of the inquiry Krausz has undertaken, this
state of affairs appears to constitute an institutional constraint that mandates
singularism" (p. 240).

In standard court cases one is forced to issue a singularist verdict when the grounds for the issuance of the verdict are typically multiplist! The grounds are typically inconclusive with respect to the singularist outcome. The requirement of singularism in criminal cases—despite underdetermining evidence—results in a practical difference in legal behavior.

At the same time, Weston observes that much of legal procedure is concerned to avoid singularist verdicts, by the practice of settlement. She says: "This process, which candidly abandons concern with truth and right to a contest of strategic power, is more decorously framed when the matter to be settled is criminal, where the settlement procedure is known as 'plea-bargaining'" (p. 241).

Weston associates preference with the manipulation of power. She says: ". . . it comes to be concluded that there "is no" law, in any sense related to right, but only the sheer play of power" (p. 253). Being concerned about the authority that is invested in legal practitioners, Weston holds that there must be something beyond the authority of designated practitioners that justifies their authority. If authority is to be authentic, it cannot be self-certifying. Weston says, "it is not clear why we should follow such . . . practices and practitioners in determining rightness in any event unless we had reason to believe that their determinations are, indeed, *right*—as distinct from effective or widely conformed to—unless we are tacitly equating these." (p. 256).

Weston thinks of rightness or admissibility in terms distinct from practices and practitioners. And she thinks she finds them in the work of Martin Heidegger. Weston says: "The only remaining possibility . . . lies in attending to the matter at hand, so that we understand rightness to obtain in relation to *it*. When we do so, we return to a consideration of the thing before us—the work of art, the dispute of law . . . and ask whether the interpretation, judgment, or answer under consideration is right with respect to *it*" (p. 265).

The problem is that the Heideggerian idea of a thing "at hand" which Weston invokes provides no criterialogical grounds to decide between singularism and multiplism. And decisions of admissibility are, finally, criterialogical. Precisely the matter at hand is contentious. And whether that matter answers to singularism or multiplism—as the thesis of relationality affirms—depends upon whether it is to count as one or more in tandem with whether proffered interpretations are to count as one or more. So what is "at hand" is not alone determinative of rightness or admissibility. Weston agrees that no help may be derived from considered ontologies for the criterial task. She says: "Krausz is quite right to conclude that these contemporary ontological theories do not bear upon the undertaking of understanding rightness. Yet it is not the case that ontological considerations may simply be dispensed with and dismissed" (p. 268).

I agree that, insofar as ontology is needed to understand the nature (in general terms) of objects of interpretation we cannot do away with ontology. But the Heideggerian ontology that Weston urges serves us no better than the other considered ontologies for securing rightness or admissibility. It does not provide the needed grounds for fixing sufficient determinacy of objects of interpretation so as to judge whether a fit between it and proffered interpretation(s) is to be found.

Let us turn to consider the strategies of pluralizing and aggregating. Mukherji correctly characterizes the strategies of aggregating and pluralizing objects of interpretation, on the one hand, and aggregating and pluralizing interpretations themselves, on the other hand, as strategies that may be deployed by singularists or multiplists. The strategies of aggregating and pluralizing available to singularists and multiplists do not settle whether a given object of interpretation should be treated as singularist or multiplist. These strategies are offered without intending to settle the matter as to whether a given object of interpretation should answer to singularism or multiplism. To Mukherji's disappointment, these strategies do not come with formal rules for their appropriate application. Mukherji asks for general grounds on which any of these strategies should be appropriately applied. He suggests that their appropriate applicability depends upon the kind of thing that is being interpreted. In contrast, I suggest that it depends upon the peculiarities of the practice in which the case is nested. Accordingly, no general grounds can be given.

Mukherji is right to have observed that aggregating and pluralizing objects of interpretation or interpretations themselves are strategies that themselves carry no general rules for correct application. But he need not fear that the matter is arbitrary, for their appropriate deployment is a matter of piecemeal deliberation within the context of pertinent practices.

Yet Sasaki worries that applying the pluralizing strategy to objects of interpretation without restraint results in solipsism. If one could not identify a common object of interpretation between interlocutors one would talk at or past each other, much like with the Tower of Babel. Accordingly, Sasaki is concerned about what one might call the "perpetual pluralist" who indiscriminately pluralizes the object of interpretation in order to avoid conflict. According to such a procedure, only a favored interpretation would be admissible because only a stipulated object of interpretation could satisfy the favored interpretation. This question-begging strategy would disallow conflict between interpreters, be they singularists or multiplists. But no reason exists why the pluralizer need be indiscriminate. Keep in mind that the appropriateness of deploying the pluralizing or aggregating strategies needs to be judged in a piecemeal way, depending upon the nature of particular practices. While no general rules may be found for the appropriate application of these strategies, arbitrariness and indiscriminacy are not entailed.

Sasaki's worry is exacerbated by his defining singularism in terms of perpetual pluralizing. He is concerned that perpetual pluralizing would result in a "self-refutation" of singularism because singularism would be rendered vacuous. And with the vacuity of singularism, the distinction between singularism and multiplism would dissipate. But while Sasaki couples singularism with perpetual pluralizing nothing requires that singularism should be attached to perpetual pluralizing. And so singularism has nothing inherently self-refuting about it. The distinction between singularism and multiplism (happily) remains.

Sasaki's argument against the perpetually pluralizing singularist could be turned on its head. He could as well worry about the multiplist who might be a "perpetual aggregator." In his or her hands any would-be singularist case would be transformed into a multiplist case by aggregating the initially considered objects of interpretation into one. Correspondingly, by parity of reasoning, multiplism would be rendered self-refuting—because, again, it would be rendered vacuous—and the singularism versus multiplism problem again would be (unhappily, I say) dissipated.

The moral that we should draw in such cases is that the singularist and multiplist should not be indiscriminate. They should not be perpetual pluralizers or perpetual aggregators. They should deploy the pertinent strategies judiciously in accord, again, with the nature and interests of pertinent practices. Just as singularism should not be defined in terms of perpetual pluralizing (where, again, objects of interpretation are bifurcated), multiplism should not be defined in terms of perpetual aggregating. Consequently, the distinction between singularism and multiplism remains.

The appropriateness of pluralizing or aggregating an object of interpretation can be a contentious matter. Consider the case of the baby in the Ganges, first offered as an example of multiplism. Paul Thom suggests it need not be so understood if the object of interpretation is pluralized. I first suggested that the Western secular interpreter is horrified by the sight of the baby floating in the Ganges, in contrast with the Hindu who, in view of the baby having been honored and "returned" to the Ganges, is not horrified by the same sight. Thom suggests that while both interpreters may be horrified, the sight might not amount to the same thing. The Hindu might see the floating baby as an honored being whose proper burial unintentionally went wrong. The honored being should have remained at the bottom of the Ganges. But the baby was not dumped! Thom's re-construal suggests the thought that it was not one and the same thing that prompted different reactions, but it was different things that prompted the respective reactions.

The example is made yet more complicated because elsewhere the Ganges is also used as a dumping site for buffalo carcasses. This additional fact might give more credence to the "dumping" interpretation of the baby, although you could still see the floating baby as a sign of a respected honor-bestowing burial practice gone wrong. The point is that the appropriateness of pluralizing or aggregating is relativized to the intentional frame through which you construe the pertinent situation. Put otherwise, the appropriateness of pluralizing or aggregating depends upon the practices in which the object of interpretation is nested.

In this case, the object of interpretation may be pluralized in a different way yet again, as when Thom raises the possibility that the object of interpretation might be the phenomenon of death. He says: "Maybe he [Krausz] wishes us to focus on the belief-systems of the Indian (described as 'Hindu/Buddhist') and the North American (described as 'secular'). Those belief-systems can be seen as different interpretations of another object of interpretation—the phenomenon of death" (pp. 115–116).

As I said, the appropriateness of pluralizing or aggregating an object of interpretation can be a contentious matter. Interestingly, Maxwell seeks to install his singularism in the case of musical interpretation by pluralizing works of music. He holds that interpreters of music create new works. He says:

> That singularism breaks down in the case of the performing arts is due not to any inadequacies in singularism, but to the strange, "hydra-headed" character of a performed work of art. . . . The performer re-creates—or co-creates—the work of art. . . . What we have, in short, in the case of the performing arts, is not one work of art and many different equally correct adjunct interpretations, but many different works of art, all sharing common features, and stemming from a common source, a common set of instructions . . . (pp. 278–279).

For Maxwell, for any given musical work one and only admissible interpretation of it can be found, because what results from co-creation is hydra-headed. So Riccardo Muti is not performing or interpreting the same work on two different occasions. Rather, on different occasions he is performing different works. According to Maxwell's account, we could not say that on two different occasions Muti can offer performance-interpretations of the same work. This is most counter-intuitive.

Here is another way in which Maxwell seeks to install his pan-singularism. It involves his aggregating candidate interpretations (in contrast with objects of interpretation). Maxwell adduces an intriguing example that—by way of aggregating interpretations—he takes to confirm his singularism. The example involves interpretations of Leonardo DaVinci's *Last Supper*. Goethe's "betrayal" interpretation and Leo Steinberg's "Eucharist" interpretation suggest a multiplist condition. But, according to Maxwell, Michael Podro's reconciliationist intervention results in an aggregating strategy that issues in a singularist condition. Maxwell says that, given Podro's intervention, "The true meaning of the *Last Supper,* in short, is bound up, not just with the existence of two, equally valid, different interpretations (betrayal and Eucharist), but with the way in which these two readings interact with one another, or are related to each other, in the form of the picture. The correct adjunct interpretation will incorporate all these meanings" (p. 276).

But notice that (on Maxwell's account) Podro is not advancing yet another interpretation—a single comprehensive one—but a strategy for interaction. Podro recommends that the betrayal and the Eucharist interpretations should "interact" and "relate" to each other, presumably in Gestalt-switch fashion. This is no new single reconciliationist interpretation, but an invitation to switch back and forth between interpretations. Interaction between interpretations is not a conjunction of interpretations. Multiplism remains.

Further, in order to satisfy Maxwell's singularism, he would need to affirm that for any would-be incongruent interpretations, they would be conjoinable without regard to the extent of their incongruence. (Maxwell would be a pan-aggregator with respect to interpretation.) He takes this to be affirmed by Podro's intervention. Presumably he would so construe my example of Anselm Kiefer, whose early paintings were interpreted alternatively as celebrating or exorcising the world's unresolved memories of the Nazi past.

In Maxwell's handling incongruence is subtended under a single admissible interpretation. In my handling, incongruence is grounds for distinguishing between interpretations. Aggregating incongruent interpretations would reduce a would-be multiplist case to a singularist case. Maxwell's view commits him to the improbable claim that in no cases is such aggregation disallowed.

Finally, Paul Grobstein introduces a neuro-physiological argument that prohibits aggregating interpretations that would result in singularism. On his account there can be no singularist cases. Grobstein's argument derives from his claim that the brain is inherently a multiplist organ. He argues that only what is seen or experienced can be countenanced as what is known or knowable. We can make no judgments about the way the world is independently of what the brain pictures it to be. The notion of an external world—having a determinate nature in relation to which the results of the brain can be tested— is inapplicable. What is seen or experienced cannot be singularist. The reason concerns the relation between the eye and the brain. The receptors of the eye do not provide all the information that the brain would need for it to form a single picture of what the eye "sees." The brain is a multiplist interpreter. It fills in what the eye incompletely provides to it. And the brain "completes" the picture it gets in one of several ways.

A singularist might respond by saying that even if the brain does not receive enough information to mandate a singular picture of the way the world is, that does not entail that no single right interpretation of it exists. That a single admissible interpretation exists is still possible. That the eye underdetermines the picture that the brain paints does not establish no single admissible interpretation is to be found. (A multiplist also may affirm multiple interpretability on grounds altogether distinct from constraints on the brain's functions.)

To this response Grobstein replies that all inquiry begins and ends with the brain, that it makes no sense to talk about the way the world is independently of what the brain can deliver. Consequently, we cannot assume an idea of a world that answers to singularism (or multiplism for that matter). The brain and what it does is all that exists. The argument that there could be a fact of the matter independently of the way the brain works is incoherent.

Grobstein dubs his view "pragmatic multiplism"—in contrast with multiplism as originally defined—in order to signal that multiplism arises from the activity of the brain itself. Objects of interpretation do not answer to one or more than one interpretation in virtue of the relation between interpretation and its objects independently of the brain. Rather, the product of the brain must answer to more than one admissible interpretation. Ideality is a product of the brain and is restricted to the brain.

In contrast, I urge that from the brain completing the information that is brought to it from the eye (or any of the senses), multiplism does not follow. A world exists external to the brains engaged in interpretive practices. And that fact is consistent with Grobstein's observation that the brain is a completing organ. As powerful as the brain is, it may just be incapable of "seeing" a singularist condition beyond itself. Accordingly, a singularist could agree with Grobstein's neurological finding to the effect that the information presented to it by the eye is incomplete, or that the eye's information underdetermines the picture that the brain paints of it. Notice further that Grobstein's "pan-multiplism" is refuted by the concession that singularist cases exist at all, such as that unsupported bodies drop at a rate of 32 feet per second squared is singularly true. The multiplicity of the brain's pictures does not entail pan-multiplism.

3. Aims of Interpretation

Our discussion of singularism and multiplism so far has presumed that these ideals compete insofar as they both seek a single aim of interpretation, namely, elucidation. The issue of the aim of interpretation must be considered. For two interpretations to compete, they must have identical aims. And interpretations that pursue different aims need not be in conflict. Notice that the multiplicity of aims does not license multiplism. Only one aim of interpretation must be assumed for singularism or multiplism to obtain. Within the terms of that one aim, the singularist denies and the multiplist affirms that a given object of interpretation may answer to more than one admissible interpretation.

LR distinguishes between the aims of elucidation and edification. Thom offers a version of the distinction by distinguishing between understanding and consolation. He says:

Consolation requires not knowledge but hope. A consoling message is not so much one we know that is true, as one we hope will be fulfilled. We must believe fulfillment of the message to be possible. But belief in a possibility is a far cry from knowledge. The consolations offered by the great religions often concern matters about which no knowledge is possible, one way or the other. Precisely because we cannot know that their claims are false, we can cling to the hope that they may be realized (p. 116).

This "same-aims-proviso" holds that for two interpretations to compete—whether singularist or multiplist—they must pursue the same aim. For example, if Hinduism were taken to pursue the elucidatory aim (alone) and Buddhism were taken to pursue the edificatory aim (alone), then the two would not exhibit multiplism. They would not "compete," despite their apparent incongruence. Alternatively, where each of these is taken to pursue a common aim (elucidatory or edificatory) they would compete.

Yet I emphasize that the core aim of interpretation is elucidation even though an interpretation may "laterally," so to say, be "used" to satisfy edificatory interests. Sasaki mistakes me to hold that interpretation aims for elucidation and edification when he says: "Krausz claims two 'aims of interpretation' exist: 'elucidation and edification.' His 'soteriology' evidently belongs to the second aim . . . . [I]n my view, interpretation has the unique aim of 'elucidation' and this is implied in its concept" (pp. 76–77).

I agree with Sasaki that the core aim of interpretation is elucidation. Yet sometimes interpretive activity may be laterally "used" in an edificatory way. But we should not mistake that interpretation may be laterally used in an edificatory way as constituting a core aim of interpretation.

One way to pursue edification as a lateral aim may be found in the interpretation of religious paintings, such as those of Giovanni Bellini.[1] The choice of a religious over a Marxist interpretation of one of these paintings, say, might be motivated by an interpreter's concern to "enter into" the sacred space depicted in the painting, for the purpose of furthering your religious experience. That would satisfy an aim that is extrinsic or lateral to the core aim of elucidation.

Yet notice that as a matter of religious doctrine you might hold that edification is part and parcel of elucidation, that religious experience is part and parcel of religious understanding. So, our separation of elucidation from edification might well amount to our having taken a stand on a religiously contentious matter.

4. Interpretation

Several contributors press for a formal definition of the idea of interpretation. Without it, they affirm, no comparative study of interpretations between practices—as regards their answering to singularism or multiplism—can be sustained. Yet "interpretation" cannot be so defined. Hilary Putnam emphasizes that the idea of interpretation is informal when he says, "We all realize that we cannot hope to mechanize interpretation. The dream of formalizing interpretation is as utopian as the dream of formalizing nonparadigmatic rationality itself. Not only is interpretation a highly informal activity, guided by few, if any, settled rules or methods, but it is one that involves much more than linear prepositional thinking."[2]

Following Putnam and Ludwig Wittgenstein and Morris Weitz, I affirm that interpretation is an "open concept" whose conditions are best thought of not as necessary or sufficient but as contingently "characteristic." Rather like "art", "interpretation" has no fixed essentialist conditions. To think of its correct application in the contexts of its uses is more fruitful. "Interpretation" should serve as a summation of an inventory of characteristic applications instead of a stipulation that precedes pertinent applications.

Yet Mukherji is suspicious (as is Giridhari Pandit) of the generality of the notion of interpretation as I deploy it, at least in the cultural realm. Mukherji says: "This means that some notion of interpretation remains invariant across the entities in this category" (p. 43). "Invariance" is too strong a term here. It suggests, contrary to Wittgenstein's notion of a cluster concept, that all the defining conditions of interpretation hold between cases, without the possibility that, serially, some of its conditions may be substituted, sensitive to the idiosyncrasies of the case. But Mukherji affirms that in the absence of invariance, interpretation could not generally apply. And without it, neither singularism nor multiplism could apply. As Mukherji says: "The notion of interpretation varies so much across literature, painting, especially music that unitary notions of singularism and multiplism would apply everywhere is implausible" (p. 43).

If no "characteristic" notion of interpretation applies (I soften Mukherji's "invariant," for the reason given), then no comparative study between cases—as to their answering to singularism or multiplism—could be conducted. And this consequence (perhaps unnoticed by Mukherji) would also hold for comparative studies of cases within as well as between practices. Preserving the applicability of "interpretation" despite its objects differing in diverse practices, is crucial.

A sufficiently unitary notion of interpretation exists, one that is characteristically enduring but pliable in the sense that it admits of local variations. Mukherji himself provides us with examples. First Mukherji adduces the case of the baby in the Ganges when he says: "we find two layers of interpretation: (a) the interpretation as a floating dead baby, and b) the interpretation regarding how we evaluate (a)" (p. 44). Mukherji suggests that there are two notions of interpretation because interpretation is applied at different levels. But from different levels being involved it does not follow that no characteristic notion of interpretation applies to both. In turn, Mukherji cites a difference between the interpretation of the baby in the Ganges and the interpretation of Van Gogh's *Potato Eaters*. Mukherji notes that in the formalist interpretation of the painting no social dimension is to be found, in contrast with the Marxist interpretation of it. Mukherji takes this to mean that different senses of interpretation are in play. But, again, from such a difference it does not follow that no characteristic sense of interpretation applies to both. In turn, Mukherji considers the case of interpretation in music in which a difference exists between interpretation in the sense of performance and a critical interpretation of a score, both of which differ from the interpretation of literature. Yet, again, such differences do not disallow that "interpretation" can accommodate the differences.

How, then, will we positively characterize the "open" concept of interpretation? First, an interpretation is of something distinct from itself. An interpretation is of a baby in the Ganges, a painting, a work of music, a poem, etc. Second, interpretive activity involves the assignment of salience, significance or value to features of designated objects of interpretation. The Marxist and the Freudian assign salience to different features of the painting, for example. The performer and critical interpreters of music assign salience to different features of the music. Third, the core aim of interpretation is elucidation. Yet these conditions are not jointly sufficient nor is each necessary for a characteristic definition of interpretation. Interpretation is not a closed concept.

Pandit goes further than Mukherji in affirming that any general theory of interpretation must be essentialist. He says, "essentialism denied at one level of analysis raises its head at the other levels" (p. 295). He holds that my general theory of interpretation and ontology cannot possibly escape the charge of essentialism in some form or the other, and that it is impossible to develop an all-embracing theory of interpretation free from all forms of essentialism.

Pandit thinks that a general theory of interpretation—one that speaks of interpretation as it applies to diverse sorts of cases where characteristic conditions might collect pertinent cases—entails an essentialism. But this is no more true of a theory of interpretation than true of a general theory of science. That a theory of science (such as Karl Popper's theory of falsifiability) would need to apply to all scientific theories does not mandate that the theory must be essentialist. Essentialism does not follow from generality.

Garry Hagberg offers deeper reasons why interpretation need not be closed or essentialist. He reports how Wittgenstein provides the reason why no essentialist definition can be given, and how we may still have license to offer a general account of interpretation in diverse practices. In different parts of his treatment, Hagberg discusses an often-assumed offensive distinction between manifestation and apparatus. This dualism coincides with the dualism between word and world. These distinctions misleadingly suggest to some that, in virtue of the presentation of a phenomenon, we may infer or grasp what is there beyond the manifestation to the apparatus. Some inherent essentialized existent is reflected in the manifestation or the word.

Following Wittgenstein, Hagberg seeks to overcome this kind of dualism, and he rightly sees me as a comrade in his effort. The notion of a manifestation in opposition to an apparatus must be deconstructed. It would be better, as he and Harrison and Hanna do, to content ourselves with what practices yield. Hagberg's message is that the model and not the practice is dispensable. The nature of a presumed hidden state or process should be jettisoned. That, in a nutshell, is Hagberg's recapitulation of Wittgenstein's practice-centered orientation.

Now, how does Hagberg's critique of the offending dualism apply to the idea of interpretation? The answer is that we should not seek some apparatus—some presumed bit of reality to which manifestations correspond or reflect or answer. If, when asking for a definition of interpretation, Mukherji and Pandit seek some discernible apparatus that needs to be captured, then that request cannot be fulfilled. Instead, we should collect representative practices and inspect them to discern patterns and tendencies and inquire about relations between them. The point is that pertinent practices will not have been collected in virtue of the foreknowledge of some privileging criterion. For the notion of interpretation is parasitic of the practices collected. A dialectical relationship holds between our understanding of the cases as the cases they are, and the category that allows us to collect them in the way we do. Accordingly, when Mukherji and Pandit require an essentialist definition of interpretation in virtue of which you may include or exclude cases of interpretation, they dislodge the dialectic in question. From our having collected pertinent interpretive practices it does not follow that we must have had a criterion in virtue of which that collection was possible. So the request to make that would-be criterion explicit cannot be met—not because of some epistemic failing, but because the criterion is not there to be had! Correspondingly, Hagberg says: "[T]he term 'interpretation' is not univocal . . . . [W]e do not follow narrow and uniform rules for its singular and correct application. The concept is used multifariously, and Krausz will not allow the unifying demands of theory to falsify the diversity of our practice" (p. 26).

Hagberg underscores the multifarious nature of interpretation in the face of its diverse practices. He notes that you can acknowledge the diversity of practices but still deploy a sufficiently general but pliable notion of interpretation. Such deployment would remain faithful to the diversity of practices. When Mukherji and Pandit ask for the criterion for the correct application of the notion of interpretation, on Hagberg's account, they are committing the sort of mistake that Wittgenstein warns us against. For, as Hagberg says, "we cannot separate the manifestations from the alleged 'apparatus'" (p. 32). The dualism needs to be deconstructed.

5. Interpretation and Its Objects

While "interpretation" is an open concept, we may enumerate characteristic features. As I have suggested, one of the characteristic features of interpretive activity, is that interpretation is of something distinct from itself. Further, both singularism and multiplism assume the distinction between an interpretation and its objects. Without it, a singularist could not affirm the proposition that for a given object of interpretation, it must answer to a single admissible interpretation. Nor without such a distinction could a multiplist affirm that some objects of interpretation answer to more than one admissible interpretation. Yet, as Sasaki says, a dialectical relation is to be found between an interpretation and its object. The object of interpretation is constituted in the interpretive process itself. The product of interpretive activity may be bracketed as an object of interpretation, and may itself answer to subsequent interpretations. For example, a painting is the product of interpretive activity. A painting is an object understood as such within a genre that has a cultural history. Once it has been bracketed as an object of interpretation, you can ask of it whether it answers, say, to a Freudian or a Marxist interpretation. The point is that the distinction between interpretation and its object of interpretation is not an absolutely fixed one. But that does not undercut the distinction between interpretation and its object that can be drawn and redrawn at different stages and levels of interpretive activity.

Yet Maxwell offers a theory of interpretation that violates the distinction between interpretation and its objects. He argues for a two-fold thesis. First, he argues that a work of art is its interpretation. (Call this his "reflexive" thesis.) This claim violates the key distinction. Second, he argues that the interpretation that is the work of art is the one and only one admissible interpretation of itself. In contrast, I hold that even if a work were its interpretation, it does not follow that the interpretation that would be the work is the only admissible interpretation.

But, with adjustment, perhaps Maxwell's so-called reflexive interpretation might be defended this way. Allow that "self-interpretation" involves an equivocation on that which is being interpreted. Allow that no "self-interpretation" exists in a strict univocal sense. Allow that a work-as-a type is an interpretation of a work-as-a-token. Allow that were an object of interpretation to refer to "itself," there would be a shift in its identity. If sense is to be made of the idea that works of art are their "own" interpretations, what is the object of interpretation would have been mediated in the interpretive activity. In this way, the distinction between interpretation and its object could be sustained, if re-figured in the activity.

Maxwell himself suggests some ground to sustain such an adjustment to his reflexive thesis. He likens the activity of interpreting to that of explaining. An explanatory scheme is comprised of an explanandum (the description of the state of affairs to be explained) and a distinct explanans (the explanation of the explanandum). Put otherwise, you distinguish what is to be explained from the explanation of it. An explanandum does not explain itself. Correspondingly in the case of interpretation, we ask for an interpretation of something distinct from the interpretation. We ask for an interpretation of a painting, or of a poem, for example.

One might think that reflexive interpretation runs into the difficulty that interpretations need to be a piece of prose. Maxwell rightly responds by observing that a performance may be an interpretation, and that a performance is not a written text. An interpretation may be in the same medium as the work that is being interpreted. But notice that that observation is not enough to license the reflexive view of interpretation, namely, that a work (without equivocation) is self interpreting. To suggest that "nothing precludes the work from being its own best interpretation" (p. 270) is a non sequitur. The possibility of an interpretation being in the same medium as the work does not license the thought that a work may be an interpretation of itself, or the thought that the work should be the single admissible interpretation of itself!

Maxwell goes further. He privileges self-interpreting works as "core" interpretations. Interpretations that are not self interpreted works are "adjunct" interpretations. Core interpretations are reflexive interpretations. They take "pride of place," as Maxwell puts it. He says, "Adjunct interpretations can only be, at most, ad hoc additions to the correct interpretation, the work of art itself" (p. 272).

Now, I agree with Maxwell that we ought to give pride of place to the work of art. Critics, historians, and writers do often get so enmeshed with interpretations of interpretations that they leave the work of art behind. This is lamentable. But the refusal by many artists to offer interpretations of their work does not establish that their work is an interpretation of itself. Maxwell takes such refusals of artists to be tantamount to their offering their work as interpretations. But no reason exists to construe such refusal in this way. The artist may just be inviting the viewer to look at the painting, to attend to it, instead of engage in interpretive activity at all. Giving pride of place to the work of art is not tantamount to endorsing the thought that the work of art provides the single interpretation of itself.

Maxwell goes still further. He reasons that if a work of art were to be an interpretation of itself (as he affirms), it should be possible for a work of art to misinterpret itself. Maxwell attempts to unpack how this is possible by considering Simone de Beauvoir's novel, *She Came to Stay*. Maxwell's discussion is meant to show how a novel can be mistaken about itself. But all that Maxwell shows is that de Beauvoir's view of the work (the unacknowledged jealousy interpretation) and Maxwell's view (the acknowledged jealousy interpretation) disagree. This does not show that the work misrepresents itself! It only shows that an author—quite distinct from the work—may have a different interpretation from that of a reader. It shows neither that a work can be its interpretation nor that it can be a mistaken interpretation.

I have said that the distinction between interpretation and its objects is a characteristic feature of interpretive activity. Yet, Cristoph Cox asserts that the distinction breaks down, and it cannot be sustained in genres other than classical music. He says: "Interpretation always involves transformation—or as Nietzsche polemically puts it 'forcing, adjusting, abbreviating, omitting, padding, inventing, falsifying and whatever else is of the *essence* of interpreting.' To put it another way, no interpreter of a text (with the possible exception of the classical musical performer . . .) ever cares to reproduce the original, which, after all, already exists" (pp. 286–287).

But from the claim that interpretation always involves transformation it does not follow that we cannot draw the distinction between interpretation and its object(s). Rather, forcing, adjusting, abbreviating, omitting, padding, inventing, falsifying, results in the production of new works (or objects of interpretation), which may in turn be interpreted. Such interpretation is rather like a collage. Instead of deconstructing the distinction, Cox shows how transformation provides ever-greater possibilities for its application. By remaking one work one makes another. The distinction reappears in further iterations.

Cox invokes the case of jazz when arguing for the deconstruction of the distinction between interpretation and its objects. Crucial differences can be found between improvisation in accord with a chart (as in jazz) and improvisation according to a more fully developed score (as in early Baroque music). But improvisation does not amount to a deconstruction of the distinction between interpretation and its objects. Improvisation results in a new work. Even if the new work is an interpretation of a prior work this would still not undercut the applicability of the distinction between interpretation and its objects. And this point holds as well for Cox's further case of the remix. Cox even concedes as much when he says, "Not one 'Body and Soul' exists, but thousands. The original . . . is buried under stronger versions . . . . [T]he 'interpreters' are simply the authors of new texts" (p. 288).

Cox favors the ontology of constructivism in the aesthetic context because, as he says, ". . . the constructionist undermines any firm distinction between interpretation and text. For the constructionist . . . the text is always itself an interpretation, a reworking of materials already on hand; and any new interpretation is an interpretation of an interpretation, with no ultimate or final *Ur*-text underlying this process" (pp. 288–289).

Cox thinks that constructivism undercuts the distinction between interpretation and object of interpretation (or work or text or text-analogue). But it does not. Constructivism merely offers a basis for the distinction different than that offered by the realist. The constructivist can draw the distinction just as well as the realist can. The distinction does not uniquely mandate realism. So to reject realism (as Cox does) does not entail a collapse of the distinction.

On the constructivist account the interpretation-text may become the object of interpretation of a subsequent interpretation, much like a meta-language can be taken as an object language with respect to a subsequent higher order meta-language. Further, nothing is to be found in the distinction between interpretation and its objects that mandates anything like the offending notion (offending to both Cox and me) of a final or ultimate Urtext.

Even for someone who (like Andreea Ritivoi, as we will see) holds that the self is constituted in interpretive activity, the distinction between object of interpretation and interpretation applies and reapplies as the self changes. The emerged self is bracketed as an object of interpretation, which then answers to subsequent interpretations.

Cox misleadingly aligns constructivism with what he calls "pragmatic" questions in contrast with elucidatory questions. No reason can be found to assume that constructivists are any less interested in elucidatory questions, nor that realists or constructive realists are less interested in "pragmatic" questions. But Cox affirms that: "On the constructionist model, the question about interpretation is not 'Does it get the original right?' but 'How does it render the original otherwise?' and 'Is this interesting? New? Significant?'" (p. 291).

But the core elucidatory questions of "sense-making" are not displaced by the "pragmatic" questions that Cox favors, namely, "Is it interesting? "Is it new?" "Is it significant?" Cox's suggestion that—in accord with constructivism—we exchange the elucidatory question for such pragmatic questions ignores the principal aim of interpretation. Affirming elucidation as the core aim of interpretation does not disallow Cox's pragmatic questions. Realists, constructivists, and constructive realists could well ask elucidatory or pragmatic questions. Cox's proposed substitution of pragmatic questions for elucidatory questions does not unseat realism. No reason exists why the constructivist should forgo asking elucidatory questions, nor why the realist should forgo asking pragmatic questions.

6. Objects of Interpretation

We have been discussing the idea of interpretation in relation to its objects. Let us turn our attention more directly to the notion of an object of interpretation. I have observed that what is conceptualized and reconceptualized as the object of interpretation may shift in the course of its history according to its intentional setting.

Thom asks whether the two-term distinction between interpretation and its objects is sufficient for the understanding of interpretive activity, whether the phrase "object of interpretation" masks a further crucial sub-distinction. He embraces a three-tier structure which distinguishes among (1) an interpretation, (2) an object-as-represented (what I have been calling an object of interpretation), and what he calls (3) a further object. He holds that an object-as-represented may be differently imputed by competing interpretations. Consequently, an object-as-represented is not one and the same thing when differently interpreted. But, in an indirect way, the interpretations still address the same further object—which affords and is represented by the object-as-represented. More fully, Thom says:

> That which is interpreted (the "object of interpretation") is represented in a particular way such that, as so represented, it can be subsumed (relative to a particular significance-system) under a governing concept that makes sense of it, and thence indirectly makes sense of the object of interpretation. What I am here calling the object I elsewhere called the "further object." That expression has led some . . . to attribute to me a belief in transcendental objects of interpretation. But I see no reason for theorists of interpretation as such to engage in metaphysical issues, of which the existence of transcendental objects is one. The object of interpretation, on my account, is a "further" object only in the sense that the object of interpretation is further removed from the governing concept than is the object-as-represented (p. 109).

Note that, according to Thom, the further object need not be independent of all representation. It is no transcendental object. In this regard a previous reading of mine stands corrected. (A corresponding reading by Pradhan also stands corrected.)

As Thom sees it, where multiplism obtains, it does so indirectly. Multiplism does not obtain directly between interpretations and the object-as-represented, for where objects-as-represented are imputed differently, different objects-as-represented obtain. A pluralist instead of a multiplist condition obtains directly between interpretation and object-as-represented.

Thom also holds that objects of interpretation "need not be existent countable entities." He mistakenly criticizes me for holding that pertinent objects prior to intentional activity must exist. I do not hold that they must exist. On this point Thom and I agree. Rather, I affirm that objects of interpretation are countable! Notice that coffee—even if there is none—can be said to be the same or different from other mass nouns like milk. And that is all that I mean by saying that such intentional objects are countable. Indeed, such countability is required for the application of singularism or multiplism. Consider the further case of the mass noun "death." Death is one thing and not another thing. In this sense death is countable as one thing, and (say) life is another thing. These are mass nouns and they are countable. If they were not countable, the conditions of singularism and multiplism could not apply to them.

Yet interesting cases exist in which countability or sameness does not apply. They include cases characteristically invoked by particular religious traditions, sometimes called the "Mysterium," or the Atman (for the Hindu) or the Anatman (for the Buddhist). Being not countable—or at least not normally counted in pertinent practices—they are disqualified as objects of interpretation that might otherwise answer to singularism or multiplism. They will have gone beyond the "limits of interpretation," and consequently beyond the "limits of rightness."

Let us keep our overriding thesis in focus. I agree with Thom that profiling (the assignment of salience) is central to interpretive activity. I agree with some tripartite distinction between interpretation, objects-as-represented, and further objects, or some analog thereof.[3] (I will not here take up the question whether Peter Lamarque's three tier scheme improves upon Thom's.) Yet my countenancing some such three-tiered account amounts to no denial of the detachability thesis. Thom agrees with my detachability thesis—the logically lean thesis concerning the non-entailment of singularism or multiplism from representative ontologies.

Again, the object of interpretation must be singular (and countable) if the object is to answer to singularism or multiplism. I do not assume that its further object must exist. Intentional objects need not entail the existence of any external object. The object-as-represented, the intentional object, must be singular. The singularity of an object of interpretation needs to be secured before the possibility of conflict between interpretations can arise. The intentional object needs to be countable, so that an interpreter can affirm that the same object-as-represented is addressed by competing interpretations.

While Thom agrees that singularism and multiplism are detachable from realism, constructivism, and constructive realism, he says that ontology (or "metaphysics") is irrelevant to interpretation theory. By this he means that as a theorist of interpretation he embraces no transcendental objects. On grounds independent of a theory of interpretation he embraces realism. But as a theorist of interpretation he refuses to engage in ontology. Yet no clear boundaries exist in what is in or what is out of a theory of interpretation. How Thom could draw the line between interpretation theory and ontology is unclear. Further, I suggest that whether you are a realist, constructivist or a constructive realist does bear on your conduct of inquiry. These ontologies provide the terms in which you set the limits of the range of admissibility, all the while it remaining that realism, constructivism, or constructive realism entail neither singularism nor multiplism.

7. The Detachability Thesis

Before considering the central thesis of detachability, several points of terminology are in order. Their misunderstanding has led some readers to misconstrue the reach of the thesis.

I have enumerated realism, constructivism, and several varieties of constructive realism. As a means of referring collectively to these theories, I have designated them as "ontological theories" or "ontology." Correspondingly, as a means of referring collectively to singularism and multiplism I have designated them as "ideality." So, when asserting that ideality is detachable from ontology and vice versa, I understand "ontology" and "ideality" as shorthand for the enumerated ontological theories and for singularism and multiplism. More fully, neither realism, constructivism, nor constructive realism entails singularism or multiplism; and neither singularism nor multiplism entail either realism, constructivism, or constructive realism.

Some readers, notably Margolis, read the short-handed formulation in an inflated way. They inflate the intended lean claim and construe it as the unintended claim that any and all possible ontologies are detachable from the ideals of interpretation. The intended lean thesis asserts only that detachability holds for the inventoried ontologies. This leaves open the possibility that some as yet unidentified ontology might not be detachable. But even if such an ontology were produced, we might still affirm that there would be a tendency toward detachability by considered ontologies. A refutation of such a tendency claim would require a more ample list of ontologies, which would uniquely entail either singularism or multiplism. What Margolis has "missed", since he asks (p. 124), is that realism, constructivism, and constructive realism do not entail singularism or multiplism uniquely, and visa versa, and that is all that the lean thesis asserts.

Now let us turn to the lean thesis itself. It concerns entailment. The thesis holds that both singularism and multiplism are compatible with realism, constructivism or the varieties of constructive realism that I have rehearsed. No unique entailment may be found in either direction between singularism and multiplism (on the one hand) and any of the inventoried ontologies (on the other hand). Yet the thesis allows relevance between these mentioned ontologies and these ideals.

Margolis, Harrison and Hanna, and I all agree that fixing the object of interpretation as the single countable object that it is, is required for the application of singularism or multiplism. But this can be done only in the context of some conduct of inquiry as provided by some ontology. For Harrison and Hanna it can be done within the terms of practices; for Nelson Goodman it can be done within the terms of symbol systems; for Michael McKenna it can be done within the terms of natural kinds, and so on. We may disagree about which candidate sets of terms to adopt. But what remains is that each provides some terms in virtue of which the discussion of fixing pertinent objects of interpretation can proceed. In this way ontology is relevant to the theory of interpretation. Notice, though, that fixing the singularity of an object of interpretation with the aid of any of the inventoried ontologies is not enough to uniquely mandate singularism or multiplism.

At the end of his paper Margolis says: "Showing that neither singularism nor multiplism entails 'realism' (in the sense supplied) is a trivial matter" (p. 126). Trivial as it may appear, the point has far-reaching consequences—thus, it is not trivial at all. It is a matter of logic that the entailment relations do not hold. And the choice between singularism and multiplism is a choice that follows the initial fixing of an object of interpretation as the re-identifiable object that it is. The identity of an object of interpretation must be "secured" by some ontology, but that is insufficient to choose between singularist and multiplist cases. While a given ontology may provide an account of the sort of thing an object of interpretation is, and indicate the outlines of a pertinent conduct of inquiry, it does not provide a criterial decision procedure for sorting which interpretations are admissible and which are not. It does not mandate either singularism or multiplism.

Margolis misleadingly assumes that the ontology that he offers for "securing" the identity of objects of interpretation concerns the choice between singularist and multiplist cases when he says: "Neither singularism nor multiplism makes any sense until we say what we take to be the nature of the countable things we are examining, in virtue of which we rightly decide whether singularism or multiplism is the better position" (p. 121).

Whether an object of interpretation answers to singularism or multiplism depends on the relation between it and the number of its candidate interpretations. My thesis of relationality makes this explicit. Whether singularism or multiplism obtains is not a matter that can be read off from the examination of the kind of object of interpretation it is. We cannot, by regarding a physical object or a painting determine that it does or does not answer to a single admissible interpretation. Whether you count a Marxist and a feminist interpretation as one or two interpretations depends not only upon addressing the kind of thing it is. Whether one should aggregate or pluralize interpretations or objects of interpretation is not settled by noting whether the object of interpretation is cultural. It depends upon local considerations of the practice. Whether you should count a given case as embodying one or more interpretations depends not solely on the nature of the object of interpretation. Its nature will not settle whether a singularist or multiplist condition obtains in a given case.

Even the ontology of Harrison and Hanna (which I endorse) offers no criterial way of identifying which particular objects of interpretation answer to singularism or to multiplism. Their practice-based account indicates where to look—to practices—for an answer to the piecemeal question whether a given object of interpretation does answer to singularism or to multiplism or to neither. Harrison and Hanna's constructive realism does not mandate the view that a given object of interpretation must answer to a singularist or multiplist condition. Once the object of interpretation is fixed within a practice there remains—as indicated by the relationality thesis—the open question of its relation to proffered interpretations.

Again, the point is that even after we indicate what we take the nature of a countable thing to be, we still do not have the grounds for deciding between singularism and multiplism. The grounds for such a decision are not provided by realism, constructivism, or constructive realism alone. Once you secure the identity of the object of interpretation it does not follow that either singularism or multiplism is uniquely entailed.

Yet, while the lean thesis of detachability concerns the non-entailment of singularism or multiplism from the inventoried ontologies, it does not follow that you ought not provide an ontology of objects of interpretation, nor that, more generally (contra Rorty), you should not engage in ontology. The relevance of ontology to theory of interpretation is found in fixing the identity or countability of an object of interpretation. Without such grounding, the question of singularism versus multiplism cannot arise. But the ontologies in question do not entail the choice of singularism over multiplism or multiplism over singularism. Weston mistakenly thinks that the detachability thesis denies the possibility of ontologizing *tout court.* But the detachability thesis does not say that you must remain agnostic about pertinent ontologies. It only affirms that none of them is uniquely entailed by either singularism or multiplism, and vice versa.

This point bears on the theory of objectivity, which Margolis challenges me to provide. On this occasion I can offer only desiderata for such a theory. The proposition, "Unsupported bodies drop at a rate of 32 feet per second squared" is objective in the sense that it is testable. An empirical method exists for determining if the proposition is false. Generally, objectivity concerns the grounds for separating or "triaging" false claims from the pool of considered claims. Realists, constructivists, and constructive realists alike can pursue that activity. They may agree about an objective method to triage distributive claims—claims concerning whether a given subject does or does not behave in a particular way—all the while disagreeing about the nature of the sort of thing it is. Accordingly, I suggest that a theory of objectivity should function at the methodological and not at the ontological level. Margolis finds this distinction unpalatable since he runs together methodology and ontology. In the last sentence of his essay he says:

> 'ideality' . . . cannot be anything but a piece of our ontological / epistemological / methodological / logical / semantic construction . . . (pp. 126–127).

Margolis also says: "In order for Krausz's argument to have any legs at all, it must be possible to separate ('detach') metaphysics ["ontology" in my idiom] and epistemology. Not only is that impossible, Krausz himself opposes the idea" (p. 126). Margolis misreads me. I do think that you should distinguish between ontology and epistemology. The grounds for asserting the distributive claim that horses but no unicorns exist are different from the account we might give of the nature of material beings. These are different sorts of enterprises. Put otherwise, a realist, constructivist, and a constructive realist can all agree that horses exist, and that unicorns do not; or that *Hamlet* is about a Danish prince and not a Bulgarian prince; or that *The Potato Eaters* is not about the World Trade Center attack of 11 September 2001. The issue of objectivity concerns the grounds for countenancing such distributive claims. But realism, constructivism, and constructive realism do not provide such grounds. Or, consider the example of the Holocaust. Some say that to deny realism, for example, is to deny the existence of the Holocaust. I say that the claim that the Holocaust happened does not commit you uniquely to realism, or uniquely to any of its alternative ontologies. The notion of "what happened" can be captured in different ways by any of these ontologies. Realists, constructivists, and constructive realists may agree that the Holocaust happened. That discussion is objective in the sense that each can agree to the evidence. Yet the disagreements between these ontologies is not at the evidential level. And the applicability of singularism versus multiplism is not at the ontological level, but at the praxial level. So Margolis mischaracterizes my position when he says that I oppose the idea of the separation between methodology and ontology.

Objectivity is a methodological matter. Such ontologies as realism, constructivism, and constructive realism have no resources to make the distributive discriminations that are required for triaging distributive claims. They do not provide a method of triage. The praxial grounds necessary for distinguishing between admissible and inadmissible claims commit us to no one of these particular ontologies. Interestingly, Margolis relents when he continues, "The dispute between singularists and multiplists is at least an epistemological and methodological dispute (to give Krausz his due); but if so, on the argument I am advancing, it can not fail to depend on metaphysical grounds as well—which Krausz denies" (p. 125). Again, not quite. Metaphysical or ontological issues are involved in fixing the identity or countability of objects of interpretation. But they do not help to choose between singularism and multiplism in designated cases. Nowhere does Margolis show how any of the considered ontologies as such help choose between singularism and multiplism.

8. Ontology

In accord with the detachability thesis RR and LR explicitly avoid endorsing any one ontology. Pressed by contributors, on this occasion I will make my ontological predilections explicit. Before doing so, I consider particular ontological claims of Margolis, McKenna, Grobstein, and Harrison and Hanna.

I have said that multiplism is not entailed by the indeterminacy of an object of interpretation, for it may be "matched" by a single indeterminate interpretation. Yet Margolis is puzzled by the idea of indeterminate objects and indeterminate interpretations. He says, "I cannot imagine ever speaking of real but indeterminate objects" (p. 122). He says further: "I take an 'indeterminate interpretation' to be no interpretation at all (or one we cannot make out); and an 'indeterminate object,' one that does not exist at all (or one we are inclined to believe is real but whose nature and existence we cannot quite make out)" (p. 122).

The sense of indeterminacy that I invoke is straightforward and is provided in *The Oxford English Dictionary* which defines "indeterminate" this way: "Not fixed in extent, number, character or nature; left uncertain as to limits of extent, number, etc; uncertain of size or character; indefinite, indistinct, uncertain."

Consider one construal of a swarm of bees. Bees themselves may have determinate boundary conditions, but swarms do not. Yet where the single interpretation recognizes that the boundary conditions of a swarm are indeterminate, a swarm of bees could answer to that single admissible interpretation. We could say that a swarm of bees is moving more or less at such and such a rate, and still count that claim as singularist. Just as swarms are indeterminate in the pertinent sense, the interpretation "that swarm is moving at more or less a fixed rate," or "that swarm looks more or less like a moving fish" is also indeterminate. Speaking of the object of interpretation as indeterminate or of the interpretation as indeterminate involves nothing mysterious. The indeterminacy is signaled by the "more or less" clause. A swarm exists and the indeterminate interpretation is an interpretation! Margolis manufactures a puzzle where none exists.

Yet Margolis does concede the possible reality of indeterminate objects after all when he says: "To exist is to be 'determinate' enough to do so! For instance, . . . an artwork or interpretation is determinate in 'number,' in the sense that it can be identified and re-identified" (p. 123). Margolis's allowance that something may be "determinate enough" suggests that on his account determinacy is a matter of degree. That is all my argument requires. Despite the indeterminacy of the swarm of bees, it may be identified and re-identified as the same swarm on different occasions. On my account, you can have an object, which is not fully determinate but determinate enough still to be counted as a single object. It can be, as Margolis himself says, "determinate in 'number' in the sense that it can be identified and re-identified." The swarm of bees may be counted as one swarm despite being indeterminate.

Here is a point on which I do stand corrected by Margolis. I have suggested that his pan-fluxism tends toward the conclusion that determinability as to nature entails determinability as to number. In response he says that ". . . that confuses reference and predication" (p. 123). I have said above that an indeterminate object may answer to a fixed number. You may alter particular properties of an object with no change in its number—as, for example, when some individual bees drop out of the swarm. So a change in its nature need not change its number. Margolis affirms that you can hold fixed the number of an object of interpretation while you may impute different properties to it. So long as you hold fixed the distinction between reference and predication, I should not worry (as I have) that Margolis's thesis of pan-fluxism tends toward the conclusion that determinability as to nature entails determinability as to number. I have come to agree with Margolis about this matter.

But, with our newly established agreement that with change of nature there need be no change in number, Margolis holds that that point decides between singularism and multiplism (p. 123). But it does not. Singularism and multiplism are ontologically constrained by the identity and countability conditions of a pertinent object of interpretation. But that is a far cry from saying that those constraints provide grounds for deciding between singularism and multiplism! The fixed number of the object of interpretation is a necessary condition for either singularism or multiplism. But it uniquely entails neither. That change in predication entails no change in reference or that a change in nature entails no change in number is compatible with realism, constructivism, or constructive realism. And, on account of the relationality thesis, whether we are talking about one or more than one object of interpretation, does not uniquely entail either a singularist or multiplist condition.

Margolis objects (as does McKenna) to my invoking Nelson Goodman's idea of world-making, as if I endorse it. But I invoke Goodman's idea of world-making not to propound it, but to offer it as a well-known example of a constructivist ontology that does not entail singularism or multiplism. Whether that ontology is in its terms "coherently adoptable" is another matter.

As regards the adoptability of Goodman's constructivism McKenna argues against Goodman in this way: "To say something about anything (including the world), it has to be said. Naturally, said things are said in languages. From these two morsels we are to move to the quite dubious point that no aspect of the world is free of the conventions of a symbol system or a conceptual scheme" (p. 134). McKenna is right that these "morsels" do not entail Goodman's constructivism. From Goodman's claim that the way things are is assertable only within a symbol system, it does not deductively follow that things are in no way independent of such symbol systems or practices. But from this conclusion not being entailed, it also does not follow that (as McKenna asserts) there is a differentiated way that things are independently of symbol systems or practices. Nor does it follow what that way is. These matters are left open. And this non-entailment does not mandate McKenna's so-called Plain Jane Metaphysics.

McKenna seeks to draw me out about the ontology that I do embrace above and beyond the confines of a theory of interpretation, however boundaries of the theory may be delineated. I have indicated my predilections to embrace a practice-centered ontology along the lines suggested by Harrison and Hanna, as appropriately qualified. Before taking up Harrison and Hanna's ontology, though, let us consider McKenna's realist ontology, and then Grobstein's.

First, McKenna seeks to disarm his readers by calling his realist ontology "Plain Jane Metaphysics," thereby suggesting that common sense is on his side. But McKenna's metaphysics has nothing plain about it. As he elaborates his view he is driven to rename it "Sophisticated Plain Jane Metaphysics." Jane turns out to be quite unplain.

McKenna seeks to ground his realist metaphysics in individuals located at the level of an "ultimate nature of reality" where, he says, ". . . we must make room for the notion of a countable, datable item, a particular, a thing, an entity—one of a possible many" (p. 130).

Further, McKenna takes it that individuals reside at the ultimate or most primitive level, where reality is taken to be cut at its joints, where kinds reside in their most un-analyzable states. Of course there are individual rocks, socks, and seagull flocks. I confess, though, that I can make no sense of the idea of an ultimate reality, and I see no reason to assume that individuals should reside in such an "ultimate nature of reality." My global anti-essentialism resists such a notion. I propose to retire it, and with it any temptation to ground individuals in it.

As well, the temptation to place "nature" (in contrast to "culture") in the "ultimate nature of reality" should be resisted. Crucial differences are to be found between natural and cultural individuals. But these kinds of individuals need not draw their credentials from a putatively privileged "ultimate nature of reality." The differences between such kinds of individuals do not constitute a difference in essentialist natural kinds that implicate an ultimate nature of reality, complete with independent joints waiting to be discovered.

But, we might ask, if we disallow the idea of an ultimate reality, what would happen to our ability to negotiate everyday life? Grant that biologists' and botanists' and physicists' and every-day pedestrians' descriptions differ according to respective interests. In everyday life we may pick out middle sized descriptions—say, of cars and trucks on busy streets—motivated by our interest to stay alive. But that does not mean that middle-sized descriptions are inherently more privileged than, say, the biologist's description or the botanist's descriptions or the physicist's descriptions.

Given his presumption of an ultimate reality, McKenna asserts that realism obtains in the natural domain and constructivism obtains in the artifactual or cultural domain. He draws a sharp distinction between nature and culture. In contrast, I suggest that the distinction between nature and culture cannot be made to fit or does not coincide with the distinction between realism and constructivism. Neither of these distinctions is exclusive, and the two distinctions are not coextensive. Accordingly, you cannot withhold realist commitments from the cultural domain, nor can you withhold constructivist commitments from the natural domain. In each domain realist and constructivist elements are characteristically mixed.

McKenna himself notes that natural elements are found in the cultural realm. "All artifacts have to have some natural constitutive basis. People perform plays on stages. Music requires acoustic excitations. Novels are realized on some paper. Poems, in conception, came from some thought, some brain. Chairs are made of wood, or other materials. Canvasses are made of something. . . . [T]he honored soul and the dumped baby were constituted out of the biological item, infant" (p. 141).

McKenna holds that you should make room for multiplism in the cultural domain. That is fine. But for that reason he countenances constructivism in the cultural domain. He does so on the mistaken assumption that constructivism entails multiplism. But it does not. A constructivist could well embrace singularism. The sort of multiplism that McKenna favors in the cultural realm is not insured by constructivism. Just as realism does not insure singularism, constructivism does not insure multiplism. The cultural realm has no monopoly on multiplist cases. Nor does the world of natural science or middle-sized objects have a monopoly on singularism.

That these domains are "mixed" as regards their objects' answering to singularism or multiplism constrains those who would be tempted to offer multiplism as a demarcation between the cultural and the natural realms. Some readers (notably David Norton) have taken multiplism to be a criterion for the cultural. Yet while multiplism is characteristic of the cultural realm, by no means is multiplism invariantly instantiated in the cultural realm. Both singularist and multiplist cases are to be found in both the cultural and the natural realms. Thus, multiplism cannot serve as a criterion of the cultural.

Note that the retirement of an essentialist "ultimate nature of reality" does not contravene all possible realisms. A realist may self-consistently deny the essentialist claim that an ultimate reality exists. There is no reason to tie realism to the thesis of an ultimate reality. Accordingly, we may still speak of "natural" kinds in a non-essentialist way. Rocks fall under a constructed category called "natural," and socks fall under another constructed category called "cultural." And the supposed "joint" between them is an emergent product of taxonomy. In this way, "made" and "found" are made compatible. The "made" may be as "real" as the "found." This point is lost on McKenna, who assumes that that which is made is not real. To say that what is found cannot also have been made is also wrong. There need be no exclusive disjunction between the constructed and the real, or between the made and the found.

While McKenna embraces multiplist realism, his realism is essentialist. He holds that essentialist objects of interpretation answer to more than one incongruent description. McKenna deploys David Wiggins's metaphor of differently sized fishing nets that you cast into the sea, some with finer weavings, others with courser weavings. The metaphor prompts McKenna to posit a prior essentialist nature of that which is caught in a given casting. Yet the metaphor leaves open the possibility that the nature of that which is caught might be a function of a prior construction. It leaves open the possibility that kinds are enacted, allowing that kinds are real. The products of such casting need not be unreal. It also leaves open the possibility that that which is arranged into kinds pre-existed before any given casting. But no "ultimate nature of reality" need be posited.

Let us consider the ontology, which Grobstein associates with his neurological findings. As already noted, Grobstein affirms a kind of realism which holds that the real is constructed in the brain. More fully, Grobstein asserts that, to a scientist, understandings are always "summaries of experiences," and, at least in principle, multiple admissible ways of summarizing a given set of observations can always be found. He takes it that the multiplicity of understandings follows from the brain being a multiplist organ. Further, since the brain cannot presume to have access to anything beyond its products, it cannot presume that reality is beyond its pictures. As Grobstein says, ". . . the brain does not know that reality exists out there, and so it cannot, without reservations, assume that it itself has been designed (by evolution) to paint pictures of it" (p. 160). According to Grobstein what the brain produces is all that exists.

But Grobstein runs together two claims. First is the "idealist" claim of our inability to know a "reality" beyond our perceptions. ("To be is to be perceived.") Second is the claim (in accord with his neurological findings) that, for a would-be world independent of our perceptions, given the neurological constraints of the brain, it cannot be singularly grasped. These are two quite distinct claims. While the second claim may be defensible (and I do not say that it is) the first is not.

Grobstein's position has further difficulties. Grobstein takes the brain to be a material thing. He does not explicitly say that the material brain must also be a product of the brain, but the claim is entailed by his thesis. But then how can a brain be a product of itself? And whose brain is it that produces the brain? And what is the status of materiality?

Finally, there remains the question of criticism and the growth of scientific knowledge. Ironically, Grobstein's remarks about criticism accord more with someone who embraces the kind of external realist ontology that he himself resists. Grobstein says: "Progress in science has instead always been measured in terms of distance from ignorance. Science proceeds not by proving truth or reality but by disproving falsity, not by painting the right picture but by painting a picture less wrong than prior pictures. [And that] . . . is the basis of the demonstrable power of science" (p. 162).

Notice that Grobstein's negativist epistemology (with which I agree) is quite distinct from his world-as-pictured-by-the brain hypothesis. When

Grobstein talks about the movement from ignorance he would need some way to account for the notion of falsity (in contrast to truth) fully in terms of the painting that the brain paints. He rules out the realist account of falsity in terms of the non-correspondence between propositions and the way the world is. The notion of the way the world is has no place in Grobstein's account. So an alternative account of falsity is required. But he does not provide one. The claim that "the world" is a product of the brain and is limited to the brain precludes the conceptual space required for criticism of the contents of hypotheses about the world.

Grobstein's ontology also precludes the possibility of giving a coherent account of the aims of cognitive inquiry above and beyond what the material brain contingently produces. His ontology provides no conceptual space to ask such normative questions as to why you should pursue astronomy over astrology. If such issues are settled exclusively in terms of the products of the brain, then normative questions cannot even arise.

But, I affirm, a world exists "out there." And its status requires a nuanced accounting, neither along the lines of McKenna nor of Grobstein. That the world reveals itself only in commerce with practices is the view of Harrison and Hanna. So I turn to consider their ontology with which I associate myself in broad outlines. I say "broad" to signal my reservation (discussed earlier) with that part of their treatment that asserts that singularism and multiplism may be jointly instantiated. That reservation aside, we should note at the outset that Harrison and Hanna's practice-centered ontology entails neither singularism nor multiplism.

Harrison and Hanna agree with two of my central claims, namely, as they put them, "(1) that realism and constructivism are not exclusive alternatives, but admit combination in several versions of constructive realism; and (2) that neither realism nor constructivism, nor any version of the two, entails either singularism or multiplism" (p. 93).

We should consider the terms in which Harrison and Hanna understand themselves to be "external constructive realists." They are not the terms in which "constructive realism" is articulated in LR. Both internal and external constructive realism as defined in LR accord with Putnam's terms, and they assume that objecthood and existence are internal to a pertinent symbol system. What, in those terms, distinguishes internal from external constructive realism is that the external version affirms that presystematic "stuff" is there, yet without countenancing that it exists. (McKenna mistakenly characterizes the distinction (p. 132). The challenge facing the external constructive realist is to make sense of the stuff being there without countenancing its existence in the only sense available, namely an internal sense. No clear way to do this has been shown.

R. C. Pradhan ramifies my treatment of the distinction between internal and external constructive realism. He indicates that LR formulates those versions in terms provided by Putnam who holds objects are internal to a conceptual framework or symbol system. For Putnam, objects as such do not appear external to conceptual frameworks. That is one reason why Putnam calls his view internal realism. At the same time, I have characterized Putnam as an external constructive realist because he also posits (or at least allows the possibility) that there is stuff not countenanced as objects and also not countenanced as existing independent of or preceding conceptual schemes.

But, again, constructive realism need not be formulated in these Putnamian terms. We get a different conception in the proposal of Harrison and Hanna who allow that objects are constructed within practices. And they are external constructive realists in the sense that they hold that those practices are practices upon an independent world. They offer a tripartite distinction among world, practices, and symbol systems, emphasizing the practice-relativity of singularism and multiplism. Their approach is best seen, again, in the context of their central example.

Harrison and Hanna affirm that there can be no appeal to the length of a physical object, for example, independent of some method of measurement or "modulus" as they call it. You don't just need a modulus to measure. You cannot make sense of the notion of the length of an object independently of a pertinent modulus. They say, "Absent a modulus in terms of which O is to be measured, the question cannot be answered" (p. 99).

In accord with their tripartite distinction, Harrison and Hanna take physical objects to "exist prior to the institution of any symbol system." While such objects predate symbol systems, they do not predate practices. As objects, they do not exist prior to practices. What then is the stuff to which pertinent moduli apply? The stuff is a world that is "conceptually undifferentiated" but not "praxially undifferentiated." Harrison and Hanna state their core thesis this way:

> In a sense, the world prior to the institution of linguistic practices *is* "ineffable," but only in the sense that, as yet, nothing can be said of it. That world is not "ineffable" in the sense of "unknowable," for it is already richly knowable as a realm of outcomes, and its characteristics *qua* realm of outcomes are precisely what will determine what propositions we will find to be true or false of it when we are sufficiently equipped with linguistic practices to have a use for such notions as propositions, truth, and falsity (p. 102).

In an unpublished correspondence this is how Hanna ramifies the thesis:

> . . . the world as it exists prior to the introduction of . . . practice, is indeed, in one sense, "undifferentiated." It is, let us say, conceptually undifferentiated. But that is not at all to say that it is undifferentiated with respect to the practical techniques and manipulations that connect the

practice to it. On the contrary, the world as it exists prior to the institution of the practice is replete with the sort of structure that reveals itself to optical, manual, auditory, or other manipulation. It is not, in other words, praxially undifferentiated. It makes sense to think of the world relative to practical techniques, including techniques of measurement, as, in effect, a realm of outcomes. . . . Such a realm will deliver the same outcome in response to a given manipulation in wholly reliable ways, ways reliable, that is, from observer to observer, given equal accuracy in the conduct of the manipulation in question.[4]

In sum, I agree with Harrison and Hanna's practice-centered ontology, including their tripartite distinction between world, practice, and symbol system. I agree with their external constructive realism, cast in such terms in which (contra Putnam) existence is not taken to be internal to practices or symbol systems. Finally, notice that their ontology—along with others rehearsed in LR—accords with the thesis of detachability. It uniquely entails neither singularism nor multiplism. Their ontology also accords with the thesis of relationality.

9. Applications

Several contributors have addressed themselves to applications of the distinctions and strategies that I have rehearsed so far. V. A. Rao, Krassimir Stojanov, and Ritivoi address issues concerning cross cultural interpretation and transition. Chaturvedi addresses issues concerning religious interpretation. And Pandit addresses the interpretation of music. I will address each in turn.

I have suggested that while no overarching standards of adjudication between cultures are available, it does not follow that there can be no way to compare and contrast pertinent considerations. Nor, more pointedly, does it follow that no conversational space can be forged between them, space in which dialogue concerning mutual interests and shared values can be found and fostered. Given our empathetic ability to imagine ourselves in the situation of others, we may understand cultures other than our "home" culture, and we may assess them (inevitably) from the perspective of our home culture.

Rao is correct to observe that I do not go so far as to nest such an ability in some universal and necessary condition of humanness. Attempts at articulating such a notion are characteristically marred by a level of abstraction that tends to render them void of content. An inverse relationship holds between the degree of universality of candidate commonalities and their content. But to characterize my view as ethnocentric in an unqualified sense is misleading.

I allow for and encourage the emergence of ever growing conversational spaces between diverse cultures and their practices. In this regard I follow

Jitendra Mohanty who proposes a conversational model of communication.[5]
Mohanty says:

> The overcoming of relativism . . . cannot consist in that *violent* act by
> which one validity-claim imperiously supersedes all others but shall
> rather consist in that gentle and tolerant view which recognizes that
> unity is always in the process of being achieved by communication and
> is just too fragile to be sustained by any violence. The world-in-itself is
> rather a regulative idea that guides communication and translation. To
> elevate any world, scientific or religious, to the status of absolute is to
> fall into the trap of relativistic arguments: the "other" would remain un-
> convinced, and communication and internal criticism would be closed
> off . . . It is in this idea of "overlapping" and "emergence" of identity,
> rather than its imposition through a metaphysical essentialism (as
> through political absolutism) that rationality is seen in operation.

In her terms, Ritivoi ramifies the conversational model. She and Mohanty agree that no universal standards exist (in contrast with informal considerations) to which we can appeal. Yet we can find crucial resources for
conversational discourse, and such discourse is improvisational and inherently informal. Such resources provide the basis for piecemeal bridge-
building. This view allows for the emergence of local grounds for consensus,
itself in historical flux as cross-cultural conversations proceed. The denial of
necessary and universal (timeless, immutable) standards does not disallow
grounds for cross cultural understanding and normative assessment *tout
court*. But Rao worries: "If knowledge exists not in its own right but as a
form of socio-cognitive process, owing its existence to social structures and
institutions, and if no standard or process of evaluation is higher than the 'as-
cent of the relevant community' (Kuhn's phrase), interpretation will be at the
mercy of 'contexts' and without a normative criterion" (p. 174). Yet my denial that there need be an operative standard of adjudication between cultures
need not result in an absence of normativity. A process of evaluation exists
that is conversational and informal. But to tie its credentials to an essentialist,
necessary, and universal standard is a mistake.

In the spirit of Rao, Stojanov invites me to extend my account of interpretation to include a theory of morality. Again, in this context, I can offer
only desiderata for such a theory, ones in keeping with my theory of interpretation. Stojanov says: "Unlike aesthetic objects, which are unique, moral
norms tend to be universal: moral agents normally claim that what they hold
for right is right in itself and applies to all human beings" (p. 219). Stojanov
distinguishes the aesthetic domain from the moral domain when he asserts
universalism for the moral domain but not the aesthetic domain. In contrast, I
am impressed by the aesthetic and the moral domains being more on a par
than Stojanov supposes. Both domains are marked by characteristic cases of

inconclusivity and non-universality. Interesting moral cases characteristically display an absence of overarching standards or universal principles that would adjudicate between contending verdicts. Those cases might include such conflicts as between some Palestinians and Israelis whose interpretations of their common situation radically differ. Or those cases might include debates over abortion or euthanasia. But, again, notice that my concerns about a universalist morality do not disallow creative efforts toward piecemeal bridge building in the context of conversational space. While I favor a strategy that "tends toward" the construction of ever more general norms, I find no reason to presume that such a tendency should converge upon universal moral principles or standards.

Stojanov embraces a realism that he thinks is entailed by the requirement that persons must be recognized as real or existing. He thinks you must assume a realist understanding of persons in order for you to engage with other persons. He says, "The constitution of the self still requires a realistic concept of the existence of other persons" (p. 221). But—as I have argued in RR and LR—the claim that something is real does not mandate realism. To say that persons with whom we relate in moments of mutual recognition must be assumed to be real does not mandate realism. Constructivists or constructive realists could just as well acknowledge the reality of engaged persons.

Further, as Charles Taylor notes, no pre-existent autonomous self exists awaiting interpretation. Rather, selves are self-interpreting and perpetually self-made.[6] For Taylor, the interpreted self is not an autonomous substantive "object" that precedes interpretive activity, but is constituted in interpretation. Accordingly, Stojanov says: "Selves are constituted as ends-in-themselves in relations of intersubjective recognition. Every such end-in-itself exists only as a point on the intersubjective net. It occurs within the process of moral deliberation" (p. 222).

I agree with Stojanov's implication that human rights and cognate notions are dialogical achievements, and that they are ineliminably tied to constituting cultural practices. Yet the on-going conversational project of bridge-building requires no universalist assumption that such notions as rights capture a fact of the matter quite independent of pertinent practices. That means that rights are a matter of perpetual re-constitution and not a "once-and-for-all" discovery.

Rao disagrees. Consistent with his Kantianism, he thinks that there must be a convergence toward pre-existent universal conditions common to all cultures and persons. Mine is a convergence that demands no singularist resolution. I reach for bridge building as a work perpetually in progress, one that builds and builds upon instead of discovers pre-existing commonalities. In contrast, Rao says: "However much the rules informing the moral code differ from culture to culture, a common thread runs through them: an implicit acknowledgement of a relation between the 'sensible' and the 'intelligible' worlds" (p. 177). The difficulty is to locate and properly characterize the common thread without inflating its ontological pretenses.

I turn to consider Ritivoi's treatment of personal programs and their relation to cultural transition. RR elucidates personal programs as stories that you tell yourself about your present place in relation to your past and your projected future, informed by your aims and interests. They are stories in which you place yourself to orient yourself to yourself as you live your life through its different stages. These stories are retold periodically for self-orientation, planning, and constituting. Ritivoi develops the notion of a personal program as deployed in cultural transition—when you go through cultural change both within and between cultures. She is motivated by the thought that multiplism is especially conducive for the interpretation of the culture that you leave and the culture that you adopt. Further, on her account, multiplism is especially conducive for the interpretation, constitution and edification of the self that is in transit within and between cultures.

If we understand the self as socially constituted, and if a shift occurs in the culture that constitutes the self, then the self is differently constituted and differently interpretable. Whether such a shift amounts to multiplism is an open question, for you might affirm—in pluralizing fashion—that in such a transition newly constituted selves could answer to serially singularist conditions. Yet we may under characteristic circumstances allow that the "self-same" self is in transition, perhaps in part because of the consistency of the autobiographical personal program in question.

Ritivoi's view resounds with Moore's thought that multiplism is especially conducive to cognitive dexterity. The ability to see things from another person's point of view is enhanced by multiplism. Yet, again, a singularist could agree with Moore that we ought to be tolerant, that we ought to be open to seeing a situation from different points of views so as to understand another person or another culture, and still affirm that one and only one admissible interpretation of a given situation is to be found. Cognitive dexterity is not uniquely tied to multiplism. This sort of singularist response could be offered to Ritivoi as well; namely, equipping someone for cultural transition might be just as well served by singularism as by multiplism. A singularist might hold that you should be aware of the differences between the culture that you are leaving and the new culture that you are adopting. A singularist might affirm that you should be aware of the constituting affects of such transitions on the self that is in transit. Yet such awareness does not disallow that one and only one admissible interpretation of the exited culture, the adopted culture, and the exiting self and the transited self, are available.

No unique entailment holds between multiplism and the edificatory resources that both Ritivoi and Moore seek from multiplism. Yet such non-entailment does not disallow a softer relationship between multiplism and pertinent edificatory resources. Multiplism may especially promote edificatory conditions conducive for transiting selves. A demonstration of such a promotion from Ritivoi or Moore would be significant.

Turning to the justification of personal programs, Ritivoi is puzzled by a passage (RR, p. 85) that suggests that the standards for admissibility of a particular move within your life program are internal to personal programs. Correspondingly, she asks how the transition to new personal programs and projects takes place, if the change is supposed to be radical and if indeed incommensurable standards of evaluation make programs incongruent.

Ritivoi is right to observe that—despite "inner necessities" presenting themselves without regard to moral approbation and that they may be integral ingredients to personal programs—the justification of a personal program as such cannot only be internal. While a move within a program is keyed to values internal to it, justification of the program as such involves considerations external to it. But such considerations need not amount to standards in a strong sense of "principles" for the conclusive adjudication between personal programs, as the directional singularist requires. What is required, as Ritivoi herself suggests, is a framework for critical discussion much needed for an identity emerging from one epoch into another, and from one cultural space into another. According to her, narrative opens a space in which a person can "converse" with himself, scrutinize the interpretation and consider potential alternatives, and in so doing, take hold of experiences and assume responsibility for the past, as well as choose life paths and make decisions for the future. In this critical space the person articulates an "internal rhetoric" that can differentiate opportune from opportunistic moves. Understanding and responding to a situation does not mean only satisfying immediate interests. It also means grasping the larger significance of the situation, including its possible consequences and moral import.

By emphasizing "internal rhetoric" Ritivoi signals that the moral consideration of personal programs concerns not so much the search for universal standards that would univocally adjudicate between one personal program over others. What is needed is the dialogical space in which informal considerations can be deliberated by the transiting self. So when she asks on what kind of grounds can such a critical discussion be carried out, we should not assume Ritivoi is asking for standards that would univocally adjudicate between moves within a given personal program or between programs. Instead, she is concerned with the dialogical space in which pertinent judgments can be intelligibly pursued. In contrast to Rao and Stojanov, she does not set justificatory demands unrealistically high.

Let us consider the bearing of our interpretive concerns on the case of religious belief and experience. Different religious traditions affirm that the "Undifferentiated Unity" or "Mysterium Tremendum" (as Chaturvedi references them) cannot be spoken of in a direct way, since it both answers to all predicates and is also beyond predication. If something is beyond predication, then it can be no object of interpretation, for it cannot be individuated and counted. In that sense, something beyond predication is beyond the "limits of interpretation," and beyond the "limits of rightness." At the same time, Chaturvedi holds that you should treat religious language cognitively, and not fully reducible to expressions of feelings or emotions. "[A]ny attempt to treat religious language in its entirety as purely non-cognitive is unsatisfactory. . . . [P]utative assertions about God, creation, and so forth cannot be said to be merely expressions of feelings or commitments to particular moral principles or to a particular way of life" (p. 304).

In contrast, Chaturvedi rehearses the Wittgensteinian non-cognitivist approach.

> He [Wittgenstein] repeatedly warns against treating a religious belief as a scientific hypothesis. In his view, "believing" in religious contexts is a matter of having particular "pictures" that guide and regulate the thinking and life of the believer. . . . For Wittgenstein believing in the context of religion is a matter of adopting particular practices and living in a certain way (pp. 309–310).

Wittgenstein takes religious belief not as a matter of cognitive assertion but as "a picture" to aid in the pursuit of your life path. Accordingly, whether my religious belief is better than yours depends upon whether mine is better able to "guide and regulate the thinking and life of the believer." According to such an understanding, no cognitive conflict exists between the so-called atheist and the believer. That difference arises only for cognitivists. Chaturvedi says:

> Wittgenstein points out that a nonbeliever does not contradict a believer. The believer does not accept something to be true that the nonbeliever contradicts. They are on different planes, they live differently and the pictures that regulate the believer's life have no role in a nonbeliever's life. . . . [D]ifferent religious views should not be treated as rival theories about the same reality (p. 310).

Yet Chaturvedi disagrees with Wittgenstein. She holds that the cognitivity of religious claims is ineliminable. Even though particular practices might play the pictorial role that Wittgenstein suggests, it remains that such a role cannot fully capture religious belief.

When Chaturvedi turns her attention to religious experience, the issue of sameness of object of interpretation rises again. "To allow the possibility that different people may interpret the same kind of experience differently is reasonable. . . . [Yet] in the case of religious experiences you can challenge the contention that different people had the same kind of experiences" (p. 306)

Is that which diverse interpreters of religious experience the same? How can you tell? One issue is whether the terms deployed by different religious traditions implicate the nature of their objects of interpretation—in which case different religious traditions would be talking about different things. Experiences of "undifferentiated unity" or the "mysterium" might be of different things. And if they are of different things then there would be no competition between different interpretations.

Chaturvedi notes, though, that universality is a characteristic presupposition of religious language. Yet such a presupposition is problematic, for it assumes that the object of interpretation for different religious traditions is the same. The notion of "undifferentiated unity" or the "Mysterium" resists the sort of individuation or countability required to make a judgment about sameness at all!

Chaturvedi notes that Radhakrishnan adopts a transcendental approach to the unity of all religions (p. 308). To do so, he must presuppose that all religions are talking about the same thing, that they have in mind the "same" soteriological condition of realization or its cognates. But, again, to certify a claim of universality would require that different religious traditions address the same object of interpretation. But there appears to be no way of judging the matter. And if you have no grounds for fixing the identity conditions of the object of interpretation, you cannot apply the interpretive ideals of singularism or multiplism to start with.

A still deeper puzzle lies here. The distinction between interpretation and its objects is a dualism that is resisted in both Hindu and Buddhist moments of realization, for example. The Hindu and Buddhist set for themselves the aim of realizing themselves. Yet both of their soteriologies seek resolution in the overcoming of duality—precisely what is involved in setting a goal for yourself. Doing so would reinstall the offending duality. That means that in the state of realization, interpreting realization is disallowed.

Yet post-dictively, after the "equipoise," you might tell a story about the "experience" of realization that was had. That story-telling would involve the re-installation of the subject-object duality. In the retelling, the subject would be said to have "had" an experience, and perhaps even tell of headway made in the project of self-realization. Yet a falsification occurs in the re-telling, for it must re-install the subject-object duality. But it would be a mistake to say that self-realization altogether cannot be taken on as a project. To say that at pertinent stages you cannot assert that you are pursuing a soteriological project is one thing. To say that self-realization is not a phase of a soteriological project is another.

More pointedly, Chaturvedi cites Swami Vivekananda whose view of realization disallows a condition necessary for the judgment of commonality of soteriological objects of interpretation. He disallows a condition necessary for the application of singularism or multiplism. Chaturvedi reports that, according to Vivekananda, "the ultimate aim of life is the realization of the *Brahman* where all consciousness of diversity and multiplism is negated" (p. 308). Vivekananda seeks to transcend all dualisms. Where such realization obtains there can be no distinction between interpretation and its objects, common or not. Further, as regards aims of interpretation, there can be no distinction between elucidation and edification. So understood, the pursuit of elucidation in contrast with edification (or vice versa) could only be sustained at a stage intermediary to the ultimate condition of realization. Interpretive activity altogether, on this view, can be keyed only to a consciousness not fully realized.

Finally, Chaturvedi leaves us with the conundrum of the simultaneous particularity and universality of religious experience. She summarizes "the dilemma faced by the modern mind" in the following way:

> [I]t cannot be denied that human beings share a common form of life. It makes sense to talk of a human way of life, which involves shared patterns of acting and being in a shared natural environment in which they live. This human form of life at the same time admits of differences within it, which refer to different particular ways of conceptualizing human experience and associated behavior patterns and actions. How to reconcile the recognition of this commonality and sharing of environment and a way of life with the diversity of interpretations along with their varying ontological commitments is a question that eludes an easy answer (pp. 310–311).

Let us return to the case of music. In his treatment Pandit connects religious issues with musical consciousness. He does so in terms of the Hindu tradition. Pandit says: "Musical works . . . belong to a higher plane of life, or of consciousness, making an implicate order, which I have called musical consciousness" (pp. 301–302).

Pandit understands musical consciousness in terms of what he calls the "zone of silence," or "a deep state of meditation." He says: "Meditative state and timelessness make for a useful metaphor in this context, since they convey an understanding of the dissolution of external time in which the external world appears to us as an object" (p. 297).

According to Pandit, the zone of silence cannot be captured by the categories of Karl Popper's three worlds, namely: World 1: physical states; World 2: mental or subjective states; World 3: objective contents of thoughts. Instead, Pandit dubs "World 4" the world in which the zone of silence is situated. This world of "pure consciousness" is not reducible to any or all of Popper's three worlds. All individuals arise from the world of the Brahman or the Hindu Source and "seek to return" to it. Musical consciousness arises from this world and seeks to return to it. Accordingly, Pundit asks: "Is it not appropriate to take . . . music as a passage of time from the origin to the destination and from the destination back to the origin?" (p. 301). Pandit asks: "Do not the work of music, the artist-listener and the musical instrument—*tout ensemble*—again and again remind us of the original text, to which all music approximates but which is authorless, or too deep and fathomable for words?" (p. 299).

Pandit takes the Source to be invariant, universal, timeless and immutable. He embraces the idea that, "Being an artist-composer is being . . . in search of a spiritual unity with the *Urtext*, absolute music itself, or pure music" (p. 297). Pandit understands the Hindu Brahman, the Source, as an essentialist Urtext.

At this crucial juncture we confront the divide between Hinduism and Buddhism. Contrary to Pandit's Hindu conception, the Buddhist affirms "that things have only one nature, i.e. no nature."[7] They are empty of inherent existence. The Buddhist denies all inherent existents and Urtexts. The Buddhist would deny Pandit's zone of silence as understood in terms of the essentialist Hindu Brahman. With this confrontation we return to our concern about the identity of that to which the Hindu and the Buddhist address themselves. Is it the case that the Hindu and the Buddhist are talking about the same thing? In the course of my reflections about this motivating example, I have come to conclude that neither have solid grounds to make judgments of sameness of that to which they point. Consequently, the question of its singular or multiple interpretability cannot arise. The question is beyond the limits of rightness.

Finally, I extend profound thanks to all the contributors to this volume. They have substantially advanced the project upon which I have been embarked. Also, it is with pleasure that I acknowledge editor Andreea Deciu Ritivoi, without whose tireless efforts this volume would not have come to fruition. I am also grateful to Giridhari Lal Pandit who organized and chaired an international conference in relation to my philosophical work in January 2001 in Delhi, India.

NOTES

1. See Bellini's "St. Francis" (New York, Frick Art Museum), "The Dead Christ and an Angel in Scarlet" (London, National Gallery), "Christ Carrying the Cross" (Collection of Duke Louis de Brissac), or "The Pieta" (Venice, Academy). Reproduced in Philip Hendy and Ludwig Goldscheider, *Giovanni Bellini* (Oxford: Phaidon Press, 1945).

2. Hilary Putnam, *Realism With a Human Face* (Cambridge: Harvard University Press, 1990), p. 129.

3. See Peter Lamarque, "Comments on Michael Krausz's *Limits of Rightness*," *Interpretation and Culture: Themes in the Philosophy of Michael Krausz*, ed. Michael McKenna, Special Issue of *Philosophy in the Contemporary World*, forthcoming.

4. See Bernard Harrison and Patricia Hanna, *Word and World: Practice and the Foundations of Language* (Cambridge: Cambridge University Press, forthcoming).

5. See Jitendra N. Mohanty, "Phenomenological Rationality and the Overcoming of Relativism," *Relativism: Interpretation and Confrontation*, ed. Michael Krausz (Notre Dame: Notre Dame University Press, 1989), pp. 336–338.

6. Charles Taylor, *Philosophy and the Human Sciences: Philosophical Papers*, Vol. 2 (Cambridge: Cambridge University Press, 1985), pp. 26–27.

7. Quoted in *The Fundamental Wisdom of the Middle Way: Nagarjuna's Mulamadhyakakarika*, trans. and com. Jay L. Garfield (New York; Oxford: Oxford University Press, 1995), p. 356.

SELECTED BIBLIOGRAPHY
OF MICHAEL KRAUSZ

Books

Limits of Rightness (Lanham, Md.: Rowman & Littlefield Publishing Co., 2000).

Varieties of Relativism (with Rom Harré) (Oxford: Basil Blackwell Publishing Co., 1995).

Rightness and Reasons: Interpretation in Cultural Practices (Ithaca: Cornell University Press, 1993).

Editor, *Is There A Single Right Interpretation?* (University Park: Pennsylvania State University Press, 2002).

Editor, *Interpretation, Relativism and the Metaphysics of Culture* (with Richard Shusterman) (Amherst, N. Y.: Humanity Books, 1999).

Editor, *The Interpretation of Music: Philosophical Essays* (Oxford: Clarendon Press, 1993).

Editor, *Jewish Identity* (with David Goldberg) (Philadelphia: Temple University Press, 1993).

Editor, *Relativism: Interpretation and Confrontation* (Notre Dame: Notre Dame University Press, 1989).

Editor, *Rationality, Relativism and the Human Sciences* (with Joseph Margolis and Richard Burian) (The Hague: Martinus Nijhoff Publishers, 1986).

Editor, *Relativism: Cognitive and Moral* (with Jack W. Meiland) (Notre Dame: Notre Dame University Press, 1982).

Editor, *The Concept of Creativity in Science and Art* (with Denis Dutton) (The Hague: Martinus Nijhoff Publishers, 1981).

Editor, *Critical Essays on the Philosophy of R. G. Collingwood* (Oxford: The Clarendon Press, 1972).

Articles and Chapters

"The Logic of Absolute Presuppositions," *Critical Essays on the Philosophy of R. G. Collingwood*, Michael Krausz, ed. (Oxford: The Clarendon Press, 1972, pp. 222–240.

"Relativism and Rationality," *American Philosophical Quarterly* 10:4 (October 1973), pp. 307–312.

"Popper's Objective Knowledge," *Dialogue* 13 (June, 1974), pp. 347–351.

"Vision, Creation, and Object," *Proceedings of the 10th Conference on Value Theory*, Ervin Laszlo and James B. Wilbur, eds. (Geneseo, N. Y.: State University College at Geneseo, 1979), 32–49.

"A Painter's View of Self-Development and Creativity," *Leonardo* 13:2 (Spring 1980), pp. 143–145.

"Historical Explanation, Re-enactment, and Practical Inference," *Metaphilosophy* 11:2 (April 1980), pp. 143–154.

"Creating and Becoming," *The Concept of Creativity in Science and Art*, Denis Dutton and Michael Krausz, eds. (The Hague: Martinus Nijhoff Publishers, 1981), pp. 187–200.

"Ferrater-Mora's Continuum," *Transparencies: Philosophical Essays in Honor of J. Ferrater-Mora*, Priscilla Cohn, ed. (New York: Humanities Press, 1981), pp. 91–95.

"Relativism and Foundationalism: Some Distinctions and Strategies," *The Monist* 67:3 (July 1984), pp. 395–404.

"The Tonal and the Foundational: Ansermet on Stravinsky," *The Journal of Aesthetics and Art Criticism* 42:4 (Summer 1984), pp. 383–386.

"Product and Progress in Artistic Creativity," *Kultura* (Michael Mitias, ed., Belgrade, Yugoslavia) 64 (1984), pp. 64–70.

"Art and Its Mythologies: A Relativist View," *Rationality, Relativism, and the Human Sciences* Joseph Margolis, Michael Krausz, and Richard Burian, eds. (The Hague: Martinus Nijhoff Publishers, 1986), pp. 189–208.

"Intentionality, Expressive Properties, and Popper's Placement of Music," *Manuscrito* (Marcelo Dascal, ed., Sao Paulo, Brazil) 9:2 (October 1986), pp. 65–76.

"Interpretation and Its Art Objects: Two Views," *The Monist* 73:2 (April 1990), pp. 222–232.

"Ideality and Ontology in the Practice of History," *Objectivity, Method and Point of View,* ed. W. J. Van der Dussen and L. Rubinoff (Leiden: E. J. Brill Publishers, 1991), pp. 97–111.

"Crossing Cultures: Two Universalisms and Two Relativisms," *Cultural Relativism and Philosophy,* ed. Marcelo Dascal (Leiden: E. J. Brill Publishers, 1991), pp. 233–242.

"History and Its Objects," *The Monist* 74:2 (April 1991), pp. 217–229.

"Intention and Interpretation: Hirsch and Margolis," *Intention and Interpretation,* ed. Gary Iseminger (Philadelphia: Temple University Press, 1992), pp. 152–166.

"Culturas encontradas: dos universalismos y dos relativismos," *Relativismo Cultural Y Filosofia,* ed. Marcelo Dascal (Mexico City: Universidad Nacional Autonoma De Mexico, 1992), pp. 315–327.

"Culture and the "Ontology" of Music: Margolis' Anarchic Reconstruction," *Iyyun: The Jerusalem Philosophical Quarterly* 42 (January 1993), pp. 165–179.

"Introduction," *The Interpretation of Music: Philosophical Essays,* ed. Michael Krausz (Oxford: Clarendon Press, 1993), pp. 1–6.

"Rightness and Reasons in Musical Interpretation," *The Interpretation of Music: Philosophical Essays,* ed. Michael Krausz (Oxford: Clarendon Press, 1993), pp. 75–87.

"R. G. Collingwood's Aesthetics," *Companion to Aesthetics,* ed. David E. Cooper (Oxford: Basil Blackwell Publishing Co., 1993), pp. 75–78.

"The Culture of Identity" (with David Goldberg), *Jewish Identity,* ed. David Goldberg and Michael Krausz (Philadelphia: Temple University Press, 1993), pp. 1–12.

"On Being Jewish," *Jewish Identity*, ed. David Goldberg and Michael Krausz (Philadelphia: Temple University Press, 1993), pp. 264–278.

"Three Meditations on Oneness: Conversations with My Selves," *Journal of the Indian Council of Philosophical Research* 12:3 (May–August 1995), pp. 39–96.

"Interviews With Ven. Lobsang Gyatso," *Journal of Indian Philosophy and Religion* 1 (1996), pp. 104–134.

"On the Idea of the Single Right Interpretation in History," *Journal of Indian Council of Philosophical Research,* Special Issue (June 1996), pp. 57–66.

"Relativism and Beyond: In Tribute to Bimal Matilal," *Relativism, Suffering and Beyond: Essays in Memory of Bimal K. Matilal,* ed. P. Bilimoria and J. N. Mohanty (Delhi: Oxford University Press, 1997), pp. 93–104.

"Choosing What One Is Cut Out To Be," *Epistemology, Meaning and Metaphysics After Matila,* (Studies in Humanities and Social Sciences), ed. Arindam Chakrabarti (Shimla, India: Indian Institute for Advanced Studies, 1997), pp. 185–199.

"Changing One's Mind, Changing One's Emotions: An Intercultural Perspective" *Philosophy From an Intercultural Perspective,* ed. Notker Schneider, Dieter Lohmar, Morteza Ghasepour, and Herman-Josef Scheidgen, (Amsterdam and Atlanta: Rodopi Publishers, 1997), pp. 107–120.

"Interview with Lobsang Gyatso" *Journal of Indian Philosophy and Religion* 2 (October, 1997), pp. 43–87.

"Rightness and Reasons: A Reply to Stecker," *Journal of Aesthetics and Art Criticism* 55:4 (Fall 1997), pp. 415–418.

"Interpretation," *Encyclopedia of Aesthetics,* vol. 2, ed. Michael Kelly (New York and Oxford: Oxford University Press, 1998), pp. 520–523.

"The Interpretation of Art: Comments on Multiplism and Relativism," *JTLA* (Journal of the Faculty of Letters, The University of Tokyo, Aesthetics) 22 (1997), pp. 33–42.

"Two Aims of Cultural Interpretation: Explaining and Healing," *Einheit und Vielfalt,* ed. Notkar Schneider, R.A. Mall, und Dieter Lohmar. (Amsterdam: Rodopi Publishers, 1998), pp. 133–144.

"Interpretation, Relativism and Culture: Four Questions for Margolis", *Interpretation, Relativism and the Metaphysics of Culture*, ed. M. Krausz and R. Shusterman (Amherst, N. Y.: Humanity Press, 1999), pp. 105–124.

"Interpretation and Its 'Metaphysical' Entanglements," *Metaphilosophy* 31:1–2 (January 2000), pp. 125–147; rep. *The Philosophy of Interpretation*, ed. Joseph Margolis and Tom Rockmore (Oxford: Basil Blackwell Publishers, 2000).

"Introduction," *Is There A Single Right Interpretation?*, ed. Michael Krausz (University Park: Pennsylvania State University Press, 2002), pp. 1–5.

"Interpretation and Its Objects," *Is There A Single Right Interpretation?*, ed. Michael Krausz (University Park: Pennsylvania State University Press, 2002), pp. 122–144.

"Making Music: Beyond Intentions," *The Linacre Journal*, ed. Rom Harré and John Shosky, Linacre College, Oxford (2002), 17–27.

ABOUT THE CONTRIBUTORS

D. P. CHATTOPADHYAYA was Professor of Philosophy at Jadavpur University, Calcutta, India. He is Chairman of the Indian Philosophical Congress, and Chairman of the Indian Council of Philosophical Research. Among his more recent publications are *Sociology, Ideology, and Utopia: Socio-Political Philosophy of East and West* (1997), *Interdisciplinary Studies in Science, Society, Value, and Civilizational Dialogue* (2002), and *Philosophy, Phenomenology, and Other Essays* (2003). He is the General Editor and Director of a fifty-volume project on the history of science, philosophy, and culture in Indian civilization.

VIBHA CHATURVEDI is Professor and Head of the Department of Philosophy at the University of Delhi, India. She is the author of *The Problem of Personal Identity* (1988), and *Wittgenstein's Fideism: Belief, Reason and Practice* (2002). She is currently working on a project relating to the doctrine of Karma and freedom of the individual in classical Indian philosophy.

CHRISTOPH COX is Associate Professor of Philosophy at Hampshire College. The author of *Nietzsche: Naturalism and Interpretation* (1999), he also writes regularly on contemporary art and music for *The Wire*, *Artforum*, and other magazines. With Daniel Warner, he is editing a sourcebook on theories and practices in contemporary music that will be published in 2004.

DAVID CROCKER is Senior Research Scholar at the Institute for Philosophy and Public Policy and the Maryland School of Public Affairs at the University of Maryland. He has been a visiting professor at the University of Munich and twice a Fulbright Scholar at the University of Costa Rica. Among his publications are *Praxis and Democratic Socialism* (1983); editor, (with Toby Linden) *Ethics of Consumption: The Good Life, Justice, and Global Stewardship* (1998), and *Florecimiento humano y desarrollo internacional: La nueva ética de capacidades humanas* (1998). He has completed a manuscript entitled *Well-being, Capability, and Development: Essays in International Development Ethics*. Crocker is a founder and former President of the International Development Ethics Association.

PAUL GROBSTEIN is Eleanor A. Bliss Professor of Biology and Director of the Center for Science in Society at Bryn Mawr College. For ten years he taught at the University of Chicago before assuming his post at Bryn Mawr as Chair of the Department of Biology, where he continued research on developmental and integrative neurobiology. Grobstein focuses largely on problems of "applied neurobiology," on implications of research on the brain for education and philosophy.

GARRY HAGBERG is James H. Ottaway Jr. Professor of Philosophy and Aesthetics at Bard College, where he is Director of the Program in Philosophy and the Arts. Author of *Meaning and Interpretation: Wittgenstein, Henry James, and Literary Knowledge*, and *Art as Language: Wittgenstein, Meaning, and Aesthetic Theory*, he has contributed to numerous journals and collections in philosophical aesthetics. He is also co-author, with Howard Roberts, of the three-volume *Guitar Compendium: Technique, Improvisation, Musicianship, Theory*, guest-editor of a recent special issue of *The Journal of Aesthetics and Art Criticism* on "Improvisation in the arts," and is co-editor, with Denis Dutton, of the journal *Philosophy and Literature*.

PATRICIA HANNA is Professor of Philosophy and Professor of Linguistics at the University of Utah, and was until recently Dean of the College of Humanities. She works primarily on the philosophy of language and philosophical linguistics. She has published many articles on these topics, and has written a book (with Bernard Harrison), *Word and World: Practice and the Foundations of Language* (2004).

BERNARD HARRISON is Emeritus E. E. Ericksen Professor of Philosophy, University of Utah, and Honorary Professor of Philosophy, University of Sussex. His books include, on philosophy and literature, *Inconvenient Fictions: Literature and the Limits of Theory* (1991), and on philosophy of language, *Form and Content* (Blackwell, 1973), and (with Patricia Hanna), *Word and World: Practice and the Foundations of Language* (2004).

MICHAEL KRAUSZ is Milton C. Nahm Professor and Chair of the Department of Philosophy at Bryn Mawr College. Trained at the Universities of Toronto (Ph.D., 1969) and Oxford, Krausz has been visiting professor at Georgetown University, Oxford University, Hebrew University of Jerusalem, American University in Cairo, University of Nairobi, Indian Institute for Advanced Studies, and the University of Ulm, among others. Krausz is the author *of Rightness and Reasons: Interpretation in Cultural Practices* (1993), *Varieties of Relativism* (with Rom Harré) (1995), and *Limits of Rightness* (2000). As well, he is editor and contributor to nine volumes on such topics as relativism, rationality, interpretation, cultural identity, metaphysics of culture, creativity, interpretation of music, and the philosophy of R. G. Collingwood. He is co-founder and former Chair of the thirteen-institution Greater Philadelphia Philosophy Consortium. In 1997 the University of Ulm awarded Krausz the Hans Kupczyk Prize, and in 2001 the University of Delhi sponsored an international conference in relation to his philosophical work.

JOSEPH MARGOLIS is Laura H. Cornell Professor of Philosophy at Temple University. He has published more than thirty books. His most recent ones include *Reinventing Pragmatism* (2002) and *The Unraveling of Scientism* (2003).

NICHOLAS MAXWELL was Reader in the Department of History and Philosophy of Science at University College, University of London. His books include *What's Wrong With Science?* (1976), *From Knowledge to Wisdom* (1984), *The Comprehensibility of the Universe* (1998), and *The Human World in the Physical Universe* (2001). Maxwell has also contributed to a number of volumes, and is the author of numerous papers published in academic journals.

MICHAEL MCKENNA is Associate Professor and Chair of the Department of Philosophy and Religion at Ithaca College. He received his Ph.D. from University of Virginia, and has published in the areas of free will and moral responsibility. His articles have appeared in such journals as *American Philosophical Quarterly* and *Philosophical Studies*. He is also book review editor of *Journal of Ethics*.

RONALD MOORE is Associate Professor of Philosophy at the University of Washington. Author of *Legal Norms and Legal Science*, co-author of *Puzzles About Art*, and editor of *Aesthetics for Young People*, he has contributed numerous articles to philosophical journals in aesthetics and other normative areas.

NIRMALANGSHU MUKHERJI teaches in the Department of Philosophy at the University of Delhi, India. He is the author of *The Cartesian Mind* and a co-editor of Noam Chomsky's *Architecture of Language*. His forthcoming books include *The Primacy of Grammar* and *Language and Naturalistic Inquiry* (with Noam Chomsky).

GIRIDHARI LAL PANDIT is Professor of Philosophy at the University of Delhi, and professor-in-charge in the Philosophy Department at the University of Delhi, South Campus, New Delhi. He has published several books, including *The Structure and Growth of Scientific Knowledge: A Study in the Methodology of Epistemic Appraisal* (1982), *Methodological Variance: Essays in Epistemological Ontology and the Methodology of Science* (1991), *Von der Oekologie des Bewusstseins zum Umweltrealismus* (1995), and many articles in the journals *Forschritte der Physik*, *Systemica*, in edited anthologies, and in proceedings of international conferences. His current project is titled *Environmental Realism: A Road to Environmental Understanding and Development*.

R. C. PRADHAN is Professor of Philosophy at the University of Hyderabad, India. His publications include: *Language and Experience: An Interpretation of the Later Philosophy of Wittgenstein, Truth, Meaning and Understanding: Essays on Philosophical Semantics, Philosophy of Meaning and Representation: Recent Developments in Analytic Philosophy, Philosophy of Wittgenstein* (edited), and *The Great Mirror: An Essay on Wittgenstein's Tractatus.* He is currently engaged in writing a book entitled *The Shadows of Grammar: A Study in Wittgenstein's Later Philosophy.* He is the Member-Secretary of the Indian Council of Philosophical Research.

V. A. RAO headed the Department of English at St Stephen's College, Delhi, for several years where he is currently Reader. His research publications include work on L.H. Myers and Joseph Conrad. He is a member of the Joseph Conrad Society (U.K.). He participated in many international conferences both in India and abroad. He is currently working on Lawrence Durrell and recovery of meaning in history.

ANDREEA DECIU RITIVOI is Assistant Professor of English and Rhetoric at Carnegie Mellon University. She has published a book on immigration and identity (*Yesterday's Self: Nostalgia and the Immigrant Identity*, 2002), and is currently finishing a book on subjectivity and action in Paul Ricoeur's philosophy. Her research focuses on personal identity and social transformation, cross-cultural hermeneutics, transitional societies in Eastern Europe, and the dynamics of individual and collective memory.

KEN-ICHI SASAKI is Professor of Aesthetics at the University of Tokyo. His books have been published in Japanese. They include: *Aesthetics on Nonwestern Principles* (1998), *Dictionary of Aesthetics* (1995), *Study of the History of Aesthetics in the 18th Century, From Watteau to Mozart* (1999), and *The Magical Power of Titles* (2001). He is President of the International Association for Aesthetics and President of the Japanese Society for Aesthetics.

KRASSIMIR STOJANOV is Assistant Professor of Philosophy at the University of Hannover, Germany, and the research director of a project on identity development, recognition, and education under multicultural conditions, sponsored by the German Research Council. His research focuses on the creation and preservation of individual and collective identities, on mechanisms of social integration in multicultural societies, and globalization.

PAUL THOM is Executive Dean of Arts at Southern Cross University, Australia. He has published widely in the philosophy of the performing arts and the philosophy of interpretation. His books include *For An Audience: A Philosophy of the Performing Arts* (1993) and *Making Sense: A Theory of Interpretation* (2000). He has also published on the history of logic, and his latest book, *Medieval Modal Systems*, will appear in 2004. He is planning a book on the philosophy of opera.

NANCY WESTON teaches moral, legal, social, political, and continental philosophy in the Rhetoric Department at the University of California at Berkeley. She holds degrees in philosophy from Stanford University and in law from Harvard, and earned her Ph.D. from the University of California at Berkeley. Her publications include "The Metaphysics of Modern Tort Theory," in *Valparaiso University Law Review* (1994), "The Fate, Violence, and Rhetoric of Contemporary Legal Thought," in *Law and Social Inquiry* (1997), and "Torts" in *The Philosophy of Law: An Encyclopedia,* C. Gray, ed. (1999). Her current research projects examine modern political challenges to the possibility of moral knowledge.

Index

VIBS

The **Value Inquiry Book Series** is co-sponsored by:

Titles Published

Philosophy

74. Malcolm D. Evans, *Whitehead and Philosophy of Education: The Seamless Coat of Learning*. A volume in **Philosophy of Education**

75. Warren E. Steinkraus, *Taking Religious Claims Seriously: A Philosophy of Religion*, edited by Michael H. Mitias. A volume in **Universal Justice**

76. Thomas Magnell, Editor, *Values and Education*

77. Kenneth A. Bryson, *Persons and Immortality*.
A volume in **Natural Law Studies**

78. Steven V. Hicks, *International Law and the Possibility of a Just World Order: An Essay on Hegel's Universalism*. A volume in **Universal Justice**

79. E. F. Kaelin, *Texts on Texts and Textuality: A Phenomenology of Literary Art*, Edited by Ellen J. Burns

80. Amihud Gilead, Saving Possibilities: A Study in Philosophical Psychology. *A volume in Philosophy and Psychology*

81. André Mineau, *The Making of the Holocaust: Ideology and Ethics in the Systems Perspective*. A volume in **Holocaust and Genocide Studies**

82. Howard P. Kainz, *Politically Incorrect Dialogues: Topics Not Discussed in Polite Circles*

83. Veikko Launis, Juhani Pietarinen, and Juha Räikkä, Editors, *Genes and Morality: New Essays*. A volume in **Nordic Value Studies**

84. Steven Schroeder, *The Metaphysics of Cooperation: A Study of F. D. Maurice*

85. Caroline Joan ("Kay") S. Picart, *Thomas Mann and Friedrich Nietzsche: Eroticism, Death, Music, and Laughter*.
A volume in **Central-European Value Studies**

86. G. John M. Abbarno, Editor, *The Ethics of Homelessness: Philosophical Perspectives*